D0846687

ADVANCED 80386
PROGRAMMING
TECHNIQUES

ADVANCED 80386 PROGRAMMING TECHNIQUES

James L. Turley

Osborne **McGraw-Hill**
Berkeley, California

Osborne **McGraw-Hill**
2600 Tenth Street
Berkeley, California 94710
U.S.A.

For information on translations and book distributors outside of the U.S.A., please write to Osborne **McGraw-Hill** at the above address.

A complete list of trademarks appears on page 499.

Advanced 80386 Programming Techniques

Copyright © 1988 by McGraw-Hill, Inc. All rights reserved. Printed in the United States of America. Except as permitted under the Copyright Act of 1976, no part of this publication may be reproduced or distributed in any form or by any means, or stored in a database or retrieval system, without the prior written permission of the publisher, with the exception that the program listings may be entered, stored, and executed in a computer system, but they may not be reproduced for publication.

234567890 DODO 898

ISBN 0-07-881342-5

Information has been obtained by Osborne **McGraw-Hill** from sources believed to be reliable. However, because of the possibility of human or mechanical error by our sources, Osborne **McGraw-Hill**, or others, Osborne **McGraw-Hill** does not guarantee the accuracy, adequacy, or completeness of any information and is not responsible for any errors or omissions or the results obtained from use of such information.

To my parents, for a brain;
my wife, for courage;
and my children, for a heart

CONTENTS

ACKNOWLEDGMENTS

Preparing any book requires the talents of many different people, but I suspect that technical books are more difficult than average. A great many people were involved in the various stages of this book's preparation. First, I wish to extend my gratitude to Messrs. Sven Behrendt, Martin Weisberg, and X. Kim Rubin for the opportunity to work on Project Crayon. I am indebted to them for their trust and confidence. I would also like to thank Geoff Caras for all of his best numbers.

Chris Feetham of Intel Corporation and Richard Smith of Phar Lap Software (it's the name of a racehorse) have both been tremendously helpful in illuminating the dark corners of their respective products. Thanks are also in order to Steven R. Turley, for lighting the fuse; Diane King, for enthusiasm; Dr. Rudy Langer, for lunch; my wife, Kathy, for her patience, encouragement, and demonic typing speed; Lewis Carroll, for inspiration; and Conan the Barbarian, for diversion.

Publishing is a profession with a long and honorable tradition. Much more work is involved in putting a book together than I could have imagined before trying this. I would like to thank the many people at Osborne/McGraw-Hill who, amazingly, do this for a living. Nancy Carlston, Lindy Clinton, and Fran Haselsteiner were instrumental in providing encouragement and gentle reminders of deadlines. Kris Jamsa agreed to cast a technical eye over the early manuscript. They are all possessed of a keen sense of what makes a good book, and of bottomless red pens.

To all of these people, I am indebted for their suggestions, encouragement, assistance, and learning. Each has helped to make this book as useful and as accurate as possible. If any errors or inconsistencies remain, the responsibility lies solely with me.

—J.L.T.

INTRODUCTION

We still have judgment here; that we but teach bloody
instructions, which, being taught, return
To plague the inventor.

—William Shakespeare, *Macbeth*

This book shows how a programmer can make use of the newest
and most advanced features of the 80386 microprocessor. Since
many of the most powerful features of the 80386 can be controlled
only at the machine level, it is assumed that the reader is already
familiar with the concepts of assembly language programming.
Furthermore, a familiarity with Intel microprocessors in general,
and the 8086 and/or 80286 in particular, will be helpful. Throughout the book, parallels are drawn between the 80386 and earlier
members of the iAPX 86 family. Based on this foundation, the
book progresses through the features of the 80386, showing how
improved or unique capabilities can be used to build a truly powerful microcomputer system.

A conscious effort has been made to avoid assumptions about
the reader's hardware (or lack thereof). In particular, there is no
reference to MS-DOS or to "PC-compatible" hardware features
that may not exist on your system. Therefore, readers who are
developing software for custom hardware, workstations, intelligent controllers, or other applications need not be continually dis-
appointed by examples or descriptions that they cannot use. The
concepts and techniques discussed in this book are relevant to any

advanced 80386 programmer, regardless of the hardware platform.

Several diagrams and memory maps have been strategically placed throughout the book to illustrate various points in the text. To cut down on confusion, all memory maps have been drawn in the same way. That is, low memory addresses are always toward the bottom of the page, and high addresses grow toward the top of the page. When data values are illustrated horizontally, the most significant bit, byte, or address is always to the left, with the least significant end to the right. Because this is a programmer's book, numeric values that are not spelled out are usually given in hexadecimal (base sixteen) rather than "normal" decimal (base ten) form. Occasionally, numbers are given in two or more radices if it will make things clearer.

I wrote this book for two reasons. First, after spending almost two years developing software for the 80386, I felt that the vast majority of 80386-based machines on the market completely wasted the unique power of the processor. Serious 32-bit computers were operating in "brain-dead" mode because of old software and old hardware architecture. I hoped that by generating enthusiasm for Protected mode 80386 programming I could help us all to benefit from some truly amazing microcomputer horsepower. Second, like innumerable others, I have read technical books that either were so badly written that reading them was painful, or were well written but contained no information of value. So, like any novice, I figured that I could do better. The result, you now hold in your hands; I am much the wiser and more humble for it.

The text of this book was written entirely by (left) hand with a Cross mechanical pencil on a ruled tablet. It was then entered into an aging PC-compatible computer running Microsoft Word version 3.00. The program source code was written with PC/VI from Custom Software Systems and assembled and linked with the excellent tools available from Phar Lap Software. The majority of these programs were then tested on a CPU-386 from Force Computers, as well as a Compaq Deskpro 386 and a PC's Limited 386[16].

It has been said that there are two kinds of programmers: those who say they hate Intel processors, and liars. Be that as it may, the 80386 opens up whole new applications to the programmer who is willing to tackle it. Once you understand how the 80386 works, and what it can do, I think you'll be as excited about it as I am.

—James L. Turley

1

BASICS

The short history of digital electronic computers has seen an explosive growth in power, speed, capability, miniaturization, and affordability, all seemingly at the same time. The first digital computers were laboratory curiosities, fabricated from vacuum tubes taken from other pieces of electronic equipment. These gave way to solid-state electronics built from resistors and semiconductor transistors. As the applications for digital electronics broadened, it became clear that some simple digital circuits were going to be needed over and over in almost every application. So, like cake mixes that are already measured and combined, integrated circuits, or ICs, were created out of useful combinations of resistors, transistors, and capacitors. These black, multilegged objects are found in almost every electronic device made today. Each IC is designed to perform some specific function, and the types available number in the tens of thousands. The single most complex type of IC is the microprocessor, which the popular media has, somewhat overzealously, dubbed a computer on a chip. And it can be argued that the most complex microprocessor available today is the 80386.

The first IC to be worthy of the name *microprocessor* was a product from Intel Corporation given the unassuming part number of 4004. The 4004 could not do much in the way of real work (a modern pocket calculator can outperform it in mathematics functions), but it had one vital feature: it could be programmed. That is, when fed a steady stream of carefully arranged 4-bit words (opcodes), the 4004 would input each one, perform some small operation, and then wait for the next "instruction" in its program. A skillful programmer could, by carefully sequencing the flow of opcodes to the microprocessor, perform some visible work, such as adding two numbers, turning small indicator lights on and off, and controlling electrical relays connected to motors.

To this day the basics of microprocessors and microprocessor programming have not changed. However, the number and complexity of the microprocessors themselves have increased dramatically, with no end in sight.

Currently, more than 15 different semiconductor companies design and manufacture microprocessors, many doing so as their primary business and source of revenue. The designs differ greatly and competition is fierce, with each manufacturer claiming greater speed, more capability, or lower cost than its competitors. By and large, the processors have grown in complexity as rapidly as they have in speed; this is reflected in the ever-increasing sets of instructions for state-of-the-art microprocessors. There is a counter movement afoot, however: the so-called reduced instruction set computers, or RISC. The theory behind these is that that although a RISC processor has few instructions (typically only six to ten different kinds), it can execute them extremely rapidly and can therefore accomplish as much or more work than a traditional complex instruction set computer (CISC) can perform in a given period of time. Examples of this style of microprocessor are the 29000 from Advanced Micro Devices, the SPARC from Sun Microsystems, the 88000 from Motorola, and the proprietary processor in the IBM Personal Computer/RT. Examples from the CISC camp are the 68020 and 68030 from Motorola (which seems to be playing both sides of the field), the Z80000 from Zilog, the 32532 from National Semiconductor, and, of course, the descendants of the 4004—the 8086, 80186, 80286, and the current flagship, the 80386, from Intel.

The 80386 is perhaps the best example to date of the complex instruction set architecture, for it is indeed complex. The programmer who is familiar with the complexities of the 80386 has control of a powerful tool.

80386 PREDECESSORS

To understand the 80386 better, it is necessary to look backward in time to the microprocessors that preceded it. Intel, perhaps more than any other vendor of microprocessors, takes pains to keep successive generations of CPUs as similar to one another as possible. This helps your task immensely, for it means that you do not have to relearn everything when you begin working with a new microprocessor; you can just pick up the new features and go. Compatibility with earlier generations is a noble goal, as long as it does not compromise performance or capability. To a remarkable extent, Intel has managed to tread this very thin line for several years, through multiple generations of microprocessors. Sometimes, as you will see, it requires a little stretching of definitions and some rethinking on the part of the programmer. For example, the 80386 has three distinct modes of operation (with some submodes as well), one of which is solely to allow compatibility with the 8088 and 8086.

After producing the 4004, Intel announced the 8008, a larger, faster version. Neither of these processors is in regular use today. Shortly after the 8008 came the 8080. The 8080 was a considerable improvement over its predecessor. It operated faster than the 8008, could do rudimentary mathematics better, and the number of opcodes it could recognize and act upon (its instruction set) was extended to such a degree that a programmer could accomplish a task in fewer steps. The 8080 was the inspiration for the Z80 microprocessor from Zilog, and it can still be found in active use today, controlling everything from dishwashers to disk drives.

The 8080 is called an 8-bit microprocessor because it directly manipulates 8 binary bits of data at once. This is analogous to an abacus with eight beads or a calculator that can work only with numbers less than 256 ($2^8 = 256$, so it could represent the numbers 0 through 255). A quantum leap came with the introduction of the 8086 microprocessor. It was a 16-bit processor, and it could directly handle numbers as large as 65,535 and could move those numbers around in the computer's memory twice as fast as an 8080 could. Whether by coincidence or by design, the 8086 (and its lower-cost cousin, the 8088) fueled a wave of personal and desktop computer purchases. With the release of these chips, every office and small business could afford to own a computer that could do reasonable work. Every IBM Personal Computer and Personal Computer/XT, as well as all of their clones, has an 8086 or 8088 at its heart.

Although invisible to the average user, the 8086 also sported an interesting architectural addition that is worth mentioning here. Normally, the phrase "16-bit microprocessor" refers to a microprocessor with a 16-bit data bus; this means that there are 16 pins on the package, which correspond to the 16 bits of binary data it can manipulate. However, every processor also has an *address bus*, which is used to generate memory addresses — the locations in the computer's memory where particular items of data are stored. A good analogy is a row of post office boxes at a post office, each box of which has a unique number. The more digits are allowed in the box number, the more boxes there can be. If the box numbers are limited to three digits, there can be no more than 1000 boxes, numbered 000 to 999 (in base ten, of course). If the boxes are numbered in base two (as they are in all good digital post offices), and the maximum number of digits is 16, there can be 65,536 boxes.

Usually, if a processor had an 8-bit data path, it also had an 8-bit address bus; 16-bit CPUs had 16-bit address buses. Technically, there is no reason why this needs to be; it's just one of those incremental changes made when a new microprocessor is designed. The 8086 and 8088 were unique in that they were 16-bit processors with 20-bit address buses. If a 16-bit address bus allows 65,536 different addresses for storing data (commonly abbreviated to 64 kilobytes, or 64KB), then a 20-bit address bus would allow 2^{20}, or 1,048,576, addresses to be generated. The ability to have 1 megabyte (MB) of memory on-line and instantly available to the processor made the 8086 attractive to programmers who were used to much larger, more expensive minicomputers.

A novel method, known as memory segmentation, was used to achieve this large address space. At the time, the ability to address 1MB of memory directly was unique and critical, but the segmentation mechanism used to achieve it seemed somewhat cumbersome and artificial. Memory segmentation is discussed later in this chapter.

The mismatched address bus and data bus sizes are by no

means unique anymore, by the way. The 68000 and 68010 micro-processors both have a 16-bit data bus with a 24-bit address bus.

The 8086/88 pair were the first members of what has since become known as the iAPX 86 family of microprocessors. The common features that bind these and all subsequent members of the family together are their mutually compatible instruction sets and their model of memory segmentation. Both of these features have undergone extensive changes and revisions, but both are immediately recognizable from one generation to the next.

In 1983 the next enhancement was announced, the 80186 and its cousin the 80188. Very similar to the 8086/88 pair, the 80186/188 included many useful peripheral I/O functions as an integral part of the microprocessor. To support these functions, some additions were made to the 8086 instruction set. Although the 80186 provided increased functionality, it maintained compatibility with the 8086, ensuring that it could execute 8086 application programs.

After the 80186/188 came the 80286. (There is no 80288; the lower-cost option was dropped.) The 80286 found immense popularity as a speed upgrade to 8086-based machines. The IBM Personal Computer AT is one example. On the surface, the 80286 appeared to be just another inevitable, incremental enhancement to the stock 8086, with a faster operating frequency and a larger address space. Inside the part, however, some real changes had taken place. The 80286 boasted a new mode of operation—Protected Mode—wherein the whole concept of a memory segment was changed and was under programmer control, the CPU could differentiate between tasks it was running, and rings of protection could be built around important pieces of program code or data. This mode was never used in the commercial mainstream, however, and the new segmentation mechanism went unexplored.

In the middle of 1986, the next logical processor advance, the 80386, was introduced. Table 1-1 shows the entire Intel family tree, from the 4004 to the present. As could be expected, the 80386 is faster than any of its predecessors, with a minimum operating frequency of 16 megahertz (cycles per second; usually abbreviated MHz). For that reason alone, the 80386, like the 80286 before it, has found immediate acceptance as a performance upgrade to now-tired 8086 and 8088 machines. The Deskpro 386 from Compaq and the IBM Personal System/2

Table 1-1.   80386 Family Tree

Chip	Introduction	Data Bus	Address Bus
4004	1971	4	8
8008	1972	8	8
8080	1974	8	16
8086/88	1978	16/8	20
80186/188	1982	16/8	20
80286	1983	16	24
80386	1986	32	32

Model 80 are but two examples of these fast, powerful personal computers. Along with the increase in speed came some welcome extensions to the processor itself. As in all of the previous incarnations of the iAPX 86 family, the changes were incremental, involving extensions to existing features—evolution instead of revolution. In this case, however, the increment was a big one. Some of the important enhancements were

- 32-bit programmer's register set
- 32-bit data bus
- 32-bit address bus
- New instructions

The longer registers and data path mean that the 80386 can directly manipulate numbers in the billions, a far cry from the limitations imposed by the 8086 and 80286. With a 32-bit address bus, the memory space has been given the same incredible magnitude. In practical terms, an 80386-based system can have more memory on-line than almost any mainframe or supercomputer has in its disk drives. These are limits that people do not expect to outgrow anytime soon!

The real news in the release of the 80386 was the addition of some new and unexpected features. More than a dozen entirely new registers were added to the 80386, and new registers mean new functions to control. These additions are what really set the 80386 apart from any of its contemporaries and make it such a powerful computing element, and it is these that this book is meant to help you harness. Highlights of the new features include

- Two new memory segment registers
- Six debugging support registers
- Three registers for control of segmentation and page translation
- Two registers for memory management unit (MMU) testing
- A third operating mode, allowing true 8086 emulation

Probably the most significant new feature is the addition of a full demand-paged memory management unit (MMU). The MMU allows us to take a whole new approach to systems design. Now a microprocessor-based computer can have capabilities normally possible only with a minicomputer. The groundwork for large-scale functions such as multitasking, demand paging, address translation, and virtual memory is all there, and you can use as many or as few of them as suit your needs. All of these topics will be covered in later chapters.

Like all of its predecessors, the 80386 maintains object code (binary-level) compatibility with previous members of its line. As the CPUs become more complex, this kind of compatibility is getting increasingly difficult to provide. The 80386 is similar enough to the 80286 that compatibility was relatively easy to achieve. Keeping complete compatibility with the 8086/88 proved too much, however, and the 80386 has to enter a special 8086 mode to execute 8086 programs. This "split personality" feature, along with the 80386's inherent multitasking ability, allows you to run 8086 code alongside 80286 or 80386 programs or even to run multiple 8086 programs simultaneously.

Clearly, the 80386 is the most powerful and capable microprocessor currently available from Intel, and perhaps from any vendor. It contains many new and complex features that you must understand well before you can fully utilize its capabilities. The following sections cover these new features one at a time. Along the way, many comparisons will be made to the 8086 (and, by inference, the 8088) to provide a reference point for the programmer who is already familiar with those processors. The experienced 8086 or 80286 programmer should be able to build on personal experience to gain a complete understanding of the 80386.

OVERVIEW OF THE 80386

First and foremost, the 80386 is a true 32-bit microprocessor, with 32-bit internal registers, a 32-bit data bus, and a 32-bit address bus. The size of the address bus theoretically allows you to design systems with 4 gigabytes, or GB (2^{32} bytes) of main memory, while the wide data bus allows 4 bytes to be read from, written to, or fetched from that memory at a time. The process used to manufacture the 80386 is currently one of the most advanced in the industry, allowing unprecedented operating frequency along with the increased complexity of an expanded instruction set, a new register set, memory management, page translation, and task management functions.

Operating Modes

One of the most interesting features of the 80386 is its ability to operate in three different modes. These modes give the processor three very different "personalities," depending on the mode in which you are using it. The modes, in order of increasing complexity, are Real Address mode, Virtual 8086 mode, and Protected Virtual Address mode.

The three modes are necessary for a couple of reasons. First, Protected Virtual Address mode (Protected mode for short) is a very complex environment that requires several segmentation and MMU-related tables to be set up in memory before it will work at all. This means that you are faced with a "chicken and egg" problem when bringing the machine up for the first time. Real

Address mode (usually referred to as Real mode) is a greatly simplified operating mode that you can use while you prepare for the transition into one of the other two modes (usually Protected mode).

Another reason for the different modes was alluded to earlier. The 80386 is fully three generations ahead of the 8086 in terms of product introductions and is at least that far removed in complexity and capability. Yet the 8086 has a large and tenacious following of programmers and users who do not want to give up their favorite programs. The segmentation mechanism used in Protected mode is too different from that on the 8086 and 80186 to allow those programs to run unmodified. Therefore, to reconcile these issues, the 80386 has sprouted an 8086/88 compatibility mode, in which half of the processor shuts down and the other half becomes an embedded 8086. This way, you can run a super-fast 8086 when you want to.

This book will dwell almost exclusively on Protected mode. Virtual 8086 mode is covered in Chapter 9, and Real mode is discussed in Chapter 13. The rest of the chapters apply to the benefits that can only be had through Protected mode operation.

Register Set

The register set of the 80386 has undergone changes in two ways. First, almost every register familiar to the 8086 or 80286 programmer has been extended to 32 bits. In fact, only four registers have made it from the 80286 completely unchanged: CS, DS, ES, and SS. Second, a whole new class of processor-control registers has been added. The new registers fall into three categories: *control registers* provide systems programmers with control over the segmentation and paging devices; *test registers* make it possible to test the inner workings of the paging translation cache, and *debug registers* support a new kind of breakpoint that, among other things, can monitor variables in memory for you. Two new memory segment registers have also been added for convenience.

Instruction Set

The instruction set of the 80386 has been expanded, mostly by making the familiar 8086/186/286 instructions more general-purpose. More addressing modes are available to the majority of instructions that reference memory, and, of course, the instructions may now use 32-bit operands. Many entirely new instructions have been added as well. These additions deal with the protection mechanism, memory segmentation, or the paging MMU. New instructions have also been added that allow programs to reference arbitrary bit strings in memory. Programmers no longer have to calculate the correct byte address of a bit-wise operand and then mask bits in and out. Further, instructions have been added that will set byte flags in memory depending on condition codes in the EFLAGS register. Last, arithmetic operations, shifts, and rotates have been expanded.

Memory Segmentation

The 80386 still maintains the segmented model of the world, with some fundamental changes. Although most applications use segmentation in some form, 32-bit address pointers allow you, for the first time, essentially to turn off the segmentation mechanism and address a "flat" 32-bit space. At the other end of the spectrum, you can now define segments of memory to be almost any size you want, from 1 byte to 4,294,967,296 bytes long! Many new possibilities exist; they are covered in Chapter 2.

Privilege Protection

Working closely with the memory management is a relatively new system of privilege checking, which first made its debut on the 80286. With this method, every piece of code and data is assigned one of four privilege levels, and the processor automatically performs privilege validation on every memory cycle. If the application is privileged enough, its memory access will be granted. If not, the processor will deny access and generate a privilege fault; the operating system will then take over. The CPU has thus done much of the hard work of building a fully secure and protected system. Chapter 3 explains how the privilege protection system works.

Paging

The addition of a paging MMU is one of the biggest increases in capability over the 80286. You can use the MMU to create three different effects in a running system: linear address translation, page-level protection, and demand paging.

Address translation means that any linear address can be translated into a physical address just before the processor drives its external address bus. This allows operating system designers to make physical memory appear to be anywhere in the 4GB address space of the 80386. It can even be moved around from time to time, if desired.

The paging mechanism also makes it possible to mark areas of memory as unavailable to the current user. In this way, the size of available storage, and even its location, can change from one user to the next. Many effects are possible, and many are useful in large-scale systems development.

Demand paging of the memory space is what allows minicomputers to create a virtual environment for their programs. Neither the program code nor the programmer writing it needs to know how much RAM is really available in the system or where it is located. If a program makes reference to nonexistent memory, the 80386 will trap the reference and call a page fault handler, which then retrieves the desired data from secondary storage (such as a disk) and places it in memory. The previous contents of memory are swapped with the data from the disk. In this way, you can create the impression of a machine with an enormous amount of main memory. Its actual size and its location are never known to the program or the programmer, but everything runs as desired. Some applications of paging and page translation are discussed in detail in Chapter 4.

Multitasking

One of the most powerful features of the 80386 is its support for multitasking. At the hardware level, the processor is designed to keep track of a nearly infinite number of separate, distinct tasks. A task could be defined for each user on the computer or for each procedure in a real-time control system. Context switching (changing from one task to another) can be accomplished in hardware with a single assembly language instruction, instead of the slow, bulky, software-controlled method of other microprocessors. Much of the complexity of an operating system can now be directed toward deciding when, rather than how to switch tasks. A definition of multitasking terms and various schemes for multitasking are given in Chapter 5.

BYTE ORDERING

Some basic assumptions about memory references and data storage should be covered before delving into some of the more advanced features of the 80386. All microprocessors can operate on, at a minimum, 1 byte (8 binary bits) of data during any given reference to external memory. The 80286, by virtue of its 16-bit data bus, can directly manipulate 16 bits of memory at once, twice the data throughput of the 8088 if both are running at the same clock frequency. In fact, the 80286 normally runs at two to four times the clock frequency of an 8088, so the difference is even more marked. With the advent of the 80386 and its 32-bit data bus, the processor can now manipulate 32 bits (4 bytes) of data at once. Coupled with its increased clock frequency (minimum 16MHz), this means that the 80386 can easily provide a tenfold increase in data throughput over the 8088.

Universally, when data bytes are stored in a computer's memory, they are assigned individual *addresses*. The addresses usually start at 0 (programmers hate to waste perfectly good numbers) and count upward until a machine-dependent limit is reached. An address would be assigned to every byte, because that was the only unit of data a microprocessor could be expected to deal with. The address of a particular byte of data is used when-

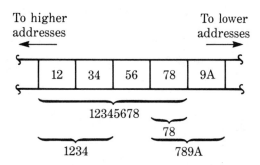

Figure 1-1.   Byte addressing

ever the machine needs to reference the value that is stored there. A conceptual problem arises, however, whenever a piece of hardware (or a person, for that matter) needs to refer to more than one byte at a time. When reading or writing, say, a 32-bit value, what address should be used? Common sense dictates that it should either be the highest-addressed byte of the set of 4 bytes or the lowest. There is constant disagreement on this point in the computer industry, and so manufacturers have gone their own ways, falling into one faction or the other. It seems unlikely that a final solution will ever be reached.

For whatever reasons, Intel has chosen to use the least-significant-address scheme in addressing multiple bytes. Figure 1-1 illustrates a series of unrelated byte values stored in sequential byte addresses. You specify in your programs the address and size of a memory value you want to reference, and the processor loads or stores the appropriate number of bytes from the correct address(es).

Of equal importance is the interpretation of a multiple-byte value once it has been located. Which byte is the most significant, and which is the least? Again, common sense would dictate that the most significant be at one end of the byte string or the other, but again there is no "correct" answer. Intel has chosen to interpret the byte with the highest address of the set as being the most significant byte, and so on. This also is illustrated in Figure 1-1. If you reference the least significant byte of the 4-byte value 12345678 (hexadecimal), you get byte 78. In short, for any arbitrary sequence of bytes (or bits, for that matter) in memory, the least significant has the lowest address while the most significant has the highest address.

DATA TYPES

Now that the addressing issue is out of the way, let's see what the 80386 thinks of the data once it gets it. Depending on the instruction mnemonics used, the context, and the programmer's own ingenuity, the 80386 may interpret the data it reads from memory

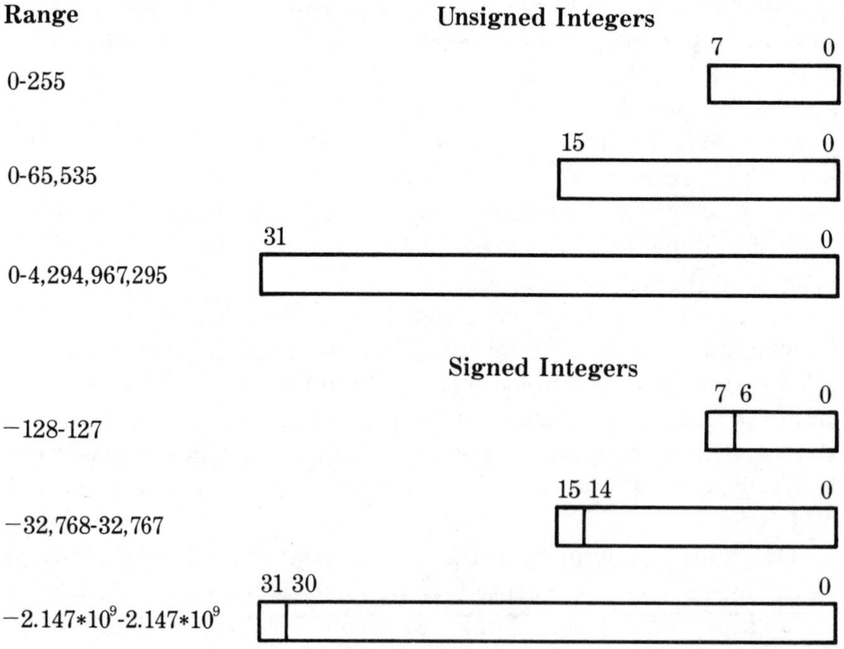

Range	Unsigned Integers
0-255	7 ─ 0
0-65,535	15 ─ 0
0-4,294,967,295	31 ─ 0

Range	Signed Integers
−128-127	7 6 ─ 0
−32,768-32,767	15 14 ─ 0
$-2.147*10^9$-$2.147*10^9$	31 30 ─ 0

Figure 1-2.   Signed and unsigned storage

(or manipulates in registers) in different ways. For example, the programmer may wish to treat an 8-bit quantity (an *operand*) as a value from 0 (binary 00000000) to 255 (binary 11111111, hexadecimal FF). This is known as an *unsigned value* because it has no positive or negative sign. A similar interpretation can be used on 16-bit and 32-bit quantities, with the value ranging from 0 to 65,535 or 4,294,967,295, respectively. Conversely, the programmer may have need for both positive and negative numbers. The 80386 handles signed numbers by interpreting the most significant bit of an operand as a sign bit. If the most significant bit of the operand is 0, then the number is positive. If it is 1, the number is negative. Which bit is most significant depends on the size of the operand, of course. Figure 1-2 shows the interpretation of signed versus unsigned values and their maximum ranges. Notice that these storage classes can represent only integers, not fractions.

Figure 1-3 illustrates all of the various forms by which the 80386 can interpret data, with the improvements over the 8086 shaded. The top of the figure shows the three most common types of 80386 operands: *byte*, *word*, and *dword*. For computer purists, the term *word* usually indicates the "native" operand size of a machine, and therefore should be 32 bits on the 80386. However, common usage has determined that a word is 16 bits, and that is the context in which it will be used here; a 32-bit operand will be referred to as a double word (dword). As was mentioned earlier, 8-bit, 16-bit, and 32-bit quantities can be considered signed or unsigned, as the programmer wishes, and they are not displayed in the figure as separate formats.

The next two formats shown are *near* and *far* pointers. Pointers are used to reference the location of some object in memory, whether a data variable, a constant, or the address of a function or subroutine. Near pointers are by far the most common, and they specify a 32-bit offset from the base of a segment in which the desired operand lies. Far pointers can be used when the program code is going to make a far jump to another segment. It specifies a new segment as well as the 32-bit offset within that segment.

The 80386 is somewhat unusual in that it has the ability to perform four-function arithmetic on numbers that are represented in binary-coded decimal (BCD) instead of the standard

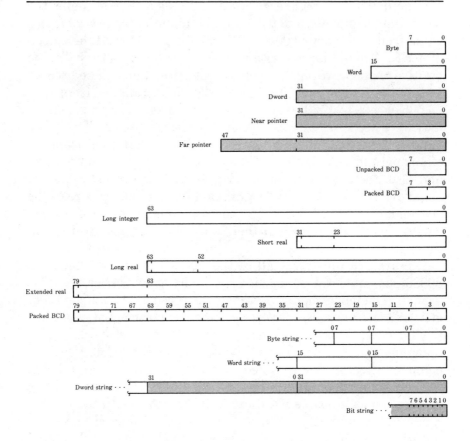

Figure 1-3. Data types

binary format. BCD number representation is used to make binary numbers more readable to human eyes. The drawbacks are that BCD numbers take up more storage than binary numbers and, while they are easy for people to read, they are hopelessly nonintuitive for a digital computer. The 80386 can handle two different BCD formats: unpacked BCD and packed BCD, both of which are illustrated in Figure 1-4. In unpacked BCD, one decimal digit (0 through 9) is stored per byte. Packed BCD stores two digits per byte, cutting down some on the waste.

Packed BCD	Value	Unpacked BCD
7 0		7 0
00000000	0	00000000
00000001	1	00000001
00001001	9	00001001
00010000	10	N/A
00100000	20	N/A
00110000	30	N/A
10011001	99	N/A

Figure 1-4.   BCD storage

Note that the maximum value that can be stored in the unpacked BCD format is 9, packed BCD allows values up to 99, and standard binary can go to 255.

The next five data formats in Figure 1-3 are technically not supported by the 80386 at all, but rather by the 80387 numeric processor extension (NPX). Because of the relatively transparent nature of the 80387 interface, however, they will be covered here. The *long integer* format is exactly like the 80386's signed byte, word, and dword formats, but it is able to represent much greater numbers. The *short real, long real,* and *extended real* formats are used to store floating-point numbers with varying degrees of precision. The packed BCD format is a large-scale extension of the BCD format just described. These formats all conform to the IEEE 754 standard for floating-point number representation on a binary computer system.

For the purposes of this book, a *floating-point number* is any number that either has a fractional part (like 3.1415926) or is so large that it must be represented in scientific notation (like 4.2×10^{69}). The 80386 is not able to manipulate these formats directly at all, and if your system has no 80387 or 80287 installed, you will have to forgo them entirely or else write some very complex floating-point emulation libraries.

One of the most acclaimed features of the entire iAPX 86 family of microprocessors is their ability to deal easily with sequences of separate but related data items stored in consecutive addresses. These vector arrays of data are called *strings*. The 80386 supports *byte strings*, *word strings*, and *dword strings*. These strings can easily be scanned for a particular value or any deviation from a value, or two such strings can be compared. These functions are especially useful for text-processing applications and for arrays of small- to medium-range integral numbers.

The final format illustrated in Figure 1-3 is unique to the 80386. In the same way that you can reference data bytes in memory by their addresses, a new class of instructions now allows you to address each bit in the entire 4GB address space of the 80386. Programmers can consider the address space of the processor as nothing more than a nearly endless string of binary digits, if desired, and manipulate it accordingly.

REGISTER SET

Usually, the first item of interest to an assembly language programmer is the register set. In the same way that there is disagreement over how to address multibyte quantities, there is a nearly religious fervor associated with most programmers' opinions about the proper design and use of a processor's register set. The register set can be completely general-purpose, with each register just like the others. The National Semiconductor 32x32 series of processors is modeled this way, as are most RISC machines, such as the AMD 29000. The Motorola 680x0 family of microprocessors takes a mostly general-purpose approach but includes some dedicated functions. Intel has historically designed processors with very rigid special-purpose register sets, on the theory that assigning special registers for the most commonly used functions cuts down on code size and increases execution speed. To a certain extent this has been true, but it can also force you to make more memory references when storing temporary variables than would be necessary under the general-purpose approach, since the limited number of general-purpose registers are already in use.

The extended register set of the 80386 provides programmers with the best of both worlds. Although there are certainly still special-purpose registers for some instructions (typically for historical or compatibility reasons), the majority of the instructions are structured so that there are preferred registers that you can override if desired. To use a different register, you insert segment override or size override bytes in the object code or use an alternate, longer form of the instruction, which uses a different addressing mode. The difference in the object code generated when a nondefault register is used is virtually invisible to the programmer, unless he or she is writing an assembler or compiler. If the default register is used for a particular instruction, it typically results in less object code being generated, thus saving on code size. It might also increase execution speed, if the rate at which code is fetched from memory is a limiting factor in your system.

Figure 1-5 shows the application programmer's general-purpose register set for the 80386. The enhancements over previous generations of processors have been shaded. The most notable change is the 32-bit extensions to the eight main registers. As before, the programmer can still refer to the least-significant byte of register A as AL (accumulator low), and the byte after it as AH (accumulator high). AX (accumulator extended) refers to the 16-bit concatenation of those two registers, as shown. The new register EAX (extended AX) refers to the 32-bit whole. There is no way to address the upper word of EAX, bits 16 through 31, as a discrete unit. This system has been carried out in the familiar pattern through the first four registers in the set (EAX, EBX, ECX, and EDX).

When you look at the next four registers, ESI, EDI, EBP, and ESP, you will notice an interesting difference. The old register names have been preserved, but now they refer only to the lower half of these registers. Unlike the four previous registers, these cannot be addressed as single-byte quantities, but 8086 and 80286

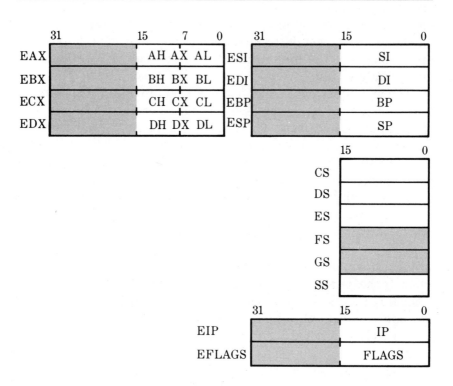

Figure 1-5.   General-purpose registers

programmers are used to this. For the first time, you have a set of pointer registers that are as wide as the address bus (32 bits). This has some ramifications for memory addressing, which will be covered in Chapter 2.

Next are the segment registers, which are still 16 bits wide, although there are two more of them now. The four basic segment registers are the only registers in the 80386 that have not changed since the 8086. The two new segments, FS and GS, do not perform any special functions; they are used as general data segment registers, much as DS and ES are.

In the same way that the pointers ESI through ESP have been extended to 32 bits, IP and FLAGS have been extended into EIP and EFLAGS. The extension to the instruction pointer is obvious, given the 32-bit architecture, but the additions to the FLAGS register imply that there must be new system resources to be monitored and controlled. This register will be discussed in more detail in the next section.

EFLAGS Register

Figure 1-6 gives a programmer's model of the EFLAGS register. The enhancements over the 8086 are shaded. The processor's interpretation of each of the bits follows. Note that none of the interpretations have changed from earlier models.

CF (Carry flag)   This bit is set by arithmetic instructions that generate either a carry or a borrow. This bit can also be set, cleared, or inverted with the STC, CLC, or CMC instructions, respectively.

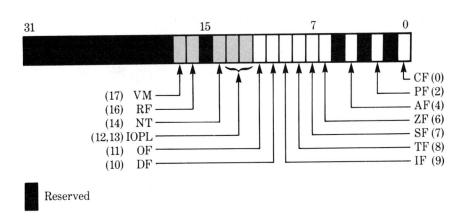

Figure 1-6.   EFLAGS register

PF (Parity flag)   This bit will be set by most instructions if the least significant 8 bits of the destination operand contain an even number of 1 bits. In other words, this flag signals a byte with even parity. Note that this flag represents the number of 1 bits in the lower byte only, not in the entire operand.

AF (Auxiliary flag)   This is like half of the Carry flag. Most comparison and arithmetic instructions set this flag if a carry or borrow occurred from the most significant nibble of the least significant byte of the accumulator (that is, bit 4 of register EAX). Its seemingly perverse function exists to aid BCD arithmetic.

ZF (Zero flag)   This flag is set by most instructions when the result of the operation is a binary zero. Comparison instructions set this flag without storing the result if the operands are equal, since comparisons are basically subtractions.

SF (Sign flag)   Most comparison and arithmetic operations set SF equal to the most significant bit of the result. This will be bit 7, 15, or 31, depending on the magnitude of the operation. The 80386 correctly sets this bit whether the values involved are considered to be signed or unsigned. If they are signed, SF will tell you whether the result is positive or negative.

TF (Trace flag)   This flag allows you to single-step through programs. When the processor detects that this flag is set, it executes exactly one machine instruction and then automatically generates an internal exception 1. When the exception handler returns, the processor executes the next instruction and repeats the process. Single-stepping continues until program code resets this flag.

IF (Interrupt flag)	When this flag is set, the 80386 recognizes and handles external hardware interrupts on its INTR pin (pin B7 on the standard pin-grid-array package). If you clear this bit, the processor ignores any inputs on this pin. Note that this does not affect the external nonmaskable interrupt (NMI) input in any way, nor does it have any relationship with internally generated faults, exceptions, traps, and so forth. The IF is set and cleared with the STI and CLI instructions, respectively.
DF (Direction flag)	This flag is set and cleared by the STD and CLD instructions. Its sole purpose is to determine whether string operations (LODS, STOS, CMPS, etc.) will automatically increment (DF = 0) or decrement (DF = 1) the index registers, ESI and EDI, after each iteration.
OF (Overflow flag)	Most arithmetic instructions set this flag to indicate that the result was at least 1 bit too large to fit in the destination. In this context, too large can also mean that a signed result was too small a negative number to be represented in the number of bits allowed in the destination.
IOPL (Input/ Output Privilege Level flags)	This 2-bit field is peculiar to the Protected mode of operation, and so first appeared on the 80286. It holds the privilege level, from 0 to 3, at which your code must be running in order to execute any I/O-related instructions.
NT (Nested Task flag)	This bit is also an artifact of Protected mode. When set, it indicates that one system task has invoked another through a CALL instruction, as opposed to a JMP. By and large, you don't care about this bit, but the 80386 does, and the chapter on multitasking will show how you can manipulate it to your advantage.

RF (Resume flag)	This flag is the first bit in the extended EFLAGS register. It has to do with the new debug features and is related to registers DR6 and DR7. By setting it, you can selectively mask some exceptions while you are debugging code.
VM (Virtual 8086 mode flag)	The space allocated to this bit in the EFLAGS register belies its importance. It has enormous impact on the way the 80386 behaves. When the flag is cleared, the 80386 can operate in full 80386 Protected mode, 80286 Emulation mode, or Real Address mode. When it is set, the 80386 is essentially converted into a high-speed 8086 until the bit is cleared again. Chapter 9 discusses this subject in more detail.

Protected Mode Registers

Figure 1-7 shows the registers associated with Protected mode operation. The global descriptor table register (GDTR), the interrupt descriptor table register (IDTR), and the local descriptor table register (LDTR) will be familiar to 80286 programmers

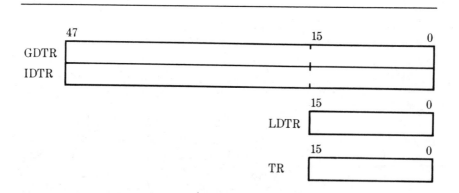

Figure 1-7.   Protected mode registers

with experience in Protected mode programming. These are essentially unchanged from their 80286 counterparts, except that their length has been extended to 48 bits to allow for 32-bit base addresses. The task register (TR) is still a 16-bit selector, just as it is on the 80286. These registers are covered in detail in the discussions of memory segmentation, protection, and multitasking in later chapters.

New Registers

No fewer than 13 new registers have been added to the programmable register set of the 80386 (with many more invisible registers added internally). They are logically divided into four categories: three control registers, six debug registers, two test registers, and two segment registers. Almost all new registers are 32 bits wide and these are shown in Figure 1-8. All of the new registers

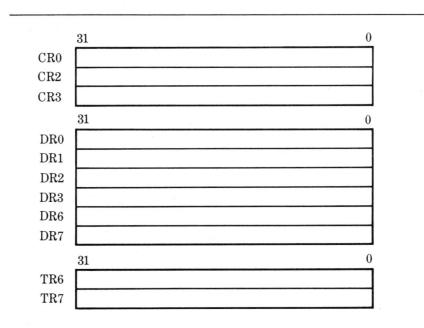

Figure 1-8. New 80386 registers

are manipulated through ordinary instructions. The 80386 instruction set has been extended to allow you to MOV data into and out of these registers.

Control Registers

Figure 1-9 shows the format of the currently defined control registers. CR1 has been left undefined by Intel and should not be used. In fact, the 80386 will generate an exception 6 (invalid opcode) if it fetches an instruction that references CR1.

Control Register 0   Control Register 0 made its debut on the 80286 as the machine status word (MSW). As the name implies, it was only a 16-bit register at the time. For strict 80286 compatibility, its lower half (bits 0 through 15) can still be referred to as MSW. CR0 is something of a garbage can register, since most of its bits are unrelated to one another. A description of each of its flags follows.

PE (protection enable, bit 0)	This bit is similar to the VM bit in EFLAGS in that it controls the 80386's mode of operation. When PE is cleared, the 80386 operates in Real mode. When set, it is in Protected mode. Setting and clearing this bit is not done often, since getting into and out

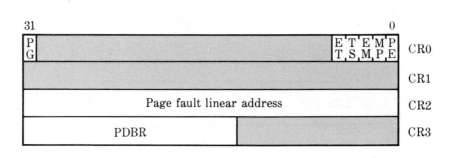

Figure 1-9.   Control registers

of Protected mode is nontrivial. Chapter 13 details the necessary steps.

MP (math present, bit 1)

When this bit is set, the 80386 assumes that real floating-point hardware is attached to it. This is typically an 80387 or 80287 coprocessor, although any numeric processor may be used with an appropriately clever hardware interface. When this bit is clear, the 80386 assumes that no such coprocessor exists, and will not attempt to use one.

EM (emulate coprocessor, bit 2)

When this bit is set, the 80386 will generate an exception 11 (device not available) whenever it fetches a floating-point instruction. You can use this exception handler to emulate floating-point hardware in software, if you want.

TS (task switched, bit 3)

The processor sets this bit automatically every time it performs a task switch. It will never clear this bit on its own, although you can do so with the CLTS instruction.

ET (extension type, bit 4)

This bit informs the 80386 whether the numeric coprocessor is an 80387. This is important because the 80387 uses a slightly different protocol than earlier coprocessors and has a 32-bit bus interface. Through some interesting magic, the 80386 is able to set this bit correctly by itself when power is applied. For details, refer to Chapters 11 and 13.

PG (paging, bit 31)

This one is new to the 80386, which is why it is in the upper word of CR0. When you set this bit, you enable the paging MMU. When you clear it, paging is disabled. You will usually not change this bit more than once in a running system. For a full explanation of paging, refer to Chapter 4.

Control Register 2   CR2 is read-only register in which the 80386 will deposit the value of the last 32-bit linear address that caused a page fault (exception 14). This address will be important to you when you write a page-fault handler in Chapter 4, because it will help you determine the cause of the fault.

Control Register 3   CR3 is defined as the page directory base register (PDBR). As such, it holds the physical address of the root of the two-level paging tables used when paging is enabled (when the PG bit in CR0 is set). Loading this register is one of the few times you will refer to actual physical addresses, as opposed to linear addresses. The paging tables must be 4KB-aligned, and so the least significant 12 bits are undefined. They will be ignored when the register is loaded and will be stored as zeros.

Debug Registers

The six currently defined debug registers implement a whole new approach to program debugging previously found on only a few minicomputers and mainframes. The debug registers are outlined in Figure 1-10. Registers 4 and 5 are undefined, and you must refrain from using them. Through careful use of the debug register set and some well-designed exception handlers, you can build some very capable and powerful debugging tools. Although Chapter 10 deals with the whole debugging tool set in more detail, the register definitions can be covered here.

Debug Registers 0 Through 3   The first four debug registers hold up to four linear address breakpoints. The addresses in these registers are compared to the processor's address-generation logic on every instruction and, if a match is found, an exception 1 (debug fault) is generated. In this way, you can monitor up to four different addresses in the system and have the processor notify you if one or more of them is referenced.

Debug Register 6   Debug register 6 is also known as the debug status register. The 80386 sets the appropriate bits in this register to inform you of the circumstances that may have caused the last debug fault (exception 1). These bits are never cleared by the pro-

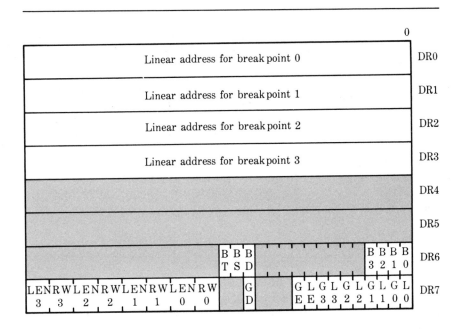

Figure 1-10.   Debug registers

cessor. You must clear the status bits manually by writing into DR6. The various status bits and their meanings are as follows:

B0 (breakpoint 0 hit, bit 0)	The processor sets this bit when it references the linear address contained in DR0, modified by the conditions set by the LEN0, RW0, L0, G0, LE, and GE fields in DR7.
B1 (breakpoint 1 hit, bit 1)	This is analogous to the B0 flag but applies to breakpoint 1.
B2 (breakpoint 2 hit, bit 2)	This is analogous to the B0 flag but applies to breakpoint 2.
B3 (breakpoint 3 hit, bit 3)	This is analogous to the B0 flag but applies to breakpoint 3.

BD (break for debug register access, bit 13)	This bit is set when the exception 1 handler is invoked by an illegal reference to one of the debug registers when the register set is locked (the GD bit is set in DR7).
BS (break for single-step, bit 14)	This bit is set if the processor has taken the exception 1 because tracing is enabled (the TF bit is set in EFLAGS).
BT (break for task switch, bit 15)	Whenever the 80386 initiates a task switch to a task that has its trace bit set in its task image (byte offset 64, bit offset 0), the processor initiates an exception 1 if this bit is set.

Debug Register 7 Debug register 7 is the debug control register. By filling in the various fields of this register, you can control the operation of the four linear address breakpoints. Each of these breakpoints is controlled by a set of four fields each, as follows:

L0 (local enable, bit 0)	When this bit is set, the breakpoint address in DR0 is monitored as long as the 80386 is running the current task. When a task switch occurs, this bit is cleared by the processor and must be re-enabled under program control.
G0 (global enable, bit 1)	As long as this bit is set, the 80386 monitors the linear address in DR0 at all times, regardless of the task. It must be cleared under program control.

Table 1-2. DR7 RWn Encodings

RW	RW Bits in Register DR7
00	Code Fetch
01	Data Write
10	Reserved
11	Data Read or Write

Table 1-3.   DR7 LENn Encodings

LEN	LEN Bits in Register DR7
00	1 byte
01	2 bytes, word aligned
10	Reserved
11	4 bytes, dword aligned

RW0 (read/write access, bits 16 and 17)

These bits qualify the type of access that must occur at the address in DR0 before the breakpoint will be taken. Table 1-2 summarizes the definition of these bits.

LEN0 (break-point length, bits 18 and 19)

In addition to the type of reference that must be made, you can further distinguish the breakpoint by specifying its size in this field. Table 1-3 shows the valid encodings for this field. Note that for the word size and dword size breakpoints, the linear address associated with that breakpoint must be word-aligned or dword-aligned, respectively.

These four bit-fields are each repeated three more times for the other three breakpoints. DR7 also contains three other bits that control the following functions:

LE (local exact, bit 8)

When you set this bit, you tell the processor that you want to know when a breakpoint hit occurs at the instant it occurs. This might seem to be a superfluous function, but the 80386 uses a *pipelined* architecture to achieve its tremendous performance, and that pipelining can make debugging a very tricky proposition. Pipelining means that the 80386 is normally well into the next instruction before the current one completes. For this reason, if the local exact bit is not set, the breakpoint may not be reported until a few instructions after the fact. When you set LE, you enable this feature only while the processor is running the current task. When a task switch occurs, this bit is cleared. This bit applies to all four linear breakpoints.

GE (global exact, bit 9)   This is similar to the LE bit but stays in effect through all tasks in the system.

GD (global debug access, bit 13)   Setting this bit is like locking the key inside a safe. Once it is set, the processor will deny all further access to any of the debug registers, either for reading or writing.

Test Registers

Figure 1-11 shows the only two test registers that are currently defined, TR6 and TR7. Do not attempt to use the others. (There are presumably six more.) The test registers are used to perform confidence checking on the paging MMU's translation lookaside buffer (TLB). The method of testing the TLB is fairly involved and requires some understanding of the inner workings of the TLB and of cache algorithms in general. Chapter 13 covers this in more detail. Intel has hinted that the arrangement of registers TR6 and TR7 might be temporary and may not be continued on future processors in the line.

Test Register 6   Register TR6 is the TLB testing command register. By writing into this register, you can either initiate a write directly into the 80386's TLB or perform a mock TLB lookup. DR6 is divided into fields as follows:

C (command, bit 0)   When this bit is cleared, a write to the TLB is performed. If it is set, the processor performs a TLB lookup.

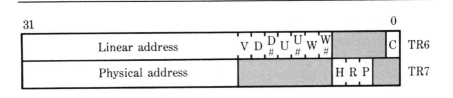

Figure 1-11. Test registers

The next 7 bits are used as tag attributes for the TLB cache, either when writing a new entry or when performing a TLB lookup.

W#	Not writable, bit 5
W	Writable, bit 6
U#	Not user, bit 7
U	User, bit 8
D#	Not dirty, bit 9
D	Dirty, bit 10
V	Valid, bit 11

Linear address, bits 12 through 31   This serves as the upper 20 bits of a linear address to be used for TLB references.

Test Register 7   Register TR7 is the TLB testing data register. When a program is performing writes, the entry to be stored is contained in this register, along with cache set information.

RP (replacement pointer, bits 2 and 3)   This field indicates which set of the TLB's four-way set associative cache to write to.

H (pointer location, bit 4)   If this bit is set, the RP field determines which cache set to write to. If it is cleared, the set is determined with an internal algorithm.

Physical address, bits 12 through 31	This field contains either the physical address to be written into the TLB or the results of a valid TLB hit.

INSTRUCTION SET

To an assembly language programmer, the instruction set is the single most important part of any microprocessor. When you write a program in a high-level language such as Pascal, C, or BASIC, the underlying instruction set of the target microprocessor is invisible to you, as it should be. One can say "I can write a program in C" to run on an Intel microprocessor as easily as on a Motorola processor, a RISC machine, or a VAX. However, it is not enough to say "I can write assembly language programs," because each machine's assembly-level instruction set is radically different from any other. More often than not, those who prefer to write programs at the assembly language level can do so for only one or two different microprocessors. Each one entails learning an entirely new language.

The 80286 programmer will not find many surprises in the 80386's instructions. If you are coming to this book straight from an 8086 environment, however, you have some catching up to do. Only a very small percentage of instructions have not been affected in some way through the generations. These are mostly instructions that have been kept for historical reasons, such as LAHF, CWD, and so on. Most of the rest have been extended in some way. Following is a list of some changes all instructions share.

- *Most instructions now operate on 32-bit registers as well as 8-bit and 16-bit ones.* General-purpose instructions like AND, OR, and NOT now use the extended registers, such as ECX, ESI, and so on, as easily as they do AX, AL, and AH. Almost all instructions have been enhanced in this way.

- *Most instructions that reference memory can use new base and index registers.* As Figure 1-12 shows, any 32-bit general-purpose register can be used as a base register, and any one except ESP can be used as an index register.

	EAX	EBX	ECX	EDX	ESI	EDI	EBP	ESP
General storage	✓	✓	✓	✓	✓	✓	✓	*
String operations	✓							
Loop counter			✓					
I/O addresses				✓				
Multiply	✓	✓	✓	✓	✓	✓	✓	✓
Divide (dividend)	✓							
Divide (remainder)				✓				
Base register	✓	✓	✓	✓	✓	✓	✓	✓
Index register	✓	✓	✓	✓	✓	✓	✓	
XLAT pointer		✓						
I/O data	✓							
String source					✓			
String destination						✓		

*Not recommended

Figure 1-12.   Register usage

- *Most instructions that reference memory can now use scaled indexing.* This is a new addressing mode available only on the 80386. Previously, you could reference memory indirectly through a base register (BX or BP), an index register (SI or DI), or one of each. Not only has the arbitrary restriction on register usage been lifted, but a new twist has been added. If you want, the 80386 will internally "scale" the index register by 2, 4, or 8 before using its contents in address calculation. This is a wonderful boon for addressing multidimensional arrays.

- *Most instructions that reference memory can now use any of six segment registers.* There are two more segment registers now, so any instruction that could previously take a segment override can take FS or GS as an override. Of course, all memory-related instructions still have default segments, as they did before. No instruction uses the FS or GS segment by default. If you do not specify FS or GS as a segment override, they will never be used.

As was mentioned before, most instructions that previously operated on the general-purpose registers still do so, but they can use the extended 32-bit registers also. Some other instructions that are affected by the larger register size may not be obvious and are worth pointing out here.

- *String instructions* LODSD, STOSD, MOVSD, CMPSD, and SCASD are new forms of the familiar string instructions; they use EAX rather than AX or AL.

- *I/O instructions* For INSD, OUTSD, IN EAX, DX, OUT DX, EAX, although the I/O space has not increased past 64KB, 32-bit I/O ports are now supported.

- *Conversion instructions* CWDE and CDQ are two new instructions for operand size conversion. CWDE (convert word to dword, extended) is a more rational form of the old CWD instruction. It sign-extends AX into EAX. CDQ (convert dword to quadword) sign-extends EAX into EDX:EAX. Its usefulness is not clear. CBW and CWD are still available.

- *Loop counter* The JECXZ, LOOP, REP, REPE, and REPNE instructions are used in loop constructs, but the 32-bit ECX register is the loop counter now, allowing 4,294,967,296 iterations through the loop. Be sure to initialize all 32 bits before starting!

- *Stack operations* PUSHFD, POPFD, PUSHAD, POPAD, and IRETD all operate on the stack. The new forms push and pop 32-bit registers rather than 16-bit registers. IRETD assumes that a 32-bit offset address is on the top of the stack.

Many familiar instructions now operate on some of the new registers in the 80386. All of the old forms have been retained, but some new ones have been added.

- *MOV* The MOV instruction now copies data into and out of the control registers, debug registers, and test registers.

- *Load full pointer*   LSS, LFS, and LGS are now valid instructions. The latter two are obviously new because the FS and GS segment registers are new. The SS register has been around since 8086 days, but LSS was not a valid instruction until now.

Finally, here are the truly new instructions. These were not available in any form before. If the program needed to accomplish any of these functions, the programmer had to write a routine to do it.

- *Bit-wise instructions*

BSF (bit scan forward)	Finds the first 1-bit in a bit stream, working from the bit address specified toward higher bit addresses.
BSR (bit scan reverse)	Same as BSF, but works backward.
BT (bit test)	Reports the setting of any arbitrary bit in memory or in a register.
BTC (bit test and complement)	Same as BT but toggles the bit after testing it.
BTR (bit test and reset)	Same as BT but clears the bit after testing it.
BTS (bit test and set)	Same as BT but sets the bit after testing it.

- *Integer multiply instruction*

IMUL (integer multiply)	This is not a new instruction, but it does have a new form. It is now possible to multiply any register by any other register, or any register by a memory operand.

- *Sign extension*

MOVSX (MOV with sign extend)	This instruction can be used to copy any 8-bit or 16-bit operand (register or memory) with sign extension to any 16-bit or 32-bit register (including the same one). This is a much more general-purpose alternative to CBW and CWD.

- *Zero extension*

  MOVZX (MOV with zero extend)   The MOVZX instruction is exactly the same as MOVSX except that the source operand is always zero-extended (as though it were always a positive signed value). This is useful when it comes time to interface 8-bit and 16-bit code to a new 32-bit operating system.

- *Set/clear byte on condition instruction*

  SETcc (set byte on condition code)   This group of instructions writes a byte of 1 bit (FF) if the condition is met or a byte of zeros (00) if it is not. All of the Boolean conditions available for conditional JMPs are legal here.

- *Double-precision shift instructions*

  SHRD, SHLD (shift right double, shift left double)   These instructions concatenate any two registers, or a register and a memory operand, and shift bits through one into the other. If two 32-bit operands are used, this has the effect of shifting up to 64 bits.

MEMORY SEGMENTATION

Like all previous members of the iAPX 86 family of processors, the 80386 supports a segmented memory architecture. In concept, this is very similar to the system of segmentation begun on the 8086 and regularly enhanced in the 80186, 80286, and now in the 80386. On the surface, the memory model appears to be unchanged—as, in fact, it must to allow downward compatibility—but the way in which segmentation has been implemented is radically different. The particulars of this are covered in detail in Chapter 2; this section reviews the concept of memory segmentation, how a programmer uses it, and its advantages for large-scale systems.

Beginning with the 8086, the addressable space of the processor (1MB, in this case) was considered to be divided into smaller parcels, or segments, each one exactly 64KB long. The locations of these segments were not in any way set or fixed by the processor. The programmer could define a segment to start on any 16-byte boundary desired. The segment would then stretch from that address to 64KB beyond that address. The programmer would make all references to memory by specifying the base of a segment and an offset within that segment. Since all segments were 64KB long, an offset never needed to exceed 16 bits (FFFF hexadecimal). In this way, a programmer could address a 1MB address space (which requires 20 bits) with 16-bit address pointers.

Rather than specify the base address of a segment on every memory reference, the programmer's four favorite segment bases could be stored in four segment registers—CS, DS, ES, and SS. Then all that was necessary was to specify a segment register that held the desired segment base, and an offset, which could come from another register or as an immediate 16-bit value in the code. To further simplify things, all instructions that could reference memory were assigned default segment registers that would be used automatically. The programmer could often override the default choice, if desired. Figure 1-13 illustrates this two-part system of memory addressing.

Because segment bases must start on 16-byte boundaries, a segment register effectively acts as "coarse tuning," and the offset address as "fine tuning." Using these two parts, a programmer can specify any address in the 1MB address range of the processor. Furthermore, any given address can be specified in no fewer than 4096 ways! For example, if the segment base were decreased by 16 bytes, the segment offset could be increased by 16 bytes, and the resulting final address would be the same. The 16-bit offset portion of the address is known as the *logical address*, while the final 20-bit result is the *physical address*.

Segment bases had to be multiples of 16 bytes because the segment registers themselves were only 16 bits wide, the same as the offset registers. If you divide a 20-bit address space by a 16-bit segment register, you get a 4-bit difference. To solve this, the 8086 processor pretends that the segment registers are really 20 bits long, with the least significant 4 bits always 0. Then, when it needs to produce a physical address from a segment base register and an offset, the addition is simple. Figure 1-14 shows the steps

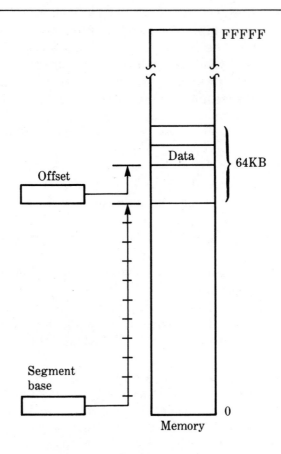

Figure 1-13.   Memory segmentation

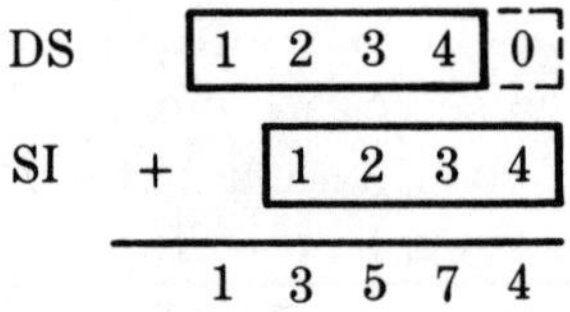

DS   [1   2   3   4 | 0]

SI   +   [1   2   3   4]

―――――――――

1   3   5   7   4

Figure 1-14.   Address calculation

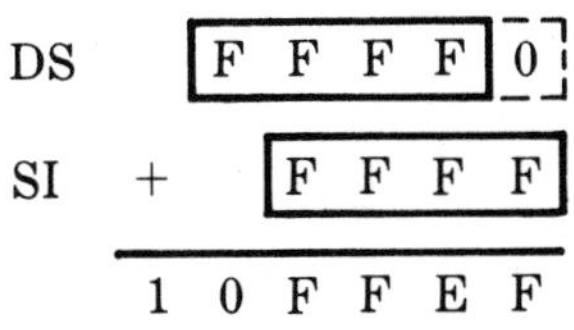

```
DS     F  F  F  F  0
SI  +     F  F  F  F
       ───────────────
       1  0  F  F  E  F
```

Figure 1-15.   Address overflow

required, using DS as a segment base and SI as the offset register.

Those of you who have programmed the 8086 or 8088 before have probably wondered what would happen if the segment base were very large—say, near the upper end of the 1MB address space—and the offset address were very large also. Because of the nature of the 8086's two-part address formation, you can see that it would be very easy to produce a physical address greater than FFFFF. Figure 1-15 illustrates just such a case. The processor handles this situation very gracefully, however. The address "wraps around" the end of the address range and starts over again at 0. While this may have been a disappointment to some, others have turned it into an intrinsic part of running code.

In the case of the 8086, an offset address either could be specified as an immediate constant coded into a program (*i.e.*, MOV AL, DS:[1234]) or could be given indirectly through a register (*i.e.*, MOV AL, DS:[BX]). If you wanted to use a register as a memory pointer, you had to use one of four registers. BX and BP were, somewhat arbitrarily, labeled base registers, while SI and DI were termed index registers (hence, no doubt, the registers' mnemonics). Most instructions also allowed you to use both a base register and an index register, and the offset address would be calculated from the sum of the contents of the two. This scheme has been maintained throughout the processor family, up to the 80386.

While the concept is the same, the 80386 has done away with artificial limitations on which registers can be used to address

Table 1-4.   Addressing Modes

Mode	Example
Immediate constant	MOV EAX, 12345678
Immediate register	MOV EAX, ECX
Direct (offset only)	MOV EAX, [12345678]
Register indirect	MOV EAX, [ECX]
Base/index + offset	MOV EAX, [ECX] + 9930
Base + index + offset	MOV EAX, [ECX][EDX] + 42
Index * scale + offset	MOV EAX, [ESI*4] + 917
Base + (index * scale)	MOV EAX, [EDX][ECX*8]
Base + (index * scale) + offset	MOV EAX, [EBX][EDI*2] + 316

memory. Recall Figure 1-12, which showed that any 32-bit register can be used as a base register and that any 32-bit register except ESP can be used as an index register. This can greatly enhance the convenience of addressing memory and allows you to try some previously difficult or impossible addressing schemes. (Imagine using ECX as an address pointer from within a LOOP construct.) To this has been added the concept of scaled indexing. If you wish, the contents of an index register (if any) can be multiplied internally by 2, 4, or 8 before being used in address calculations. This makes it much easier than before to reference arrays of elements that are not all 1 byte large, or to reference two-dimensional arrays. Table 1-4 demonstrates all of the possible places that a given instruction might get an operand, including constant values. Note that the final three memory-addressing modes are new features in the 80386.

One final point to remember is that the 80386 now has a paging MMU that is capable of translating addresses just before they are used to address physical memory. This means that there is another level of indirection in the address computation process, in addition to the segment:offset calculation. As before, the offset portion of an address will be referred to as the logical address. When the logical address is computed and added to the base address of a segment, the result is a linear address. A linear address does not become a physical address until after it passes through the MMU to the external address bus. If page translation has not been enabled, then the linear address and the physical address are one and the same, as they are on an 8086 or 80286. You must be cautious, however, because these terms are not always synonymous. The next chapter covers the logical-to-linear translation, and Chapter 4 discusses the linear-to-physical translation.

2

MEMORY
SEGMENTATION

The previous chapter reviewed the major components of the
80386, including the register set, instruction set, memory management, and some new features. This chapter and the next cover
the 80386 memory segmentation mechanism in detail, describing
how areas of memory are defined and used. This chapter ignores
issues relating to privilege protection, which is discussed in detail
in Chapter 3.

In a sense, a discussion of the 80386's segmentation mechanism
involves two levels of understanding. First, there is the general
theory of memory segmentation, which was covered at the end of
the previous chapter. Second, there is the method of segmentation
used in Protected mode, which uses a similar concept but is very
different in execution.

DEFINITION
OF A SEGMENT

In the model of memory segmentation used in the 80386, it is no
longer possible to represent all of the information that defines a
segment in a 16-bit segment register. In particular, when multi-

ple privilege levels and intertask protection are required, some mechanism other than a 16-bit segment register clearly must be used. To that end, the 80386 uses an entirely different method of defining memory segments than that used in the 8086. Oddly enough, this system is still somewhat downward compatible with previous generations of the iAPX 86 family.

The most fundamental difference in the 80386's segmentation model, and perhaps the biggest conceptual hurdle for the 8086 programmer to overcome, is the fact that a user's program can no longer access any address in the processor's memory space merely by asking. Programmers working with the 8086 architecture understood that the processor had a 1MB address range, defined as a sequence of 64KB-long segments. All the programmer had to do to reference any arbitrary address in memory was load a segment register with the desired segment base address and then index into that segment, using offsets from 0 to FFFF. To access a higher or lower range of addresses, the programmer simply had to increase or decrease the base address contained in the segment register. Someone wanting to traverse the entire 1MB address space would have to shift the segment register a minimum of 16 times (16 * 64KB = 1MB).

It is interesting to note that the kind of memory segmentation scheme used in the 8086, in which address space is there for the asking, offers no real way to enforce any kind of memory protection, except through external hardware. Further, the existence of "real" physical memory to reference at any given address is irrelevant in this kind of architecture. The programmer is expected never to produce an address that does not correspond to physical memory or I/O. If an 8086 program does reference nonexistent memory, the system's response depends entirely on the design of the bus decoding hardware. The processor might read bogus data, an interrupt might be generated (by external hardware) to signal a bad address reference, or the system might just hang, waiting for data that will never come.

The 80386 represents a major break with this model of the memory map. On an 80386 system, a program, no matter how privileged, cannot access an area of memory unless that area has been "described" to it. Memory space is no longer there for the asking. Not every address that a program could produce is allowed. A program that tries to traverse the entire 4GB address space of the 80386 merely by incrementing an index repeatedly would probably be greeted by a segment violation exception at some point along the way. This model of the address space is the foundation on which the rest of the architecture of the 80386 is built, and it pervades all of the segmentation, protection, and multitasking features that are covered throughout this book.

As you can see, the concept of a segment is very different on an 80386 system running in Protected mode than it is on an 8086 system. The definition of a segment is much more fluid in the 80386 architecture. The processor does not arbitrarily enforce segment boundaries and alignment, as it did in the 8086. Instead, the 80386 provides a mechanism whereby the systems programmer defines what each segment will be. Included in the definition of each segment are its starting address, its length, its intended use, and other attributes.

You can now define segments to be almost anything you want. For instance, segments need not be exactly 64KB long; in fact, you can define them to be any length, from 1 byte to 4GB! A 1-byte segment is exactly what it implies—a segment with only one valid offset, 0. Conversely, a 4GB segment spans the entire linear address space on the 80386, from 0 to FFFFFFFF. This suggests that you could use a 32-bit index to traverse the entire address space without ever needing to modify the segment register.

Segments are given a starting (base) address, which can be any arbitrary address in the 32-bit linear address space. This is analogous to the segment base address that an 8086 program might load into a segment register. The base address defines the actual linear address that will be accessed when a program references offset 0 within the segment. Sixteen-byte alignment is no longer required and, indeed, is not always desirable. This way of defining segments gives the programmer complete control over memory usage and space requirements.

Segments are also assigned to have attributes. One attribute defines what the segment is to be used for, such as code, data, a stack, or some other purpose; another attribute specifies a privilege level from 0 to 3; and so on. The significance of the privilege level attribute is discussed in Chapter 3.

Segments are

- Areas of memory
- Defined by the programmer
- Used for different purposes, such as code, data, and stack

Segments are not

- All the same size
- Necessarily paragraph aligned
- Limited to 64KB

Segment Descriptors

A segment is described by a special structure called a *segment descriptor*. Exactly one segment descriptor must be defined for each segment of memory to be used in a running system. As was mentioned in the previous section, the description of a segment includes its base address, its length, its type, its privilege level, and some miscellaneous status information. All of this information is stored in the segment descriptor. Figure 2-1 shows an idealized version of a segment descriptor.

A segment descriptor defines all there is to know about a segment of memory. When you create a segment descriptor, you define an area of the address space as usable, under the restrictions of the descriptor definition. For instance, you can define a segment to span the address range from A400 to CE04 and another segment to cover addresses 230000 to 230FFF. You can define virtually any number of segment descriptors.

Bear in mind that if you do not describe an area of the address space in a descriptor, that address range is not addressable at all, and the processor will refuse to access it. If one of your programs erroneously (or deliberately) generates such an invalid address,

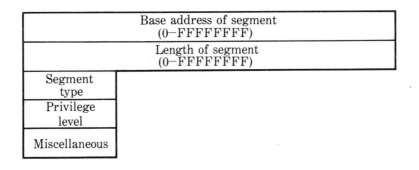

Figure 2-1.   Segment descriptor fields

the processor will trap the offending instruction before attempting to read or write the undefined address. Clearly, the ability to define segment descriptors carries considerable power and responsibility for system security.

A segment descriptor

- Describes a segment
- Must be created for every segment
- Is created by the programmer
- Determines a segment's base address
- Determines a segment's size
- Determines a segment's use
- Determines a segment's privilege level

The format of a segment descriptor is not quite as simple as Figure 2-1 might suggest. The actual format of a prototypical segment descriptor is given in Figure 2-2. Bits 16 through 39 hold the lower 24 bits of the segment's base address. The upper 8 bits of the base address are located in bits 56 through 63. By internally concatenating the two portions of the base address field, the processor can determine the linear address at which the

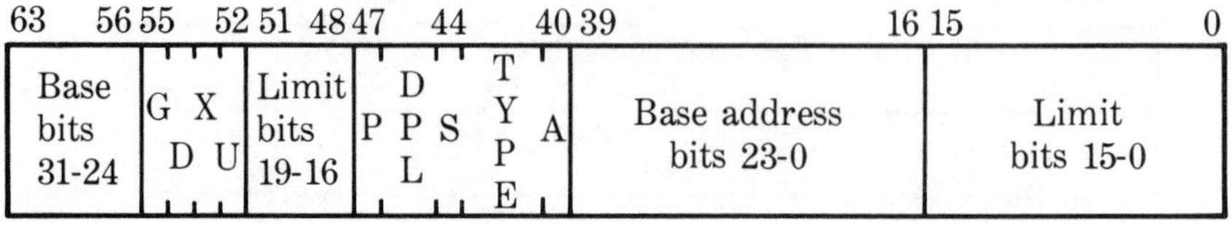

63 56	55 52	51 48	47 44	40	39 16	15 0
Base bits 31-24	G X D U	Limit bits 19-16	D P P S L	T Y P E A	Base address bits 23-0	Limit bits 15-0

Segment Types
000   Data, read only
001   Data, read/write
010   Stack, read only
011   Stack, read/write
100   Code, execute only
101   Code, execute/read
110   Code, execute only, conforming
111   Code, execute/read, conforming

Figure 2-2.   Segment descriptor format

segment starts. This is the linear address the processor will calculate when you reference offset 0 in that segment.

After the base address, the next most important field of a descriptor is the limit field, which also is broken into two parts. Intel has defined the limit field as the length of the segment in bytes minus 1. This definition saves space in the descriptor; the actual segment length is not used. For example, a segment that is 1 byte in length would have a limit of 0. A 4GB segment would have a limit of FFFFFFFF, thus saving a bit in the descriptor's limit field. Another way to remember the definition of this field is to think of it as specifying the largest valid offset for that segment. If the limit field has a value of 037, the largest offset address you could legally produce would be offset 037. (Remember that offset values start at 0.)

Bits 0 through 15 of the descriptor hold the lower 16 bits of the segment's limit. To complicate things further, the remaining 4 bits of the limit are located in bits 48 through 51 of the descriptor, making a total of 20 bits for the limit. Since 2^{20} bytes = 1MB, it might appear that you are, after all, limited to 1MB segments or smaller. But this is not so. As you learn about the rest of the fields within a segment descriptor, the reasons for this should become clear. The following provides a brief description of bits 40 through 55 of the descriptor. Each will be examined in detail throughout the chapter.

A (Accessed, bit 40)	The 80386 automatically sets this bit whenever a memory reference is made using the segment that this descriptor defines.
Type (Segment type, bits 41 through 43)	This 3-bit field indicates the type of segment you are defining. Common types are code, data, and stack.
S (System, bit 44)	If this bit is clear, it indicates that this is a system segment descriptor. If it is set, this is a nonsystem (code, data, or stack) segment descriptor. The difference between system and nonsystem descriptors is covered later in this chapter.
DPL (Descriptor Privilege Level, bits 45 and 46)	This 2-bit field indicates the level of privilege associated with the memory space that the descriptor defines. DPL 0 is the most privileged, DPL 3 the least.
P (Present, bit 47)	If this bit is clear, the address range that this descriptor defines is considered to be temporarily not present in physical memory.
U (User, bit 52)	This bit is completely undefined, and the 80386 ignores it. Intel promises that programmers can use this bit as they please.

X (Reserved by Intel, bit 53)	This bit is the opposite of the previous bit. It must not be defined, and your software must not use it.
D (Default size, bit 54)	When this bit is cleared, operands contained within this segment are assumed to be 16 bits in size. When it is set, operands are assumed to be 32 bits.
G (Granularity, bit 55)	When this bit is cleared, the 20-bit limit field is assumed to be measured in units of 1 byte. If it is set, the limit field is in units of 4096 bytes.

Figure 2-3 shows an example of a valid segment descriptor. Try to determine the size and usage of the segment it defines.

The first five fields described in the previous list are commonly referred to as the access rights (AR) byte. This byte spans bits 40 through 47, or the sixth byte, if you prefer, in the descriptor. Not all 256 permutations of this byte are valid on the 80386. AR byte values of 00 and 80 are reserved by Intel and will always be treated as invalid by the iAPX 86 processors. A segment descriptor with an invalid or undefined value in the AR byte is not an error per se, but the 80386 will generate a fault if you actually try to use such a descriptor.

Some of the bit-fields in a descriptor warrant a little more explanation. The Accessed bit of a descriptor is set automatically

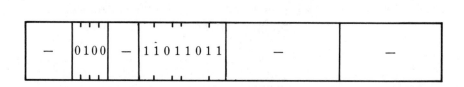

Figure 2-3.   Sample segment descriptor

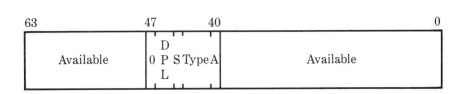

Figure 2-4.   Not-present segment descriptor

by the 80386 any time the segment of memory that this descriptor defines is used. The processor never clears this bit, however. You can use this fact to keep some simple frequency-of-usage information if you write code that periodically tests and then clears this bit in each of the descriptors. Over an extended period, the total number of times that this bit was found to be set in each descriptor should give you some pretty accurate information as to what descriptors, and hence what areas of memory, are being used most often.

The Present bit tells the processor whether the address range that this descriptor covers is considered to be present in physical memory. This bit is essentially a "descriptor-is-valid" flag. If you do not set the Present bit when creating a descriptor, the 80386 will refuse any subsequent attempts to use this descriptor in an instruction, making the address space covered by the descriptor unusable. An interesting fact to remember is that when a descriptor is marked not present, the processor ignores the rest of the descriptor, with the exception of the Access Rights byte (which must always be valid), as shown in Figure 2-4. This gives you 7 bytes to do with as you please. Some suggested uses for this free space are discussed in later chapters.

The Default bit is one of the features scattered throughout the 80386 architecture that allows compatibility with earlier processors. In particular, this feature allows you to run 80286 code in 80386 Protected mode. If the segment is defined as containing code and the D bit is clear, the processor interprets the contents of the segment as 16-bit 80286 code. If the D bit is set, it assumes that the segment contains 32-bit 80386 code. For a data or stack segment, a similar transformation takes place. When D = 0, stack operations are 16 bits wide, and SP is used as the stack pointer for all implicit stack operations (CALL, PUSH, and so on), instead of ESP. In addition, the maximum stack size is limited to FFFF (64KB), rather than to FFFFFFFF (4GB).

The Granularity bit allows you to build a segment larger than 1MB. With half of each descriptor taken up by the base address field, there is not enough room for a full 32-bit limit field. A 20-bit field is enough to specify limits up to 1MB with single-byte precision. After that point, the limit field must be interpreted in units of 4KB. If the G bit is set, the 80386 internally shifts the limit field 12 bits to the left and inserts 1s in the 12 least significant bit positions. Therefore, when the G bit is set, a limit field of 320 becomes 320FFF. Even though this doesn't allow fine-tuning with single-byte accuracy, if you're defining a segment that is larger than 1MB, it usually will not matter that it's a few kilobytes too large.

If the Granularity bit is set, the minimum size of a segment is 4KB −1 (FFF) if the limit field is 0. Thus, if you want to define a segment that is somewhere between 4KB and 1MB in size, you could define its limit with either single-byte accuracy (G = 0) or 4KB accuracy (G = 1).

Segment descriptors define

- Base address (32 bits)
- Segment limit (20 bits)
- Type of segment (4 bits)
- Privilege level of segment (2 bits)
- Whether segment is physically present (1 bit)
- Whether segment has been accessed before (1 bit)
- Granularity of limit field (1 bit)
- Size of operands within segment (1 bit)
- Intel reserved flag (1 bit)
- User-defined flag (1 bit)

Unlike the 8086 definition of segments, not all Protected mode segments are created equal. Certain attributes are associated with Protected mode segments that define what they can and cannot be used for. This attribute information is contained in the segment's descriptor, along with the segment's base address and its length. The most significant attributes are contained in the Access Rights byte; they are the System bit (bit 44) and the Type field (bits 41 through 43). When the System bit is 0, it indicates that the descriptor is a system segment descriptor, discussed in the next chapter. When this bit is 1, it means that the segment is to be used for code, data, or stack, as defined by the Type field. Figure 2-2 showed the 3-bit type and listed the eight possible encodings for this field. The differences in these eight types will be discussed carefully, since they will normally make up the bulk of any descriptors you create.

Type = 0 defines a data segment with read permission but no write permission. That is, it defines a virtual ROM space. Whether or not the physical space within this segment memory is really writable is irrelevant; the 80386 will not allow any write operations when referring to this segment.

Type = 1 is similar to Type = 0, except that the segment it defines does have write permission and so is a more traditional data segment. Read and write operations can be performed at will. A read/write data segment can be used for just that — storing data. Neither this segment type nor the previous one includes execute permission, and so you cannot store code in this segment. This prohibition is very strict. The 80386 will not fetch code from a segment that has not been defined with execute permission. You can't trick the 80386 into a FAR JMP or CALL to one of these segments, either. Although this may seem to be another annoying restriction, it is exactly this kind of typecasting that allows you to build solid, robust operating systems.

Type = 2 or 3 defines a stack segment. This is really just a variation of the data segments just described. The interesting difference between stack segments and data segments with the same permissions is the 80386's interpretation of the stack descriptor's limit field. Recall that the limit field specifies the length of a

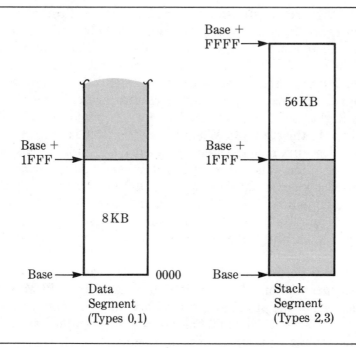

Figure 2-5.   Data segment and stack segment

segment in bytes minus 1 unless the Granularity bit (bit 55) is set, in which case it gives the length of the segment in 4096-byte chunks minus one 4096-byte chunk. Thus, the addressable range of a segment stretches from the base address to the base address plus the limit definition. Valid offset addresses range from 0 to the limit. Any offsets greater than the limit are not considered part of the segment and are not addressable.

In a stack segment, this model is precisely reversed. If the Type field specifies stack (type 2 or 3), then the limit field determines what area of the segment is *not* addressable. In a stack segment, all offsets must be *greater than* the limit. Figure 2-5 shows a data segment and a stack segment, each with a limit of 1FFF. In the case of the data segment, all offsets less than or equal to the limit are valid. The first addressable byte is at offset 0, and the last is at offset 1FFF, making the data segment 2000 bytes (8KB) long. In the case of the stack segment, all offsets greater than the limit are valid. The first addressable byte is at offset 2000, and the last is at FFFF. Offset address 0 is not valid, and the stack segment is E000 bytes (56KB) long.

With a data segment, you know that the lower limit is set by the base address field of the descriptor and the upper limit is set by the limit field. For a stack segment, you have seen that the lower limit is set by the limit field. What sets the upper limit? You have two choices. If the D bit (bit 54) in the descriptor is 0, the upper limit of the stack segment is equal to the base address plus the constant value FFFF (64KB). If the D bit is set, the upper limit is equal to the base address plus FFFFFFFF (4GB). Because all offsets must be greater than the limit, a stack segment has maximum size when the limit is 0. A stack segment has the minimum size when the limit is either FFFF (D = 0) or FFFFFFFF (D = 1), producing a null segment—a segment with zero length.

You will recall from the earlier discussion of the D bit that if a stack segment descriptor's D bit is set, the 32-bit stack pointer ESP is used for all stack references, and all PUSHes and POPs are 32 bits wide. If the D bit is not set, the 16-bit SP is used instead, and all stack-related operations are only 16 bits wide. That means that if you want to use a 32-bit stack, which is strongly recommended for new development, you must set the D bit of the stack descriptor, thus giving yourself a 4GB upper limit on the stack segment. Furthermore, the 80386 requires that if the D bit of a stack descriptor is set, the G bit *must* be set also. If the D bit is clear, the G bit *must not* be set. Hence, you not only have to define a 32-bit stack segment with an upper bound of FFFFFFFF, you have to specify the limit in units of 4KB.

This is not quite as restrictive as it might sound. To see why, first consider the issue of a segment whose upper limit is always 4GB above the base address. Obviously, since the 80386 has only a 4GB linear address space, something's got to give if you define a stack segment base to be anything other than 0. What happens to the upper limit if you define a stack with a base address of, say, 10000? The limit definition wraps around the end of the address space and ends up at FFFF. The rule of thumb, then, when defining 32-bit stack segments, is to define the base address 1 byte *above* where you want the segment to end. On the 80386, adding 4GB is exactly like subtracting 1 byte.

The second issue to consider is the fact that the D bit and G bit must have the same setting, dooming you to 4KB granularity on your 32-bit stacks. Unfortunately, there is no apparent way around this restriction. If you don't expect to use up more than 4KB of stack space, simply define the stack descriptor's limit field as FFFFE. With the large granularity, this will expand to a limit of FFFFEFFF. Because all stack offsets must be greater than the limit, your stack space extends from that address plus 1 (FFFFF000) to FFFFFFFF.

Why all of the bizarre rules for a stack segment? You are not even required to define a stack segment in order to use a stack. There is no rule against putting the stack pointer, ESP, in the middle of a normal data segment (as long as it's writable). But since stack pointers typically start at the highest address in the segment and grow down, problems arise if you run out of stack space and need to increase the size of the stack's segment. Take the case of a normal data segment, which you can expand by increasing the value in the limit field of its descriptor. Doing this allows you to use higher addresses than before. Stacks grow downward, however, and so after expanding the data segment, you would have to shift the entire stack frame up so that it was again in the upper reaches of the segment. Apart from the danger involved in fooling with the stack in this way, you would also have to translate every stack-related reference at run time to make up for the shift in addresses—not an exciting prospect. If, however, you define the segment as a stack from the beginning, simply decreasing the limit field of the descriptor gives you room to grow down. When a bat grows larger, it is sometimes easier to lower the floor than to raise the ceiling, to avoid disturbing the bat.

The remaining types, 4, 5, 6, and 7, define executable segments. As the name implies, this is where your code lives. Note that read permission is optional for executable segments. If read permission is denied (type 4), the segment must contain pure code; no constants are allowed, since they cannot be read out. Only code fetching is allowed. This is useful if you wish to protect your object code from prying eyes. If read permission is given (type 5), you can embed constants in the code itself. Note that writing is never allowed to an executable segment. Self-modifying code is not possible, nor is maliciously modified code, which is the whole point.

The two executable segment types are repeated with the conforming attribute set (types 6 and 7). Conforming simply means that these code segments voluntarily forgo their privilege level protection; this is covered in detail in Chapter 3.

The solution to the size and usage of the segment shown in Figure 2-3 is that it is a 32-bit code segment with read permission; the privilege level is 2, and the segment has been accessed.

Segments can be defined in eight basic types:
- Executable code segments with or without data read permission
- Executable code segments with or without privilege protection
- Data segments with or without write permission
- Stack segments with or without write permission

Descriptor Tables

As was mentioned earlier, you can pretty much create as many segment descriptors as you want, and you can always add more descriptors as system or user needs dictate. Now you need to know how the processor keeps track of all these separate, unrelated pieces of information.

The segment descriptors that you define must be grouped and placed one after the other in contiguous memory locations. This group arrangement is known as a *descriptor table*. The order in which they are placed in the table is not important. The table can have one descriptor in it, or it can have as many as 8192, making the table 64KB long! There are three types of descriptor tables, each used for a different purpose, and so you must consider the

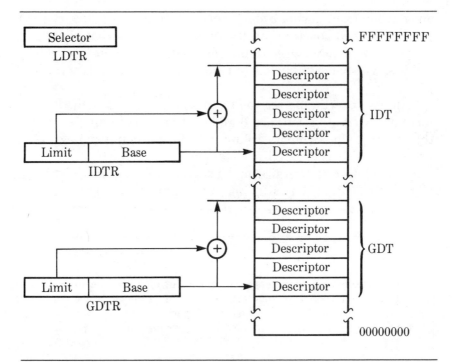

Figure 2-6.   Descriptor tables and descriptors

intended use of a segment before deciding which table to include it in.

The global descriptor table (GDT) is the main, general-purpose table of descriptors. The GDT can be used by all programs to reference segments of memory. The interrupt descriptor table (IDT) holds segment descriptors that define interrupt- or exception-handling routines. The IDT is a direct replacement for the interrupt vector table used in 8086 systems. Exactly one GDT and one IDT must be defined for the 80386 to operate in Protected mode.

Lastly, the local descriptor table (LDT) can be defined on a per-task basis in a multitasking system, but its use is purely optional. The LDT, if defined, can be used in addition to the GDT to expand the number of available descriptors and, hence, the addressable range of selected tasks. Each task usually gets its own LDT, but tasks can also share a few different LDTs. LDTs need not be defined at all if system requirements do not warrant it or if hardware-supported multitasking will not be used. Chapter 5, which covers multitasking, describes how LDTs can be used for this. Figure 2-6 demonstrates the relationship between a descriptor, the descriptor tables, and the linear address space that they describe.

Descriptors are stored in three tables:

1. Global descriptor table (GDT)
   - Maintains a list of most segments
   - May contain special "system" descriptors

2. Interrupt descriptor table (IDT)
   - Maintains a list of interrupt service routines

3. Local descriptor table (LDT)
   - Is optional
   - Extends range of GDT
   - Is allocated to each task when multitasking is enabled

After you have placed each descriptor in a descriptor table, you need to inform the processor of the whereabouts of the tables. You can place the descriptor tables anywhere in the processor's address space, and you need not keep them together. To allow the processor to locate the GDT, IDT, and current LDT (if any), you load the 80386's three special-purpose registers, GDTR, IDTR, and LDTR, respectively. Each of these registers is large enough internally to store the 32-bit linear address of the base of its descriptor table and the table's limit. The base address of a descriptor table is the linear address of the first byte of the first descriptor in the table. The limit (the length of the table minus 1) must be specified so that the processor can tell how long the table is and therefore how many descriptors it is supposed to contain. Because each descriptor is 64 bits (8 bytes) long, the table limit should equal (descriptors / 8) -1. See Appendix B for a more complete description of the LGDT, LIDT, and LLDT instructions.

SEGMENT SELECTORS

Once the descriptors are defined, how does the processor make use of them? How does the casual user, who wants only to make the program run, access them? This is the portion of the 80386 memory management that allows some measure of downward compatibility with the 8086, even though, as you have seen, the segmentation mechanism seems to be completely incompatible.

As much as the segmentation mechanism may have changed, the processor's segment registers are still only 16 bits wide. You know that to define a segment now takes no fewer than 8 bytes, and even that requires some fudging on the segment length field. Obviously, a segment register can't hold an entire descriptor, and the 8086's simple system of bit-shifting a segment register to determine a segment is certainly long gone.

It is sometimes said that the more things change, the more they stay the same. This certainly appears to be the case with the segmentation mechanism on the 80386. The problem of getting from segment register to segment descriptor to memory segment has an elegantly straightforward solution, one that looks surprisingly like the system used on the 8086. Recall that on the 8086 a segment register was bit-shifted to the left 4 bits (multiplied by 16) in order to produce a segment's base address. On the 80386, a segment register is bit-shifted to the *right* 3 bits (divided by 8) to select a descriptor in a descriptor table.

The rule is as follows: by taking any arbitrary value in a segment register and shifting it 3 bits to the right, you produce a 13-bit value, n. That segment register refers to the nth descriptor in the descriptor table.

You now see that on the 80386 the relationship between a segment register (in the processor) and a segment descriptor (in memory as part of a descriptor table) is one of pointer to structure. The segment registers act as 13-bit pointers into the array of segment descriptors. A 13-bit pointer can define a value between 0 and 8191, which is why there can be a maximum of 8192 descriptors in any given descriptor table (making the table 64KB long). But why use only 13 bits of a segment register instead of all 16? If the lower 3 bits of a segment register are shifted out, wouldn't eight consecutive segment values all index to the same descriptor? And to which of the descriptor tables does the segment register refer?

You can find the answers to these questions by looking at what the lower 3 bits of the segment register are used for. The 3 least significant bits of a segment register are indeed significant to both the segmentation and protection hardware of the 80386. The last two (bits 0 and 1) are used to define the privilege level, from 0 to 3. The privilege-checking system is discussed in detail in the next chapter. All you need to know now is that the privilege level bits have no effect on which descriptor a segment register points to, so you can ignore them for now.

The other as-yet-undefined bit (bit 2) indicates which descriptor table you want to reference. If this bit is 0, the segment register references the nth descriptor in the GDT. If this bit is 1, it references the nth descriptor in the LDT. Thus, to answer the questions raised earlier, eight consecutive segment values do not select the same descriptor, but four consecutive ones do, and the descriptor table is indicated in bit 2 in the segment register itself.

On the 8086, any value loaded into a segment register automatically became a segment base address. On the 80386, any value you load into a segment register is considered to be an index into either the GDT or the LDT. A new term has been coined for the contents of a segment register to describe its function more accurately. Any 16-bit value that you write into a segment register is called a *selector*, because it selects a segment descriptor from a descriptor table. The fields within a selector are as follows. These fields are shown schematically in Figure 2-7.

INDEX (Descriptor index, bits 3 through 15)	This value selects one of 8192 descriptors in a descriptor table.
TI (Table indicator, bit 2)	When this bit is 0, the index portion refers to a descriptor in the

	GDT. When it is 1, it refers to a descriptor in the current LDT.
RPL (Requested privilege level, bits 0 and 1)	This 2-bit field is used for privilege checking by the protection mechanism.

A selector value of 0008 would point to the second descriptor in the GDT. So would the values 0009, 000A, and 000B. Changing the RPL field affects the protection mechanism, but the selector still points to the same descriptor. If you walk through the selector values, you find that 000C, 000D, 000E, and 000F all refer to the second descriptor in the LDT (if any). Incrementing the selector value to 0010 causes it to point to the next descriptor in the GDT. Although a selector value of 0000 is valid, the first entry in the GDT is reserved by the processor and should be all zeros. This is known as the *null descriptor*. Thus, even though selector values 0000 through 0003 may be legal, they are null selectors, and do not refer to useful segments.

As Figure 2-8 shows, the entire path of logical-to-linear address translation has now been defined. A hypothetical program is shown reading an operand from the DS segment. The offset is contained in register ESI (the logical address). The processor must first examine the value that you have previously loaded into DS. The TI bit is not set, so the processor uses the index portion of DS (bits 3 through 15) as a pointer into the GDT to find the correct data segment descriptor. The base of the GDT,

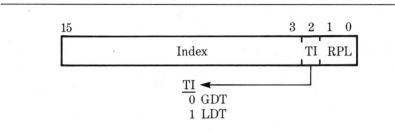

Figure 2-7. Selector format

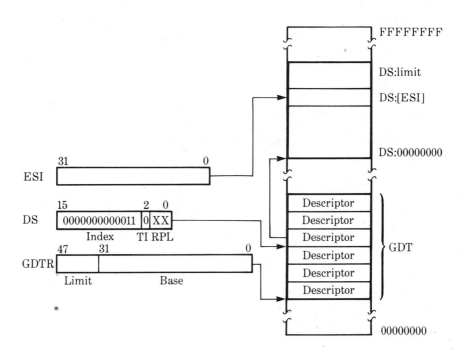

Figure 2-8.   Memory addressing

as well as its upper limit, can be located through the GDTR. The processor then concatenates the fragments of the base address field in the data segment descriptor and comes up with the base address of the DS segment. To this base address it adds the offset in register ESI. This is the linear address where the operand is actually located.

In the interest of time, and to cut down on massive amounts of external memory traffic, the 80386 does not actually perform all of these table lookup tasks on every memory reference. Instead, it caches the entire 8-byte descriptor internally when the segment register DS is first loaded with that descriptor's selector. From that point on, until DS is changed, the processor has all of the necessary information cached for quick reference. This is true of all six segment registers. All of this is invisible to the programmer, of course, except for one aspect: if you make a habit of modifying descriptor tables on the fly, be certain that all of the processor's segment registers are flushed and recached, or stale information may be used.

80386 has six segment registers:

- One for current code segment (CS)
- One for current stack segment (SS)
- Four for general data segments (DS, ES, FS, GS)

Segment registers select segment descriptors:

- Thirteen bits select descriptor
- One bit selects descriptor table
- Two bits aid privilege checking

Loading Segment Selectors

As was mentioned earlier, there is a direct correlation between the value loaded into a segment register (the selector) and the descriptor to which it refers. Any given selector value selects one and only one descriptor. Each descriptor, however, can be selected by as many as four consecutive selector values, because the RPL field does not affect descriptor selection. Changing a few bits in a segment register can have major consequences in memory addressability. It's not difficult to see that many values that would be completely reasonable for an 8086 yield meaningless results in Protected mode on the 80386. If only four descriptors have been defined in the GDT, for example, any selector value greater than 001B would be invalid because it would refer to a nonexistent descriptor beyond the end of the table. Similarly, if no LDT has been defined, any selector in which the TI bit is set (0004, 000C, or 0014, for example) would also be invalid. What happens when you try to use a segment register with such a selector in it? Nobody knows, because it doesn't ever happen.

Any time that a segment register is modified, whether by direct manipulation in your code or indirectly by some automatic action such as an interrupt, the 80386 performs some routine "sanity checks" on the selector before actually loading it into the segment register and caching its descriptor. Some of these tests have to do with privilege level checking and will be discussed in the next chapter. The rest are carefully designed to keep you from loading meaningless selectors.

In all cases, the processor checks to see whether the index field of the selector in question is within the limits of the table indicated by the TI bit. That is why the descriptor table limits are stored right along with their base addresses. In addition, if you are trying to load a data segment register (DS, ES, FS, or GS), the descriptor type it points to must be readable. No execute-only segments are allowed, although execute/read ones are permissible. In the case of the SS register, the segment must be readable and writable (read-only stacks are just about useless), but it does not necessarily have to be defined as a stack. If you are loading the CS register, the segment must be defined as executable. If the selector passes all of these tests, the 80386 checks the Present flag (bit 47) of the descriptor to see whether the segment in question is really there. If it is, the segment register is finally loaded with the new value, and the descriptor it refers to is cached, as described previously. If any of these tests fail, the processor raises an exception and nothing is changed.

If the indicated descriptor would be beyond the limits of the appropriate descriptor table, the processor raises a general protection fault, exception 13, and the offending selector is pushed onto your stack as the error code. (See Chapter 7 for a description of error codes.) If the descriptor is not the correct type for the segment register, that is, executable for CS, writable for SS, and readable for all others, you get a general protection fault. For all registers except SS, if the descriptor is marked not present (P = 0), the 80386 forces an exception 11, not-present fault, and pushes the selector. For SS, you get a stack segment fault, exception 12, instead. Loading a segment register with selector values between

0000 and 0003, the null selector, is all right unless it's going into CS or SS. In that case, you get a general protection fault.

The fact that segment registers are no longer harmless paragraph addresses for the segment is, for the most part, not relevant to the applications programmer. You can still load and manipulate segment registers with normal MOV, PUSH, and POP instructions, just as you could before. In addition, there are some new instructions for loading segment registers: LDS, LES, LFS, LGS, and LSS. However, the values the programmer loads are going to be very different. The results of loading a segment register with a given value when running in Protected mode are radically different than those to which an 8086 programmer is accustomed.

Consider the relationship between a selector, the descriptor to which it points, and the address space to which the descriptor points. First of all, incrementing the value of a segment register doesn't cause it to point to the next segment descriptor in the descriptor table; rather, it increments the RPL field of the selector. This could possibly affect the privilege-checking mechanism. If you want to select the next descriptor, you must increment the current selector by 8. Second, because there is absolutely no relationship between consecutive descriptors in a table (unless you deliberately set it up that way), even if you did point your segment selector to the next higher descriptor, it probably wouldn't define the next sequential range of addresses. In short, there is no obvious way to tell what address space (if any) a segment register points to based on its contents (the selector). Segment selectors, therefore, are nothing more than 16-bit tags for a given address space.

Given all of this information, it would seem that the task of the 80386 assembly language programmer is nearly hopeless. Without intimate knowledge of the arrangement of the GDT and LDT, there is no way to manipulate segment registers with any kind of certainty. How is the programmer to assign values to segments in order to reference variables or procedures if the selectors are assigned at random?

This is where the new generation of 80386 compilers, assemblers, and linkers comes in. Gone are the days when an assembly language programmer who happened to know where a video buffer was located in memory could blithely load the DS and ES segment registers with its paragraph address and perform a string MOV to fill the buffer. There is *no way* for the applications programmer to reference physical memory on the 80386. All memory references, whether to code, data, or stack, are segment-relative, and all segments have their own base addresses, which are not stored in the segment registers as they are on the 8086. Segments must now be referred to symbolically. Segment registers are not (or at least should not be) loaded with immediate constants hard-coded into the source code but rather are loaded with symbolic names. At program link time (or "binding," in Intel parlance), these symbols should be resolved by the linker. But even this assumes that the linker knows how the descriptor tables are going to be arranged on the target system. More often than not, segment resolution has to wait until the program is loaded; all segment references are then resolved dynamically by the loader.

If you are an applications programmer, you simply need to relearn a few habits, and you can leave the rest of the work to the linker or loader. If you are writing the operating system, however, these burdens fall directly on you.

When loading segment selectors, the 80386 checks that

- The selector index is within the descriptor table limit
- The selector references the correct descriptor table
- The descriptor is of the correct type
- The selector uses the correct privilege level

Selector Sleuthing

At run time, the curious programmer can examine the actual selector values that the linker or loader has assigned to the code segments. Given a selector, you can find out certain information. You can at least determine which descriptor table it refers to by testing bit 2, and bits 3 through 15 tell you which descriptor it references within that table. Of course, if you have access to the descriptor tables themselves, you can always read and decipher them directly. More often than not, however, this is not an option. You can also determine the type of descriptor it might be pointing to by using the LAR (Load Access Rights) instruction. LAR takes a selector, looks up its descriptor in the appropriate table, and returns the values of the following fields:

G	Granularity bit
D	Default size bit
X	Intel reserved bit
U	User-defined bit
P	Present bit
DPL	Descriptor Privilege Level field
S	System bit
Type	Descriptor type field
A	Accessed bit

Note that this includes the entire access rights byte plus the D and G bits. In fact, this instruction tells you everything about the segment except its base address and its limit.

The limit you can discover with the LSL (Load Segment Limit) instruction. Like LAR, LSL takes a selector and returns some information, in this case, the limit of the segment, in a 32-bit register of your choosing. It will even do the 4KB-to-1-byte conversion for you if the G bit in the descriptor is set.

If your needs are simpler, and all you want to know is whether or not a segment is readable or writable, two further instructions can help you. VERR (Verify for Read) will tell you whether it is possible to read from the segment whose selector you are testing, and VERW (Verify for Write) will perform a similar function, reporting writability. There is no way at all to determine the base address of a segment, which makes physical memory addressing impossible. Keep in mind also that, depending on the privilege level of the program that is doing the asking, the 80386 may refuse to return any of this information. Chapter 3 discusses the privilege checks that are performed.

Segment selectors can be "reverse engineered" to determine

- The segment's limit
- The segment's type
- The segment's read/write permission
- The segment's privilege level
- The segment's accessed status
- The segment's operand size
- The status of reserved and user-defined flags

LOCAL DESCRIPTOR TABLES

As was mentioned earlier, there are three distinct types of descriptor tables: global, local, and interrupt. There must be exactly one GDT and one IDT while the processor is running in Protected mode. The programmer can, if desired, have others defined in memory, on reserve, but only one of each can be considered active at any moment—the ones pointed to by the GDTR and IDTR registers. You can also define 0 to 8191 local descriptor tables, although, as with the other tables, only one is considered active at a time.

LDTs act like extensions to the GDT, but they are assigned to individual tasks when hardware-supported task switching is used. (See Chapter 5.) Any program can, when running, use descriptors in the GDT and in the LDT assigned to its task. If no LDT has been assigned, all descriptors must come from the GDT, and the programmer must avoid loading a segment selector with the TI bit (bit 2) set. Therefore, having an LDT defined for a task effectively extends its addressable range. This feature can be used to allow only certain tasks to access special address spaces, such as a video buffer or disk controller.

LDTs are created exactly like GDTs or IDTs. They are vector arrays of descriptors. The way in which the processor locates them is much different, however. Whereas the 80386 has special

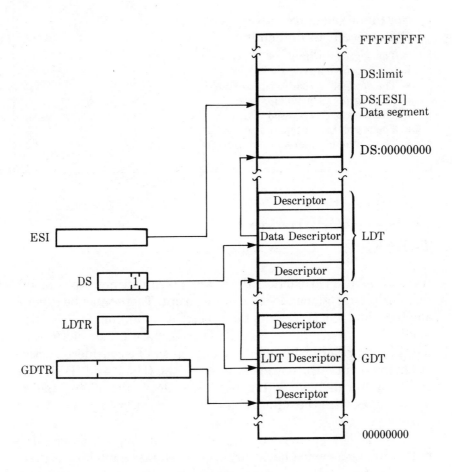

Figure 2-9.   Local descriptor table

48-bit registers to hold the base and limit of the GDT and IDT (which typically don't change very often), the current LDT (which may change with every new task) is tracked by a 16-bit selector. This selector (LDTR) must refer to a special LDT descriptor in the GDT. In the same way that a code segment descriptor defines the upper and lower bounds of a segment of memory containing code, an LDT descriptor in the GDT defines the base address and limit of another descriptor table—an LDT. The GDT can contain any number of LDT descriptors, one for each LDT to be defined. In this way, the processor can keep track of the current LDT by loading a selector that points to a descriptor that in turn defines the location and size of another descriptor table. Any memory references that use a segment that has the TI bit set in its selector will then be resolved through this LDT. Figure 2-9 illustrates this doubly indirect scheme. Don't panic—LDT descriptors cannot appear in LDTs. Only so much indirection is tolerable in silicon.

LDT descriptors are one example of the system segment descriptors mentioned earlier. When the S flag (bit 44) is not set in a descriptor, it signifies a system segment descriptor, as opposed to a code, data, or stack descriptor. System segment descriptors have no Accessed bit. Instead, the type field is expanded to 4 bits. If the value in the Type field is 2, the descriptor is an LDT descriptor, as illustrated in Figure 2-10. The base address field holds the 32-bit linear base address for the LDT, and the limit field defines the length of the LDT minus 1, just as the limits for the GDT and IDT are defined. Note that the full 20 bits for the limit are allowed, plus the G bit, so you could define an LDT that was more than 64KB long if you really wanted to. It would not be flagged as an error by the processor, but it wouldn't be wise, either, since having selector values checked against the limit of a descriptor table is one of the things that keeps errant programs from crashing the system by specifying invalid selectors.

Note also that the LDT descriptor has a Present bit just like any other descriptor. If the descriptor is marked not present, all of the descriptors within that LDT are, by inference, also not

63	55	51	47	39	15	0
Base address 31-24	0000	Limit 19-16	P 0000010	Base address 23-0	Limit 15-0	

Figure 2-10. LDT descriptor format

present. The 80386 will not even allow you to load the LDTR register with the selector of a not-present LDT.

To put an LDT in service, you simply load the LDTR with the appropriate selector for the LDT descriptor for the LDT you want to use. In that respect, the LDTR is just like the other segment registers. If you attempt to load the LDTR with anything but a selector to an LDT descriptor, the 80386 generates a general protection fault, and the offending selector is pushed on your stack as the error code. If the descriptor's P bit is 0, you'll get a not-present fault, also with the selector as the error code. Loading the LDTR with a null selector (values 0000 through 0003) is perfectly legal and informs the processor that you are not currently using an LDT.

So far in this discussion, no reference has been made to the IDT. This is because program code must never refer to a descriptor in the IDT. That's why there is only one Table Indicator bit in a selector. The IDT exists to allow the 80386 to find appropriate exception handlers by itself, should an interrupt or exception occur. It is not used as a third general-purpose descriptor table. Chapter 7 deals with exceptions, interrupts, and the IDT in more detail.

Local descriptor tables
- Hold segment descriptors
- May be used in addition to the global descriptor table
- Are defined by a special "system" descriptor in GDT
- May be larger or smaller than GDT
- May not define other LDTs

SEGMENT ALIASING, OVERLAPPING, AND MORE

The 80386 allows you to create segments that are read-only, execute-only, read/write, or execute/read. There is no combination of attributes that will give you a "traditional" 8086-style segment that is simultaneously readable, writable, and executable. As you will see, however, this effect can be created through other means.

With 8086-style memory segmentation, it is common practice to reference the same physical location in memory using different segment registers. A trivial case would be if both DS and ES contained the same paragraph address, say, 0100. Referencing offset 0234 in the DS segment would then provide exactly the same results as referencing offset 0234 in the ES segment. In both cases, physical address 1234 is accessed. If, instead, ES contained the paragraph value 0120, and you referenced offset 0034, the result would still be the same: 1234. You can produce the same effect on the 80386 through the judicious creation of segment descriptors.

Typically, segment descriptors are created at system initialization time to define all of the areas of memory you expect to use and their expected uses (code, data, or stack). You might define a single code segment to hold your executable portion, one or two data segments, and a stack segment large enough to hold a worst-case stack frame. By and large, these segments would occupy distinct areas of physical memory. You could, if you wished, assign them to contiguous addresses, end to end, so that the end of one segment coincided with the beginning of another.

Figure 2-11 illustrates this common application, with a 6KB code segment at low memory, followed by two 12KB data segments. The stack segment is defined 4KB beyond the end of the second data segment and grows down. You would say that these segments are disjoint because they do not overlap and only one unique segment:offset combination references any given byte.

What would happen if you modified the descriptor of the first data segment to increase its limit by 4KB? The upper end of the first data segment would be 4KB into the second data segment, and the two segments would overlap, as shown in Figure 2-12. This is not an error. The 80386 imposes absolutely no restrictions against overlapping segment definitions; all or only part of the segments can overlap.

When two or more segment definitions overlap in this way, you can use the result to your advantage. You can reference any location in the union (overlap) of the two segments in the figure by two different means. Reading from offset 0 in the second data

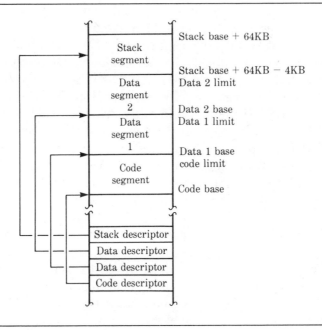

Figure 2-11.   Disjoint memory segments

segment will produce exactly the same result as reading from offset 3000 (12KB + 1) in the first data segment. Likewise, you can write to offset 3FFF in the first data segment and read the result at offset 0FFF in the second.

Although it is not allowable to write into a segment that has been defined as executable, there is nothing wrong with writing into a segment that has been defined as writable and that just happens to cover the same linear address range as an executable segment. If a data segment descriptor and a code segment descriptor have the same base address and limit fields, you can write into your code space and execute your data space. This is known as *aliasing*.

To carry this to an extreme, you could define a data segment with read/write privileges, a base address of 0, and a limit of FFFFFFFF. Loading the selector for this descriptor into a segment register would allow you to read and write every address in

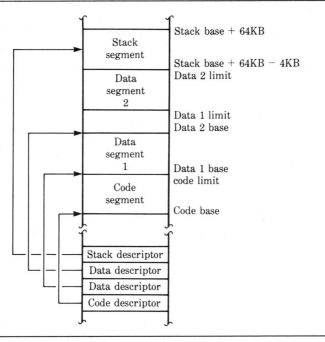

Figure 2-12.   Overlapping memory segments

the entire 4GB linear space of the 80386! You would have effectively aliased every other segment in the system. There is no guarantee that there will be any memory there to talk to (systems with 4GB of main memory are scarce), but you can define segments that describe nonexistent space as easily as you can define overlapping space.

Overlapping and aliasing are useful when the operating system wants two or more programs to share some part of a data structure. The case of a data segment aliasing a code segment is another good example that might allow you to write self-modifying code. Aliasing is also useful for illustrating a point that has not yet been made. As with all other memory, the space occupied by a descriptor table is not addressable without a descriptor to define it. If you don't create aliases of your descriptor tables as data segments before entering Protected mode, you will never see them again. Keeping these segment definitions well guarded is of paramount importance, since giving every program in a system read/write privileges for the GDT, LDT, and IDT would normally be suicidal.

EXAMPLES

The following program demonstrates how you can create the descriptors and descriptor tables necessary to partition a hypothetical system like the one in Figure 2-12.

```
code    SEGMENT ER PUBLIC USE32

        ASSUME  CS:code
        ASSUME  ES:bigdata
        ASSUME  SS:stack

        ; This program will manufacture 5 new descriptors, and
        ; add them to an existing GDT in slots 10 through 14.
        ; It will also place two descriptors in a newly-created
        ; LDT. An LDT descriptor will be created and placed in
        ; the GDT which points to this descriptor table.
        ; Completed memory map to match that shown in Figure 2-13.

        ; Assumptions:
        ; 1) We are already operating in Protected Virtual Address Mode.
        ; 2) Our ES segment points to a "global alias" i.e. a 4 Gb data segment.
        ; 3) GDT slots 10 through 14 are not already being used.

start:  CLI                                 ;disable interrupts
        SUB     ESP,6                        ;make room on stack
        SGDT    PWORD PTR SS:[ESP]           ;store GDT base & limit

        MOV     ESI, OFFSET desc_1           ;source = descriptor definitions
        MOV     EDI, DWORD PTR SS:[ESP] +2   ;EDI = base address of GDT
        ADD     EDI, 10 * 8                  ;dest = GDT slot 10
        MOV     ECX, 5 * 2                   ;count = 5 descriptors

        REP     MOVS DWORD PTR ES:[EDI], DWORD PTR CS:[ESI]

        ADD     WORD PTR SS:[ESP], 5 * 8     ;increase size of GDT
        LGDT    PWORD PTR SS:[ESP]           ;load GDT base & new limit

        MOV     ESI, OFFSET desc_1           ;source = descriptor definitions
        MOV     EDI, 0200h                   ;destination = ES:[0200]
        MOV     ECX, 2 * 2                   ;count = 2 descriptors

        REP     MOVS DWORD PTR ES:[EDI], DWORD PTR CS:[ESI]

        MOV     AX, 14 * 8                   ;LDT descriptor is in GDT(14)
        LLDT    AX                           ;load LDTR

        ADD     ESP, 6
        RET

; ------------------------------------------------
; Code Descriptor
desc_1  DW      17FFh           ;limit =    x17FF
        DW      0000h           ;base  = xxxx0000
        DB      10h             ;base  = xx10xxxx
        DB      10011010b       ;Present, DPL 0, Executable, Readable
        DB      01000000b       ;Byte granular, 32 bit code, limit = 0xxxx
        DB      00h             ;base  = 00xxxxxxx
```

```
; Data Descriptor 1
desc_2  DW      3FFFh           ;limit =    x3FFF
        DW      1800h           ;base  = xxxx1800
        DB      10h             ;base  = xx10xxxx
        DB      10010010b       ;Present, DPL 0, Data, Writeable
        DB      01000000b       ;Byte granular, 32 bit data, limit = 0xxxx
        DB      00h             ;base  = 00xxxxxxx

; Data Descriptor 2
desc_3  DW      2FFFh           ;limit =    x2FFF
        DW      4800h           ;base  = xxxx4800
        DB      10h             ;base  = xx10xxxx
        DB      10010010b       ;Present, DPL 0, Data, Writeable
        DB      01000000b       ;Byte granular, 32 bit data, limit = 0xxxx
        DB      00h             ;base  = 00xxxxxxx

; Stack Descriptor
desc_4  DW      0FFFEh          ;limit =    xFFFE
        DW      8800h           ;base  = xxxx8800
        DB      10h             ;base  = xx10xxxx
        DB      10010110b       ;Present, DPL 0, Stack, Writeable
        DB      11001111b       ;Page granular, 32 bit stack, limit = Fxxxx
        DB      00h             ;base  = 00xxxxxxx

; LDT Descriptor
desc_5  DW      000Fh           ;limit =    x000F
        DW      0200h           ;base  = xxxx0200
        DB      00h             ;base  = xx00xxxx
        DB      10000010b       ;Present, LDT descriptor
        DB      00000000b       ;Byte granular, limit = 0xxxx
        DB      00h             ;base  = 00xxxxxx

code    ENDS

END
```

Because this is the first sample of program code, some orientation may be in order. The first several lines of the program are pseudocode for the assembler's benefit. They tell the assembler that it is in fact assembling code and also where segment registers will be pointing to. All of this is typical and should be familiar to 8086 or 80286 programmers. The one unique aspect is the USE32 declaration. Because most 80386 assemblers can also produce 80286 and, in some cases, 8086 code, you need to tell the assembler that you want to produce 32-bit code.

The program starts out by disabling interrupts; this is always a good idea when you are fooling around with descriptors. To keep intersegment references to a minimum in this example, temporary variables will be stored on the stack rather than in named variables in another data segment. Because the SGDT instruction stores 6 bytes, space for it will be allocated on the stack.

Next comes the initialization for a string move. Register ESI points to the source—the five descriptors embedded in the code as constants. Register EDI gets the base address of the GDT from the stack, and then 80 bytes are added to that, since, in this example, writing is to begin at the tenth descriptor slot and each descriptor is 8 bytes long. Register ECX gets the number of times that the MOVSD instruction is to be repeated—five descriptors times two dwords per descriptor. Notice the segment override for the source of the MOVSD instruction. It is necessary to specify here that the source operands lie in the current code segment. Otherwise, the 80386 will read from the DS segment by default.

After the five descriptors have been copied into the GDT, the program needs to inform the processor that the size of the GDT

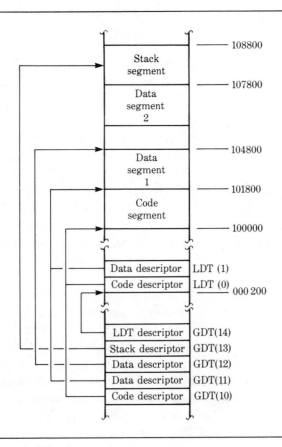

Figure 2-13.   Sample memory map

has increased by 40 bytes. It does this by changing the value of the GDT limit field left over from the SGDT instruction, and reloading it with LGDT.

Just for fun, the code creates an LDT in which the first two descriptors from the GDT (code segment and data segment 1) reappear. This LDT has been placed at the arbitrary address 0200. Just putting it there is not enough, however. The 80386 must be informed of the active LDT with an LLDT instruction that uses the selector to the LDT descriptor in the GDT as an operand. Because the LDT descriptor is in GDT slot 14, correct selector values would be 0070 through 0073.

After this program fragment has completed, you should have an address map like that shown in Figure 2-13. Note that the code segment and the first data segment could be referenced with selectors pointing to either the GDT or the new LDT.

The use of data or code aliasing may not be required or desirable in all systems, but it is a good thing to be aware of. Most operating systems or kernels need to keep a few carefully guarded segment aliases around, if only so that they themselves can modify the descriptor tables from time to time. A common practice, and a good habit to cultivate, is to dedicate the first descriptor in every table to an alias of that table.

The next sample program shows a few of the many ways that you can generate segmentation faults.

```
code    SEGMENT ER PUBLIC USE32

        ASSUME  CS:code
        ASSUME  DS:data1

        ; This program will experiment with addressing modes,
        ; deliberately generating errors.

        ; Assumptions:
        ; 1) The current address map matches that in Figure 2-12 or 2-13.

        MOV     ESI, 0
test1:  MOV     AL, BYTE PTR DS:[ESI]        ;read a byte from memory
        INC     ESI                          ;increment offset
        JMP     test1                        ;loop forever (until error)

        MOV     AX, DS                       ;copy selector into AX
        MOVZX   EAX, AX                      ;zero extend into high word
        LSL     ESI, EAX                     ;ESI gets limit of DS segment
test2:  MOV     AL, BYTE PTR DS:[ESI]        ;read a byte from memory
        DEC     ESI                          ;decrement offset
        JMP     test2                        ;loop forever (until error)

test3:  MOV     AX, 0
        MOV     DS, AX                       ;DS = null selector
        MOV     EBX, DWORD PTR DS:[ESI]      ;try to read from memory
```

```
test4:  MOV     AX, 3
        MOV     DS, AX                          ;DS = another null selector
        MOV     EBX, DWORD PTR DS:[ESI]         ;try to read from memory

test5:  MOV     EBX, DWORD PTR CS:[ESI]         ;read a dword from CS segment
        PUSH    CS
        POP     DS                              ;DS = code segment selector
        MOV     EBX, DWORD PTR DS:[ESI]         ;read a dword from DS segment

test6:  MOV     DWORD PTR CS:[ESI], EBX         ;try to write into code segment
        MOV     DWORD PTR DS:[ESI], EBX         ;try to write into code segment

test7:  MOV     AX, 11 * 8
        MOV     DS, AX                          ;DS = selector for GDT(11)
        MOV     AX, 12 * 8
        MOV     ES, AX                          ;ES = selector for GDT(12)
        MOV     WORD PTR DS:[3000h], 1234       ;write a 16-bit constant
        MOV     BX, WORD PTR ES:[00]            ;read from aliased space
        CMP     BX, 1234                        ;same ?

code    ENDS

        END
```

Recall from the earlier discussion of the differences between 8086 and 80386 segmentation that the 80386 in Protected mode does not tolerate segment wraparound. The first routine in the previous program reads a byte from offset 0 in the current DS segment, increments the address pointer, and repeats this process indefinitely. On an 8086, this would be an endless loop. On the 80386, you get a segment length violation somewhere along the way.

The next test, labeled test2, does just the opposite. It carefully determines the limit of the DS segment with the LSL instruction. Then it steadily decrements its address pointer and repeats forever. In actual use, this loop would fail just after it read from address offset 0. A segment won't wrap around the other way, either.

Labels test3 and test4 try reading from the DS segment when DS has a null selector in it. Loading the selector is allowable, but attempts to read from the null segment will fail.

The code at location test5 shows that it is perfectly all right to read data from a code segment and that it is permissible to load the selector to a code segment into a data segment register. The 80386 will allow you to read from this code space as long as it has read permission. The two instructions at test6 will both fail, however, because you cannot write into a code segment, even if its selector is in a data segment register.

At the beginning of test7, the DS and ES segment registers

are reloaded with valid selectors for GDT slots 11 and 12, respectively. If the memory map in Figure 2-13 is correct, the program should be able to write to the upper end of the DS segment and read the result at the low end of the ES segment. In this case, the two segments overlap by 4KB.

The last example for this chapter shows how you can determine the base address of a segment, given its selector.

```
code     SEGMENT ER PUBLIC USE32

         ASSUME  CS:code
         ASSUME  DS:GDT_alias
         ASSUME  SS:stack

         ; This function returns the base address of a segment
         ; whose selector is in AX.
         ; Presently, this will only work for GDT selectors.
         ; We will not worry about preserving registers here.

         ; Assumptions:
         ; 1) We are already operating in Protected Virtual Address Mode.
         ; 2) Our DS segment points to an "alias" of the GDT as readable data.

getbase:
         SUB     ESP, 6                        ;make room on the stack
         SGDT    PWORD PTR SS:[ESP]            ;store base & limit of GDT

         MOV     BX, WORD PTR SS:[ESP]         ;BX = GDT limit
         SHR     BX, 3                         ;BX / 8 = number of descriptors
         MOV     EDI, DWORD PTR SS:[ESP] +2    ;EDI = base address of GDT

         BT      AX, 2                         ;test selector's TI bit
         JC      error              ;sorry, no LDT selectors allowed!

         SHR     AX, 3                         ;AX / 8 = table index
         CMP     AX, BX                        ;index within limits of GDT ?
         JA      error              ;sorry, invalid selector!

         MOVZX   EAX,AX                        ;clear high word of EAX
         MOV     EBX, DS:[EDI][EAX*8] +2       ;EBX = base address bits 0 - 23
         ROL     EBX, 8                        ;rotate high byte to low byte
         MOV     BL, DS:[EDI][EAX*8] +7        ;read base address bits 24 - 31
         ROR     EBX, 8                        ;rotate back again

         MOV     EAX, EBX                      ;return answer in EAX

         ADD     ESP, 6                        ;re-align stack
         RET

code     ENDS

         END
```

Remember that this is just about the only item of information that cannot be obtained through other means. This particular function is not completely general-purpose, because it cannot handle selectors that refer to descriptors in the LDT. You are encouraged to expand this example to deal with LDT-based segments as well.

A few of the 80386's new instructions are in evidence here, in particular MOVZX and the use of scaled index addressing.

So far, you have seen that the segmentation mechanism used in Protected mode of the 80386 is considerably more complex than that used on the 80286 and an order of magnitude more so than the 8086 system of bit-shifting segment registers. Protected mode segmentation is the basis for almost all that is to come, for the 80386 depends on these segment definitions to do its work. You will learn to depend on them as well as you build robust, protected systems.

Another facet of Protected mode operation is also closely tied with the segmentation hardware and has so far been glossed over. The privilege protection mechanism adds even more security to the definition of memory and who may use it. This and other privilege-related issues are discussed in the next chapter.

3

PRIVILEGE LEVELS

Take a look at the inner workings of any modern minicomputer or mainframe, and you'll see the concept of a privilege hierarchy woven into every level of the operating system or executive. Any multiuser or timesharing system must have a protection scheme to keep each user's work from interfering with another's. Sometimes this takes the form of multiple rings of protection, in which certain commands or programs can be executed only by trusted users such as a system administrator.

Such protection schemes can render the system relatively safe from accidental mishaps, such as a novice user deleting important files, or from deliberate misuse or tampering by a malicious programmer who tries to bring the system down or send the CPU into an endless loop.

There are as many different techniques for implementing system-level protection as there are systems to protect, and whole books have been devoted to the subject. It is generally agreed, however, that the protection mechanism should be an integral part of the system, affecting every stage of the design. Ideally, the protection mechanism would be supported directly in hardware, perhaps in the memory management unit. That way the computing system and the protection mechanism can form a cohesive whole, instead of having protection software tacked on after the fact.

Intel chose to integrate security with hardware in its design of the 80386. All of the necessary elements have been designed in to the processor and MMU to create a useful and respectable system of protection. (Hence, the Protected mode of operation.) At the same time, the tools provided are not so narrowly defined that there is only one true way to implement them. Indeed, you can ignore the protection and security features entirely and work with a relatively unprotected system.

This chapter discusses and illustrates the 80386's hardware protection features and functions available to operating system designers, application writers, or would-be system crashers. It examines one way in which the protection features can be used to create a remarkably robust microcomputer system.

Computer system security measures prevent

- Users from interfering with one another
- Users from examining secure data
- Program bugs from damaging other programs
- Program bugs from damaging data
- Malicious attempts to compromise system integrity
- Accidental damage to data

PRIVILEGE PROTECTION

The existence of any protection hardware on a commercial microprocessor is unique and is one of the features that makes the 80386 attractive to system designers and programmers. The 80386 protection mechanism can be divided into two broad parts: memory management, discussed in both the previous chapter and the next one, and privilege protection, covered here.

The memory management hardware catches most programming errors, such as bad or illegal address generation, runaway subscripts, call/return stack corruption, and the like. The privilege protection mechanism catches more subtle errors and malicious attempts to compromise the integrity of the system.

At its heart, the privilege protection system consists of four levels of privilege, numbered from 0 to 3. Privilege level (PL) 0 is the most privileged, and PL 3 is the least privileged. Almost every time an assembly level instruction is executed, some aspect of privilege protection comes into play. The types of checks the privilege system performs fall into three categories. When running in Protected mode, the 80386 continually checks that the application is privileged enough to

- Execute certain instructions
- Reference data other than its own
- Transfer control to code other than its own

These three restrictions form the basis of the tools the 80386 provides for the building of a protected system. Let's look at how they are implemented.

Executing Privileged Instructions

Instructions that modify the Interrupt flag, alter the segmentation, or affect the protection mechanism are privileged instructions. They are allowed only if the program is running at PL 0 (the highest level of privilege). Otherwise, the 80386 generates a general protection fault (exception 13), and the operating system has to deal with the application, in most cases terminating it.

References to Other Data

In many cases, applications in a multitasking environment share data. Programs are not allowed to read or write data items that have a higher privilege level. Applications can, however, use data at the same or lesser privilege levels. Any attempt to reference more-privileged data results in a general protection fault.

Transferring Control to Other Code

As they do with data, many programs in a multitasking environment share pieces of code, such as run-time libraries. The prohibition for code is similar to the one for data but is even more restrictive. Programs are not allowed to CALL or JMP to code that does not have exactly the same privilege level that they do. Programs must therefore restrict flow of control to code at their own privilege level. Otherwise, a general protection fault occurs.

DEFINING PRIVILEGE LEVELS

Now that these ground rules have been laid out, you are ready for some basics. First, you need to know what defines a privilege level, where this definition is found, and how an application can tell which privilege level its code is running at.

Privileges are assigned by segment. Each segment of code, data, and stack has a privilege level associated with it. Everything contained within a segment has the same privilege level. Privilege, therefore, is global within a segment. For instance, you cannot define a data segment with 20 variables in it and have 4 of the 20 be more privileged than the rest.

A segment's privilege level is defined in the Access Rights byte of that segment's descriptor. Bits 45 and 46 hold the DPL field — the Descriptor Privilege Level. Actually, the term *DPL* is a bit misleading. The descriptor itself has no privilege level associated with it. The DPL defines the privilege level of the memory space that the descriptor defines. But since the level is found in a segment's descriptor, it is called the descriptor privilege level.

If the descriptor defines a data segment (type 0 or 1), all of the data within that segment has the privilege level contained in the DPL field. If it is a code segment (types 4 through 7), all of the code within that segment is considered to be at the DPL field's privilege level. This last fact is especially important. Recall that in Chapter 1, Figure 1-6 showed the various flags in the EFLAGS register. No field in that register defines the current privilege level of the processor. (There is an IOPL field, but that's different. It will be covered later on.) If the processor itself has no privilege level, what then determines the current privilege level? It is determined by the level of the code that is currently running, and that level is stored in the DPL field of the code segment descriptor. If the processor gives control to a code segment with a different DPL in its descriptor, it operates at the level of the new segment.

Descriptor Privilege Level

- Privilege levels apply to entire segments.

- The privilege level is defined in the segment descriptor.

- The privilege level of the code segment determines the current privilege level.

At any given point, the processor's privilege level is determined by the DPL of the code segment from which it is currently fetching and executing code (and the processor is always executing code). This will be referred to as the Current Privilege Level, or CPL. You can remember this as the Code Privilege Level if you prefer.

It follows, then, that privilege levels for all segments, whether code, data, or stack, are determined statically by the creator of the segment descriptors. They are not something you can change dynamically, unless, of course, you have access to your own descriptors!

Given this newfound knowledge, you are ready to take a close look at the first type of privilege checking, the use of privileged instructions.

Privileged Instructions

There are 19 privileged instructions on the 80386 but, as with many other things, some are more privileged than others. Privileged instructions are those that affect the segmentation and protection mechanisms, alter the Interrupt flag, or perform peripheral I/O. In order to execute any instructions of the first two types, the code must be at CPL 0. That is, the instructions in Table 3-1 can be used only in code segments for which the descriptor's DPL field equals 0.

The third type, instructions that perform I/O, are shown in Table 3-2. These are similar to the instructions in Table 3-1, except that CPL does not necessarily have to be 0 for them to be executed. Instead, applications can perform these I/O instructions if the CPL is less than or equal to the IOPL field in EFLAGS. Remember, 0 is the most privileged level, and 3 is the least privileged. A numerically smaller PL means a higher privilege. Having these instructions be IOPL-sensitive allows you to decide for yourself just how important it is to restrict access to I/O devices. If the IOPL is 3, then any program can alter I/O devices. If the IOPL is 0, only the most trusted code segments can contain I/O instructions.

Table 3-1.　Privileged Instructions

Instruction	Action
HLT	Halts the processor
CLTS	Clears task-switched flag
LGDT, LIDT, LLDT	Loads GDT, IDT, LDT registers
LTR	Loads task register
LMSW	Loads machine status word
MOV CRn,REG/MOV REG, CRn	Moves to/from control registers
MOV DRn,REG/MOV REG,DRn	Moves to/from debug registers
MOV TRn,REG/MOV REG,TRn	Moves to/from test registers

Table 3-2. IOPL-Sensitive Instructions

Instruction	Action
CLI	Disables interrupts
STI	Enables interrupts
IN, INS	Inputs data from I/O port
OUT, OUTS	Outputs data to I/O port

Because IOPL is part of the EFLAGS register instead of a descriptor or other non-normally-available resource, it might appear that the I/O protection scheme isn't very well thought out. If your application program was denied access to I/O (CPL > IOPL), then you could easily push a copy of the EFLAGS register onto the stack, manipulate it like any other memory operand, and then pop the modified image back, as follows:

```
PUSHFD                                    ;push 32-bit EFLAGS
OR        DWORD PTR SS:[ESP], 00003000h   ;set IOPL to 3
POPFD                                     ;pop 32-bit EFLAGS
; Go do I/O now...
```

Fortunately (or unfortunately, depending on your goals), this simple trick won't work. The POPF and POPFD instructions themselves aren't privileged, but they do operate differently depending on the PL of the code executing it and on the current setting of IOPL. Any program is allowed to execute POPF and POPFD, but unless that code is in a PL 0 segment, the two IOPL bits of EFLAGS will not be changed. No fault or error is generated to warn you of this modification; it simply won't perform as expected. The following program fragment illustrates this:

```
PUSHFD                                    ;push 32-bit EFLAGS
OR       DWORD PTR SS:[ESP], 00003000h    ;set IOPL to 3
MOV      EAX, DWORD PTR SS:[ESP]          ;copy stack top to EAX
POPFD                                     ;pop 32-bit EFLAGS
NOP
PUSHFD                                    ;push EFLAGS again
CMP      EAX, DWORD PTR SS:[ESP]          ;compare copy to real thing
JE       level0
         ; else we're at PL 1, 2 or 3...
```

A similar ploy might come to mind for modifying the IF bit. CLI and STI are normally IOPL-sensitive, too. If you find that you can't execute them directly, you might try modifying EFLAGS to get the same effect:

```
PUSHFD                                  ;push 32-bit EFLAGS
AND       DWORD PTR SS:[ESP], 0FFFFFDFFh ;clear bit 9
POPFD                                   ;pop modified EFLAGS
          ; interrupts disabled ...
```

This too has been taken care of, however. In order for POPF or POPFD to change the setting of IF, CPL must be less than or equal to IOPL. Thus, IF changes are IOPL-sensitive no matter which way you do them.

To summarize, in order to change IF, you must have I/O permission (CPL ≤ IOPL), and to change I/O permission, you must be running at privilege level 0 (CPL = 0).

Privileged Data References

The second type of privilege checking that the 80386 performs involves data references. Even the smallest utility program needs some read/write space to store local variables or a stack. By ensuring that applications access data that is not more privileged than they are, the 80386 makes it much more difficult to contaminate important data structures.

The rule is that programs can reference data only within a segment in which the DPL is greater than or equal to the CPL. In other words, the DPL of a code segment descriptor must have a smaller value (higher privilege) than the DPL of a data segment descriptor, or they must be equal. If you make an illegal reference that violates this rule, the 80386 generates a general protection fault (exception 13).

How does the 80386 enforce this? It does so in two ways. First, privilege validation is performed whenever you load a selector into one of the data segment registers (DS, ES, FS, or GS). If the DPL of the segment to which your selector refers is less than the CPL (the DPL of your code segment), the 80386 rejects the selector immediately and generates a general protection fault. The destination segment is left unchanged.

Second, when you attempt to actually use the selector to make a memory reference, the 80386 checks that the type of access you're requesting (read or write) is allowed for that segment. This is where errors such as writing into code segments or read-only data segments are trapped. Note that these cannot possibly be caught when you first load the selector, because the 80386 has no way of knowing ahead of time if you are going to misuse the segment.

When you are loading the stack segment register (SS) with a selector, the 80386 tightens the rules a bit. You can load SS only if the stack segment's DPL exactly equals the CPL. You're not allowed to use an underprivileged stack. In addition, the segment must be readable, writable, and present for the selector to load. The usage-by-usage checks mentioned earlier should never be required for stack references; all of the validation will have been done when the selector was loaded.

RPL Field

As was pointed out in the previous chapter, each selector points to exactly one descriptor, but four different selectors can identify the same descriptor. This is because the last 2 bits of every selector are reserved for the RPL field—Requestor's Privilege Level—and these bits do not affect the segment selection process. They do, however, affect privilege validation.

You can use the RPL field to weaken your current privilege level when loading a selector, if desired. Generally, when loading selectors, you will want RPL to be equal to CPL. When data and stack selectors are loaded, the 80386 does not compare the target descriptor's DPL to your CPL directly but rather compares it to your CPL or the selector's RPL, *whichever is greater*. Thus, if you load a selector that has its RPL set greater than it needs to be (greater than CPL), you effectively exclude yourself from accessing a data segment that you otherwise might have been privileged enough to use. Why do this? A use for this feature will be revealed later in this chapter.

What about the opposite effect? If you load a selector with RPL = 0, can you then gain access to privileged data segments? No; it's not that easy. If a selector's RPL is less than the CPL, it has no effect. Remember, for privilege checking, it's always the numerically greater (less privileged) of CPL and RPL that is compared to the target descriptor's DPL. Thus, if you load a selector with RPL < CPL, you accomplish nothing.

Privileged Code References

The third restriction imposed by the privilege-checking mechanism on the 80386 is the prohibition against transferring control to a code segment with a different privilege level. This is perhaps the single most important aspect of the privilege-checking mechanism, and it is certainly the most complex. It also has a few exceptions, as you will see.

By restricting flow of control to code segments that have the same privilege level, the 80386 keeps you from arbitrarily changing privilege levels at will. If the CPL could be changed that easily, the other protection mechanisms would be meaningless. You are essentially kept at your own level of trust, and allowed to transfer control only to code that is equally trusted. Usually, this will be other portions of your own programs, but it could also be services provided by the operating system, such as math libraries or shared functions.

Changing the flow of control to code contained in another segment is performed by the intersegment, or FAR, forms of JMP, CALL, and RET. In particular, these instructions are

    JMP immediate 16:32
    JMP ptr 16:32
    CALL immediate 16:32
    CALL ptr 16:32
    RETF

Intersegment control transfers are different from intrasegment, or NEAR, transfers in that they change the content of CS as well as that of EIP. Therefore, as far as the processor is concerned, intersegment transfers are just a special form of selector validation, with the selector going into CS.

Whenever you want to load a new selector into CS (that is, perform an intersegment transfer), the 80386 checks that the target descriptor is indeed a code segment (that it has the executable attribute). Read permission is not required. Next, it checks that the DPL of the target descriptor is exactly equal to the CPL. You can still use the RPL field of the selector to weaken your CPL, but doing so would guarantee failure. RPL should always be set to CPL or less in such cases. When in doubt, set the RPL to 0; then it will have no effect. In addition, the destination code segment must be marked present, and the new value for EIP must be within the limits of the new code segment. If all of this checks out, the 80386 resumes execution at the intended destination address.

If any portion of the checks fails, the 80386 generates a general protection fault (exception 13), or a not-present fault (exception 11) if the segment descriptor is marked not present.

To move between code segments requires

- Intersegment JMP instruction
- Intersegment CALL instruction
- Intersegment RET instruction

The destination segment must be

- A code segment (executable permission)
- Defined with the same privilege level
- Marked present

Determining Current
Privilege Level

Throughout this chapter there have been many references to CPL, the current privilege level, and how it is determined by the DPL field of the descriptor for the segment from which the processor is currently executing code. It is often convenient, and sometimes necessary, for your programs to determine the exact privilege level at which they are running. How can they do this if they don't have access to the descriptor tables (which is the usual case)? Easy—examine the RPL field in register CS. The 80386 always maintains these bits at the application's current privilege level, regardless of how CS might have been loaded. Two examples of this technique are shown in the following listing:

```
MOV    AX, CS              ;copy code selector into AX
AND    AX, 03h             ;drop all but RPL bits

; -- or --

PUSH   CS                  ;push code selector
POP    AX                  ;pop into AX
AND    AX, 03h             ;drop all but RPL bits
```

CHANGING PRIVILEGE
LEVELS

Thus far, you have seen that the 80386 can operate at any one of four privilege levels and that the current level is determined by the privilege level associated with the code it is currently running, which, in turn, is set by the DPL bits when the segment's descriptor is created. Furthermore, it appears that the 80386 is very strict about code running at a given level, transferring control only to code at the same level. The obvious question now is, How do you change privilege levels?

There are two ways to change privilege levels—one very simple, and one very complex yet tremendously useful. The simple way involves *conforming code* segments, described next. The complex way involves special segment descriptors known as *call gates*.

After discussing conforming code, the remainder of this chapter deals with the intricacies of call gates and their impact on system design.

Conforming Code Segments

A code segment is considered conforming if bit 2 of the Access Rights byte of its descriptor is set. These are type 6 and 7 descriptors. A conforming code segment can have read permission or not, just like a normal nonconforming code descriptor.

Conforming code segments have no inherent privilege level of their own; they conform to the level of the code that CALLs them or JMPs to them. For example, if a program in a PL 3 segment transfers control to a conforming code segment, then the conforming code runs with CPL equal to 3. If the same segment is invoked by PL 0 code, it runs with a CPL of 0. For this reason, conforming code segments should never contain privileged instructions like those in Table 3-1 or Table 3-2, unless your general protection fault handler is prepared to deal with the complexities of code that sometimes runs and sometimes doesn't, depending on the privilege level of what ran before it!

When control is transferred to a conforming code segment, the RPL bits of register CS are not changed to match the segment's DPL, as they normally would be. Instead, they still reflect the correct CPL—the DPL of the last nonconforming code segment that was executed. This is the *only* time that the RPL bits in the CS register might not match the DPL bits in the currently executing segment.

Conforming code segments

- Can be defined with different privilege levels
- Do not impart additional privileges
- Do not remove existing privileges
- Do not alter RPL bits in the code segment register
- Can be shared by code at all privilege levels

Even though conforming code segments do not have any particular privilege level associated with them, there is still one restriction regarding when a conforming segment can be used. The DPL of the conforming code segment descriptor must always be less than or equal to the current CPL. That is, you can transfer control only across or up. You can never transfer control to a segment whose DPL is greater (less privileged) than the current segment.

To understand why this is so, you need to think ahead to what would happen when the program or subroutine in the conforming code segment was through and you wanted to return back to your normal fixed-privilege code. If you had used a JMP to get to the conforming code, and it was at an outer privilege level, it presumably would use a JMP instruction to return. That, however, would necessitate transferring control to an inner, more privileged level, which is not allowed. Alternatively, if you had used a CALL instruction to transfer control to the conforming code, the subsequent RET would have to return to a more privileged level—also not allowed. Thus, even though it seems foolish not to allow control transfer to less privileged levels, it is actually in keeping with the systemwide protection scheme that the 80386 supports.

Call Gates

The conforming code concept allows some degree of freedom in changing from one segment to the next. Although it doesn't actually change your privilege level but conforms to the level of its caller, it does allow programs running at different privilege levels to share one piece of code. This is ideal for shared libraries and the like so that you don't have to create four identical copies, one for each privilege level. This is, in fact, the best use for conforming code segments. To effect a real change in privilege level, you need to use something known as a call gate.

A call gate is a special system descriptor that acts as an interface layer, or intermediary, between code segments at different privilege levels. It defines certain points in the more privileged code to which control can be transferred. Call gates are the only way to change privilege levels on the 80386. No gate, no transfer. Figure 3-1 shows the format of a call gate descriptor.

63	47	40	36	31	15	0
Destination offset 31-16	D P P 01100 L	000	WC	Destination selector	Destination offset 15-0	

Selector	Destination code segment
Offset	Offset within destination code segment
WC	Word count, 0-31
DPL	Descriptor privilege level
P	Descriptor Present flag

Figure 3-1.   Call gate descriptor

Unlike code, data, or stack descriptors or the system-type LDT descriptor you have seen so far, call gate descriptors do not define any memory space. They have no base address or limit fields. Technically, they are not descriptors at all, but it is convenient to be able to place them in descriptor tables. Selectors pointing to call gate descriptors cannot be loaded into data segment registers (DS, ES, FS, or GS) or the stack segment register (SS). They can, however, be loaded into CS. In fact, you must load them into CS in order to transfer control to a segment at a different privilege level.

As you have seen, the 80386 is very particular about allowing data or code references outside of the application's own privilege level. The call gate is the only mechanism that allows interlevel control transfers, and it leaves nothing to chance. First, only FAR CALL instructions can be used to change privilege levels; JMPs are not allowed. (Hence, the name.) Second, the CALL must reference a call gate, not the destination code segment. Applications can never reference a code segment of a different privilege level directly. Figure 3-2 shows both the correct and incorrect ways to request an interlevel transfer.

The call gate defines the code segment to which control is to be transferred and the exact offset within that segment where execution will begin. You are not allowed to specify the desired offset in your programs. That would permit too much chance of corrup-

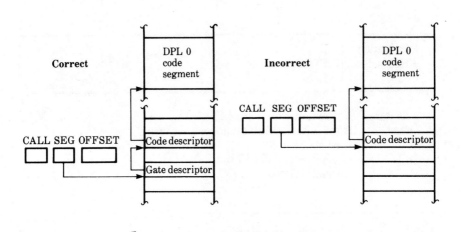

Figure 3-2.   Calling higher privileged code

tion if control were transferred into the middle of a subroutine or, worse yet, into the middle of an instruction. Having the full segment and offset specified within the gate leaves no chance of transferring control to anywhere but the predefined locations. One call gate must be defined for each segment:offset location that can be called by less privileged code.

Call gates

- Are defined like segment descriptors
- Occupy a slot in the descriptor tables
- Provide the only means to alter the current privilege level
- Define entry points to other privilege levels
- Must be invoked with a CALL instruction

Call instructions that reference call gates are indistinguishable from other FAR CALLs, even to an experienced code disassembler. They can be coded with the segment and offset given as immediate operands, or they can be placed in memory and referred to indirectly. The only difference is that the 16-bit segment selector portion of the instruction points to a call gate descriptor rather than a code segment descriptor. Because all selectors look the same, knowledge of the arrangement of the GDT (or LDT) is required to tell one from the other. The following code fragment illustrates two forms of FAR CALL that may or may not reference a call gate.

```
        CALL      0010:12345678            ;FAR CALL, immediate seg:offset
        ;

        CALL      gateptr
        ;

gateptr LABEL     PWORD
        DD        12345678h                 ;32-bit offset
        DW        0010h                     ;16-bit selector
```

A selector value of 0010 selects GDT descriptor 2 (index = 2, TI = 0, RPL = 0). If GDT(2) is a code descriptor, the two instructions shown perform a FAR CALL to another segment with the same privilege level. (If it is not of the same privilege, both of these instructions generate a general protection fault.) If GDT(2) is a call gate, however, CS is loaded with the selector specified within the gate descriptor, and EIP is loaded from the call gate's offset field. Neither the selector nor the offset given in the CALL instruction is used. Execution commences at that new location, which, by the way, is not known to you unless you can read the descriptor tables. Control will return to your "home" segment when the processor encounters a FAR RET instruction. Figure 3-3 shows the steps involved.

From the point of view of the less privileged applications programmer, the function(s) performed by the call gate are a "black

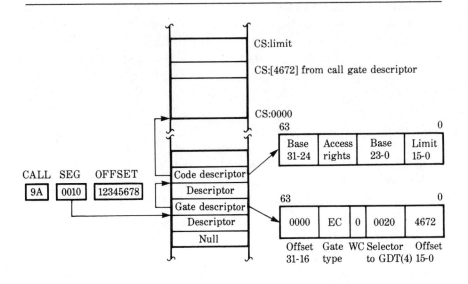

Figure 3-3. Calling through a call gate

box" in the truest sense. The programmer would typically write something like this:

```
;
EXTRN    system:FAR
;
CALL     system                    ;perform system function
;
```

The linker, or possibly a loader, would fill in the symbolic name "system" with the selector for a call gate and an unknown offset, which the processor will ignore. The programmer has no way of knowing whether the FAR CALL refers to another segment of equal privilege or to a call gate. If the CALL refers to a gate, there's no telling what segment the program will be transferred to, or what offset within that segment. If the programmer could find this out, he or she could not read the object code because it is in a more privileged segment and therefore not accessible. Besides, the code segment probably wouldn't be defined with read permission anyway.

This level of indirection serves several purposes. First, it maintains absolute security in the higher privilege code. Presumably, the gated procedures will have been thoroughly debugged and can be trusted not to cause errors of their own. Because their entry points are closely guarded, there is very little possibility that the routines could be trashed by their callers. Second, the gates render the actual procedure code invisible to programs at outer privilege levels, as was illustrated earlier. The less that is known about protected functions, the better. Third, since the gate is the only unit that the caller addresses directly, you can change the function it refers to without changing the gate interface. The gated function can be relocated in different versions of the operating system, for instance, and the caller's code would not have to be modified at all.

Call Gate Accessibility

You have seen that to transfer control to a more privileged segment, applications have to use a call gate, and the call gate, not the program, defines the target code. But you may not even be allowed to use the gate. Call gates have "tolls," and the application may not be able to get through.

When you are loading a data segment register, the DPL of the target segment's descriptor must be greater than or equal to the CPL. That way, you are allowed to reference only data with an equal or lesser privilege level. The same rule holds true for call gates. Call gates have a DPL field even though they don't define any memory segments. The destination code segment has its own descriptor with its own DPL that defines the privilege level of the code you want to call. The DPL of the gate descriptor itself is used to qualify who can use the gate. The rule is as follows:

Target DPL $\leq$ Max (RPL, CPL) $\leq$ Gate DPL

Figure 3-4 illustrates the four relevant privilege fields and the checking required.

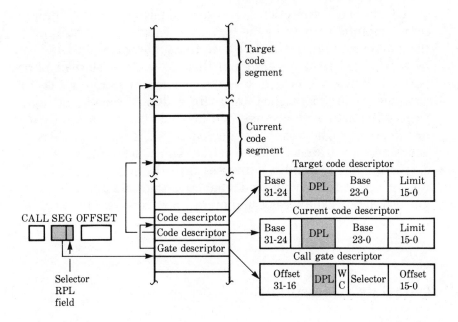

Figure 3-4.   Privilege validation checks

For example, if you are currently running in a PL 2 code segment (CPL = 2), and you want to call a PL 0 procedure (target DPL = 0), you must use a gate to that procedure with a DPL of 2 or 3. If the gate descriptor had a DPL of 1, it could be used only by PL 1 and PL 0 code segments to call the procedure, and PL 2 and PL 3 code segments could not access the gate and therefore the code behind it. Some of the possibilities are illustrated schematically in Figure 3-5.

Note that the privilege rules for call gates allow you to call a segment with the same privilege level as the current CPL as well as one with a higher level. This degenerate case has the same effect as a normal FAR CALL without the intervening gate. In

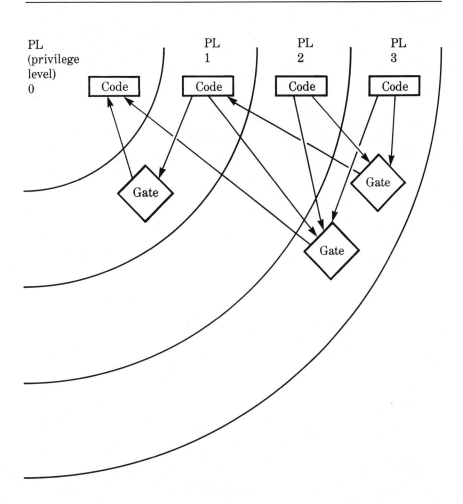

Figure 3-5.   Call gate privilege

fact, if the destination code segment has the same privilege level as the current segment, you can even use a FAR JMP instruction to reference the call gate. Like the CALL, this offers no advantages over the more direct form of FAR JMP. This is the only case in which a JMP instruction can refer to a gate; it does not violate the earlier rule that only CALL instructions can cross privilege levels.

Privilege requirements to use a call gate:

- Call gate DPL must be greater than or equal to the current privilege level
- Call gate DPL must be greater than or equal to the RPL of the gate selector
- Call gate DPL must be greater than or equal to the target code segment DPL
- Target code segment DPL must be less than or equal to the current privilege level

---

Changing Privilege Levels, Changing Stacks

With a change in privilege level comes a change in the addressable domain of a program. For example, when your program runs at PL 2, it can access data and readable code segments only at PL 2 and 3 and must use a PL 2 stack. If it makes a call, through a gate, to a PL 1 segment, the program can then access PL 1, 2, and 3 segments. But what about the stack segment? The privilege rules stated earlier that the PL of the stack segment must exactly match the PL of the code segment at all times. (Conforming code segments might appear to be an exception to this rule, but they have no inherent privilege levels of their own.) What happens to the stack when you change privilege levels? The 80386 performs an unusual operation to avoid sabotaging the rest of the protection mechanisms—it changes stacks.

When you make a call through a gate that causes a change in privilege, your old stack segment and pointer are abandoned, and a new stack is used that corresponds to the new, inner privilege level. When control is returned to your old, outer level code, the use of the original stack is restored. The best part is that all of this is invisible to the program code on both sides of the gate, even if you are passing parameters on the stack!

The first step in understanding this new twist is knowing where the new stack comes from. To learn that, you need to look at yet another special system descriptor that defines an area of memory called a Task State Segment.

Figure 3-6 shows the format of a Task State Segment (TSS), and the special TSS descriptor that defines it is given in Figure 3-7. A TSS is like a scratchpad for the 80386. In it, the processor

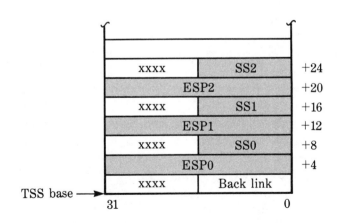

Figure 3-6.   Task state segment

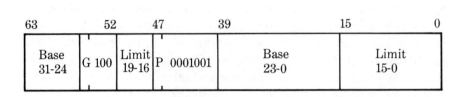

63		52	47		39		15		0
Base 31-24	G 100	Limit 19-16	P 0001001		Base 23-0		Limit 15-0		

Figure 3-7.   TSS descriptor

stores everything it needs to know about a task. For the purposes of this chapter, a *task* is all of the code running on the 80386 at all privilege levels. The TSS is covered in great detail in Chapter 5. For now, you will be looking only at the six fields that are shaded in Figure 3-6. These six fields hold the stack segment selectors and stack pointers for privilege levels 0, 1, and 2. There is no pair of fields for a PL 3 stack. The following paragraphs describe how these fields work.

If your CALL instruction through a gate is successful (no privilege violations occur) and the destination code segment has a higher privilege level than the current segment (that is, you are not calling "straight across"), the 80386 begins a new stack. The segment selector and the pointer for this stack are taken from the TSS. If you are calling a PL 1 procedure, for example, the new stack selector and stack pointer are taken from SS1 and ESP1, respectively.

Your old stack selector and stack pointer are immediately pushed onto this new stack. Figure 3-8a shows this first step. Next, the 80386 consults the WC field of the call gate descriptor. The processor automatically copies that number of dword (32-bit) parameters from your old, outer stack and pushes them on the new stack in the same order, as shown in Figure 3-8b. Next, the old CS selector and EIP offset are pushed onto the new stack like any other CALL instruction. See Figure 3-8c.

Finally, CS is loaded from the selector field of the call gate descriptor, EIP is loaded from the offset field, and execution commences at the new address.

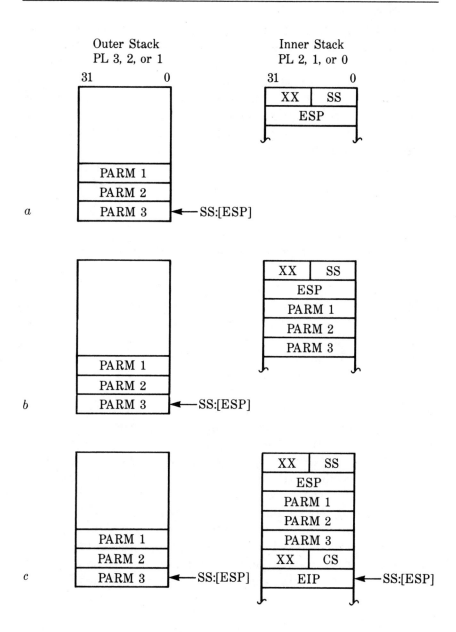

Figure 3-8. Interlevel stack switch

The result is that the new procedure is called with the return address and parameters on the stack, exactly as if it had been called directly. These steps are all performed automatically whenever a privilege transition occurs and are calculated to make the change as transparent as possible.

The 80386 also performs some additional reality checks during all of this that programmers who expect to create call gates must keep in mind. First, it checks that valid stack pointers are defined in the TSS for all three privilege levels (or at least for those levels that will be used). Second, it verifies that the three stack segments are of the correct privilege level. The selector in SS0 must point to a PL 0 stack or data segment and have its RPL field set to 0. The same is true for the PL 1 and PL 2 stack selectors. Remember, code and stack segments must be at the same privilege level. (The code DPL must equal the stack descriptor DPL.) Third, it makes sure there is enough room on the new stack for the caller's old stack pointer (8 bytes), any parameters to be copied as defined by the WC field in the gate (0 through 124 bytes), the caller's return address (8 bytes), plus any stack space the procedure itself might need. The fourth check, which should be obvious, is the requirement that the three stacks (four, counting the caller's) are not in the same place. It would be a shame to have the 80386 do all this work for you, only to walk all over the caller's stack. Aliasing of stack segments is not recommended.

The procedure can now run along and do its work, using whatever resources are available to it on the stack or in the new, more privileged segments that it can now address. Of course, the higher privileged procedure can also access any lower privileged segments, including the caller's stack and data segment(s). If the procedure needs more information than what is available to it on the stack, it can examine any memory area in which the caller could possibly have stored data. For large parameter blocks, the caller may need to pass a pointer and a parameter count and let the procedure retrieve parameters indirectly. All of the processor registers will be exactly the same as they were before the call except for CS:EIP (which is true of any FAR CALL) and SS:ESP. If the new procedure wants to make use of higher privileged segments that its caller could not address, it has to load new segment registers as necessary. When the procedure is finished and is ready to return to its caller, it must use either a FAR RET or a FAR RET n, which removes n bytes from the stack before returning. Bear in mind that the latter form is *required* if parameters were pushed on the stack by the call gate (WC $\neq$ 0).

The internal procedure for an interlevel RET is primarily just the reverse of that for a CALL. The steps are as follows:

1. Pop CS:EIP from the inner-level stack.

2. Increment ESP by n bytes to remove parameters.

3. Pop SS:ESP from the inner-level stack.

4. Increment ESP by n bytes again to remove parameters from the outer-level stack.

During these steps, the standard privilege checking is done to be sure that the RPL of the return CS is greater than the CPL (outward return) and that the RPL of the return SS is exactly equal to both the DPL of its descriptor and the RPL of the return CS. This ensures that the higher privileged procedure has not corrupted its own stack before returning. It also prevents you from trying to back into a higher privilege level by pushing the appropriate values and executing an intersegment RET.

An interlevel RET executes one final step that aids security. Just before control returns to the old, less privileged code, the data segment registers (DS, ES, FS, and GS) are checked to see if the called procedure might have left selectors to more privileged segments in them. If so, the segment register is loaded with the null selector (0000). This keeps high-level procedures that are sloppy with their registers from giving less privileged procedures access to memory that would normally be off-limits.

DEFENSIVE PROGRAMMING

As you can see, the built-in protection mechanisms are indeed complex and thorough, especially considering that you don't have to write any software to support them. Some things, however, are impossible to trap with silicon. The remainder of this chapter takes the viewpoint of an operating system designer and implementer trying to seal up any remaining cracks in the protection system.

The major risk lies in the fact that any procedure called through a gate is, by definition, more privileged than its caller. Therefore, you must be careful not to provide the caller with any of the benefits of that increased privilege (except, of course, to perform the function for which the procedure exists). This is especially true if your procedures run at CPL 0.

The best approach is to test all parameters passed to you completely before performing any significant work. It is also wise to test these parameters as early as possible. In no event should your code "hand off" parameters to another, higher level procedure before they have been tested. If they were in fact destructive, the higher level procedure would fail and you would look like the culprit.

- *Check loop/iteration counters.* All loop counters should be checked against upper and lower bounds (usually unsigned). Remember, ECX, as well as all of the other registers, is 32 bits wide. It takes a 16-MHz 80386 nearly an hour to count down from FFFFFFFF!

- *Check for 8-bit and 16-bit parameters in 32-bit registers.* Oftentimes, a parameter needs only a small amount of register storage, and the caller won't bother to fill the entire 32-bit register. Be certain to either sign-extend or zero-extend these kinds of parameters, as appropriate. Don't depend on anything!

- *Keep interrupt latency to a minimum.* If your procedure requires interrupts to be disabled, be certain that the amount of time IF is cleared is not under the caller's control. Do not disable interrupts within loops. Do not disable interrupts before instructions that do not take a finite amount of time to execute, such as WAIT and ESC opcodes.

- *Never accept code from a stranger.* Do not write functions that take executable code or pointers to code as parameters. If the caller can't run the code itself, why is it asking you to?

- *Verify all memory references.* This can be done in several ways. A common trick or mistake is to pass a segment:offset pointer to a more privileged segment and request that a number of bytes of data be read from or written to that address. A typical example would be a disk I/O function that accepts a file handle, a byte count, and an address to which the data is to be written. Although your procedure might be privileged enough to write to the destination address, does the caller have the proper permission?

The best way to verify segment selectors that are passed as parameters is to use the ARPL instruction. ARPL compares two selectors and adjusts the RPL field of the first one if it is more privileged than the second. Typically, the first selector is one you were given as a parameter and the second is what you know the caller's privilege level should be. This is easily found right near the top of the stack, since the RPL field of the caller's CS register is always maintained at its CPL, and the caller's CS is at SS:[ESP] + 4 at the time your procedure is called. A nice side effect of ARPL is that it sets the Zero flag if a change was required to the selector—a dead giveaway that you were passed an invalid parameter. An example of how this can be implemented is shown below:

```
         PUBLIC  system

system   PROC    FAR
         ; Assumptions:
         ; 1) First parameter (nearest top of stack) is a selector.
         ; 2) Next parameter is an offset address into the first segment.
         ; 3) Third parameter is a function request.

         MOV     BX, WORD PTR SS:[ESP] +4              ;BX = caller's CS
         ARPL    WORD PTR SS:[ESP] +8, BX              ;compare RPL fields
         JZ      error                        ;sorry, RPL too small!

         MOV     FS, WORD PTR SS:[ESP] +8              ;load selector into FS
         ASSUME  FS:NOTHING                            ;tell the assembler
         MOV     ESI, DWORD PTR SS:[ESP] +12           ;ESI = 2nd parameter
         MOV     ECX, DWORD PTR SS:[ESP] +16           ;ECX = 3rd parameter
         ; go do some work ...


system   ENDP
```

Another ruse is to pass an offset address that is beyond the limits of its segment. This will cause a general protection fault unless you test the address first with an LSL instruction.

In addition, be sure to check for read and write permission before actually using a selector. VERR and VERW can help avoid general protection faults.

- *Check EFLAGS before proceeding.* In particular, ensure that DF (Direction flag) is set correctly. Don't string-move 12KB of data only to find that it has gone to the wrong place. It's usually a good idea to set the flags back the way they were before returning, to avoid antagonizing the caller.

- *Final RET or RET n instruction must match the gate's WC field.* Because all call gates copy a fixed number of parameters from the caller's stack to yours, the final RET or RET n instruction must pop exactly the right number of bytes off both stacks. The value of n should equal WC/4, because WC is counted in dwords (0 through 31) and n is counted in bytes (0 through 255). If WC and n do not agree, both your stack and the caller's will be corrupted. The caller must also push the appropriate number of parameters before calling. If not, its stack will be corrupted on return, although yours will be okay.

- *Do not use call gates for functions that pass a variable number of parameters.* See the previous guideline. If necessary, pass an argument count and argument pointer instead.

- *Functions cannot return values on the stack.* Both your stack and the caller's will be shrunk by the number of bytes specified in the final RET instruction. When the caller regains control, it looks as though no parameters were ever on its stack. Return values should be passed in registers.

- *Save and restore all segment registers.* This is more to protect the caller than the callee. If you change any of the data segment registers to point to segments that you can access but the caller can't, the 80386 will automatically zero them on return to keep you from passing on ownership of a privileged segment. Moreover, the caller will regain control with one or more of its data registers clobbered through no fault of its own. This can be hard to track, since null selectors are perfectly all right until they are used. If the caller does not use, say, GS very frequently, it can be difficult to track down why its code produces general protection faults later on.

4

PAGING

For the 80386 programmer who craves the ultimate in control, yet another stage in the address translation system is available. The internal memory management unit (MMU) that is an integral part of the 80386 microprocessor can be used to add another level of indirection (and complication) to the existing segmentation and protection mechanisms. The technique for doing this is known as paging.

The use of the paging feature is optional. It is available in both the Protected Virtual Address mode and the Virtual 8086 mode of operation. As you will see in Chapter 9, its use in Virtual 8086 mode is almost required, especially if you want to run multiple virtual 8086 tasks on a single 80386. In Protected mode, however, the use of paging depends on the intended design of the completed system. Some significant benefits can be had through paging, especially if you are designing a multiuser system or an open-architecture, bus-structured system, in which physical memory resources might not be fixed. This chapter presents the features available to you through the paging hardware. It also looks at some of the software necessary to support it and some sample applications.

First of all, it is important to understand that you can use the internal paging MMU on the 80386 to achieve three distinctly different effects. You might choose to use paging for any one of these features, or you might want all three. A section dealing with a particular aspect of the paging hardware and its usefulness has been devoted to each. The three major capabilities of the paging hardware on the 80386 are

- Address translation
- Page-level protection
- Demand paging

Historically, the MMU of a microcomputer system has been implemented either as a custom-designed circuit of discrete semi-conductor components or as a separate, external very large-scale integrated circuit (VLSIC). The former approach allows a system hardware designer to tailor the MMU design to its intended use, making tradeoffs for available resources such as board space, cost, performance, and so on. The latter approach has been very popular for those system designers who don't want to reinvent the wheel and can get along quite nicely with a standard MMU provided by the microprocessor company.

The 80386 is unique in that the MMU is actually integrated on the same die, or silicon chip, as the processing element itself. (The Fairchild Clipper also has an MMU as an integral part of the computing element, but it is located on a physically separate die.) The benefits of this are many: it saves precious real estate on the printed circuit boards because another large-scale device does not have to be fit in. Proper connection and communication between the two elements is guaranteed. The CPU/MMU combination can operate faster as a unit because information does not have to be transferred continually between the two devices. And, in the case of the 80386, the MMU can be switched off if it is not required.

The 80386 internal memory management unit

- Performs address translation

- Performs page-level protection

- Performs demand paging (virtual memory)

- Saves space over an external MMU

- May be disabled through software

REQUIRED ELEMENTS

Before getting under way, let us take a look at the parts of the 80386 that are involved in the paging functions. The clever reader may deduce that those registers that are new to the 80386 are dedicated to the major new function of paging, and that deduction would largely be correct. Specifically, the 80386 uses control registers CR0 through CR3 to control the paging MMU. In addition, you must create a new batch of memory-resident tables to control paging, much like the segment descriptors used in "simple" memory management. Last, you may need to write a page fault handler for the newly defined exception 14.

Register CR0 is the old Machine Status Word (MSW) on the 80286. Besides having its name changed, it has been extended to 32 bits; thus, predictably, the part related to paging is in the upper half of CR0. When you set bit 31 of CR0, paging is enabled; it is disabled when you reset this bit. (Paging is disabled by

Figure 4-1. Control register 0

default.) See Figure 4-1. Because of the nature of paging, you must exercise caution when setting or clearing this bit. A later section of this chapter deals with enabling and disabling paging in detail.

Register CR1 is another undefined register and should not be used. CR2 is used exclusively by your page fault exception handler. It holds information that tells your software what linear address was being translated when the fault occurred. This is covered later in this chapter and in Chapter 7, which deals with exception handling.

CR3 is also called the Page Directory Base Register, or PDBR. It points to the "root" of the page tables, used in address translation, page protection, and demand paging. It too is covered in a later section.

Remember, the MOV instructions required to read or write the control registers are privileged, and so only PL 0 programs can access the paging registers. This is the safest arrangement, for, as you will see, the ability to affect the paging mechanism is at least as dangerous as the ability to affect segmentation or protection.

ADDRESS TRANSLATION

Address translation is the major use for an MMU in a microprocessor-based system. In the case of the 80386, its effect is very much like that provided by the segmentation mechanism: linear addresses are converted to physical addresses without the programmer's knowledge for better performance. In processors without a segmented memory architecture (such as the Motorola 680 × 0 family), MMU paging is the only way to achieve this effect. In the 80386, it simply allows yet another level of indirection.

In the memory segmentation system described in Chapter 2, a program's logical address is automatically converted to a linear address through the operation of the segmentation mechanism. Every memory reference is considered to be part of a memory segment, and every segment has a base address associated with it. When a program makes a memory reference, the segment's base address is added to the logical address (the only part the programmer sees) to yield a linear address, of which the programmer has no knowledge. This address translation is done on every reference to memory, by every program at every privilege level, yet it is invisible to everyone except those who create the translation tables (the segment descriptors). When page translation is not enabled, this linear address is the final result. Logical addresses become linear addresses, and linear addresses are driven onto the processor's external address bus and used to address physical memory. This was the case with the 80286 and, in a much simpler form, the 8086/88 and the 80186/188.

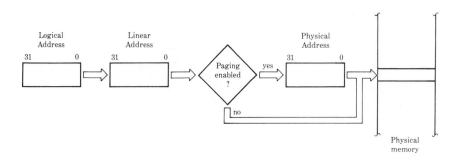

Figure 4-2.   Logical to linear to physical address translation

On the 80386 with paging enabled, the linear address is only the halfway point. Linear addresses can now be translated again into physical addresses. It is this physical address that will finally be driven onto the address bus to the outside world. See Figure 4-2. Like segmentation, paging allows you to redirect, or "translate," every memory reference to suit your particular needs. One common application is to create the impression of a large, contiguous memory space when, in fact, the system's memory is scattered and fragmented; this application will be used to illustrate the most basic form of paging.

No matter what the intended goal or effect is (address translation, page-level protection, or demand paging), paging is implemented much like segmentation, but it is not nearly as complete. Because it is implemented "on top of" the segmentation, however, the net result is extremely flexible control over the memory model of the system.

The paging mechanism augments, rather than replaces, the segmentation mechanism. Page address translation, when performed, is done in addition to the translation performed by the segmentation hardware, as was described previously. Any page-level protection features will not supplant the more complete segment-related protection but act as additional checks. Likewise, the virtual memory demand paging features go above and beyond any you may have implemented at the segment level.

Segmentation can't be turned off in Protected mode, but paging can. Its use is strictly optional. If you never set the most significant bit of CR0, you can ignore all of the paging issues in this chapter. For many systems, the memory allocation and protection features of segmentation alone may be adequate. Conversely, you can choose to create the opposite effect—paging without segmentation. If the only segment descriptors consist of one 4GB data segment and one 4GB code segment in the GDT, both at DPL 3, then segmentation is all but disabled, and external memory appears as one big, flat address space, with no partitioning or privilege protection. In this degenerate case, paging (if enabled) would provide the only memory protection.

Table 4-1. Segment Protection Versus Page Protection

	Segmentation	Paging
Base address	any	4KB aligned
Size	any	4KB
Privilege levels	4	2
Write protection	yes	yes
Present status	yes	yes
Accessed status	yes	yes
Dirty status	no	yes

Like segmentation, paging depends on special memory-resident tables. These tables perform many of the same functions that segment descriptors do. The values you choose to write into these tables have a major effect on what the paging hardware in the 80386 will do for you. You enable paging by creating the tables in memory and initializing registers CR3 and CR0. Although paging is described in three different contexts in this chapter, there are no modes of paging. The net effect(s) depends entirely on the contents of the tables. Table 4-1 summarizes the memory attributes of paging as compared to segmentation.

Paging requires two kinds of tables: page directories and page tables. Both types are made up of 32-bit descriptors. Unlike tables of segment descriptors, each page directory or page table must contain exactly 1024 descriptors, making each directory or table exactly 4096 bytes long (4KB, or 1000 hexadecimal, or MMMMXCVI in Roman numerals). Henceforth, a descriptor in a page directory will be referred to as a page directory entry (PDE), and one in a page table will be called a page table entry (PTE). The format of a PDE is shown in Figure 4-3a, and that of a PTE is given in Figure 4-3b. The format of their respective tables is fairly straightforward and is left to the reader's imagination.

PDE Descriptor

A page directory entry is broken out into several fields. Starting from the most significant end, they are as follows:

Page Table Address The most significant 20 bits of a PDE point to the physical (not logical or linear) address of the base of a page table. Because there are only 20 bits in the address, the 80386 assumes that the lower 12 bits are all 0's, effectively forcing 4KB alignment on the page table being pointed to.

User Bits 9, 10, and 11 are not used or interpreted by the 80386. You can use them as you wish. Some possible uses are discussed in the section on demand paging.

Accessed The processor automatically sets bit 5 whenever this PDE is used in address translation or another page-related function. It is never cleared unless you write code to do it manually.

User/Supervisor Bit 2 is the User/Supervisor (U/S) protection bit. If this bit is set, the memory pages that this PDE covers are accessible from all privilege levels. If it is cleared, the pages are accessible only by PL 0, 1, and 2 (supervisor) code.

Read/Write Bit 1 is the Read/Write (R/W) protection bit. If the U/S bit is clear, this bit has no effect; supervisor-mode access is never restricted. If U/S is set, this bit determines whether the memory pages covered by this PDE are write-protected. If R/W = 1, write privileges are allowed from PL 3 code. If R/W = 0, read and code fetch operations only are allowed.

Present The least significant bit of a PDE is the Present bit. If this bit is set, the page table pointed to in bits 12 through 31 is present in physical memory. If this bit is clear, the page table referred to is not present, and the rest of this PDE is available for use by your software. See Figure 4-3c for the format of a not-present page descriptor.

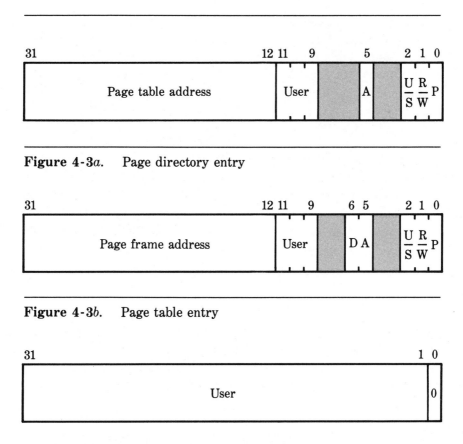

Figure 4-3a.   Page directory entry

Figure 4-3b.   Page table entry

Figure 4-3c.   Not-present page descriptor

As you can see, the format of a PDE is vaguely similar to that of a segment descriptor but is much simpler. There are no "type" bits, only read/write permission. There is a Present bit and, as in a segment descriptor, if the Present bit is not set, most of the rest of the descriptor is available to you for whatever uses you can devise.

The U/S bit implements a simple two-level privilege system (PL 3 versus not PL 3). Most important, the bulk of a PDE, like that of a segment descriptor, is taken up by an address pointer to something else. That something is a page table. Like a page directory, a page table is a vector array of 1024 descriptors, but the PTE brings you one step closer to the real memory.

PTE Descriptor

The format of a PTE is as follows:

Page Frame Address   Bits 12 through 31 point to the base of a 4KB page frame—a "page" of target memory. The 12 least significant bits of this address are assumed to be 0, enforcing 4KB page alignment on all pages.

User   Bits 9, 10, and 11 are reserved for your use. You can use them as you wish.

Dirty   The Dirty bit (bit 6) is automatically set by the processor whenever the page frame which this PTE covers is written into. The processor never clears this bit. By periodically testing and then clearing these bits, you can find out what pages of memory are being written to most often.

Accessed   Bit 5 is set by the processor whenever this PTE is used in a paging-related function. It is never cleared by the processor. You can keep track of the most-often-used pages of memory by periodically testing and clearing this bit in all PTEs.

User/Supervisor   Bit 2 enforces simple privilege protection on the page that this PTE covers. If this bit is set, access is allowed from all privilege levels. If it is cleared, access is allowed from all privilege levels except level 3.

Read/Write   Bit 1 enforces write protection for nonsupervisor pages. If the U/S bit is clear, this bit has no effect. If U/S is set and R/W is not, code running at PL 3 may not perform data writes into the page that this PTE covers. If U/S and R/W are both set, write permission is given.

Present   The least significant bit of a PTE indicates whether the 4KB page frame to which it points is physically present. As in a PDE, when a PTE is marked not present, the rest of the PTE is available for your own uses.

Clearly, the format of a PTE is almost exactly the same as that of a PDE. The only real difference is the fact that a PTE has a Dirty bit. Bit 6 is undefined in PDEs. A more subtle difference is the fact that the address field of a PDE (bits 12 through 31) points to the base of a table of PTEs, whereas the address field of a PTE points to the base of a page of memory. Based on this newfound knowledge, you can now examine the steps performed in address translation.

Physical pages of memory have these attributes:

- Linear address

- User/supervisor privilege

- Read/write permission

- Present status

- Accessed status

- Dirty status

Using Page Translation

As was mentioned earlier, the paging mechanism works like the segmentation mechanism but on a simpler scale. The fact that page descriptors are half the size of segment descriptors bears this out. Two major points of departure are the 20-bit page address fields and the total absence of a limit field. Both of these shortcomings are very neatly dealt with if you enforce a rule that all pages of memory must be exactly 4KB long and aligned on 4KB boundaries. This way, there is no ambiguity about where one page ends and another begins. Pages are like floor tiles, all exactly the same size with one fitting right next to the other. No overlapping is possible. Thus, what you have is a user-defined, free-form system of segments overlaid on a basic processor-enforced system of pages. Figure 4-4 shows this arrangement of memory pages.

The paging tables allow you to remap, or translate, linear addresses before they are used to access real, physical memory. You can translate every single address in the entire 4GB address space if you want to. Translation is always done in units of 4KB. That is, addresses from 0000 to 0FFF can all be translated to some other address range as a block. Addresses from 1000 to 1FFF can all be

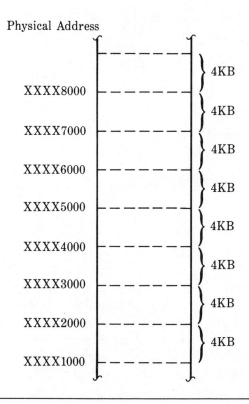

Figure 4-4.   Pages of physical memory

translated to some other address as well. You can continue in this way, shifting the address of every block of 4096 bytes to some other address range, for as much of the 4GB address space as you require.

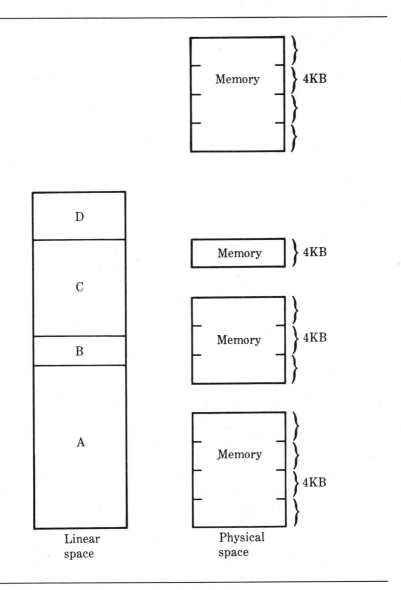

Figure 4-5. Linear space versus physical space

Figure 4-5 shows a schematic representation of a sample linear address space (the type you are used to) on the left and the physical address space (what the processor really generates) on the right. At every 4KB boundary, the addresses of the next 4KB block of linear memory can be translated to any other 4KB block of physical memory. All of the addresses in the block move as a group. It is not possible to translate 512 bytes to one address and the remaining 3.5KB to another. Unlike segmentation, paging allows only one level of granularity: 4KB. The 4KB block of physical memory is known as a *page frame*, or simply as a *page*.

This is a good time to point out that the segmentation mechanism and the paging mechanism don't know anything about each other. The fact that the paging granularity and the coarse segmentation granularity are both 4096 bytes is purely coincidental. Segment boundaries and page boundaries have nothing in common. For this section on address translation, segmentation will be ignored entirely. The later sections on protection and demand paging deal with the relationships between segments and pages.

When a linear address is translated into a physical address, only the most significant 20 bits (12 through 31) are changed. No matter how bizarre the paging, bits 0 through 11 of your linear address are never modified. Hence, paging only performs "coarse-tuning," leaving the "fine-tuning" alone. Twelve address bits corresponds to a 4KB space, and so page translation can translate your address only in units of 4KB—one page. All of these sizes are beginning to make sense.

How is this translation carried out? This is where the page directory and page tables come in. The translation is done in two stages, making it even more indirect (and tougher to follow) than memory segmentation. To translate a linear address to a physical address, you need exactly one page directory and one page table. As the diagram in Figure 4-6 shows, register CR3 points to the base of a page directory. A PDE (1 of 1024 in the page directory) points to the base of a page table. A PTE (also 1 of 1024) points to the base of a page frame. This is where translation stops. Because a page frame is always exactly 4KB long, and because the least significant 12 bits of your linear address are not translated, you are left with exactly one unique physical address.

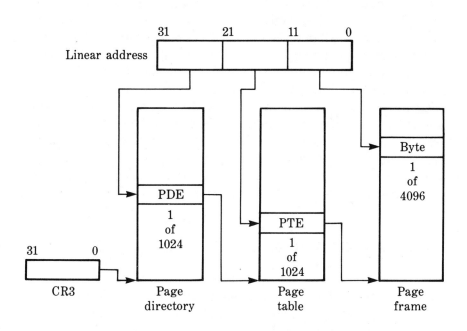

Figure 4-6.   Linear-to-physical address translation

Now comes the tough part: which PDE in the page directory is used, and why? And which PTE in the page table is used? You know that both tables must contain exactly 1024 descriptors (PDEs or PTEs). The quantity 1024 is equal to 2^{10}, so you need a minimum of 10 bits to be able to select a unique entry from each table. Ten bits for the page directory plus 10 bits for the page table makes 20 bits. Those 20 plus the 12 untranslated ones add up to 32—exactly the number of bits in a linear address. How convenient.

As Figure 4-6 shows, the MMU internally divides a linear address into three fields: two fields of 10 bits each and one field of 12 bits. The most significant 10 bits of the linear address (bits 22 through 31) are used to select one PDE from the page directory.

The next most significant 10 bits (12 through 21) are used to select one PTE from the page table to which the PDE is pointing. The least significant 12 bits select one of 4096 bytes of memory from the page frame to which the PTE is pointing. Voila! You have successfully translated a linear address into a physical one.

An alternate definition of this procedure, which some people may prefer, is to regard the PTE as the source of the 20 most significant bits of a linear address. In essence, the MMU concatenates the 20-bit address field from the PTE with a 12-bit address field from the linear address. The address field of the PDE does not contribute any address bits itself. It is used purely for the purpose of internal table location and then discarded.

Building Page Tables

Let us consider now how these tables are arranged and where you might put them. Register CR3 points to the physical base address of a page directory (which, like all page-related organs, must be page-aligned). Since each PDE is 4 bytes long, the page directory occupies 4KB ($2^{10} \times 2^2$) of address space. Each of the 1024 PDEs points to the base address of a page table. Each page table is also 4KB long. If you define 1024 of these tables, you eat up 4MB ($2^{10} \times 2^{10} \times 2^2$) of space for MMU tables! If this amount of storage was required for paging, it might not seem worthwhile. Fortunately, this is not the case.

Recall that page translation takes effect after segmentation. Paging only translates linear addresses, and linear addresses have to come from *successfully* translated logical addresses. If there's a problem with a particular logical address, the 80386 deals with it at the segmentation stage (general protection fault, stack fault, and so on) before it ever reaches the page translation stage. You can use this knowledge to trim down severely the amount of storage you need for page translation tables. If you know (through your intimate knowledge of the segmentation tables) that certain linear addresses will never be generated, then you don't need to build page tables for them. It is the rare system that uses the entire 4GB linear address space of the 80386 as real memory, so this table trimming is the rule rather than the excep-

tion and is perfectly valid. To see how to determine which tables
you can delete, take a look at a hypothetical system.

Figure 4-7 shows a schematic representation of the linear
address range of the system. Everything looks normal; it has a
few code segments, some more data segments, and a few stack
segments. It even has a code segment up at the extreme high end

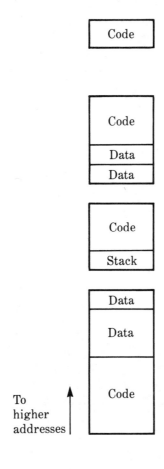

Figure 4-7.   Linear address map

of the linear address space for a boot ROM. A pretty fair amount of space is covered, but compared to the 4GB address range, it has barely made a dent. If you look at the way the segment definitions are arranged, you see that they fall into four blocks of contiguous segments, with some gaps in between. Some of the gaps are small, and some are quite large, such as the space between the end of the last data segment and the beginning of the boot ROM code segment. You can guarantee that it is impossible ever to generate a linear address outside of these ranges. If there is no linear address, there is no need for a translation table. By thinking through how the translation tables are used, you can see just how much you can do without.

Figure 4-8 shows the first few PDEs in a page directory. Recall that Figure 4-6 showed that the most significant 10 bits of a linear address are used to select a PDE from the page directory.

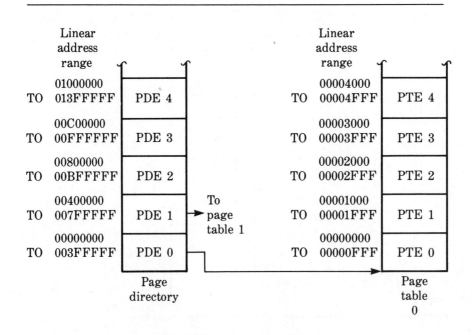

Figure 4-8. Linear address mapping

That being the case, you know that the first entry (PDE 0) will be used for all linear addresses from 00000000 through 003FFFFF. The next entry (PDE 1) will be used for linear addresses from 00400000 through 007FFFFF, and so on. The 1024th page directory entry is used in the translation of linear addresses from FFC00000 through FFFFFFFF. Every PDE, therefore, covers a 4MB address range. At 4MB apiece, 1024 of these are just enough to cover the 4GB linear address range of the 80386. If you know that a linear address will never fall into a given 4MB range of addresses, you have no need to define the page table to which that PDE would point, and thus you save the space for 1024 PTEs, or 4KB. Every 4MB address range that is guaranteed to be invalid saves you one 4KB page table.

What about the PDE itself? You might be able to dispose of unused page directory entries entirely, but this is usually not possible. Normally, both of the page-related tables need to have exactly 1024 descriptors in them, whether they're all valid or not. If there are gaps in your address space, as there were in Figure 4-7, the unused PDEs act as placeholders. PDEs aren't like segment descriptors, which you can pack together in random order in a segment descriptor table. The MMU looks for a particular PDE (or PTE) based on its position within the page directory (or table). If the 10-bit index from the linear address indicates, say, the 1004th PDE, then there had better be a valid descriptor in that position. Hence, for the example memory map, you would have to define valid PDEs at the low end and at the high end of the page directory, with a lot of placeholders in between.

You can get away with shortening a page directory if the total possible linear address range is truncated. That is, if you know that no linear addresses will be generated above, say, 00480000, you don't need to define any more than the first two PDEs. Of course, you don't need to define page tables for the 1022 unused PDEs, either. Strictly speaking, the 80386 MMU still thinks that the page directory is 4KB long and has 1024 entries, but if it's never going to reference them, who cares?

You can pull a similar trick if the total linear address range is limited to the high end or is even somewhere in the middle. If linear addresses below a certain point will never be generated,

you can effectively leave the lower end of the page directory undefined by loading CR3 with an address that is lower than the actual
address of the first PDE. This must be calculated carefully, however, so that the first valid PDE will appear to be in the correct
position in a full 1024-entry page table. Figure 4-9 shows an
example of this.

All of these rules hold true for PTEs in a page table as well.
Let's take a look at how linear addresses are broken out between
page directory entries and page table entries. Recall that Figure
4-8 showed that each PDE in sequence was used for each consecutive 4MB range of linear addresses. In a similar fashion, each
PTE in a page table covers a 4KB linear range.

If you know that only some fraction of a 4MB linear address
range will ever be used, you can effectively truncate a page table

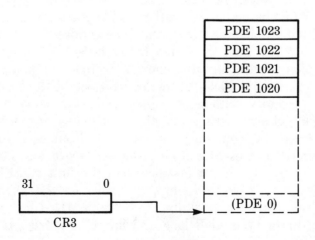

Figure 4-9. Truncated page directory

in the same way that you truncate a page directory. As before, this is true only if there are no holes in the address space. If there are gaps, PTEs must still be used as placeholders. The table must always appear to have 1024 entries.

Between these two forms of table reduction, you should be able to cut the size of the MMU tables from 4,195,328 bytes (4MB for 1024 page tables, plus 4KB for a page directory) to about 1KB per megabyte of linear memory. That's less than one tenth of 1% allocated to MMU tables.

As was pointed out before, the page directory and the page tables are both position-sensitive. The location of a PDE (or PTE) in the page directory (or table) is everything. This fact is important when it is time to decide how you want to translate linear addresses and create your paging tables.

Because of the way PDEs and PTEs are indexed by the MMU, any given linear address can be translated in exactly one way. Page translation is deterministic. By mentally dividing a linear address into its three component fields, you can find out exactly what path the 80386 will take in translating it. This allows you to manufacture your descriptors to get just the effect you want.

Like segmentation, page translation modifies addresses from those the programmer expects into those you want him or her to use. The incentive for doing this might be better system performance, protection from other users, easier operating system control, or whatever. One of the most common uses for page translation is to make a fragmented memory space appear contiguous, even to the segmentation mechanism.

Consider the physical memory map in Figure 4-10. It illustrates a machine in which memory is spread around; none of the chunks is larger than 128KB. What could you do if a program created a data structure that was larger than 64KB? It would obviously have to be located in one of the larger physical memory segments or else broken into two or more logical segments. That's not a very elegant solution, and it requires cooperation from the program code. Worse, what happens if a user wants to load and run a 134KB program? It too would have to be broken into two or more logical code segments, with FAR JMP and CALL instruc-

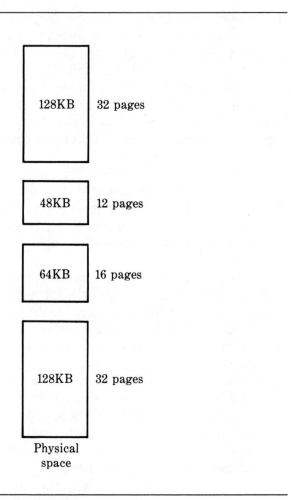

Figure 4-10.   Fragmented physical space

tions used to hop back and forth between them. This is not very sophisticated. With paging enabled, however, there are at least two different solutions to these problems, and both of them are completely invisible to the user. The first is page address translation. The second involves virtual memory, which is explained toward the end of this chapter.

If you create your page directory and page tables (those that are required) to resemble the ones represented in Figure 4-11, you can make the fragmented physical memory resources appear to

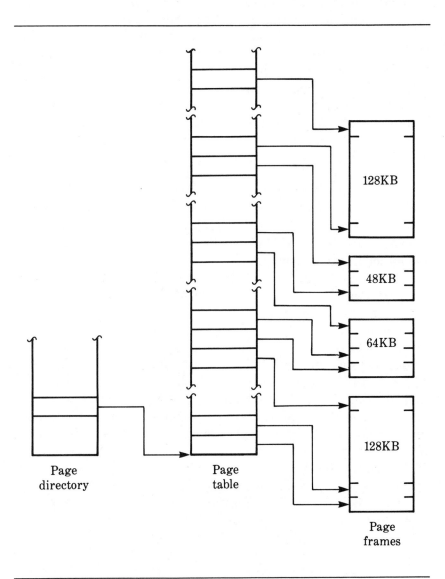

Figure 4-11.   Producing contiguous linear addresses

be contiguous. Each consecutive PTE is marked present and points to physical memory. The physical memory is not contiguous, of course, but the linear addresses will be. As the hypothetical program creates a larger and larger data structure, it can steadily generate ever-larger linear addresses, blissful in its ignorance of the real physical addresses that are actually being generated to access memory. As long as the page translation tables aren't changed during run time, this image of the memory space will be self-maintaining.

It is important to remember that even the 80386's own segmentation mechanism is fooled by this address translation. If you refer back to previous sections on segmentation and address calculation, you will find that at no time is there a reference to physical addresses, only linear ones. You are cautioned that these two terms do not mean the same thing if page translation is in effect. In fact, the address loaded in register CR3 and the 20-bit address fields contained in PDEs and PTEs are the *only* direct references the 80386 makes to actual physical addresses. All other addresses are either linear or logical.

Another use of the address translation feature of paging is for aliasing. Page-level aliasing is much like segment-level aliasing. Although the address granularity is hampered, you can still create some interesting and useful effects. If you map two or more linear address blocks into the same physical address page (or pages), physical memory will be aliased. For example, Figure 4-12 shows a linear address map on the left and a physical address map on the right, with the paging tables in between. In one instance, two PTEs point to the same physical page frame. This gives every byte in that page two linear addresses. Which addresses are duplicated depends entirely on the positions of the PTEs within the page table and the position of the page table within the structure of the page directory. In another instance, two PDEs point to the same page table. They thus share a translation table, giving every address in their respective 4MB spaces access to the same physical space. Aliasing with page tables like this is also called *shadowing*.

By the way, there is nothing wrong with creating PDEs and PTEs in such a way that linear addresses are translated into their

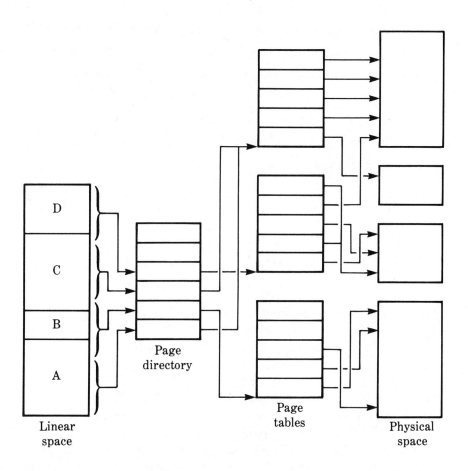

Figure 4-12.   Page-level aliasing

own physical addresses, that is, not translated at all. This is known as *direct mapping* or *identity mapping* and can be used if paging is enabled on the 80386 for some purpose other than address translation.

Linear addresses are translated into physical addresses

- Address bits 22 to 31 select one of 1024 PDEs in the page directory

- Address bits 12 to 21 select one of 1024 PTEs in the page table

- Address bits 0 to 11 select one of 4096 bytes in the page

- Register CR3 locates the base address of the page directory

- PDE locates the base address of the page table

- PTE locates the base address of the page

ENABLING AND DISABLING PAGING

Page translation adds another level of reality to the idea of memory addresses. The programmer knows about logical addresses only because they are generated directly in the code, either as immediate address offsets or indirectly through a register. The operating system designer who creates the segment descriptors deals only with linear addresses. When the descriptors are created, each segment is given a base address and a maximum length. These are unknown (and irrelevant) to the applications programmer. The programmer who designs the paging tables is the only one who handles physical addresses. This requires some understanding of the physical realities of the system's hardware and of performance considerations. For example, it may be wise to map low linear addresses to a high-performance cache memory or local RAM. Higher addresses can be relegated to off-board or extension memory with lower performance, or something similar.

The page directory and necessary page tables must be created and stored in a convenient place. (Remember, the paging tables take up linear address space, and there must be segment descriptors aliasing them as read/write data!) You can keep the paging tables in RAM, or they can be permanently burned into a ROM, along with power-up reset code. In any event, paging is usually the last major feature of the processor to be enabled when the system is brought up. To enable paging, use a privileged MOV instruction to set the most significant bit of CR0. The moment this is done, paging takes effect. If you are using page translation (if linear space is not identity mapped), some unexpected things may happen at this point.

When you are using paging, memory will appear to be in one place while actually being in another. When writing paging instructions you run the risk of moving your program to an address where you can't find it. Therefore, you should set aside a range of addresses that will never be translated and you should be in that "safe spot" at all times.

After the PG bit (bit 31) is set, page translation takes effect on the next instruction, and if the linear addresses from which you are executing are not at the same physical addresses they were before page translation took effect, you're going to wind up somewhere unexpected. For this reason, it is strongly recommended that you take the following three steps:

1. Disable interrupts, including NMI if you can do so on your system. This ensures that subsequent steps will not be interrupted at an inopportune time.

2. Enable paging only from a page that is identity mapped, that is, one in which the linear addresses are the same as the physical addresses after paging is enabled. (Linear addresses always equal physical addresses without paging.)

3. Flush the instruction prefetch queue immediately after the MOV instruction that enables paging. The 80386 fetches instructions from your code segment ahead of time, before they are actually used. After paging is enabled, any address references that those instructions contain may no longer be valid.

A recommended sequence for enabling paging is shown here:

```
        PUSHFD                              ;save current interrupt flag
        CLI                                 ;disable interrupts
        MOV     EAX, page_directory_base    ;EAX = physical address
        MOV     CR3, EAX                    ;load PDBR
        MOV     EAX, CR0                    ;read current machine state
        BTS     EAX, 31                     ;set PG bit
        MOV     CR0, EAX                    ;load CR0
        JMP     foo                         ;flush prefetch queue
foo:    NOP
        POPFD                               ;restore interrupt flag
```

Note that the instruction **prefetch queue** is emptied with a simple
JMP to the next sequential instruction. All flow-of-control type
instructions cause the 80386 to abandon its prefetch queue, since
it takes the instruction to mean that the prefetched instructions
won't be used after all. The 80386 cannot tell that the JMP doesn't
actually change the flow of control.

Disabling **paging** involves the same hazards that enabling it
does. Again, be sure that your code will be mapped to the same
physical space after the page translation is turned off, and flush
the prefetch queue afterward.

PAGE-LEVEL PROTECTION

The previous section glossed over the lower 12 bits of the PDE and
PTE descriptors. In address translation, just about the only interesting part of a paging descriptor is its 20-bit address field. But
the paging mechanism of the 80386 can be used for effects
besides, or in addition to, address translation. This section covers
the interpretation and usefulness of the last 3 bits in PDE and
PTE descriptors.

Present Bit

Bit 0 is the Present bit for both PDEs and PTEs. When this bit is
set, it indicates to the MMU that the page table indicated by the
PDE is present in physical memory or that the page frame indicated by the PTE is present. This is the normal case and has been
assumed until now. Consider the case of a PDE first.

If you do not set the Present bit of a PDE when you create it, then any time that the 80386 tries to use this PDE in a page-related function it will generate a page fault (exception 14). The paging function it was attempting will be aborted, no memory will be accessed, and control will be turned over to the page fault handler. Note that if this bit is not set, the 80386 will never be able to access any of the 1024 PTEs in the page table to which this PDE points. In fact, if the Present bit is not set, the entire PDE is invalid, and you can use the remaining 31 bits in any way you please. When there are holes in the linear address space and you intentionally omit page tables, it is strongly recommended that you clear the Present bit of the PDE that would ordinarily point to the missing page table.

The use of the Present bit in a PTE is essentially the same but on a smaller scale. When a PTE is marked not present, it indicates that the 4KB page frame to which it would normally point is not present. As it does with a not-present PDE, the 80386 generates a page fault when it encounters such a PTE, the instruction is aborted, and no memory reference is made. It is recommended that if certain PTEs in a page table will not be used, you clear their Present bits as well.

In both cases, when the MMU encounters a not-present paging descriptor, the linear address that was being translated is left in register CR2. Your page fault handler can use this register and the error code that is pushed onto the stack to help it determine the proper course of action. In most cases you would load the memory contents required from disk (paging). Interrupts and exceptions are dealt with in Chapter 7.

Present bit

- Used to implement virtual demand paged memory systems
- Page table entry: 4KB of physical memory is not present
- Page directory entry: 4MB of physical memory is not present
- Remainder of page descriptor is available to programmer

User/Supervisor Bit

The User/Supervisor (U/S) bit is as close to an equivalent of the segment descriptor's privilege level (DPL) as paging gets. When this bit is set in a PDE, the 4MB space that the PDE covers is accessible to programs running at all levels of privilege. If it is not set, the physical space is accessible only to programs running at the supervisor level. For the purposes of page-level protection, supervisor privilege is defined as any level except 3. You can use this feature to deny access to a range of physical space even if the segmentation mechanism and segment-level privilege protection allows it. Like address translation, page-level protection is applied after its segment-level counterpart. Therefore, the page-level protection features can be used only to make access more restrictive. They cannot loosen permissions already denied by the segmentation.

When the U/S bit is cleared in a PTE, nonsupervisor access is denied only for that page frame. When this bit is set, user access is granted. However, if the PDE that points to the page table containing this PTE does not allow user access (U/S = 0), the PTE's bit becomes irrelevant, because user access has been denied for the whole 4MB block. Again, permissions can be made only more restrictive.

If the U/S bits in either the PDE or the PTE cause a privilege violation, the processor will generate a page fault. The linear address in question is copied into CR2, an error code is pushed, and the exception 14 handler is invoked.

User/supervisor bit

- Supervisor access = CPL 0 through 2 only
- User access = all privilege levels
- Page table entry protects 4KB of physical memory
- Page directory entry protects 4MB of physical memory

Read/Write Bit

Bit 1 of a PDE or PTE sets read/write permission for a 4MB block or for a 4KB page frame, respectively. Oddly, this bit has an effect only if U/S = 1. In other words, read/write permission does not apply to supervisor-level programs; they are exempt. In a PDE, if U/S = 1 and R/W = 1, all privilege levels can freely read and write into the physical space spanned by this PDE. If the R/W bit is clear, write permission is not allowed to PL 3 code. Supervisor-level (PL 0, 1, and 2) code is not affected.

In the case of a PTE, if the U/S = 1, R/W = 1, and the corresponding "parent" PDE's U/S = 1 and R/W = 1, write permission is allowed for that page frame. If write permission is denied by the PDE, then the R/W bit of the PTE (and of the 1023 other PTEs in its page table) is ignored. This protection is above and beyond any write privileges granted by the segment descriptor (or descriptors) that describe the linear space being checked. If the segment descriptor does not allow write permission and the program attempts a write access, it will be caught at the segmentation stage with a general protection fault, and the page-level protection would be redundant.

By using these latter two bits, you can effectively map out physical space in units of 4KB and make it off-limits to PL 3 code. By not setting the U/S bit of a PDE, you deny all PL 3 code access to 4MB of memory. By not setting U/S in a PTE, you exclude PL 3 code from using a 4KB page. This is roughly equivalent to creating a code or data segment descriptor with a DPL of 2. The Present bit is not privilege-sensitive, however. If a page or block of pages is marked not present, they are not present for everyone.

Read/write bit

- Does not affect supervisor privilege levels (CPL 0 through 2)
- Protects write permission from CPL 3
- Page table entry protects 4KB of physical memory
- Page directory entry protects 4MB of physical memory

PAGING MMU CACHE

Clearly, a lot of table lookups must be done when paging is enabled. Two levels of paging tables must be consulted for every memory reference, even if the linear addresses are identity mapped and there are no privilege restrictions. That means there are two outside memory references for every one your programs actually request. To keep the processor's performance from degrading by 200%, the MMU portion of the 80386 maintains some internal memory—a cache—to help with paging. The cache holds up to 32 PTEs inside the chip itself. Whenever a program produces a linear address that maps to a PTE already in the cache, the MMU can use the cached information it has internally, thus saving two outside memory references.

Programs cannot control which 32 PTEs the 80386 will cache. Instead, the MMU caches every PTE it uses until the cache is full. Because each PTE spans a 4KB physical memory space, the 80386 can find all of the paging information for 128KB of physical memory instantly when the cache is filled. What happens to the 33rd page table entry? This is where the magic comes in.

The MMU cache is maintained as a 32-entry four-way set-associative cache. This means that the 80386 sorts the PTEs into four sets of eight so that it can find them faster. (And finding them fast is the whole idea, right?) A lot can be (and has been) said about the relative merits of four-way set-associative cache management, but none of it is going to help you to any practical extent, so the finer points will be skipped here.

At some point after the processor has been running for awhile with paging enabled, it will probably need to look up more than 32 PTEs. When it does, and it is forced to go to outside memory for the 33rd one, it will want to add that PTE to the cache. To do that, the 80386 examines the 32 existing cache entries and throws out the least recently used one. It then puts the new one in its place. Without any intervention from your code, it has probably made the best possible decision for maximum performance. This system of updating a cache is known as LRU—least recently used.

The 80386 always maintains 32 entries in the cache (which is also called the translation lookaside buffer, or TLB), assuming that it has had occasion to look up at least 32 PTEs. Because the freshest ones are always kept in the cache, it's a pretty safe bet that the necessary entries will be there as your programs run.

Keeping page table entries in an internal cache can be a double-edged sword, however, if you are planning to make several changes to the page directories and/or page tables while the system is running. Consider the following scenario: you have created all of the necessary paging tables and enabled paging. As your program runs merrily along, the MMU loads all of the PTEs that are referenced until the TLB is full. Thereafter, it starts selectively replacing old ones with new ones as needed. For whatever reason, your program decides that it needs to modify some PTEs, maybe marking them not present or changing privileges, addresses, or whatever. That done, the program goes on about its business, operating under some modified system of paging. Or is it modified?

If some of the page table entries you altered were already in the cache, the MMU will still be using the old, unmodified versions. The 80386 isn't smart enough to know when page table entries have been modified and automatically recache them. To do that, it would have to reread all of the page tables constantly, which defeats the whole purpose of keeping them in a cache in the first place.

Whenever the page tables are modified on the fly, you should reload CR3 after all of the work is done. A quick way to do this is as follows:

```
MOV EAX, CR3
MOV CR3, EAX
```

This doesn't materially affect the paging, but it does cause the 80386 to invalidate its entire TLB, because it thinks you're loading a pointer to new page tables. (It doesn't know that you're loading CR3 with the same address it had before.) Apart from this precaution, the operation of the MMU cache, or TLB, is completely invisible. It is one of the many little features that give the 80386 its impressive performance.

Translation lookaside buffer

- Speeds up linear-to-physical address translation

- Holds the 32 most-often-used page table entries

- Maintained with an LRU algorithm

- Programmer must maintain cache coherency

DEMAND PAGING AND VIRTUAL MEMORY MANAGEMENT

So far, this chapter has covered the use of paging to accomplish address translation and privilege protection. Now these two ideas will be combined to create something new. Using the 80386 MMU to perform demand paging, you can create a system with nearly unlimited virtual memory.

Demand paging, virtual memory, swapping, and some other concepts that will be used in this section were once reserved for the realm of minicomputer operating system design. Never before have the tools been present in a commercially available microprocessor to accomplish these functions. As you will see, the 80386 can be used to create a respectable system even by minicomputer standards.

Virtual memory management is a term used to describe a technique whereby the computer appears to have much more memory than it actually does. (Virtual means being in effect but not in fact.) In particular, it allows a programmer to create programs that might require several megabytes of memory space and yet run them on a computer system with only, say, several kilobytes. The advantages of this technique are many. If the program (and the programmer) really believes that nearly unlimited memory is available, then very large scale projects become possible. Huge databases can be kept on-line in memory (or so it might seem), large structures or arrays are possible, large portions of code or data can be kept in one segment instead of many, and so on. By maintaining the image of a great amount of memory without really having it, you can keep system costs way down. Why build a system with 370MB of memory if the largest of programs will run with only 2MB? In addition, virtual memory allows programs and data structures to be portable from one machine to another machine with a different memory configuration, provided they both support virtual memory.

The entire basis for virtual memory is the obvious but often overlooked fact that a computer can be in only one place at a time. That is, it can execute only one instruction, acknowledge one interrupt, or read or write one memory address at any given moment. Only the instruction, interrupt, or memory address in question really needs to exist at that time. For all the CPU knows, the rest of the system has disappeared. You can run a train across the country by pulling up the rails behind it and laying them down again in front as it rolls. The faster you can relay the track, the better, but the train will make it either way. It only needs to have rails directly underneath.

In the same way, you can "pull up" currently unused memory space and put it where the processor needs it. You can do this with as much memory as you need and as often as is necessary to satisfy the currently running program(s). As far as the application software is concerned, the 80386 system has as much memory as it needs, wherever it needs it. In reality, the same physical memory is being used and reused. This is a wonderful feature, especially for multiuser systems, but there are some tricks to using it.

A few major elements are needed to get virtual memory working. First, there must be a way to know when a program has requested the use of nonexistent memory. Second, there must be a way to allocate currently used memory to fulfill the request. Third, there must be a reliable system for saving the contents of that memory to some secondary storage medium. Fourth, there must be some method for making the reallocated memory appear to be where the program thinks it should be. Finally, there must be a way to restore the reallocated memory space to its original state if the program requests access to it again.

Each of these steps is something of a science unto itself, and it is left to the systems programmer to determine the best policy for implementing them. For the applications programmer, the whole subject is intentionally mysterious, because the idea is to present an image that is much larger and more impressive than the real thing. ("I am the great and powerful Oz ...")

Step 1: Determining Memory Requirements

Theoretically, a program would get the best performance if it was loaded in its entirety into the system's best high-performance memory and could use as much of that memory as it wished for massaging data. More often than not, however, this isn't possible. Either there are other programs in the system already, such as the operating system, memory-resident programs, and other users' programs, or there simply isn't enough memory present to go around. This is where virtual memory can help. If you can't give a program all of the memory space it wants, perhaps you can give it some minimum amount and shuffle that around as the program executes.

How do you determine what kind of memory a program wants? That information is usually difficult or impossible to determine. Most programs dynamically create some data storage space as they run or request storage space from the host operating system. Simple ".COM" files under MS-DOS have pretty basic require-ments. You can be certain that they will never require more than 64KB to run. Other file types are not so obliging. Under UNIX or XENIX, an executable file gives no indication of its run-time storage requirements. It just starts requesting memory until it has as much as it needs (or bombs because it can't get enough). The best bet, then, is to make no assumptions about memory requirements and to allocate some standard minimum amount of space. If the program makes large demands on memory as it runs, you can deal with them on demand.

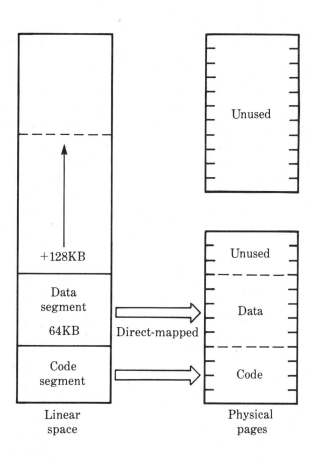

Figure 4-13.   Physical space before reallocation

Figure 4-13 shows an example of a running program that has been allocated a code segment large enough to hold the program and a standard 64KB data segment. During the course of execution, the program requests that the operating system (not pictured) extend its data segment by 128KB. This might be accomplished by a CALL instruction to a call gate that guards an entry point to the operating system. The UNIX function *malloc* is a typical example. The operating system obliges by extending the limit field of the program's data segment descriptor. Now the program starts to fill the new space with data. As it creeps up through the segment, it is eventually going to reference nonexistent memory. If the paging tables have been constructed correctly, the processor will generate a page fault at the first not-present address.

That page fault is the 80386's cue that this program has made a reference to physical memory that was declared not present in either the page directory or the page table. The 80386 copies the linear address in question into register CR2 and invokes your exception 14 handler. The specifics of how the fault works are covered in Chapter 7. This discussion deals strictly with paging concepts. Your page fault handler should then begin the next step in virtual memory management.

Step 2: Allocating Memory

You have a program that has innocently produced a linear address that was not mapped to any physical address. To keep up the illusion of virtual memory, your software needs to pick some area of memory to "insert" into the requested address space. Obviously, you can't physically move memory chips around and make some appear in the required place. Instead, you use the page-translation mechanism to make some other area of *physical* memory appear to be in the correct *linear* address space. The assumption is that you have already run out of unused physical memory. It's all being used for something—user program, boot ROM, operating system code, GDT, IDT, and so on. Something has to give.

Again, the criterion used to decide what gets yanked is entirely up to the system software designer, and it depends on many factors. This hypothetical system uses a very simple least-recently-used algorithm. When the page fault occurs, the operating system initiates a search through the page tables for a PTE that does not have its Accessed bit set (bit 5). If the Accessed bit has not been set by the processor, that 4KB page frame has never been referenced (at least, not since the last time the bit was cleared).

For an LRU system of page replacement to work well, your software must periodically clear the Accessed bit of all page table entries. Better yet, have it check the bit first before clearing it and keep a tally of how often it was found to be set. Then, when it comes time to select a page for reallocation, the PTE with the fewest accesses would be a prime candidate. If you do not need to count any higher than eight, the three user-defined bits in each PTE (bits 9 through 11) might be convenient.

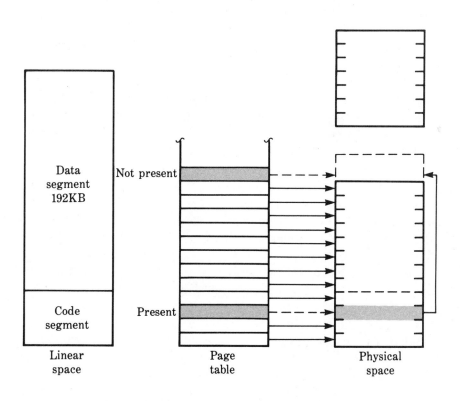

Figure 4-14.   Page selected for reallocation

At last, an unaccessed page is found! Figure 4-14 shows that this PTE maps a 4KB portion right out of the middle of the user's code. Apparently, this program contains a lot of functions that have not yet been called. This is the page that will be remapped.

Step 3: Saving the Contents of Reallocated Memory

If the page of physical memory that is currently in the middle of this program is going to be remapped into the program's data space, it's a safe bet that the program will write to that memory. What happens to the code that used to be stored there? It will be overwritten. Clearly, you can't arbitrarily terrorize the program by allowing it to write over itself, and so you must copy the contents of this page elsewhere.

The contents of the page frame can be copied wherever is convenient for your system. Overwhelmingly, microcomputer systems use hard disk drives as their swap devices. Before the page is remapped, its contents can be copied to a 4KB file reserved on disk for just that purpose. Then, when the code fragment is finally needed (if ever), it can be retrieved from the swap file.

In some cases, copying the contents of a reallocated page to a swap device is not even necessary. Take the case of the hypothetical system, in which a page of code was selected for reallocation. Presumably, this program was originally loaded from some other device, probably also a disk. Because code space can never be written to, you can guarantee that the 4KB of code in this page frame is exactly the same as the original file from which it was loaded. If you want, you can forgo copying it to the swap device and instead retrieve it from the original file again when it is needed. This is bound to save disk access time and improve overall system throughput. A similar shortcut can even be taken for read/write data segments. Every PTE has a Dirty bit (bit 6) as well as an Accessed bit. The 80386 sets the Dirty bit of a PTE every time it writes into the page to which that PTE points. If a page is selected for reallocation and its Dirty bit is not set, there may be no need to swap it out if another copy of the data exists elsewhere. These kinds of decisions fall under the category of system tweaking and are best left to real-life trial and error.

Step 4: Remapping a Page of Memory

The remapping stage is really the crux of the virtual memory system. If there were no way to translate addresses from linear to physical, there would be no way to keep up the appearance of infinite memory resources. It is through this translation and retranslation that the system's physical memory resources can be made to work double (or more) duty.

Now that a page has been found and its contents are safely tucked away somewhere, it can be dropped into place where the suspended program expects to find it. Before mapping the page into the new linear space, you must be certain to remove it from its current linear space. This is as simple as clearing the Present bit of the PTE. Recall Figure 4-3c, which showed that if a PTE is marked not present, the 80386 doesn't care what is stored in the rest of it. If it suits your needs, you can store any 31-bit quantity you wish in the rest of the PTE. The disk address of the swap file is one common usage. Save the original contents of the PTE first, however. You may want them later.

Next, you have to map the page to a new linear address space. This is simply a matter of changing the PTE that generated the page fault to begin with. Presumably, it was marked not present, although a privilege violation could also have caused the fault. For the time being, this discussion will be confined to not-present pages. You need to change the page-frame address field (bits 12 through 31) to point to the physical base address of the page frame. You can copy this number directly from the page's original PTE if you haven't already written over it. Then you need to set the Present bit, because the page is now, indeed, present in physical memory. Figure 4-15 illustrates the changes to the two PTEs.

As a final step, the paging cache (the TLB) should be flushed and reloaded, because two PTEs have been modified. Your software can now allow the processor to resume execution of the pro-

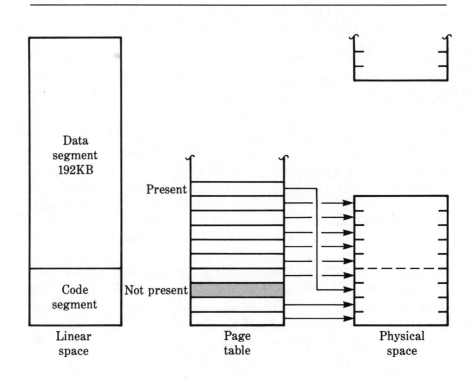

Figure 4-15.   Physical space reallocated

gram that caused all the fuss. Normally, this is done with an IRET instruction.

One side note on the page cache: if the only change you're making to the page directory or page tables is to mark one or the other present when it was previously not present, then flushing and recaching is not necessary. The MMU will never cache a not-present PTE or any PTE pointed to by a not-present PDE. Thus, if you're only setting Present flags, the change will be noted automatically the next time the processor has occasion to look up that entry.

Step 5: Restoring Reallocated Pages

What do you do when the program finally makes a JMP or CALL into the section of code that was mapped out? This should be treated exactly like the extended memory reference that caused the page to be swapped out in the first place. Your software should choose a page of physical memory to allocate to the hole in the code segment, swap out that page's current contents, if necessary, and remap it into the linear space vacated earlier. If the not-present PTE holds the disk address where the code fragment was stored, retrieving the contents should be a simple matter.

Now you have all of the necessary background and tools for creating a system that supports virtual memory. The whole system goes on and on like this, always swapping pages of physical memory around on demand, like a person moving a bucket under a leaking roof. The difference is that you always have a sufficient number of buckets.

Demand paging and virtual memory

- Creates the illusion of nearly infinite memory
- Achieved by "swapping" pages of physical memory
- Processor requests page marked not present
- Page is chosen for reuse
- Contents of page are swapped out
- Page is readdressed
- Program is restarted

USING SEGMENTATION AND PAGING TOGETHER

Throughout this chapter, the various uses for the 80386's paging MMU have been discussed without regard for memory segmentation. In Protected mode, paging is optional but segmentation is not. Therefore, any real-life running system that uses paging is also going to be using the memory segmentation mechanism in

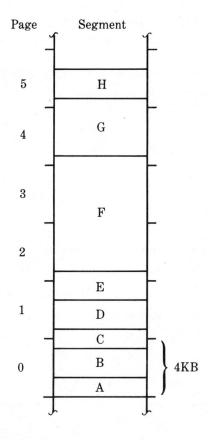

Figure 4-16.   Example memory map

some capacity. This section covers some things you may want to consider when designing the segmentation and paging tables.

Figure 4-16 shows a linear memory map (a segmentation map) of a typical system. Marks every 4KB along the edge show where the physical page boundaries are. The segments are assigned identification letters from A through H. The pages are numbered from 0 through 5. Note that in some cases a segment is contained entirely within one physical page (segments A, B, D, and H), while in other cases a page is contained within one logical segment (page 3). Still another combination is a segment spanning a page boundary (segments C, E, and G). If you implement segmentation boundaries without regard for page boundaries, this kind of arrangement is inevitable. Segment base addresses can be created at any linear byte address desired, with almost any arbitrary length, while pages are fixed both in size and in location.

There is nothing wrong with the memory arrangement shown in Figure 4-16. Indeed, it is this flexibility that allows systems programmers to build their own particular balance of system memory management. The arrangement shown is probably the most difficult to manage effectively, however, precisely because of its loose, nonaligned nature.

Suppose that page 3 needs to be swapped out. That is, its PTE is going to be marked not present, and the physical space it occupies will be reallocated elsewhere. This scenario is exactly like the one described in the earlier discussion of demand paging, in which a page was taken out of the middle of a code segment, and it is probably the easiest situation to handle. The entire physical page is contained within one logical segment, so only one segment of code, data, or stack is affected. When the currently running program needs to reference that particular portion of segment F, the demand paging handler takes over and fills the void.

Change the situation slightly and assume that page 2 is the one being remapped. Physical page 2 currently holds the upper address range of segment E as well as the lower range of segment F. After this page is swapped out, it may need to be swapped in again if a reference is made to either of those address spaces. Technically, this is handled no differently than the previous situation (a missing page is a missing page), but the page is roughly twice as likely to be needed in the future. After it gets swapped out to fulfill some other memory request, it may be needed again before too long. This can affect overall system performance, if swapping pages out to disk occurs more often than is necessary.

A worse situation would arise if page 1 was chosen for reallocation. Page 1 contains all of segment D and half of segments C and E. It is possible, depending on what these segments were used for, that one of these segments would be in use at all times. In other words, as soon as page 1 was swapped out, the current program might try to JMP to segment C, read a parameter from segment E, or PUSH a value into segment D. If possible, try to avoid swapping out pages that contain all or part of a stack segment. Stacks are typically very active pieces of memory, and swapping one out is begging for trouble.

Another particularly bad situation arises when a page of memory that a program uses constantly is reallocated to fill another location that the program also references constantly. An example would be a matrix of data values and the code that performs some iterative operation on them. If physical memory is pulled out from under the code to fulfill the data requirements, the program becomes "swap-bound." Every instruction in the program will force a page fault, and the two pages will be swapped and reswapped ad nauseum. This is known as thrashing. Avoid this.

Finally, assume that page 0 has been swapped out and is now not present. Furthermore, say that segment A is an alias to the GDT and segment B is an IDT alias. This means that not only will the descriptor tables not be present when system-level PL 0 programs want to read or write to them (to modify segment descriptors, for example), but they won't be present when the *processor* wants to access them, either. Above all, system tables should not be swapped out. Marking the page that contains the IDT as not present is a sure-fire way to shut down the processor.

> **Aligning segment boundaries with page boundaries**
>
> - Segments can be page-aligned
> - Segments can be unaligned
> - Aligned segments allow easier memory allocation
> - Unaligned segments allow more flexibility

EXAMPLES

The three sample programs shown in this section can be used as a set to build up paging tables in a running system. The following program shows a small function that returns the index of the first unused slot in the global descriptor table. This can be used as part of a linear (segment-level) memory management and allocation function. It requires no input parameters and returns a signed 32-bit result in EAX. If the result is positive, it is the index of the first empty slot in the GDT. If it is negative, there are no free slots left.

```
code    SEGMENT ER PUBLIC USE32
        ASSUME  CS:code

; Return index to first free GDT descriptor in EAX
; or -1 if none left.
; Assumptions:
; 1) Segment selector in DS points to an alias of the GDT as readable data.

find_free_GDT    PROC    FAR

        PUSH    EBX                             ;save work registers
        PUSH    ECX

        MOV     BX, DS                          ;BX gets alias selector
```

```
          MOVZX    EBX, BX                             ;extend BX to all 32 bits
          LSL      ECX, EBX                            ;ECX gets alias segment limit
          SHR      ECX, 3                              ;limit / 8 = number of slots

          JECXZ    not_found                           ;null length GDT -- exit
          MOV      EAX, 0                              ;start at GDT(1)
next:     INC      EAX
          CMP      BYTE PTR DS:[EAX*8] + 5, 0          ;Access Rights Byte = 0 ?
          LOOPNZ   next                                ;repeat as necessary

          JNZ      not_found

found:
          POP      ECX
          POP      EBX
          RET                                          ;return value in EAX

not_found:
          POP      ECX
          POP      EBX
          MOV      EAX, 0
          DEC      EAX
          RET                                          ;return -1 in EAX

find_first_GDT   ENDP

code      ENDS

          END
```

The next program builds segment descriptors in the GDT. The caller passes it the desired segment parameters (base, size, and so on) in an easy-to-understand form, and the program formats the input parameters properly to create a valid descriptor. One of the functions it performs is to ensure that the DPL of the new segment is no more privileged than the program that called it.

```
code      SEGMENT ER PUBLIC USE32
          ASSUME  CS:code

; Create segment descriptor in GDT.
; All pertinent information is passed in registers.
; Returns 16-bit selector in AX, or -1 if error.

; Assumptions:
; 1) Segment register DS holds selector to GDT alias as read/write data segment.
; 2) Base address is passed in EAX (32 bits).
; 3) Segment length (not limit) is passed in EBX (32 bits)   0 = 4 Gb.
; 4) Segment type is passed in CL (3 bits).
; 5) Segment DPL is passed in CH (2 bits).

; Define eight descriptor type values...

DRO       EQU      0                         ;data, read only
DRW       EQU      1                         ;data, read/write
SRO       EQU      2                         ;stack, read only
SRW       EQU      3                         ;stack, read/write
CEO       EQU      4                         ;code, execute only
CER       EQU      5                         ;code, execute/read
CEOC      EQU      6                         ;conforming code, execute only
CERC      EQU      7                         ;conforming code, execute/read

make_descriptor PROC     FAR

          PUSH     EDX                       ;save word registers
          PUSH     EAX
```

```
        CALL    find_first_GDT          ;find index of first empty GDT slot
        MOV     EDX, EAX                ;EDX gets free slot or -1
        POP     EAX
        OR      EDX, EDX
        JL      error                   ;sorry, no space left in GDT !
base_address:
        MOV     DWORD PTR DS:[EDX*8] +2, EAX     ;write base address 23 .. 0
        ROL     EAX, 8
        MOV     BYTE PTR DS:[EDX*8] +4, AL       ;write base address 31 .. 24
        ROR     EAX, 8

        DEC     EBX                     ;segment length becomes segment limit
        CMP     EBX, 0FFFFFh            ;limit less than 1 Mb ?
        JA      page_granular           ;no -- go page granular
byte_granular:
        MOV     WORD PTR DS:[EDX*8] +0, BX       ;write limit 15 .. 0
        ROL     EBX, 16
        MOV     BYTE PTR DS:[EDX*8] +6, BL       ;write limit 19 .. 16
        ROR     EBX, 16
        AND     BYTE PTR DS:[EDX*8] +6, 0Fh      ;drop G, D, X, U bits
        OR      BYTE PTR DS:[EDX*8] +6, 40h      ;set D bit

        JMP     segment_type
page_granular:
        SHR     EBX, 12                 ;shift limit right twelve bits
        MOV     WORD PTR DS:[EDX*8] +0, BX       ;write limit 15 .. 0
        ROL     EBX, 16
        MOV     BYTE PTR DS:[EDX*8] +6, BL       ;write limit 19 .. 16
        ROR     EBX, 16
        AND     BYTE PTR DS:[EDX*8] +6, 0Fh      ;drop G, D, X, U bits
        OR      BYTE PTR DS:[EDX*8] +6, 0C0h     ;set G and D bits

segment_type:
        MOV     BYTE PTR DS:[EDX*8] +5, 0        ;clear Access Rights Byte
        CMP     AL, CERC
        JA      error                   ;sorry, invalid segment type !
        SHL     CL, 1                   ;shift to make room for A bit
        OR      BYTE PTR DS:[EDX*8] +5, CL       ;write Type and A bits·

priv_level:
        MOVZX   AX, CH                  ;AX gets requested DPL level
        MOV     BX, WORD PTR SS:[ESP] +4        ;BX gets caller's CPL
        ARPL    AX, BX                  ;adjust AX if necessary
        SHL     AL, 5                   ;move DPL field into position
        OR      BYTE PTR DS:[EDX*8] +5, AL       ;set DPL bits
        OR      BYTE PTR DS:[EDX*8] +5, 90h      ;set Present and System bits

        MOV     AX, DX                  ;AX gets GDT index
        SHL     AX, 3                   ;index * 8 = selector
        ARPL    AX, BX                  ;adjust RPL field if necessary
        POP     EDX
        RET

error:
        POP     EDX
        MOV     EAX, 0
        DEC     EAX
        RET                             ;return -1

make_descriptor ENDP

code    ENDS

        END
```

The next program builds a page directory and two page tables and then enables paging. To keep things simple, all linear addresses are identity mapped. No actual address translation takes place. The physical address map is shown in Figure 4-17. There are 4MB of RAM at the low end of the address space and 64KB of code at the upper end. Note that the program must create only two page tables, one for the upper end and one for the lower end. Consequently, only the first and last PDEs in the page directory are defined.

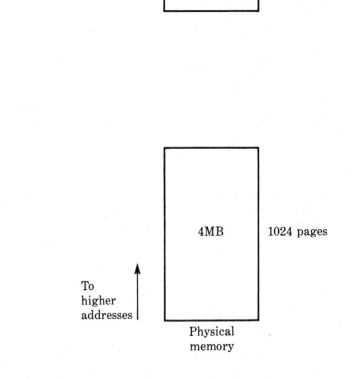

Figure 4-17.   Target memory map

```
code    SEGMENT ER PUBLIC USE32
        ASSUME  CS:code

; This program produces paging tables and enables paging.
; Memory space will be identity-mapped i.e. no actual translation.

; Assumptions:
; 1) Physical memory from 1000 through 3FFF is not currently in use.

; Define eight descriptor type values...

DRO     EQU     0                       ;data, read only
DRW     EQU     1                       ;data, read/write
SRO     EQU     2                       ;stack, read only
SRW     EQU     3                       ;stack, read/write
CEO     EQU     4                       ;code, execute only
CER     EQU     5                       ;code, execute/read
CEOC    EQU     6                       ;conforming code, execute only
CERC    EQU     7                       ;conforming code, execute/read

page_enable     PROC    FAR

; Create page directory...
        MOV     EAX, 1000h              ;base address = 1000
        MOV     EBX, 1000h              ;size = 4096 bytes
        MOV     CL, DRW                 ;read/write data segment
        MOV     CH, 0                   ;privilege level 0
        CALL    make_descriptor
        OR      EAX, EAX
        JL      error                   ;couldn't make descriptor

        MOV     ES, AX                  ;ES gets new segment selector
        MOV     EDI, 0
        MOV     EAX, 0
        MOV     ECX, 1024
        REP     STOSD                   ;start by zeroing out table

        MOV     DWORD PTR ES:[0], 00002003h     ;1st PDE -> 1st page table
        MOV     DWORD PTR ES:[0FFCh], 00003003h ;1024th PDE -> 2nd page table

; Create first page table...
        MOV     EAX, 2000h              ;base address = 2000
        MOV     EBX, 1000h              ;size = 4096 bytes
        MOV     CL, DRW                 ;read/write data segment
        MOV     CH, 0                   ;privilege level 0
        CALL    make_descriptor
        OR      EAX, EAX
        JL      error                   ;couldn't make descriptor

        MOV     ES, AX                  ;ES gets new segment selector
        MOV     EDI, 0
        MOV     EAX, 00000003h          ;first page frame address = 0
        MOV     ECX, 1024
table1:
        STOSD                           ;write one PTE
        ADD     EAX, 1000h              ;increment page frame address
        LOOP    table1                  ;repeat 1024 times

; Create second page table...
        MOV     EAX, 3000h              ;base address = 3000
        MOV     EBX, 1000h              ;size = 4096 bytes
        MOV     CL, DRW                 ;read/write data segment
        MOV     CH, 0                   ;privilege level 0
        CALL    make_descriptor
        OR      EAX, EAX
        JL      error                   ;couldn't make descriptor

        MOV     ES, AX                  ;ES gets new segment selector
        MOV     EDI, 0
        MOV     EAX, 0
        MOV     ECX, 1008
        REP     STOSD                   ;zero first 1008 PTEs
```

```
        MOV     EAX, 0FFFF0003h        ;1009th page frame address = FFFF0000
        MOV     ECX, 16
table2:
        STOSD                          ;write one PTE
        ADD     EAX, 1000h             ;increment page frame address
        LOOP    table2                 ;repeat 16 times

; Enable Paging...
        MOV     EAX, 1000h             ;physical address of page dir = 1000
        MOV     CR3, EAX               ;load into CR3

        PUSHFD                         ;save EFLAGS
        CLI                            ;disable interrupts temporarily

        MOV     EAX, CR0               ;copy CR0 into EAX
        BTS     EAX, 31                ;set bit 31
        MOV     CR0, EAX               ;** Enable Paging **
        JMP     flush                  ;flush prefetch queue
flush:  NOP

        POPFD                          ;restore EFLAGS
        RET

error:
        RET

page_enable     ENDP

code    ENDS

        END
```

All of the example programs are assumed to be running at privilege level 0, and are called through call gates. Each one can operate on various other assumptions, outlined in the respective program listings.

5

MULTITASKING

Multitasking has become the microcomputer buzzword for the latter half of the 1980s. In September 1987, Microsoft introduced Windows/386, and OS/2 was released in early 1988. The major selling feature of both of these operating environments is that they allow multitasking. That is, they enable the host computer to perform more than one task at a time. The term *task* is often rather vague and loosely defined, so some clarification is in order. This chapter defines a task and multitasking, shows you how the 80386 supports multitasking, and illustrates how you can perform multitasking in your own programs.

Because multitasking was not possible on microcomputers until very recently (and has never been as well supported as it is on 80386 machines), it is necessary to look to minicomputer systems for a good example of multitasking. On a typical minicomputer, several computer operators, or users, generally share the system. Each user commonly has on his or her desk a terminal that is connected to the computer. One user in the personnel department may calculate company payroll, another in finance may do financial modeling, and another in engineering may use the computer to help in the design of its replacement. All of these people are using the same computer at the same time. This scene is fairly typical, and most programmers have seen similar arrangements or, indeed, been one of the users.

How is one computer able to serve so many people? The answer lies in the fact that a digital computer runs at extremely high speed and is thus able to share its attention among more than one person at a time. Since virtually all modern computer systems (those using the Von Neumann architecture) can perform only one step at a time, in sequence, the computer is actually serving only one user for a short time and then moving on to the next user, and so on. Each user is allotted a *time slice*, usually a small fraction of a second. When a user's time slice is up, the computer directs its attention to the next user's work until that slice has expired. Eventually, the computer will return to the first user, pick up where it left off, and do as much work as it is able in a time slice.

This technique is known as *timesharing*, and it is how nearly all computers that support multiple users operate. Each user believes that he or she is getting the machine's undivided attention. There is no outward indication of the true nature of the work the computer is performing. This technique works as well as it does both because of the extreme processing speed in a minicomputer and because the average computer user doesn't actually "use" the machine most of the time. (How many times have you stared at the keyboard or monitor while the computer could have been doing compute-intensive work?) In the same way that a movie projector creates the illusion of smooth, continuous motion by momentarily flashing still pictures on a screen, a timesharing computer system appears to be running only your own personal application program, with no interruptions. In fact, all you are getting is brief "flashes" of processor time.

Timesharing

- Allows multiple users to use the same computer
- Provides economical use of processing resources
- Is invisible to the users
- Can work for any number of users

The two elements most critical to maintaining this illusion both require cooperation from system software. The first is determining when to change from one user to the next. The simplest way to do this is to allocate each user a fixed time slice, say, $1/10$ second. The computer will then divert its attention to the next user in line 10 times per second. If there are 10 users, each one will be serviced once per second. In real life, this turns out to be a wasteful way to regulate processing time, because users who are staring at keyboards (or who are away from their terminals altogether) get exactly as much CPU time as users who are compiling 348KB of FORTRAN code. The different methods of allocating time slices are not particularly germane to this book, so they won't be discussed here.

The second element crucial to successful timesharing is the ability to restart a user's program every time its time slice comes around. When a user's time slice expires, the computer system must have a way to save the current state of the program. It must then be able to restart the next user's program exactly as it was left when its time slice expired, and so on. Usually, saving the state of a running program requires saving the contents of all of the processor's registers as well as any read/write memory variables. The next instruction to be executed must be noted with the equivalent of a bookmark. Everything possible must be done to "freeze" the current state of a running program so that it can be "thawed" at any time with no ill effects. The frozen state of a program is known as its *context*, and the act of freezing the state of one program and thawing the next one is a *context switch*.

The timesharing machine will have a private area of memory that is accessible only to the operating system, where it will store all of the information necessary to revive or restart each program. This is known as a *context store* or *state frame*. To minimize the time and complexity involved in changing contexts, it is desirable to save and restore as little information as possible for each program while still allowing seamless changes in execution from one context to the next. Thus, to avoid saving and reloading every user's entire code and data space to and from disk on every time slice, the computer's main memory is partitioned. All currently running programs are allotted a certain area of memory as their own. Then, when the time comes for a context switch, the machine merely leaves that partition of memory as it is and begins working with the next program in the next partition. As long as one program does not interfere with another's memory partition, every partition should be found just as it was left. Leaving dormant programs in main memory like this reduces context-switch time considerably. In fact, the only volatile part of a program's context that still needs to be saved is the contents of the processor's registers when the time slice expired. Depending on the processor, this usually isn't very much information, and so the state frames can be kept small.

A context switch

- Is necessary to perform timesharing

- Saves the state of the current program

- Loads the state of the next program

- Allows any program to be restarted at any time

Note that by partitioning memory between running programs, the machine is essentially storing their entire states, code and all, with the tradeoff being that the maximum number of programs running is limited by available memory. This is a fair trade, since it is usually easier and cheaper to add memory to an existing computer system than it is to install a new computer. Even this limitation can be overcome through the use of demand paging, described in the previous chapter.

The 80386 equivalent of almost every aspect of a minicomputer timesharing system has been introduced already. The memory partitioning can be accomplished with memory segmentation. One program can be prevented from interfering with another through segmentation or with the privilege protection system. Limited memory space can be overcome with paging. The only aspects not covered so far are the management of a context store and the transition from one context to another. On the 80386, these correspond to the task state segment and the task switch instructions. This chapter explores these and other multitasking features of the 80386 and discusses how they can be used to create some very advanced programs and operating systems.

TASK STATE SEGMENTS

On the 80386 the basic unit of a multitasking system is the task. From a programmer's point of view, the definition of a task is somewhat vague. A task can be a single program, or it can be a group of related programs. If the 80386 system is to have multiple users, a task can be assigned to each user. In general, multiuser implies multitasking, but the reverse is not necessarily true. Windows/386, for example, allows a single user to run multiple tasks.

Multitasking versus multiuser

- Multitasking = Many different tasks on one computer

- Multiuser = Many different people using one computer

- A multitasking computer can perform many tasks for one user

- A multiuser computer can perform many tasks for many users

From the point of view of the 80386, the definition of a task is very clear. A task is any collection of code and data that has a Task State Segment (TSS) assigned to it. There is a one-to-one correlation between TSSs and tasks.

The TSS is the 80386 equivalent of the context store or state frame described earlier. It is where the 80386 stores a task's vital information when that task is not running; it is also where the 80386 finds all of the information necessary to restart that task when its turn comes again. When a task lies dormant, its TSS holds all of the information required to restart it at any time.

A TSS is nothing more than an area of read/write memory, like a small data segment. This segment is not accessible to the general user program, however, even at privilege level 0. The space defined within a TSS is accessible to the 80386 only. This is its private "cold storage."

TSS Descriptor

Like other, more traditional, areas of memory, the task state segment is defined by a segment descriptor in a descriptor table. TSS descriptors can appear only in the GDT, never in the IDT or in LDTs, for reasons that will become clear later on. The format of a TSS descriptor is shown in Figure 5-1, and that of a task state segment is given in Figure 5-2.

The TSS descriptor is basically like any other segment descriptor, with a Base Address and Limit field. The Base Address determines the (linear) starting address of the task state segment. It must point to physically writable memory. If paging is (or will be) enabled on your system, the TSS should be mapped to a "present" page of RAM.

The Limit field determines how long the task state segment will be. The 80386 requires 104 bytes of storage in order to perform a context save, and so the Limit field of a TSS descriptor must never be less than 00067 (hexadecimal). It can always be made larger (up to 4GB); some uses for an enlarged TSS are brought up later in this chapter. The TSS DPL field does not imply a privilege level for the task state segment itself; TSS segments are not accessible to any

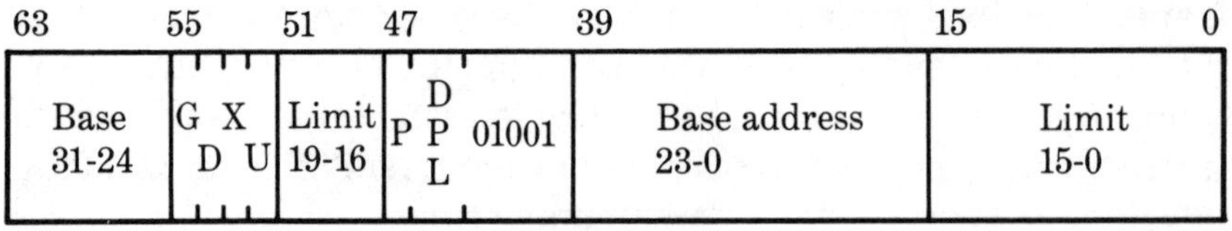

63	55	51	47	39	15	0
Base 31-24	G X D U	Limit 19-16	D P P 01001 L	Base address 23-0	Limit 15-0	

Figure 5-1.   Task state segment descriptor

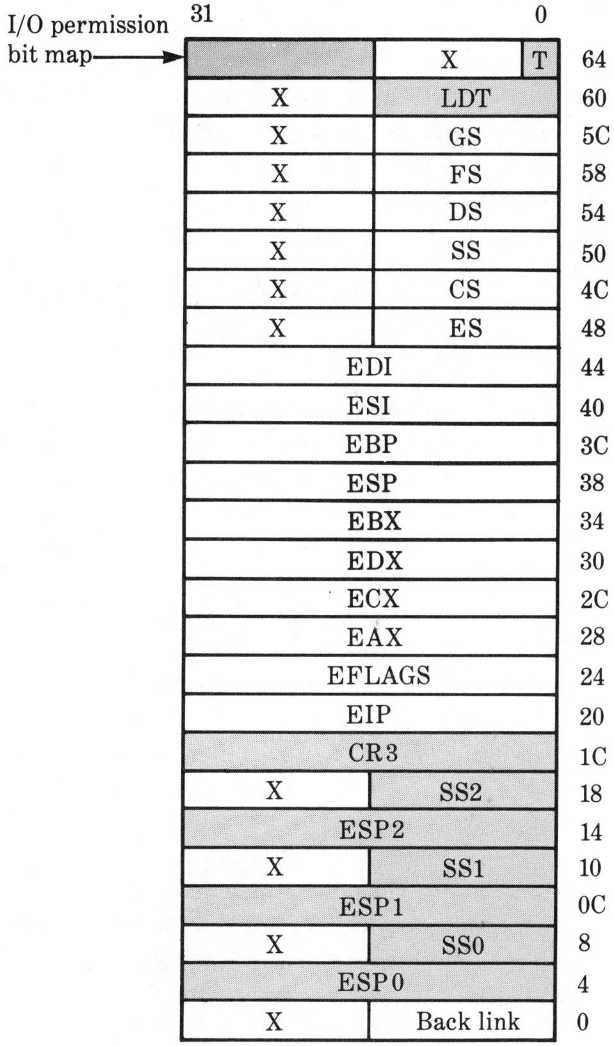

I/O permission bit map →	X	T	64

```
  31                                      0
┌──────────────────┬──────────┬──┐
│      (shaded)     │    X     │T │ 64   I/O permission bit map →
├──────────────────┼──────────┴──┤
│        X         │    LDT      │ 60
├──────────────────┼─────────────┤
│        X         │    GS       │ 5C
├──────────────────┼─────────────┤
│        X         │    FS       │ 58
├──────────────────┼─────────────┤
│        X         │    DS       │ 54
├──────────────────┼─────────────┤
│        X         │    SS       │ 50
├──────────────────┼─────────────┤
│        X         │    CS       │ 4C
├──────────────────┼─────────────┤
│        X         │    ES       │ 48
├──────────────────┴─────────────┤
│            EDI                  │ 44
├─────────────────────────────────┤
│            ESI                  │ 40
├─────────────────────────────────┤
│            EBP                  │ 3C
├─────────────────────────────────┤
│            ESP                  │ 38
├─────────────────────────────────┤
│            EBX                  │ 34
├─────────────────────────────────┤
│            EDX                  │ 30
├─────────────────────────────────┤
│            ECX                  │ 2C
├─────────────────────────────────┤
│            EAX                  │ 28
├─────────────────────────────────┤
│          EFLAGS                 │ 24
├─────────────────────────────────┤
│            EIP                  │ 20
├─────────────────────────────────┤
│            CR3                  │ 1C
├──────────────────┬─────────────┤
│        X         │    SS2      │ 18
├──────────────────┴─────────────┤
│           ESP2                  │ 14
├──────────────────┬─────────────┤
│        X         │    SS1      │ 10
├──────────────────┴─────────────┤
│           ESP1                  │ 0C
├──────────────────┬─────────────┤
│        X         │    SS0      │ 8
├──────────────────┴─────────────┤
│           ESP0                  │ 4
├──────────────────┬─────────────┤
│        X         │  Back link  │ 0
└──────────────────┴─────────────┘
```

Figure 5-2.   Task state segment

programs. Instead, it fulfills a function similar to that of the DPL in a call gate descriptor: it determines what software can reference the task that this TSS descriptor defines.

Task State Segment

The task state segment itself is the interesting part. The diagram of the TSS in Figure 5-2 is divided to show where the 80386 will store its various registers within the segment. All eight general-purpose registers are saved, along with the six segment registers. It is illuminating to note that the eight general-purpose registers are saved in the same order in which a PUSHAD instruction would save them on a stack. Apparently, some microcode is being reused here. The 32-bit instruction pointer, EIP, is also stored. This is necessary so that the task can be restarted at the point at which it stopped. Saving EFLAGS guarantees that conditional instructions will behave properly when the task is restarted. The three upper-level stack pointers are also stored here, as is noted in the discussion of privilege transitions in Chapter 3. The fact that CR3 is stored in the TSS would seem to imply that the page directory (and, hence, all page-related information) can be changed on a per-task basis, which is exactly correct. Also in the TSS is a selector to an LDT. This, too, might change on a per-task basis. In fact, that's the whole idea behind using LDTs—separation of address space between tasks.

The last three fields to be covered are at the extreme ends of the TSS. The Back Link field is used by the 80386 to keep track of a task chain. The I/O Permission Bit Map field refers to an additional privilege-related function. Both of these are covered in later sections. The field marked "T" is used in debugging, which is covered in Chapter 10.

Whenever the 80386 starts executing a new task, it reads in all of the information contained in the first 104 bytes of the task's TSS. Most of the data is copied directly into its registers, as indicated, while some is cached internally for later use. Execution then commences at the address indicated by the contents of the CS and EIP registers. In effect, loading a TSS and running a new task is just like performing a FAR RET instruction from a subroutine and loading registers from the stack, but on a much larger scale. On a subroutine return, most of the processor's registers are unchanged, so that parameters can be passed back and forth. If the subroutine needs to preserve some of the caller's registers, it must be explicitly coded to do so.

For a task switch, the opposite approach is taken. Absolutely no information crosses task boundaries. Two tasks are as separate as they can be and still run on the same processor. This is necessary both to keep one task's work from contaminating another's and so that tasks can be stopped and started at any time, in any order, without side effects.

When the current task has used up its time slice, the 80386 must, of course, save all of the current context information back into the TSS. However, only the unshaded portions of the TSS are updated. The shaded sections are only read from, never written to. This is done to save context-switching time. The portions that are shaded were not deemed volatile enough to warrant being saved on every context switch. Ideally, of course, only those bits of those registers that had actually changed during execution would be saved, but you have to draw the line somewhere.

If these sections of the task state segment are never updated by the 80386, how do their values ever get set? This is actually part of a larger chicken-and-egg problem: how are the original values loaded into a TSS in the first place?

Initializing Task State Segments

As advanced as the 80386 task-management hardware is, it still needs some intervention from old-fashioned programmers. The TSS descriptors need to be defined, task state segments must be located in sensible places in the address space, and the TSSs need to be initialized. Given that the segments are not real memory segments in the normal sense (you can't load a selector to a TSS descriptor without getting a general protection fault), how do you initialize them? You make an alias for them.

If your task state segments are all defined end to end in linear memory, one data segment alias should take care of them all. A better idea is to create one alias segment per task state segment, with exactly the same base address and limit. That way, there is less danger of fouling up more than one TSS at a time. Alias management will also be easier if you interleave the TSS descriptors with the alias descriptors in the GDT, so that you always know which alias belongs to which TSS (and vice versa).

After the aliases are created, you must load the TSSs with their initial values before multitasking can begin. The same chore arises when the 80386 is already multitasking and the supervisor/operating system wants to add another task. There are two ways to accomplish this. You can either write the data in "manually," storing the desired initial values for EAX, EBX, and so on, or you can load the whole TSS at once by making the 80386 store its current state into it. You can do this by forcing a task switch, but this method has the disadvantage that in order to task-switch out (and save the current state in a TSS), you must also task-switch into a new task (and load state information from a different TSS). Thus, at least one TSS must still be created by hand.

The original values stored in a TSS may or may not be critical. In between time slices, the TSS holds the task's context at the point at which it was preempted, and it is normally not modified. But when the TSS is first created and the task is started for the very first time, the initial contents of the TSS may affect the program's behavior when it begins executing. Obviously, the CS and EIP fields must point to the segment and offset of the first instruction in the program. The data segment register fields should probably be loaded with the task's data segment selectors. The SS field almost certainly must be initialized with a valid selector with the correct privilege level. The eight general-purpose register storage areas are typically zeroed, unless the program depends on different initial values when it is first started. The three alternate stack segments and pointers should also point to valid stacks unless you are certain that only one privilege level will ever be used within this task. If the task uses an LDT, this field must be initialized to select it, and CR3 should be set to the appropriate address value if paging is (or will be) enabled.

Perhaps just as important as the information that is stored in each task's TSS is the information that is not stored. Note that CR0 (MSW) and CR2 are not saved in the TSS, indicating that they are global and do not change when a task switch occurs. This means that paging and other features are either on or off for all tasks. Because CR3 is reread on a task switch, the paging information can change from task to task, but paging will still be in effect throughout the system. Likewise, neither the debug registers (DR0 through DR7) nor the test registers (TR6 and TR7) are affected by a task switch. GDTR and IDTR are not task-sensitive either. Only the LDT may change automatically on a context change.

To create a task

■ Choose an area of memory for a context store

■ Define a task state segment

■ Store original values for the segment registers

■ Store original values for the general-purpose registers

■ Store original value for the instruction pointer

MOVING BETWEEN TASKS

A task switch can be initiated by software (the JMP and CALL instructions), as the result of a processor fault or exception (a General Projection fault or divide-by-zero error), or by an external interrupt (a time-slice clock interrupt, for example).

Forcing a task switch in software is very similar to calling a call gate. Conceptually, however, a very different function is performed. When calling another function through a call gate, the caller usually passes some parameters, expecting the called function to perform some useful work and then return to the caller, possibly returning some parameters. When invoking a task switch, the program is deliberately putting itself to sleep and awakening another, unrelated, dormant task. The new task receives no parameters from the old task. Indeed, it does not know that it has ever been frozen. The new task is typically under no obligation to reawaken its caller at any time. The 80386's concept of a task was devised to distance unrelated sections of code and data as much as possible. It is intentionally difficult for one task to affect another in any way.

Task Gates

Task gates, like call gates, are special system descriptors. A task gate descriptor does not define a memory segment but instead acts as an interface point between user code and a task state segment. The format of a task gate is shown in Figure 5-3. Notice that a task gate is much simpler than even a call gate. In fact, the only parameter a task gate defines is the selector to a TSS (and the Access Rights byte that defines this as a task gate descriptor). When you use the selector to a task gate in your code, you are indirectly referencing a TSS descriptor, which uniquely identifies a task. Like the selector to a call gate, the selector to a task gate can be used in place of a selector to a code segment in FAR JMP and FAR CALL instructions. Such a JMP or CALL is indistinguishable from "normal" FAR JMPs or FAR CALLs unless you know that the selector refers to a task gate descriptor. The current program must also be privileged enough to invoke the task gate, as it must to invoke a call gate. The privilege rule is as follows:

$$\text{MAX (CPL, RPL)} \leq \text{task gate DPL}$$

Note that unlike the DPL of a call gate, the DPL of the target descriptor (in this case, of the TSS descriptor) is not checked. Just to cover all bases, the privilege level of the code segment that the new task is going to use is completely irrelevant. This is in keeping with the concept of separation of tasks. Because the new task is not doing any work for the old task, their respective privilege levels are unimportant. The DPL of the task gate descriptor simply prevents PL 3 hacks from causing task switches.

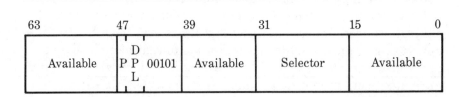

63	47	39	31	15	0
Available	D P P 00101 L	Available	Selector	Available	

Figure 5-3.   Task gate descriptor

Direct to TSS

There is another way to force a task switch, one that departs from the call gate model. Instead of using a task gate selector as the object of an intersegment transfer instruction, you can use the selector of the TSS descriptor itself. In other words, you can reference a task gate selector in your FAR JMP or FAR CALL, or you can reference the TSS descriptor's selector directly, bypassing the gate entirely. The privilege rule for this form is as follows:

$$\text{MAX (CPL, RPL)} \leq \text{TSS DPL}$$

This rule is exactly the same as the one stated previously, except that the 80386 tests a different descriptor. Thus, depending on the form you use, the 80386 tests either the TSS descriptor or the task gate descriptor, but never both.

What is the difference between the two? There is none. Both forms behave identically. What, then, is the advantage of having task gate descriptors at all? It is apparent only when multitasking is in use (which makes a certain amount of sense). Because there is only one TSS descriptor per task, and it must be located in the GDT, all programs or tasks have access to it and could cause a task switch, assuming they were privileged enough. If, however, you define a few task gates for that TSS descriptor and locate them in various LDTs, you can effectively restrict task-switching privileges to only those tasks with the gate in their LDTs as well as to those that run at PL 0 (which can always access the TSS descriptor in the GDT directly). This allows a PL 2 program, for instance, to force a task switch, but only if the task gate is in its LDT, and it can switch only to that particular task. Creating task gates also allows interrupts and exceptions to cause task switches automatically, if the task gates are put into the IDT. This is covered in detail in Chapter 7.

Task Register

When a task switch occurs, the 80386 must save its complete context in a TSS and load a new context from another TSS. Execution will automatically resume at a new location, since CS and EIP are two of

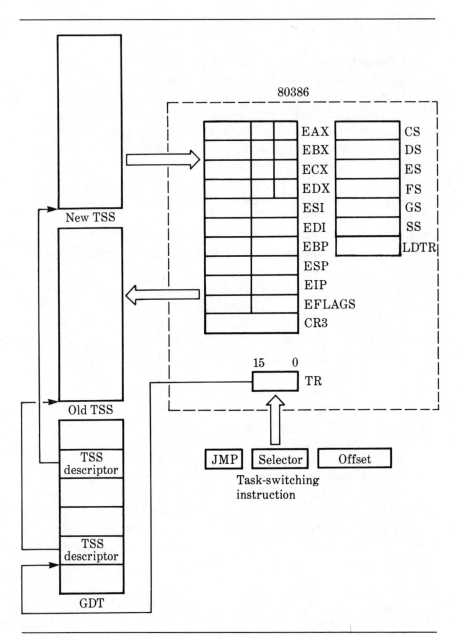

Figure 5-4.   Task switch operation

the registers loaded. The new TSS is identified by the TSS descriptor, which may have been referenced either directly or indirectly through a task gate. But how does the 80386 know which TSS to save the old state in? A selector to the current task's TSS descriptor is kept in TR (task register) at all times. When a new task begins, the 80386 updates TR with a selector to the new task's TSS, but not before the current context is saved in the TSS pointed to by TR. In this fashion, TR is always current and is self-maintaining. See Figure 5-4. Any application can use the STR instruction to store the contents of TR into a register or memory, thereby determining which task it is. Typically, this information is meaningless to the casual user, but there it is.

Updating TR on every task switch presents another chicken-and-egg problem. If TR holds the selector to the current TSS, and it is updated on every task switch, how does it get loaded the first time? You must use the privileged instruction LTR to initialize TR. Otherwise, the 80386 will not know where to store its context on the very first task switch. After this point, the processor should be allowed to maintain TR on its own.

The advanced programmer should be aware of a few other subtle changes that take place automatically on every task switch. After loading a new context from a TSS and updating TR, the 80386 then marks the new TSS as "busy." A busy TSS is one that is currently executing, or that is part of a call chain, discussed later. It marks the TSS busy by setting bit 41 in its descriptor (bit 1 in the Access Rights byte). Note that the Busy bit is part of the TSS descriptor; it is not stored in the TSS itself, because it is not strictly part of the executing task's context.

The 80386 will refuse to task-switch into a task that is already marked busy. This keeps it from switching into the currently running task. Tasks are not reentrant, and task switches therefore cannot be recursive.

On every task switch, the processor also automatically sets the TS (Task Switched) flag in register CR0. This bit will never be cleared unless you do so in the new task. The TS bit can be used by system software to manage the coherency of other systemwide resources, such as an 80387 floating-point mathematics coprocessor.

Task register

- Sixteen-bit processor register
- Always holds the selector for the current task
- Old task state is saved in current TSS
- New TSS selector is stored in task register

Nested Tasks

A third change may take place, depending on the circumstances that caused the task switch. If it was caused by a FAR CALL instruction or by an exception, fault, or trap, the new task is considered to be nested within the old task that invoked it. This is analogous to a subroutine that is called or an interrupt handler that is invoked by an external interrupt, fault, or trap. In any of these cases, when the task executes an IRET instruction, the 80386 automatically task-switches back to the task that invoked it. In this way, tasks can be loosely nested to almost any level. This effect does not occur if the task switch was the result of a FAR JMP instruction.

In order to nest tasks, which are usually very independent entities, the 80386 must maintain the equivalent of a call/return stack. Without some mechanism of linking the tasks, the processor would have no way of unwinding the sequence of task switches. For this reason, the TSS contains a 16-bit field that is not strictly part of an executing task's context. At offset 0 in every TSS is a Back Link field. Whenever two tasks are nested, the new, called task has the selector of the TSS of the calling task stored in its Back Link field.

The 80386 also sets the NT (Nested Task) flag in the EFLAGS register. Technically, the 80386 uses NT as a flag so that it can tell whether the Back Link field in the current TSS is valid. Should it encounter an IRET instruction, this is the only means the 80386 has of determining whether it should perform a task switch or a normal IRET. Conceptually, NT indicates that this is a "child" task and that the Back Link field is the ID of its "parent." Because NT is part of EFLAGS, which is saved during a task switch, it follows that a child

Table 5-1.   Effect of Task Switch on TSS

Before / After	NT Bit		Back Link Field		Busy Bit	
	Old TSS	New TSS	Old TSS	New TSS	Old TSS Descriptor	New TSS Descriptor
JMP	X / X	X / 0	X / X	X / X	1 / 0	0 / 1
Call Interrupt Exception	X / X	X / 1	X / X	X / Note 1	1 / 1	0 / 1
IRET	1 / 0	X / X	Note 2 / X	X / X	1 / 0	1 / 1

1 = Bit must be set/will be set
0 = Bit must be clear/will be cleared
X = Unimportant/unaffected
Note 1 = Back link will be set to old TSS selector
Note 2 = Back link must be set to new TSS selector

task that is interrupted or that uses up its time slice will still be able to return to its parent when its turn comes around again.

Note that a RET instruction will not "unnest" tasks, even if they were nested by CALL instructions. Only the IRET instruction has this feature.

When unnesting tasks after an IRET, the 80386 saves the processor state in the outgoing, child TSS, loads TR from the child's Back Link field, and loads a new context from the indicated TSS. The incoming parent TSS should be marked busy. If it is not, the 80386 will raise an invalid TSS fault (exception 10). This is an exception to the normal rule that incoming tasks must not be busy, but it makes sense because of the nature of the relationship between the tasks. Table 5-1 summarizes the relationship between incoming and outgoing TSSs under various task-switching conditions.

If any of the "before" conditions are violated, the processor will abort the task-switch operation and report an invalid TSS fault. A lot of other things can go wrong during a task switch and cause the 80386 to abort it; these are covered in detail in Chapter 7, which deals with error handling. This chapter takes the optimistic view that all task switches work as desired. Before long, however, you will want to familiarize yourself with Chapter 7.

Nested task switches

- Nested tasks act like subroutines
- CALL instruction to task gate will nest tasks
- Interrupt or exception to task gate will nest tasks
- JMP instruction will not nest tasks
- New TSS gets old TSS selector in Back Link field
- New task gets nested task bit set in EFLAGS register
- New task must return to old task with IRET instruction

TASK SCHEDULING

Now that all of the features have been covered, the tools discussed, and the problems pointed out, it's time to build a hypothetical multi-tasking system. For starters, let's design a simple one, with two (count 'em) tasks. One task will turn on a green LED, and the other will turn on a red LED. They could just as easily be tasks that do square-root calculations, but these will serve as illustrative examples for now.

Assume that you are in Protected mode and have all the privilege you need in order to modify the GDT. First, you need to create two task state segments to hold the dormant states of the two tasks. Because you intend to timeshare between the two tasks, both tasks will never be dormant at the same time, but TSS sharing is not allowed. The code for task 1 looks like this:

```
task1:  MOV     DX, GREEN_LED
        MOV     AL, ON
        OUT     DX, AL                      ;turn on green LED
        MOV     DX, RED LED
        MOV     AL, OFF_
        OUT     DX, AL                      ;turn off red LED
        JMP     task1
```

Task 2 is very similar but has the ON and OFF constants swapped. You may already have noticed an interesting feature. Neither task's code is concerned with preserving registers, that is, DX and AL. They have no reason to, since the task-switching mechanism takes care of that for them. You can (and should) write tasks as though there was no other software in the system.

A second item of interest is that both programs run in infinite loops, repeating their two I/O instructions over and over. Why repeat the I/O instructions if you assume that an LED stays on when turned on and off when turned off? Why not just turn one LED on and the other off and "spin" at the end of the program, as follows?

```
            ...
            OUT     DX, AL
forever:    JMP     forever
```

The reason is that this program may be switched out at any time, to be replaced by a program that reverses the condition of the LEDs. If each task did not continually write the same data out to the LEDs, task 1's work would be overwritten by task 2, and then both would sit in endless do-nothing loops. Even though your tasks' code can always depend on the processor's registers being exactly as they left them, you can make no such assumptions about shared resources such as I/O addresses or shared memory.

The next step is to initialize the two TSSs so that they hold the values necessary to start both programs properly. For this example, CS and EIP are just about the only things that need to be correct. The programs do not depend on any initial values in the general-purpose registers or even in the data segment registers. Each TSS should, however, have a valid stack segment (SS) and stack pointer (ESP). If you want, you can store the code for both tasks in the same code segment, with task 1's program at offset 0 and task 2's code at, say, offset 100. They can share a stack segment, too, as long as the two stack pointers are started a safe distance apart.

Everything is in readiness. Register TR is loaded with the selector to task 1's TSS, and a FAR JMP is executed to task 2's TSS. The red LED comes on . . . and stays on. What's wrong with this picture?

A couple of things are wrong. First, there is no provision for changing from one task to another. The tasks don't do it voluntarily with JMPs or CALLs, nor is a time-slice or other interrupt defined to make it happen automatically. The other problem is that when TR is loaded and the first task switch is made, the information written into task 1's TSS is obliterated.

The trouble with starting multitasking is that the current state of the processor *must* be saved somewhere, even if you don't want it. There are at least two solutions to this. First, you can create a third, "garbage" TSS in which the original state of the processor is stored as you begin the first task. The TSS will probably never be used again, and so it's a waste of 104 bytes, but it works. The second workaround is to make the creation-and-initialization code part of the first task. In other words, you can append the program in task 1 to your setup code and "fall through" into it when initialization is complete. This saves a TSS and has no ill side effects.

The Scheduler as an
Interrupt Service Routine

Now, given that neither task is voluntarily going to preempt itself and force a task switch to its twin, you need to create a time-slice interrupt and write a handler for it that will suspend the currently running task and start the other.

Even though interrupts have not been dealt with much so far, most 8086 programmers are familiar enough with them to understand how Interrupt Service Routines (ISRs) operate as procedures within the context of the currently running program. On a multitasking 80386 system, this definition needs to be broadened to state that ISRs execute under the context of the currently running program in the currently running task. As always, ISRs should be written so that they do not disrupt the program or task that was interrupted.

If this time-slice ISR is treated as a typical ISR procedure, you must assume that it could be called at any time, while either task is running. It needs to deal with any hardware-related functions, such as resetting the timer, and then force a task switch to whichever task is *not* currently running. There are any number of ways in which the ISR can determine which task is the current one, that is, which task was interrupted when the time-slice interrupt came. The ISR could execute an STR instruction to examine the task register. Alternatively, it could examine the two TSS descriptors in the GDT to determine which one was busy. A third possibility would be for the ISR to maintain a local variable or flag and toggle it every time the ISR is called. If the flag is clear, it will invoke task 1; if it is set, it will invoke task 2. These examples should be used for comparison only; your implementation may vary.

Assuming that the ISR has somehow chosen which task is going out and which is coming in, how do you implement the mechanics of the switch? If you simply execute an IRET to terminate the ISR, program flow will return to the point of interruption, which will be the endless loop of I/O instructions. That won't get you anywhere. You need to modify the return stack so that the IRET "returns" you to a FAR JMP instruction that causes a task switch. An example is shown here:

```
switch_to_task_1:
            MOV     DWORD PTR SS:[ESP] +0, OFFSET start1
            MOV     WORD PTR SS:[ESP] +4, SEG start1
            IRETD
start1:     JMP     PWORD PTR task1ptr

; ------------------------------
switch_to_task_2:
            MOV     DWORD PTR SS:[ESP] +0, OFFSET start2
            MOV     WORD PTR SS:[ESP] +4, SEG start2
start2:     JMP     PWORD PTR task2ptr

; ------------------------------
task1ptr    LABEL   PWORD
    DD      0                           ;32-bit offset (ignored)
    DW      task1_tss_selector          ;16-bit TSS selector

task2ptr    LABEL   PWORD
    DD      0                           ;32-bit offset (ignored)
    DW      task2_tss_selector          ;16-bit TSS selector
```

This will work just fine—once. Remember that on any task switch, the current state is saved in the TSS, and when that task resumes, execution commences as if nothing had happened. Where is your interrupted task going to resume execution? Right after the FAR JMP that caused it to be task-switched out. Because no instructions are specified there, you're liable to start executing empty space. If your code segment descriptor was defined "tightly" to cover just the required code and nothing more, you will get a general protection fault instead, as the 80386 tries to fetch instructions from off the end of the code segment. One small addition to the ISR cures the problem and makes the programs and the ISR fully "circular." No matter where execution is stopped, it will resume properly. The following listing shows this change:

```
switch_to_task_1:
                MOV     DWORD PTR SS:[ESP] +0, OFFSET start1
                MOV     WORD PTR SS:[ESP] +4, SEG start1
                IRETD
start1:         JMP     PWORD PTR task1ptr
                JMP     task2        ;repeat this task

; ------------------------------
switch_to_task_2:
                MOV     DWORD PTR SS:[ESP] +0, OFFSET start2
                MOV     WORD PTR SS:[ESP] +4, SEG start2
start2:         JMP     PWORD PTR task2ptr
                JMP     task1        ;repeat this task

; ------------------------------
task1ptr        LABEL   PWORD
     DD         0                    ;32-bit offset (ignored)
     DW         task1_tss_selector   ;16-bit TSS selector

task2ptr        LABEL   PWORD
     DD         0                    ;32-bit offset (ignored)
     DW         task2_tss_selector   ;16-bit TSS selector
```

Now the example has been sufficiently patched up that it should run properly, toggling LEDs at every time-slice interrupt.

The Scheduler as a Task

You can also take an entirely different approach to the scheduler. Rather than implementing it as an interrupt-service routine, you can promote it and give it a task of its own. This has several advantages, especially in real-life multitasking systems, where the scheduling software is apt to be more complex than this example. If the time scheduler is a task unto itself, it does not have to operate in the context of the task that was interrupted or be so cautious about preserving registers. The scheduling task may well have its own LDT, allowing it to maintain its own private data stores and code library. It can run at a different privilege level and might share data with the operating system. Indeed, for many simple real-time kernels and executives, the scheduler *is* the operating system.

In addition to these advantages, there is another benefit to this approach that makes dispatching the new task somewhat simpler and more elegant than in the example ISR. The next example uses the nested task feature to illustrate this.

To implement the scheduler as a task, you need to define and initialize a third TSS, set it up with the proper instruction pointer to your scheduling code, and put a task gate descriptor in the appropriate slot in the IDT. When your time-slice interrupt arrives, the 80386 immediately performs a task switch, saving the state of the interrupted task and loading the state of the scheduler task. This in itself is an improvement, since the interrupted task has had its entire context saved already, and the scheduler doesn't have to be concerned with contaminating it. Because the task switch was caused by an interrupt, the scheduler's task is considered a nested task. (You can verify this by testing the NT bit in EFLAGS.) As a nested task, the scheduler will have its caller's TSS selector stored in the Back Link field of the TSS. If the scheduler can read its own TSS, it can determine which task was running and then force a task switch into the other one.

Performing the switch is now even easier than it was in the ISR procedure. Whenever a nested task executes an IRET instruction, the 80386 unnests it by returning control to the task specified in the Back Link field. If the scheduler has write permission to its own TSS, it merely exchanges the TSS selector in the Back Link field with the TSS selector of the task it wants to run and executes an IRET. This not only cleanly terminates the interrupt, it performs a "directed" task switch as well! The following listing illustrates the minimum amount of code required to implement the scheduler as a third task.

```
code     SEGMENT ER PUBLIC USE32

         ASSUME   CS:code
         ASSUME   DS:TSS_segment

back_link         EQU     0                      ;offset of back link in a TSS

scheduler:
         MOV      AX, WORD PTR DS:[back_link]     ;read own back link
         CMP      AX, Task_1                     ;parent = Task 1 ?
         JE       switch_to_task_2

switch_to_task_1:
         MOV      AX, Task_1
         JMP      switch

switch_to_task_2:
         MOV      AX, Task_2
         JMP      switch

switch:
         MOV      WORD PTR DS:[back_link], AX     ;change back link
         IRETD                                   ;cause task switch
         JMP      scheduler                       ;repeat

code     ENDS
         END
```

Performing task scheduling with a task

- Allows old task state to be saved automatically

- Prevents scheduler from interfering with applications

- Allows scheduler to use its own address space

- Allows scheduler to back into new task

BUSY BIT, NT BIT, BACK LINK FIELD, TS BIT

As you can see, some interesting tricks can be played on the 80386's internal task-scheduling system. In the previous example, the Back Link field of a TSS was changed to make the 80386 return to the "wrong" task. It was the right task for the purposes of the program, but it was not the task that was interrupted. One detail of this scheme is not obvious but is crucial to avoid crashing the system. The

Busy bit of both TSS descriptors must be set at all times. The 80386 thinks that it is returning control to an interrupted task, and if that task's TSS descriptor isn't marked busy, the 80386 detects foul play and generates an invalid TSS fault (exception 10).

From the point of view of defensive programming and system design, you should pay attention to the Back Link fields of all TSSs. Normally, tasks are not given read/write permission to their TSSs. This should be an invisible, operating system-managed resource. The scheduler task is an example of a program or task that can legitimately modify its own TSS. Access to the NT bit in EFLAGS is not restricted, however. The lowliest PL 3 hack can set or clear this bit, which can cause disastrous effects if a subsequent IRET instruction is executed. The best approach is probably to initialize the Back Link fields of all new TSSs with the selector to a "safety net" task. Then, if NT gets set when it shouldn't (either accidentally or maliciously), control will return to a predefined task (which should probably terminate the offending program).

The TS (Task Switched) bit in CR0 is set any time tasks change. This bit is never cleared by the 80386. Because CR0 is a protected register and CLTS (clear TS) is a privileged instruction, most applications will be unaware of, and unable to affect, this flag. The 80386 and system software can use it to enable extensions to the automatic hardware task-switching mechanism. For instance, when an 80387 is connected with the 80386, its context is not automatically saved on a task switch. This needs to be done, however, if two or more tasks are using the 80387. The 80386 uses TS to determine whether the 80387 task belongs to the current 80386 task. If TS is set, it knows there has been a task switch since the last time the 80387 was used, and so it raises an exception to allow system software to save the 80387's state somewhere. After the 80387 context has been safely stored, TS should be cleared.

EXTENSIONS TO THE TSS

Saving the state of a coprocessor like the 80387 is an example of one good use for an extended TSS. As was stated earlier, the TSS descriptor must define the task state segment to be at least 104 bytes long (Limit = 00067). To define a TSS to be any smaller than that is an error because the 80386 requires that much space to store its context. Like other memory segments, however, a TSS has no maximum size limit. You can define TSSs up to 4GB long, and they can even overlap to some degree, if desired. The extra space is completely user defined; you can use it for anything you want. Technically, since task state segments are not readable or writable at any privilege level, simply extending the limit of the TSS doesn't buy you anything. What you really want to do is extend the limit of your TSS alias segment or segments. The extra space can store the 80387 context, the names of open disk files, paging information, and even arbitrary text, such as "Rich's Task." Any data stored above offset 103 is ignored by the 80386 when it is reading or writing to a TSS.

I/O PERMISSION BIT MAP

The only remaining portion of the TSS structure that hasn't been covered so far is the 16-bit field at offset 0066 (102 decimal). This holds the offset of the beginning of the I/O Permission bit map, an optional addition to the privilege-checking mechanism described in Chapter 3. It is implemented on a task-by-task basis and affects the hardware privilege checking only for I/O instructions. The affected instructions are shown in Table 5-2.

   Without the I/O permission bit map, a given program or task can execute these I/O instructions only if its CPL is less than or equal to IOPL. IOPL is stored in EFLAGS and thus might change with each task. When the I/O Permission bit map is defined for a task, code within that task has a second chance. If the standard I/O permission check fails, the processor consults the I/O permission bit map for the particular I/O address(es) in question. If the permission bits for the I/O addresses equal 0, then the I/O instruction is allowed. If they do not, the I/O instruction is not allowed and the 80386 generates a general protection fault.

   The I/O permission bit map is just that — a sequence of bits. Each bit corresponds to a single, byte-wide I/O address. The least significant bit of the first byte corresponds to I/O address 0 and so on. Because the 80386's I/O space is 64KB, a full I/O permission bit map

Table 5-2. IOPL-Sensitive Instructions

IN	Input from I/O port
INS	Input string from I/O port
OUT	Output to I/O port
OUTS	Output string to I/O port
CLI	Clear Interrupt flag
STI+	Set Interrupt flag

occupies 8KB of memory. Fortunately, this is not always necessary. The bit map can be truncated at any byte boundary. All bits not included in the bit map are assumed to be 1s. Therefore, I/O read and write privileges are not allowed for "truncated" I/O space.

You can place the bit map anywhere in memory, but it must be near (within about 64KB) the TSS of the task that will use it. The 16-bit field at offset 0066 in the TSS defines the start of the I/O permission bit map relative to the start of the TSS. The bit map ends after 8KB or at the end of the task state segment, whichever comes first. By deliberately making the TSS descriptor too short to hold an entire 8KB bit map, you can truncate the table. Because the offset of the bit map is relative to the beginning of the TSS, offsets less than 0068 are not a good idea, unless you want the TSS Back Link field to define permission for I/O addresses 0 through 15 and so forth. After the last byte of I/O permission information, there must be a terminating byte of 1 bits (FF). Since the terminator is considered part of the table, be sure that it fits within the limit of the TSS.

The I/O permission bit map gives tasks free access to certain unprotected I/O ports without requiring that IOPL be lowered to allow access to all I/O ports. Also, since the bit map can be placed almost anywhere near the TSS, you can have several TSSs share a single bit map, with some careful manipulation of the tasks' TSS limits and I/O permission bit map offsets.

I/O permission bit map

- Allows I/O space to be protected like memory space

- Is allocated by task

- Each task can have a different I/O permission bit map

- Allows specific I/O access if CPL > IOPL

CHANGING PRIVILEGE LEVELS
WITHIN A TASK

As Chapter 3 showed, any time that there is a change in code segments, there is the potential for a change in privilege level. With a change in privilege level comes a change in stack. The privilege level of the current stack segment must always match the privilege level of the current code segment. Conforming code segments are excepted from this rule. This is important to remember when you are first creating task state segments. Be sure that the code segment and stack segment selectors have compatible privilege levels.

A change in code segment may come about voluntarily, as when a program references a call gate to get a temporary boost in privilege. It may also happen involuntarily when an external interrupt or processor fault occurs and the exception handler is not at the same privilege level as the interrupted task. A privilege shift, and hence a stack change, occurs in both cases. For this reason, all TSSs should be carefully initialized so that they will be able to "host" any higher-privileged code. Specifically, this means providing alternate stack segments and stack pointers for PL 0, 1, and 2 in the TSS. These stack segments must be large enough to hold a worst-case stack frame.

When an external interrupt is received or a processor fault is generated, the 80386 may or may not perform a task switch immediately. If the exception is handled with a task gate (as in the second scheduler example), the interrupted task will be unaffected. If the exception is not handled with a task gate, however, the exception must be treated as a traditional ISR within the context of the task it interrupted. The nuts and bolts of handling interrupts and the advantages of using task gates in the IDT are covered more thoroughly in Chapter 7. When you are building TSSs, be certain that every task that could possibly be interrupted has the resources to host every non-task-switching exception handler that could possibly interrupt it.

CHANGING LDTS

An LDT selector is stored as part of every TSS. When the 80386 loads context information, it may load a new LDT selector as part of the task-switch procedure. This is what makes the local descriptor tables local. Regardless of privilege, if a particular segment descriptor appears only in a certain LDT, tasks that do not use the same LDT cannot use that descriptor. This can be a very effective way of isolating the memory space of different tasks. If your multitasking system is also a multiuser system, each task might correspond to a user, and the LDT might hold all of the descriptors to that user's memory. For multitasking on a single-user system, each task might correspond to an application program that the user is running, and the LDT might hold the code, data, and stack segments for that application.

It is possible to define a system with almost no descriptors in the GDT and with all of the code, data, and stack descriptors spread around in various LDTs. In a system like this, no segments are shared, and everything is local to a task. This represents the ultimate in task separation. The next chapter discusses various methods of sharing code and data and of passing parameters between tasks.

6

COMMUNICATING
AMONG TASKS

In Chapter 2, which dealt with segmentation, you saw that the memory space available to a program is limited by the segment descriptors it can use. Because each segment descriptor defines an area of memory, the ability to use a segment descriptor implies access to the memory space that that descriptor defines. Keep in mind that a program uses a given descriptor by loading a selector to that descriptor into one of the 80386's six segment registers.

A program might not be able to use a descriptor because it (the program) is not privileged enough. In most cases this occurs when the memory space that the descriptor defines is deemed "too sensitive" to be trusted with that program. Another instance in which a program may be unable to access a given segment of memory is when the descriptor for that segment is logically not available. It may be marked not present. This occurs when virtual memory or paging is used. Also, the descriptor may be located in an unusable descriptor table. That is, it might not be in the GDT or in the current LDT. When this occurs, no amount of privilege can help the program to reach the descriptor. The memory is simply not defined in one of the currently available segments. This represents the greatest amount of address space separation possible on the 80386.

Segment descriptors located in the GDT are accessible to all programs in all tasks, barring any privilege considerations. Segment descriptors in an LDT are accessible only to the program(s) within the tasks that use that LDT. If each task has a different LDT (determined by the LDT selector field in its TSS), they will have largely separate address spaces. The tasks will share only memory that has been defined by GDT-based descriptors.

In a protected, multiuser system, this clear separation is probably desirable for maximum safety. The risk of one program crashing another is minimal if they do not share code, data, or stack space. You may want to take the opposite approach if there is no particular reason to partition off the memory between tasks or if your tasks require a high degree of cooperation. The middle ground might be a multitasking, windowing environment with a full WIMP (Windows/Icons/Mice/Pointers) interface, in which a few supervisor tasks need to share code and data but application programs must be carefully separated. In this chapter, you will see how this broad spectrum of goals can be met.

The two extreme cases can be dealt with fairly rapidly. The bulk of this chapter explores the gray area in between, involving tasks that require some amount of overlap.

TOTAL SEPARATION OF ADDRESS SPACES

Total separation of address spaces between tasks is relatively easy to achieve. Each task's required segments, including any code segments needed to service non-task-switching interrupts or faults, should be defined and located in an LDT. The LDT descriptors must be kept in the GDT, of course. Before task switching begins, store the LDT selectors in the appropriate TSSs, and off you go. The GDT should hold nothing but LDT descriptors and TSS descriptors. If there is a PL 0 supervisory task, its LDT should contain, at a minimum, an alias for the GDT and IDT. Otherwise, you will not be able to perform any segment maintenance or debugging once the system is running.

As each task switch occurs, either because of an external time-slice interrupt or because of some orchestrated software-controlled scheme, the 80386 will load a new LDT, cache new segment descriptors, and load a new register context. Assuming that each segment descriptor in each LDT is unique and that none aliases another, there is no way for one task's programs to affect those in another task. The data storage space cannot be read or written from another task, code segments cannot be read or called, stacks cannot be manipulated, and even the 80386's internal registers are not carried from one task to the next.

Unless programs are capable of creating descriptors (requiring an alias of the GDT or of the current LDT), this arrangement is basically fixed. If a task has no method of affecting another task's operation, it is impossible to transfer data between tasks or to orchestrate any kind of cooperation between them.

Separate address spaces for each task

- No sharing of data or code

- One task cannot affect another task

- Tasks cannot communicate

- All descriptors are in local descriptor tables

- Each task uses a different local descriptor table

- No descriptors in the global descriptor table

TOTAL OVERLAP OF ADDRESS SPACES

The opposite of the previous arrangement would be to have all tasks share exactly the same address space. Each task would be able to access the same logical space as every other task. In this kind of model, much of the distinction between tasks disappears. In fact, it's not clear that multitasking under these circumstances offers any advantages over a single-task system. The tasks essentially become large-scale subroutines with no protection between them, save that provided by the privilege protection mechanism. All code and data become a global resource.

Interestingly, there are at least three ways to create this kind of a system. The first, and most obvious, way is to put all of your segment descriptors in the GDT. You can dispense with LDTs entirely by placing a null selector in each task's TSS field for the LDT selector. The 80386 will resolve all segment references through the GDT, and all programs in all tasks will use selectors that point to the GDT (TI = 0).

A second way is to put all segment descriptors in an LDT but have all tasks share the same LDT. The TSS descriptors and the lone LDT descriptor must still be placed in the GDT, of course. By placing the same LDT selector in each task's TSS, you create the same effect as you would if all of the descriptors had been in the GDT, except that now all selectors must point to the "current" LDT (TI = 1).

The third alternative is also the most wasteful. Rather than having all tasks share a single LDT, you can give each task its own LDT but have it contain the same descriptors as every other task's LDT. That is, every segment has several aliases—one per task. Essentially, you create one LDT with all of the necessary descriptors, as in the previous method, and then duplicate it as often as necessary so that each task gets its own copy. This offers no conceivable advantage over the previous example, unless you want to have each task start out identically and then modify their descriptor tables as they run.

Identical address spaces for each task

- All data and code are shared
- One task can affect another task
- Tasks can exchange information
- All tasks can use only the global descriptor table
- All tasks can share a single local descriptor table
- All tasks can use identical local descriptor tables

PARTIAL OVERLAP OF
ADDRESS SPACES

By far the most common implementation of multitasking on the 80386 lies somewhere between the extremes described in the previous two sections. Often, in a multitasking environment, some amount of cooperation is desired among tasks. This is true for both single-user and multiuser systems.

To communicate among tasks, you must be able to transfer data from one task to another, and to do that, their address spaces must overlap to some degree. The amount of the overlap depends entirely on what you want to accomplish. Two tasks might share a descriptor to a 1-byte-long data segment and use it as a simple flag or semaphore. Alternately, it is not unusual for two (or more) tasks to share large data and code segments of 1MB or more. Rather than aliasing entire segments, you can define the descriptors of two tasks such that their two data segments intersect at some point, thus sharing part of a segment. Again, the implementation depends on your goals. This chapter discusses *how* to communicate between tasks, not *what* to say.

Generally speaking, two tasks can share either code or data, or they can share some of each. The shared space may be available to only two tasks, a collection of a few tasks may have access to the shared space, or all tasks may be allowed access. These decisions are up to you, and all are simple to implement on the 80386. Any time that tasks are sharing memory space, you need to address some general issues. Managing any shared resource can be a major part of system design and deserves special consideration.

All memory sharing centers around segment descriptors. For any given program to have access to memory, it must be able to use a segment descriptor. The way in which the descriptor is defined controls the amount of memory the program can address and what it can be used for. The descriptor must be placed in an accessible table (the GDT or the current task's LDT), and the program must have sufficient privilege to use it. All of these factors can be adjusted when you create and allocate segment descriptors and descriptor tables. When a program has the use of a segment descriptor, it has the "key" to that memory. Managing shared memory is thus a matter of managing descriptors.

You can control which tasks have access to a given segment by controlling which LDTs contain a descriptor for that segment. If three tasks are going to share a data segment, then three copies of the segment's descriptor should be made, one for each task's LDT. If all three are not going to have equal read and write privileges, you can modify the descriptor for some tasks. You might remove write permission from one task's copy of the descriptor, for instance, while leaving all other descriptor fields the same. Likewise, some of the sharing tasks might get an abbreviated version of the segment descriptor, with a smaller Limit field than the others. This allows you to further control memory accesses on a task-by-task basis. The key is in defining the descriptors.

Sharing Code

Sharing code among tasks is a very common application of segment sharing. By sharing code space among tasks, you can avoid the need to maintain multiple copies of certain pieces of code that are commonly used. An example of such code might be a floating-point emulation library for those systems that do not have an 80387 (or other floating-point coprocessor) installed. Floating-point emulation routines can be extremely tedious and difficult for the average programmer to write, yet they may be called regularly by various math-intensive programs in multiple tasks. Rather than requiring every program to contain its own floating-point functions (and every programmer to write them from scratch), a complete system would have all reasonable floating-point code functions prewritten and debugged and available in a library that could be used by any program that needed them.

For this library of code to be accessible to multiple programs in multiple tasks, the code segment that contains it must be shared. You can have it be shared either by locating the library segment's descriptor in the GDT, thus making it public domain, or by placing the descriptor in the LDT of every task that requires it.

The privilege level associated with the library descriptor must be chosen carefully. It must be low enough (that is, numerically large enough) to allow each task to make use of the code without incurring privilege violations. In the case of a floating-point library, you might want to set DPL to 3, since emulation libraries are harmless and there is no danger of math functions falling into the wrong hands. If the DPL were any higher, low-privileged programs would be prohibited from performing complex arithmetic functions, a rather arbitrary restriction.

If the shared code instead contained functions to perform, say, descriptor modification, it would certainly need a higher level of privilege protection. Then, the code could be accessible from various tasks, but only to programs with the proper privilege.

If you share code by placing multiple code descriptors in the sharing tasks' LDTs (the preferred method), it is not necessary to give each copy of the descriptor the same DPL. This would allow programs in one task easier access to the shared code than programs in other tasks. Although this may serve some purpose in your system, it should be used with caution. First, you must consider whether the shared code will be accessed from the individual tasks through a call gate or through direct CALL or JMP instructions. Whichever method you use, it must be the same for all possible sharing tasks. If the shared code is to be used through a privilege-boosting call gate, it should return control through a FAR RET instruction. If one of the sharing tasks has different privilege requirements from the others, however, programs in that task might be capable of using a direct CALL or JMP instruction, bypassing the gate and fouling the return stack. Be sure that all entry and exit points are consistent and compatible. Shared code segments like this are prime candidates for the conforming code segment attribute.

When you assign different privilege levels to different tasks, the code contained in the shared space will execute at the privilege level of the task that invoked it. This could be fatal if the code contains privileged instructions. Also beware of shared code that contains IOPL-sensitive instructions. Even though IOPL is not related to privilege level, it can change from task to task, and so shared code that performs I/O instructions may work from some tasks and fail from others. Either define all TSSs with the IOPL field in EFLAGS the same way or avoid IOPL-sensitive instructions in shared code.

To further complicate matters, each task's TSS can have a different I/O permission bit map. If the shared code performs reads or writes to particular I/O addresses, those addresses may be valid for some tasks and off-limits for others.

One final point you must remember when code is shared among tasks is that a running task can generally be preempted at any time. The task might be frozen in the middle of executing shared code, and the new, incoming task might also need to execute the shared code. In short, all shared code must be completely reentrant. More so than the "normal" code within a task, shared code must be written so that it can be stopped and started at any time and can be used simultaneously by several tasks. In practice, this means that you need to avoid dependence on data values, variables, and so forth. Because these properly fall under the heading of shared data, that aspect will be covered later in this chapter.

Code space is not writable by definition, so there is no danger of users, tasks, or programs trashing shared code. This makes shared code somewhat more manageable than shared data. Sharing data space allows various tasks to pass data back and forth by writing to and reading from a common area. Code sharing, by contrast, allows no intertask communication.

Normally, an entire code segment is shared. The floating-point library or whatever is given its own segment and invoked through FAR CALLs or FAR JMPs. To allow it to be shared, you place the code's descriptor in every sharing task's LDT. It is certainly possible, however, to share portions of a segment by modifying each task's copy of the shared segment's descriptor. By adjusting the Base Address and Limit fields, you can "bracket" only the parts you want to expose to a particular task. Obviously, you need to be certain that you haven't inadvertently trimmed off required portions of the code segment. Also, modifying the base address of a segment can affect the way the code in that segment runs. This can be tricky.

> **Sharing code segments among tasks**
>
> - Allows sharing of common functions and procedures
> - Code descriptor can be placed in GDT
> - Code descriptor can be placed in different LDTs
> - Shared code can execute at different privilege levels
> - Shared code must be reentrant
> - Shared code cannot be modified

Sharing Data

Sharing data space is the *only* way that any useful information can be passed between tasks. If each task has a separate address space that does not overlap that of any other task, there is no place where the tasks can exchange data. They must have some agreed-upon transfer area using shared data space, like that shown in Figure 6-1. (Conceivably, two tasks could transfer data through read/ write I/O locations, but even these might be mapped out through the I/O Permission bit map.) This is exactly as it should be. It is usually desirable to have as much separation between tasks as possible to keep the unwanted interactions between them to a minimum. You get a much more secure system when separation is enforced in the hardware with provisions made for communication than you would if task separation were enforced by software.

The shared data space might be an entire data segment or only a portion of a segment. Different tasks might also have different definitions for the shared space. For instance, one task might be given both read and write permission for the shared data segment, and the other tasks might be given read permission only. This creates a situation in which there is one "broadcaster" and several "receivers." Obviously, these dissimilar arrangements are

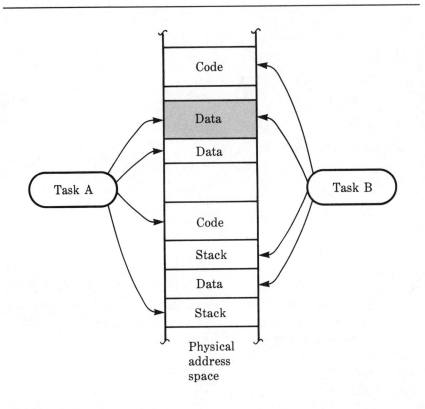

Figure 6-1.   Shared data space

possible only if you place the shared segment's descriptor in the
sharing tasks' LDTs. If you place a descriptor in the GDT, it
becomes public domain and will be seen as having exactly the
same attributes from any task.

You can also define the various LDT-based descriptors to have
different DPL fields. As does changing the DPL of shared code
descriptors, this enforces different privilege requirements in the
programs from different tasks. Unlike shared code, however, a
varying DPL will not affect the contents of a data segment.

Changing the Base Address and Limit fields is also safer with this method.

Sharing data space has its own unique problems that do not affect shared code because code is not modifiable. When a shared resource is also a modifiable resource, special care must be taken to ensure that all tasks are kept up to date on any changes.

Data space that is shared between tasks is aliased. You will recall from the discussion of memory segmentation in Chapter 2 that an alias is any descriptor that defines a linear address space that is already defined by another descriptor. In other words, aliasing creates overlapping segments. By placing multiple descriptors for the same space in the sharing tasks' LDTs, you alias that segment.

Any changes made to the definition of the segment that affect its descriptor must be made to all of its alias descriptors as well. For example, whenever the 80386 uses memory, it sets the Accessed bit (bit 40) in that segment's descriptor. This information might be used by an operating system to accumulate segment-usage statistics, or it might be used by a demand-paging mechanism to determine whether the contents of a page selected for swap-out need to be copied to secondary storage before the space is reused. If the page has been accessed, it may be necessary to copy it to avoid lost data. When a segment has multiple aliases, however, only one descriptor has its Accessed bit set when the 80386 uses it. All of the others still show unused status. This causes a statistical skew in the first case and loss of data in the second.

Another example would be a segment that grows in size as the programs that use it run, such as a message buffer that is not emptied rapidly enough. As data fills the buffer, it eventually reaches some "high-water mark," and the size of the segment is increased. The operating system might simply extend the segment descriptor's Limit field, or it might move the whole segment to larger quarters by changing its base address and then increasing its limit. In either case, you can see that it is critical that all of the segment's aliases be updated immediately.

Sharing data among tasks

- Allows the sharing of common data values and structures

- Allows communication among tasks

- Data descriptor can be placed in the GDT

- Data descriptor can be placed in different LDTs

- Shared data can have different access permissions

- Shared data in cache must be kept coherent

- Shared data descriptors must be kept coherent

A third nightmare concerns the data itself. Presumably, if two or more tasks are sharing data space, at least one of them is writing into it and at least one is reading from it. These tasks can generally be interrupted or preempted at any time, and so the data they share might be updated at any time, from the point of view of a running program. A task that is reading shared data should reread it as often as possible to keep abreast of any changes that may have been made while it was suspended. This is particularly true if the task is polling a special mailbox location that is used to initiate some action. The following two program fragments show two ways in which a program could poll a byte of shared memory looking for the number 37.

```
wait1:   CMP     BYTE PTR DS:[4B696D52h], 37h   ;read byte from memory
         JNE     wait1                           ;repeat


         MOV     CL, BYTE PTR DS:[4B696D52h]    ;load byte from memory
wait2:   CMP     CL, 37h                         ;compare to constant
         JNE     wait2                           ;repeat
```

Experienced assembly language programmers will recognize that the second example runs faster because it tests an internal processor register instead of a memory operand and therefore would usually be preferred. An optimizing compiler for a high-level language such as Pascal or C would also normally choose the second form because of its greater speed. This is exactly the kind of optimization you must avoid when reading from shared memory, however. The operand must be reread on every pass through the loop. Otherwise, only one external operand fetch will be performed, and the same number will be tested over and over, resulting in an endless loop if the operand doesn't match the desired value.

An assembly language programmer can avoid this pitfall simply by using the first form when coding polling routines. This can be difficult from a high-level language. Your compiler may not optimize this loop at all, and so there may be no problem. If it does optimize it, you may be able to turn optimization off with a compiler switch. If you are writing in C and your compiler is fairly new (as it would almost have to be to produce 80386 code), you can do this by using the "volatile" type modifier in your variable declaration. It was designed for exactly this purpose.

Yet another problem can arise when two or more tasks exchange data through shared data space. Suppose that you have two tasks and that they both work on a single, shared data structure. The data is arranged as a sequence of 32-bit records, and each record has a flag bit associated with it (say, bit 31), signifying that the record is currently being used and may be prone to frequent updates. The two programs run merrily along, reading records, setting their respective flag bits, modifying the data, storing it, and then clearing the flags. If one of the programs needs to read a record but finds the record's flag bit set, it waits patiently until the flag is cleared, using a polling technique not unlike that shown in the previous example. Suppose further that your first program has read (and carefully locked) records 1, 2, and 3. It now wants to read record 4 but finds it already locked. The second program has read (and locked) records 6, 5, and 4, and now wants to read record 3. The first program is waiting for the second to unlock a record and vice versa. The two will be caught in this "fatal embrace" forever.

Unfortunately, you can't prevent this by changing any data segment attributes. You just have to avoid writing any code that might create such a situation. Either a maximum timeout should be enforced, or both programs should release all locked records before requesting a new one.

MAINTAINING ALIASES

Most of the complications involving data pointed out in the previous section had to do with maintaining alias coherency, that is, ensuring that changes made to one descriptor for a shared segment were reflected in all of the other alias descriptors. These include changes to a segment's Base Address and Limit fields and to its Accessed and Present bits. Herewith is a partial list of possible solutions to these problems. You can choose to implement one of these schemes or devise something of your own.

Alias List

The major obstacle to keeping all segment aliases current is finding the aliases. One solution is to maintain a simple list of aliases. If a given descriptor in the current LDT has an alias in another task, set the descriptor's User bit (bit 52). Then create a simple list of the aliases. You could store the list in an extended TSS, right before the I/O Permission bit map. Each entry in the list

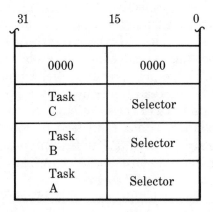

Figure 6-2.   Aliased descriptor list

would be 32 bits long: 16 bits for the selector of a sharing task's TSS and 16 bits for the selector in that task's LDT to the alias descriptor. Terminate the list with 4 bytes of 0s. Figure 6-2 illustrates this concept. This works well if you know that each task will share at most one segment. Otherwise, multiple lists would have to be created, one for each shared segment.

Multiple Lists

Multiple lists can be implemented as an extension to the system just discussed. If a descriptor is aliased, set its User bit, as before. Keep a simple directory of segment aliases in the extended space of the task's TSS. If the aliased descriptor resides in slot 4 of the LDT, your program would consult entry 4 in the directory, which gives the offset to the base of an alias list. An example is shown in Figure 6-3. This allows for a task that shares multiple segments with other tasks.

Descriptor Pairing

When you are creating LDTs, put valid descriptors only in every other slot, and reserve the odd-numbered slots for alias information. If a descriptor is not aliased, the "descriptor" immediately following it will be all 0s. (Note that this will not upset the 80386, since an AR byte value of 00 denotes an invalid descriptor.) If the descriptor is shared, use the next descriptor in the LDT to hold alias information. You have 7 bytes to hold whatever you want. The AR byte must be legal; 00 and 80 are recommended values. You could even use the Base Address and Limit fields to point to the beginning and end of an alias table, arranged like those in the previous examples.

This technique, shown in Figure 6-4, wastes half of your LDT, of course, but only if very little of a task's address space is shared. If you can compact the necessary alias information into 7 bytes, you can store it in the "descriptor" directly, abolishing the need for a separate table.

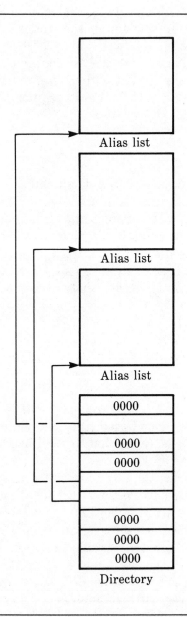

Figure 6-3.   Multiple aliased descriptor lists

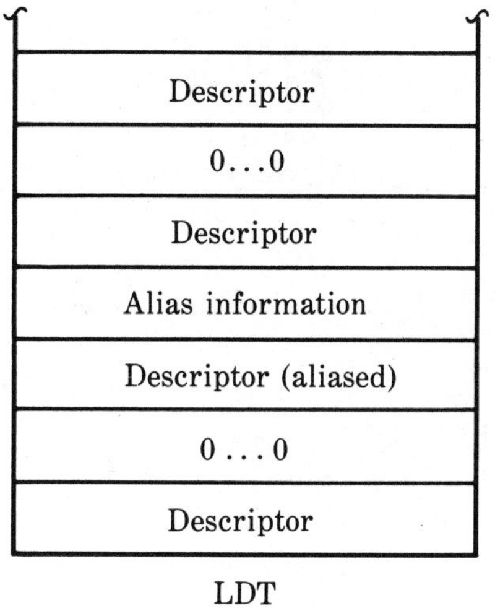

Descriptor
0...0
Descriptor
Alias information
Descriptor (aliased)
0 ... 0
Descriptor

LDT

Figure 6-4.   Interleaved alias information

Centralized Alias Information

Rather than maintaining separate alias information with each task, you could keep all of the necessary information in one place. Presumably, the tasks themselves would not be concerned with this information anyway. It would be the operating system's responsibility to keep shared-segment descriptors current, and so storing the relevant information in one privileged location might be preferable.

Shadow Descriptor Table

Rather than interleaving good descriptors with pseudodescriptors, you might want to maintain a second, "shadow" descriptor table somewhere in the supervisor's space. The shadow table would be arranged exactly like the task's LDT, but it would hold aliasing information instead of descriptors in every 8-byte slot. An example is shown in Figure 6-5. Maintaining a one-to-one correlation between the descriptors in the task's LDT and the shadow table's aliasing information would make it easy to determine whether or not any particular segment was shared, and with which tasks.

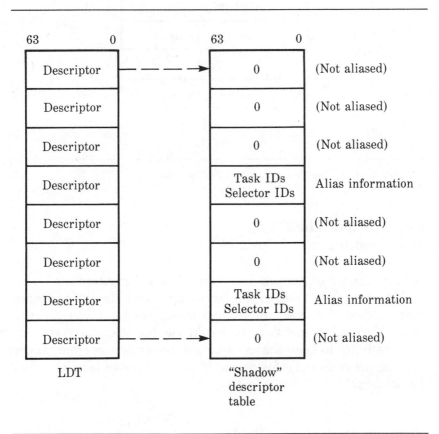

Figure 6-5.   Shadow descriptor table

Table Search

The least appealing approach is to keep no alias information at all. Then, when a descriptor's attributes are modified, you could initiate a search through all currently defined LDTs for a descriptor with similar Base Address and Limit fields. This brute force approach is tougher if some tasks have been paged out and are not present in physical memory.

When a descriptor is modified deliberately through software (such as when a Limit field is changed), it is important that all aliased versions of the descriptor be modified as soon as possible. Certain more subtle, automatic changes initiated by the 80386 (such as setting an Accessed bit) can be nearly impossible to detect immediately, yet the information may be just as important. Some possibilities for trapping this kind of change are as follows:

- Dedicate one program or task to watching the descriptor tables constantly.

- If paging is enabled, watch the Dirty bit of the pages containing the descriptor tables.

- If paging is enabled, mark the pages containing descriptor tables as being not present, and try to handle the nearly infinite stream of page faults that will result.

A much more rational approach to updating the Accessed bit in aliased descriptors is to wait until the issue forces itself. Because the Accessed bit is the only part of a descriptor affected, this should not hurt system performance much. A previous section discussed how the Accessed bit might be used for statistical analysis or for page-out selection (which is really the same thing). When the time comes to tabulate these figures, scan through your carefully maintained alias information, making note of any Accessed bits that have been set, and propagate them through the appropriate aliases.

MODIFYING UNSHARED DATA

Thus far, this chapter has covered various ways in which a task can communicate with another through shared data. One task writes information into an agreed-upon address space, and another task eventually reads it and acts upon it. A good deal of intertask cooperation can be implemented this way. There are some other, more underhanded, ways to affect another task — techniques that should be reserved for the operating system or not used at all.

Presumably, the operating system, executive, or kernel is able to read and write to any linear address space it pleases. If it doesn't already have a global alias, it can certainly create one in its own descriptor table. Through this, it can write directly into a dormant task's data space, stack, TSS, or even code. (You know that the other task is dormant because your code is running now!) In this way, you can directly manipulate another program's variables and data structures. This kind of tampering implies detailed knowledge of the workings of the victim's programs.

Modifying Stacks

It is possible to modify the stack of a dormant task, thereby causing it to return to a place other than the one at which it was called. This, too, requires that you understand completely how the task's stack frame is defined, and it is not recommended for the faint of heart.

Modifying TSSs

The final tactic involves manipulating the TSS fields of a dormant task. By changing the EIP or CS register images, you can have the task "wake up" somewhere other than the place at which it was preempted. Exercise caution so that this does not run afoul of the stack. If the task was frozen in the midst of a subroutine call, the next RET instruction will return it to its caller.

A less harmful technique is to change the contents of one of the general-purpose registers. This is especially useful if the receiving task is expecting it and will take some action on the contents of, say, register ECX. With this method, the endless-loop program shown earlier in this chapter could have been made to terminate by having the value of the register "mysteriously" change at some point in the loop. LDT entries can be changed (as they must be to implement any of the features discussed in this chapter) and entire LDTs replaced. Changing a task's Back Link field is a nice trick, either to unnest tasks (be sure to clear NT as well) or to nest them differently.

There is no reason why a task cannot modify its own TSS. If the operating system task examines its own TSS, it will find its own state when it was last frozen. This is true of all tasks that can read their own TSSs. The state stored there does not reflect the task's current state but rather its condition when it was last saved.

If reading your own TSS is important, try to limit your examinations to one register or field only. There is usually no guarantee that any two instructions in your code are really executed sequentially with no interruptions. The worst-case scenario would be if you were to examine your own task's CS and EIP fields to determine where (or when) you were last preempted. This requires two separate read cycles from memory. If your task is frozen after you've read CS but before you've read EIP, you are going to get bizarre results, since the values are coming from two separate task-switch operations.

This is one example of how an unexpected interruption of your program can have peculiar results. Interrupts are a necessary part of almost any microprocessor system, however, and they should be understood fully if you are to get the most out of your 80386. The next chapter covers all manner of interrupts, faults, exceptions, and traps.

In this chapter, you have seen how you can allow multiple 80386 tasks, which are normally separated, to communicate with one another. Intertask communication requires shared physical memory, which requires careful attention to your segmentation and paging tables. Although it may take some careful planning and a little creativity, intertask communication allows you to create very powerful systems for business, graphics, industry, real-time control, comunications, and networking.

7

HANDLING FAULTS
AND INTERRUPTS

This chapter deals with *exceptional conditions*—conditions that the 80386 thinks are important enough to warrant stopping your programs in midstream. Such conditions are not expected and are not predictable, but must be dealt with before your program can resume.

External hardware may signal exceptional conditions, or the 80386 may detect an exceptional condition itself. In either case, the 80386 suspends processing and follows a precisely defined sequence of steps in order to resolve the situation. Most of these steps are left for the programmer to define. Just as you must know what to do in the event of a fire or an earthquake, you must decide on the steps to be taken for each exceptional condition ahead of time and then lay them aside until they are needed. When an exceptional condition arises, the 80386 will then be prepared to follow your instructions immediately. These steps are your exception handlers.

Some exceptions are caused by external, hardware-related events in the system, and are signaled to the 80386 through special pins on the microprocessor package. These events are called *interrupts*. A hardware interrupt may tell the 80386 that a parity error has occurred in the memory, that there is a problem with a disk drive, or that system power is about to fail. Hardware interrupts may also signal events that are not so catastrophic, such as that a key has been pressed on a terminal, that it's time to switch tasks, or that it's midnight. Whatever the cause, the 80386 will immediately stop whatever it is currently doing and begin processing your predetermined sequence of steps for that particular interrupt. This may mean mapping out a bad area of physical memory, making a last-ditch attempt to save vital data on a hard disk, or simply reading a character and putting it in a buffer. The response is up to you, and this chapter explains how you can define that response and control the processor's actions.

The 80386 itself may also initiate exception processing if it detects something that needs immediate attention before processing can continue. These are termed *software exceptions*, and they are generated when a privilege violation occurs, an attempt is made to execute floating-point instructions when no coprocessor is present, or a program tries to overrun one of its segments. In all of these cases, and in more to be covered throughout this chapter, the 80386 suspends execution and turns control over to your exception handler. Processor-initiated software exceptions are handled just like hardware-initiated interrupts. The only difference is the source of the exception.

Hardware interrupts

- Are created by devices outside the 80386
- Signal an event that needs attention

Software exceptions

- Are created by 80386 software
- Signal an error in processing

Hardware interrupts can be divided into two categories: *maskable* and *nonmaskable*. See Figure 7-1. A maskable interrupt is signaled when the 80386 INTR pin is driven by external hardware to its active state. The 80386 examines the state of this pin

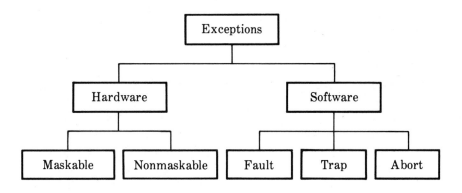

Figure 7-1.   Classes of exceptions

after every instruction it executes. When it is executing repeated string instructions, it checks after every iteration. You can tell the 80386 to ignore this pin by clearing the interrupt flag (IF) in the EFLAGS register.

The nonmaskable interrupt is connected to the 80386's NMI (nonmaskable interrupt) pin. As the name implies, NMI cannot be masked under any circumstances. In all other respects, the processor treats NMI like INTR.

Maskable hardware interrupts

- Are signaled through the INTR pin

- Can be ignored by clearing the IF bit in EFLAGS

Nonmaskable hardware interrupts

- Are signaled through the NMI pin

- Cannot be ignored

Software-initiated exceptions come in three types: *faults*, *traps*, and *aborts*. The differences among them are relatively subtle and of interest only to programmers who need to write exception-handling software. Faults are exceptions that the 80386 can catch before the actual error occurs. These include privilege violations and segment overruns. After the exception-handling software for a fault is finished, the 80386 reexecutes the instruction that caused the fault.

Traps are exceptions that are caught after the fact. When the exception-handling software completes, the 80386 resumes execution with the instruction following the one that caused the trap. Most debugging breakpoints are treated as traps.

Aborts are failures for which no cause can be pinpointed. Normally, it is not possible to restart the failing code. The program that generated the abort must be terminated or aborted. Some coprocessor errors and the double fault are classified as aborts.

Software faults

- Are detected by the 80386 before an error occurs
- The faulting instruction can be restarted

Software traps

- Are detected by the 80386 after an error occurs
- The trapping instruction cannot be restarted

Software aborts

- Are detected by the 80386 after an error occurs
- The aborting program may need to be terminated

EXCEPTION PROCESSING

Let's take a close look at what happens when the 80386 encounters an exceptional condition. Regardless of whether the exception is caused by hardware or software, all exception processing involves two stages. First, the 80386 performs certain "reflex" operations that are the same for all exceptions and are not under programmer control. Second, the 80386 passes control to the predefined exception-handling software for the exception in question. At that point, the interrupt or software exception is your responsibility (or that of the operating system developer). After the 80386's automatic operations are examined, some of your options for creating exception handlers will be covered, along with some pointers and suggestions.

The first step in all exception processing for the 80386 is to identify the source of the exception. All exceptions must be given an identifying number, or *vector*, which allows the 80386 to choose which one of the exception handlers to use in order to rectify the situation. Vector numbers range from 0 to 255 (FF). If the 80386 encounters a software exception, it assigns it a number automatically. (See Table 7-1.) A general protection fault, for example, is always assigned exception number 13. Missing coprocessor exceptions are given vector 7, and divide-by-zero errors take number 0. Note that the first 17 vectors (0 through 16) are each assigned to a fixed software-initiated exception. These correspond to the 17 things that can go wrong internally with the 80386.

If the exception was caused by an external hardware interrupt, a vector is not assigned automatically. Instead, the 80386 allows the hardware in question to identify itself by performing an external interrupt acknowledge bus cycle. The interrupting device is expected to pass its vector to the 80386 as a byte of data.

Once the 80386 has an identifying vector, it uses this number to select one of 256 programmer-defined exception-handling routines. You should write code to deal with each of these cases. To

Table 7-1.   Protected Mode Exceptions

Vector	Description	Class	Error Code?
0	Divide error	Fault	No
1	Debug	Fault/trap	No
2	Nonmaskable interrupt	Trap	No
3	Breakpoint	Trap	No
4	Overflow	Trap	No
5	Bound	Fault	No
6	Invalid opcode	Fault	No
7	Device not available	Fault	No
8	Double fault	Abort	Yes
9	Coprocessor overrun	Abort	No
10	Invalid TSS	Fault	Yes
11	Segment not present	Fault	Yes
12	Stack fault	Fault	Yes
13	General protection fault	Fault	Yes
14	Page fault	Fault	Yes
15	Reserved	Trap	No
16	Coprocessor error	Fault	No
17-31	Reserved		
32-255	Maskable interrupt and INT *n* vectors		

choose the correct exception handler (also called an interrupt service routine, or ISR), the 80386 consults the IDT.

Exception vectors

- Every exception is assigned an 8-bit vector.

- The vector selects 1 of 256 exception handlers.

- Hardware interrupts assign their own vectors.

- Software exceptions have preassigned vectors.

You will recall that the IDT was the forgotten descriptor table. It must be defined and located in memory, but programs can never reference it. There is no way for a selector, with a single TI bit, to select a descriptor in the IDT. Now you can see that the IDT is necessary after all. It contains descriptors, like any other descriptor table, but must hold exactly 256 of them—one for each exception vector. After the 80386 acquires a vector (either from external hardware or by assigning one itself), it uses that number as a direct index into the IDT. If a divide-by-zero error occurs, the first descriptor (IDT slot 0) is used. If a hardware device passes a vector of FF, the last descriptor is used. The chosen IDT descriptor then points to your ISR for that exception, and the 80386 soon passes control to that code. See Figure 7-2.

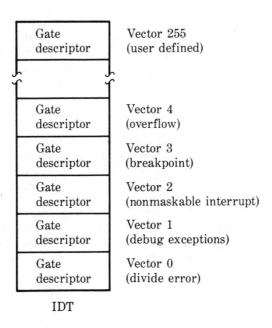

Figure 7-2.   Interrupt descriptor table

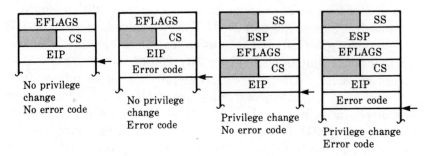

Note: Arrow represents new top of stack.

Figure 7-3.   Exception stacks

Before it passes control, however, the 80386 pushes at least 12 bytes onto the ISR's stack. In this sense, exception handling is a lot like a FAR CALL (intersegment transfer). Figure 7-3 demonstrates the information that is stacked before control is turned over to your ISR. As it does with a FAR CALL instruction, the 80386 pushes both the code segment selector and the offset of the return address. Precisely which instruction this points to depends on whether the exception is a fault, a trap, an abort, or an interrupt. These bytes are the minimum information necessary to enable a return to the interrupted code.

Another similarity to an intersegment CALL is that the 80386 pushes the information onto the stack of the target code, not that of the interrupted code. If this requires a privilege change, the old stack segment and pointer are pushed also. Unlike its handling of a CALL, however, the 80386 always pushes EFLAGS just before the return address. This is done because certain exceptions will alter flag bits when exception processing begins. Some software exceptions cause a special error code to be saved on the stack as well.

All told, the ISR may see from 12 to 24 bytes on the top of its stack when it starts running. At that point, the routine is on its own. The ISR executes just as any other piece of code would. It runs at the privilege level indicated by its code segment's DPL field and can use whatever segments of memory are available in the GDT and the current task's LDT at that privilege level. No special powers are given to ISR code, and there are no special restrictions. ISR code can make FAR JMPs or CALLs to other segments, traverse privilege levels (through gates, of course), and perform I/O. For most purposes, ISRs are no different from any other program or subroutine.

When the ISR is finished with its appointed function, it returns control to the interrupted code with an IRET (interrupt return) instruction. Before dealing too specifically with your ISR code, let's take a closer look at the IDT and see how to create an effective one.

Interrupt service routines

- Operate exactly like programmed subroutines

- Must save all registers that are used

- Are invoked by exceptions instead of CALL instructions

- Terminate with IRET instead of RET instructions

THE INTERRUPT
DESCRIPTOR TABLE

As you saw in Chapter 2, the interrupt descriptor table is treated much like the GDT or an LDT. Like other descriptor tables, the IDT contains descriptors, at 8 bytes each, and the 80386 keeps track of its location in memory and its limit (total size minus 1 byte) in the IDTR register. Like the GDTR register, IDTR is not stored in a TSS and does not change with task switches. This makes the IDT just as global as the GDT. Unlike the GDT or LDT, however, programs can never select a descriptor in the IDT. Only the 80386 itself ever references descriptors in the IDT, based on exception vectors, as was mentioned previously.

The IDT is a direct replacement for the simple interrupt vector table used on earlier iAPX 86 processors, up to and including the 80186/188. Like the earlier table, the IDT should define 256 ISRs, one for every possible exception vector. This would give the IDT a limit of 07FF. You can create an IDT shorter than this, but it is not recommended. If an exception occurs and the vector (whether assigned or acquired) indicates a descriptor beyond the limit of the IDT, a general protection fault (exception 13) will occur. In addition, if an interrupt occurs and a hardware problem with the data bus prevents the passing of a vector, the 80386 will often read all 1 bits (FF) as a vector and try to read the 256th descriptor in the IDT. If your IDT is short, this will force a general protection fault. Of course, if your system's data bus is no good, your problems probably go way beyond this inconvenience.

You could conceivably define an IDT with more than 256 descriptors, but since exception vectors are limited to 8 bits, the excess descriptors would never be used, and so the usefulness of doing this is questionable.

Each descriptor in the IDT must point to a programmer-supplied exception-handling or recovery routine, but the IDT cannot contain code descriptors. In fact, only three kinds of descriptors can be used in the IDT. They are

- Trap gate descriptor
- Interrupt gate descriptor
- Task gate descriptor

If any other type of descriptor is found in the IDT when an exception occurs, the 80386 generates a general protection fault.

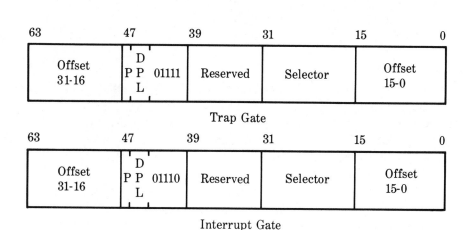

Figure 7-4.   Trap gate and interrupt gate descriptors

Task gate descriptors were defined in Chapter 5. Trap gate and interrupt gate descriptors are introduced here for the first time. Figure 7-4 shows the format of these two descriptor types. Note the marked similarities between these and a call gate descriptor. All that is missing is the 5-bit Word Count field. Because interrupts and exceptions are, by definition, unexpected events with no particular relationship to the work the current program is doing, this seems only natural. Just as a call gate does, each interrupt and trap gate holds only a selector to a code segment and a 32-bit offset where execution is to begin. This should point to the first instruction of your ISR.

Also like call gates, interrupt and trap gates have privilege levels associated with them. The DPL field of a trap, task, or interrupt gate determines the minimum privilege level required to pass through the gate. In most systems, it is recommended that this field always be kept at 3. Otherwise, certain programs or tasks would not be able to handle exceptions if their privilege level was not high enough. Since the occurrence of interrupts and exceptions generally cannot be predicted, if you use a higher privilege level you are setting yourself up for some truly nasty protection faults. A worst-case scenario would be a system in which the gate in IDT slot 13 (the general protection fault vector) had a DPL less than 3. If a PL 3 program were to cause, say, a segment limit overrun, the 80386 would attempt to invoke the general protection fault handler and find the gate too privileged for it to use. This is a privilege violation, and so the 80386 would invoke another general protection fault. Finding the gate still too privileged to use, the processor would give up and shut down, causing a total system crash.

Since it is precisely the lower-privileged programs that generate the majority of software exceptions, you should at least keep the first 17 gates accessible to all privilege levels. Remember, programs can never call these gates voluntarily; they can be used only by the 80386 to find an ISR.

Exception handler privilege levels

- Exception handlers and gates obey the same rules as call gates
- The exception gate's DPL must be no less than CPL
- The exception code's DPL must be no greater than CPL

DECIDING ON THE TYPE OF GATE TO USE

Because only three types of descriptors are allowed in the IDT, you do not have a lot of leeway in creating exception gates. However, looking up the gate in the IDT is the last of the 80386's reflex actions before it turns control over to your ISR. The type of gate you use here can make a difference and may give your ISR a head start in handling the exception. The next sections discuss the trap gate and interrupt gate, which are almost identical. Then task gates are reevaluated for the effect they have on exception processing.

Trap Gates

Trap gates are very similar to the now-familiar call gates, covered in Chapter 3. The most noticeable difference is the absence of a Word Count field for passing parameters. The similarity is not entirely coincidental; the 80386 handles exceptions almost exactly the same as it does FAR CALL instructions. In the case of an interrupt or exception, however, you haven't asked for the change in flow of control; it is forced upon you by some internal or external stimulus.

When an exception occurs and the exception vector selects a trap gate in the IDT, the 80386 saves some of its internal state, as was shown in Figure 7-3. Then the 80386 performs an intersegment transfer of control to the segment and offset contained in the trap gate descriptor. The segment selector in the trap gate must point to an executable code segment; it cannot refer to another gate or descriptor of any kind (such as a TSS). Obviously, that code segment must be available to the processor at the time the exception occurs. This might be tougher than it sounds. If the selector in the trap gate indicates a code descriptor in the LDT (TI=1), that descriptor must be in the current task's LDT. Because the occurrence of most exceptions is unpredictable, creating a trap gate that points to an LDT-based descriptor is a risky proposition if multitasking is being used. A different LDT might be in use when the exception occurs. A much safer technique is to keep all code segment descriptors for ISRs in the GDT. Alternatively, you could alias the ISR code segments, putting alias descriptors in every task's LDT. Whatever scheme you use, be sure that an exception handler's code segment descriptor is "visible" wherever and whenever that exception is possible.

The code segment does not necessarily have to be marked present, either at the segment or page level. If it is marked not present, the 80386 will generate a not-present fault (exception 11 or 14) while attempting to locate the ISR. If your not-present fault handlers can resolve this and make the necessary segment or page present, the 80386 will be successful when it tries again, and the net result will be only a minor delay for the original exception handler.

Once the processor has found the ISR's code segment and has pushed all of the necessary information on the stack, execution begins with the first instruction pointed to by the offset field in the trap gate. As is the case with a call gate, you must ensure that this field points to something rational. Execution continues until an IRET instruction is encountered. The 80386 pops the 48-bit return address and EFLAGS off of the stack (along with the 48-bit outer stack pointer, if a privilege change has taken place) and returns to the interrupted code. Everything should now return to normal and the interrupted program should be unaware that anything has happened.

Interrupt Gates

An interrupt gate operates exactly like a trap gate in all respects except one. When an exception vectors through an interrupt gate, the 80386 clears IF (interrupt flag) after it pushes the return address and EFLAGS but before it executes the first instruction of the ISR. In a trap gate, all flags, including IF, remain exactly as they were when the exception occurred.

By clearing IF as it passes through an interrupt gate, the 80386 masks all further *hardware-initiated* interrupts until the ISR is done, the final IRET is executed, and the original EFLAGS image is popped off of the stack. Note that the setting of IF does not affect software-initiated exceptions. You cannot tell the 80386 to ignore general protection faults by clearing the interrupt flag. In addition, the IF bit cannot mask the external NMI input pin. NMI can never be disabled.

The auto-disable feature of interrupt gates can be crucial when your ISR is written to service a hardware-related interrupt. Suppose that you have a clock/calendar chip in your system that generates an interrupt to the 80386 once every second, so that your software can keep track of the time. Normally, an IC like this will drive its interrupt output pin to the active state when it decides it is time and will release it when told to do so by your clock-tick ISR. If hardware interrupts were not masked automatically just before your ISR began executing, the 80386 would never get to the first instruction of your ISR code. Instead, it would pass through the gate, stack information, locate the first instruction of your ISR, check for interrupts, and find a hardware device requesting service. The whole process would then repeat indefinitely, and the same interrupt would be acknowledged over and over. Usually this stops only when the 80386 runs out of stack space. Since it will still try to acknowledge the clock interrupt without a stack, it will finally shut down. All of this takes place in a few milliseconds.

Because the 80386 is designed to check for interrupts after every instruction, there is no way to prevent this spiral nosedive unless you use an interrupt gate. Even if the very first instruction in your ISR is a CLI or one that disables the clock chip, it will not be fast enough.

Apart from this distinction, interrupt gates and trap gates operate identically. When in doubt, you might want to err on the side of caution and use an interrupt gate.

Task Gates

The third alternative for an exception gate is a task gate, and it operates quite unlike the previous two types. Although task gates were discussed in Chapter 5, you can now see how to use them in exceptional circumstances.

When an exception vector selects a task gate, the 80386 performs an immediate task switch. The task awakened is determined by the TSS selector stored in the task gate descriptor. The TSS selector of the current task, which is now dormant, is copied into the Back Link field of the new task. The new task will have its NT (nested task) bit set in EFLAGS. When the exception-handling task completes and executes an IRET instruction, the 80386 reawakens the interrupted task based on the back link information. Like any task gate descriptor, the selector field must hold the selector to a TSS descriptor in the GDT. TSS descriptors in an LDT are not allowed, nor are task gates to other gates.

If all of this sounds a lot like the description of a task switch due to a FAR CALL instruction, it should. The 80386's reaction to the task gate is the same. Note that unlike a FAR CALL, an exception cannot vector directly to a TSS descriptor; an intermediate gate must be used. Like the descriptors for the other exception gates, the task gate descriptor has a privilege level associated with it, and it must not be greater (numerically smaller) than the task being interrupted. In essence, the interrupted task is trying to perform a FAR CALL (albeit involuntarily) to another task through a task gate, and all of the normal protection rules apply.

Handling exceptions with task gates (and therefore with different tasks) has some real advantages over using trap or interrupt gates:

- The entire context of the interrupted task is saved automatically.
- The exception handler does not need to be concerned with contaminating the interrupted code.
- The exception handler can run at any privilege level.
- The exception handler can run in an environment that is known to be good.
- The exception handler can use its own private code and data space because it can have its own LDT.

There are a couple of drawbacks as well, however:

- The 80386 requires more time to perform a task switch than it does to stack a few bytes.
- A task gate cannot specify where in the task to begin execution. Dormant tasks always resume where they left off.

- It is difficult to retrieve any information about the interrupted code when it is in a different task.

As the last point shows, the total separation of tasks can be an asset or a liability, depending on how much your ISR needs to know about the code that was interrupted. If the need to know is great and you still want to handle the ISR as a distinct task, Chapter 6 shows some methods for sharing code and data among tasks.

If the exception-handling task needs to extract information from the task that was running, the first step, of course, is to determine which task that was. This can be very easy. If the exception-handling task can read its own TSS, it can examine its own Back Link field to read the TSS selector of its parent task. If you are concerned about the exception handler reading privileged information, you might define a read-only data segment descriptor in its LDT that is only 2 bytes long, covering just the Back Link field.

By separating the ISR from the interrupted code and placing it in a different task, you gain some advantages in both protection and addressability. If the ISR handles a hardware interrupt, as in the earlier clock/calendar example, you can give it a different I/O Permission bit map than the other tasks, allowing access to the clock/calendar chip. The ISR could also maintain in its LDT one or more data segment descriptors that define space not available to other tasks. A disk I/O handler is one example of an ISR that may require access to a memory buffer that is unavailable to other tasks.

Even if the ISR does not require access to special, private space, you may want to create a task for it so that it does have a permanent address map that is known to be good. Otherwise, the ISR must run in the address space of the program or task that was interrupted. This is the case with ISRs that are handled with trap or interrupt gates. A non-task-switching ISR must restrict itself to using segment selectors for descriptors in the GDT. Unless you know which task was interrupted and what the current LDT looks like, you should avoid using segment selectors that reference the LDT in these types of exception handlers.

Like a task switch caused by a program's FAR CALL instruction to a task gate or to a TSS descriptor, a task switch caused by an exception will nest the exception-handling task within the interrupted task. The outgoing task will remain in the busy state, and the incoming task will be marked busy. The incoming task will also have its NT bit and Back Link field set to reflect its nested status. The IF bit in the new task's EFLAGS register is not affected. Its setting depends entirely on what was stored in the EFLAGS image in the TSS. You can create the same interrupt auto-clear effect as an interrupt gate by defining the exception-handling task with IF cleared. This might be mandatory if the task is designed to service a hardware-generated interrupt.

When some or all exceptions are handled with task gates, you must pay particular attention to avoiding recursive exceptions. As long as the ISR task is running, both it and its parent task will be marked busy. During this time, you must be able to guarantee that another exception of the same type will not occur. Task state segments are not reentrant. It is an error to try to switch to a task that is already busy, even if you did not actually request the task switch. A task that handles coprocessor-not-available faults (exception 7), for example, must never generate coprocessor-not-available faults. Likewise, if you vector general protection faults through a task gate, debug the ISR carefully, making certain that it will never generate general protection faults of its own.

EXCEPTION HANDLERS AND PRIVILEGE LEVELS

As you have seen, all exceptions must be handled through gates. Trap gates and interrupt gates operate very much like call gates. All three IDT gate types have an internal DPL field as part of their respective descriptors. The DPL of the gate determines the minimum privilege level necessary to use the gate. It is recommended that this field always be set to 3 so that all exception processing can proceed unimpeded regardless of the privilege level of the currently executing code.

For trap and interrupt gates, the 80386 performs another privilege check just before it begins executing the ISR. Like a call gate, an interrupt or trap gate must transfer control to a segment of greater or equal privilege. An ISR is not allowed to run at a lower privilege level than the program that was interrupted (unless it is in a separate task). Because of the unpredictability of interrupts and other exceptions, you must be able to guarantee that a privilege violation will not occur. Two methods are possible:

- Define all non-task-switching ISRs in PL 0 code segments
- Define all non-task-switching ISRs in conforming code segments

If you use the latter technique, the ISR will inherit the privilege level of the interrupted code. This can range from CPL 0 to CPL 3, or whatever range of privilege levels you use in your system. Because the privilege level of a conforming code segment ISR is fluid, you must avoid all privileged and IOPL-sensitive instructions. Even more so than other non-task-switching ISRs, you must also be cautious about what segment selectors you use. Not only are you restricted to segment descriptors in the GDT, you must use only PL 3 segments, since the ISR might very well be running at PL 3.

For these reasons, the recommended solution is to handle all exceptions with PL 0 code. The GDT-only restriction still holds, but at least you can use all of the segment descriptors if you need to, and you don't need to worry about privileged instructions.

As is the case with a call gate, if an exception through a trap or interrupt gate causes a change in privilege level (always up), a stack change takes place as well. The 80386 takes the new stack segment selector and offset from the privileged stack fields of the current TSS. If the ISR runs at PL 0, the 48-bit stack pointer will be found in the SS0 and ESP0 fields, for example. Having located the new stack, the 80386 first pushes the old SS and ESP registers, followed by the standard EFLAGS, CS, and EIP registers.

When exceptions are handled by separate tasks through task gates, the privilege level of the handler's code is unimportant. Only the privilege level of the task gate descriptor itself is checked.

ERROR CODES

As Figure 7-3 showed, many software-initiated exceptions cause the 80386 to push an additional 4 bytes onto the exception handler's stack. This extra piece of data is known as an *error code* and is meant to provide useful diagnostic information to the ISR. Exception 8 and exceptions 10 through 14 always cause an error code to be pushed. The 80386 generates this error code internally when the exception occurs. No other exceptions ever push an error code.

The error code for exception 8 is always 0, and so not much can be said about it here. For exceptions 10 through 13, the error code is a 16-bit quantity that is "garbage-extended" to 32 bits to keep the stack aligned. See Figure 7-5. The format of these error codes is very similar to that of a selector. This makes a certain amount of sense, since exceptions 10 through 13 are all descriptor-related errors. Whenever the 80386 detects an invalid TSS fault, a not-present fault, a stack fault, or a general protection fault, it pushes an error code that identifies the offending descriptor onto the top of the ISR's stack. Although the format of these error codes is similar to that of a selector, the difference is important. Instead of an RPL field in the two least significant bit positions, an error code has an I bit and an EX bit. The format of a descriptor-related error code is as follows:

EX (External, bit 0)   When this bit is set, it indicates that the exception was initially caused by an external (hardware) interrupt or that it occurred when the 80386 was already handling another exception.

I (IDT, bit 1)   This bit is like a second TI bit. When set, it indicates that the index portion of the error code refers to a descriptor in the IDT.

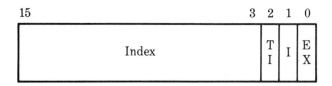

Figure 7-5. Error code for exceptions 10 through 13

| TI (Table Indicator, bit 2) | This is just like the flag of the same name in a segment selector. When set, the index portion of the error code refers to a descriptor in the current LDT at the time the exception occurred. When clear, the index selects a GDT descriptor. This bit is undefined when I is set. |
| INDEX (Descriptor Index, bits 3 through 15) | This field uniquely identifies a descriptor in the GDT, LDT, or IDT, depending on the status of the I and TI bits. |

Table 7-2 summarizes the significance of the TI and I bits.

In some cases, the 80386 will not be able to generate a meaningful error code, and so will push a 0. This should be treated as a null or invalid error code and not as an indication that GDT slot 0 is bad. If the error code indicates a descriptor in the LDT (TI=1, I=0) and the exception was handled through a task gate, keep in mind that the error code refers to a descriptor in the old task's LDT, not in the error-handling task's LDT.

Table 7-2.   Table Indicated by Error Code

00	GDT
01	IDT
10	LDT
11	IDT

Exception 14 (page fault) always causes an error code to be pushed. The format of a page fault error code is different from that of the descriptor-related exceptions (10 through 13). The 80386 pushes a 3-bit error code that is garbage-extended to 32 bits to align the stack. The format of a page fault error code is shown in Figure 7-6. The significance of these bits is as follows:

P (Present, bit 0)
This bit is the logical AND of the Present bits in the PDE and PTE used in the last linear-to-physical address translation. If it is clear, one or the other was marked not present.

R/W (Read/Write, bit 1)
When this bit is set, it means that the 80386 was attempting to write to memory when the page fault occurred. If it is clear, the 80386 was trying to read from memory.

U/S (User/Supervisor, bit 2)
When this bit is set, the 80386 was operating at user privilege level. That is, it was executing PL 3 code. When clear, this bit indicates that the processor was at supervisor privilege level (PL 0 through PL 2).

Table 7-3 summarizes the combinations of the three page fault error-code bits. Unlike the error codes for exceptions 10 through 13, a page fault error code of 0 is perfectly valid.

Figure 7-6.   Error code for exception 14

RESPONSIBILITIES OF
AN EXCEPTION
HANDLER

Whenever an external hardware interrupt that is not masked occurs or the 80386 detects an internal software-related exception, the processor immediately begins the automatic exception-processing sequence described earlier. You, as a programmer, can do nothing to affect this reflexive action. The earliest point at which software can have an effect is in the definition of the gate type: trap, interrupt, or task. After the gate is located, the 80386

Table 7-3.   Determining Page Fault Cause

000	PTE or page not present during supervisor read
001	(not an error)
010	PTE or page not present during supervisor write
011	(not an error)
100	PTE or page not present during user read
101	User read access denied
110	PTE or page not present during user write
111	User write access denied

passes control to your exception-handling software (ISR). At this point, the system's reaction to any given exception is under your complete control. The 80386 has identified the exception condition for you and started execution of the correct ISR. The rest is up to you.

When an exception vectors through a trap or interrupt gate, the ISR runs in the context of the interrupted code. No task switch takes place. At most, a privilege change occurs if the ISR is in a higher-privileged code segment than the interrupted code. Only a return address and EFLAGS are saved on the stack, perhaps with an optional error code and a lower-privileged stack pointer. Typically, the ISR's job is to remedy the exceptional condition as quickly as possible and return to the interrupted code with no side effects.

A non-task-switching ISR should operate like a function call that returns no parameters. You must be certain to preserve all 80386 registers, including segment registers. You should also avoid generating any additional exceptions of your own. An endless string of errors can result if one ISR generates an exception that turns control over to another ISR that generates exceptions, and so on. Especially in a real-time system, exception response time (interrupt latency) must be kept to a minimum. Above all, latency must be consistent and deterministic. A given exception should take the same amount of time to process, regardless of any other circumstances that may prevail.

When writing ISRs for exceptions 8, 10, 11, 12, 13, or 14, be sure to pop the error code off of the stack before executing the final IRET instruction. The 80386 cannot return control to an error code, although it will try, resulting in a general protection fault.

If you are writing ISRs that will be handled with task gates, remember that when you execute an IRET instruction the ISR task state is frozen at that point until the next similar exception. Be sure that there is a JMP instruction or something similar immediately after the IRET that will return control to the beginning of the task's code. Otherwise, your ISR will work only the first time and will probably generate a general protection fault the second time it is called.

Because the 80386 will not switch into a task that is already busy, you need to be cautious about recursive exceptions when those exceptions are handled with tasks. This may mean running the ISR with interrupts disabled (in the case of hardware interrupts) or carefully debugging your ISR under various conditions (for software exceptions).

HALT AND SHUTDOWN

Two other exceptional conditions are not interrupts or exceptions in the normal sense. These are the *halt condition* and the *shutdown condition*. Neither one is assigned an exception vector, and no ISR needs to be written for them (nor, indeed, can be). To understand the halt and shutdown conditions, you must consider the three states possible for the 80386 microprocessor:

- Running (normal condition)
- Temporarily not running (halt condition)
- Unable to run (shutdown condition)

Normally, you assume that the processor is running; it is fetching instructions, responding to interrupts, and so on. If the 80386 encounters a HLT instruction (opcode F4), it immediately ceases running. All external address and data bus activity stops, and it will not fetch or execute any instructions. The 80386 is idle and does nothing. When (or if) an exception occurs, the 80386 wakes up, handles the exception, and continues processing with the next instruction after the HLT. Since the 80386 is not executing any code, software exceptions are impossible. Therefore, only hardware interrupts will bring it out of a halted condition.

The shutdown condition is the 80386's reaction to a catastrophic system failure. Like halt, a shutdown is not a normal exception. Unlike halt, a shutdown condition cannot be specified with a special instruction. A processor shutdown is to be avoided at all costs. The only way to resurrect an 80386 that has shut down is through an NMI or an external reset. (Early versions of the 80386 did not respond to NMI when a shutdown occurred, only to a reset.)

The processor enters the shutdown condition when there is no way for it to continue processing. For example, if a PL 0 program runs over the edge of its stack segment, a stack fault results. If the stack fault handler is also at PL 0 in the same task, the 80386 has no place to push a return address, EFLAGS, or an error code. Because it cannot continue, it shuts down. A similar deadlock can arise if an exception is handled with a task gate and the ISR generates another, similar exception while running. The 80386 cannot vector to an already busy task, and so it gives up and enters the shutdown condition. There is no clean way to restart an 80386 that has shut down. It is the system programmer's responsibility to ensure that it cannot happen.

Halt condition

- 80386 performs no processing

- Entered with an HLT instruction

- Exited with a hardware interrupt

Shutdown condition

- 80386 cannot continue processing

- Entered with a catastrophic failure

- Exited with a hardware reset NMI

USING EXCEPTIONS FOR EMULATION

Neither hardware interrupts nor software exceptions are to be avoided per se. Hardware interrupts can signal anything from imminent system demise to the successful transmission of a character to a printer. Software exceptions can be generated by gross software failure or a simple INT *n* instruction, used for making a system call. Both types can be and often are used for constructive purposes in running systems.

Exception 7 is raised by the 80386 when an attempt is made to execute either 80287 or 80387 instructions when neither one is present in the system. For your purposes, this may be a software error and cause for termination of the failing program, but you could instead choose to emulate the functions of a coprocessor in software. This provides a very clean, invisible means of simulating an 80387 that even assembly-level programs cannot detect. If a coprocessor is present, application programs could use it; if not, a coprocessor would be emulated. The only difference would be in execution time. Not one byte of application code would need to be changed.

Exceptions 11 and 14 are used to signal not-present segments and pages, respectively. Either or both can be an error or an integral part of your virtual memory mechanism. Chapter 4 showed how you can make use of exception 14 to implement demand paging.

Exception 6 indicates that the 80386 has fetched from the code segment one or more bytes that are not valid instructions. This usually *is* a system failure or at least a good reason to terminate the offending program. However, there is nothing to keep you from using an invalid-opcode fault handler to implement your own custom extensions to the instruction set. You could, for instance, decide that the 2-byte opcode sequence 0F 30 will perform some special function on your system. Be careful how you implement this, however. In the first place, deliberately using an undefined opcode could spoil your chances of using this software on an 80486, where it may become a valid instruction. Second, not all of the opcodes shown as invalid in the opcode maps from Intel and other sources really are invalid. Opcode 82, for example, performs a logical OR function, and opcode D6 performs no observable function but isn't trapped as invalid, either. If you want to create extensions to the instruction set, use INT *n* instructions instead.

EXCEPTION REFERENCE

The rest of this chapter covers each of the predefined exceptions in detail. Note that all of these except NMI are software-initiated exceptions; hardware-initiated exceptions supply a vector to the 80386 during the interrupt acknowledge cycle.

All exceptions are classified as faults, traps, or aborts. For faults, the return pointers (CS and EIP) that are saved on the error handler's stack point to the faulting instruction, with any prefixes. Therefore, when control is returned, the 80386 will reexecute that instruction. Trap handlers will find the return pointer pointing to the instruction that follows the trapped instruction. Any change in flow of control will already have been taken into account. Exceptions classified as aborts may not have meaningful return pointers at all. The 80386 does not support the restarting of aborted code anyway, so it usually doesn't matter.

Of course, any hardware interrupt can pass a vector for one of these exceptions, but this is not recommended. Likewise, an INT *n* instruction can use any vector. You may find this very useful for simulating various hardware interrupts or for debugging your exception handlers. However, it is tough to do for exceptions that are supposed to push an error code.

Exception 0—Divide Error.
Class: Fault. Error Code: No

The 80386 automatically generates this exception if it detects a DIV or IDIV instruction with a divisor of 0. Division by 0 yields an undefined result in traditional finite mathematics, and so the 80386 will not attempt it. An exception 0 will also be generated if the result of an otherwise legal division operation will not fit in the accumulator (AL, AX, or EAX).

Exception 1—Debug.
Class: Fault/Trap.
Error Code: No

This is a catchall for a number of debugging aids. The 80386 takes this exception on any of the following conditions:

- Hardware breakpoint found (data)—trap
- Hardware breakpoint found (code)—fault
- Instruction trace enabled—trap
- Task-switch trap enabled—trap
- Debug register access violation—fault

A more complete description of these conditions and their uses can be found in Chapter 10.

Exception 2—NMI.
Class: Trap. Error Code: No

This is the only hardware interrupt assigned a permanent vector. Whenever the 80386 receives an active NMI signal, it internally generates vector 02, forgoing the standard interrupt acknowledge cycle and thus saving time. NMI is usually reserved for ultra-important, "the machine is on fire" kinds of circumstances. NMI cannot be masked, unlike normal hardware interrupts, except under very special conditions.

When the 80386 has received an NMI and is executing the NMI handler, it ignores all further hardware interrupts, including NMI, until the handler completes. If another NMI is received while an NMI handler is running, the 80386 remembers it and acts on it as soon as the current handler is done.

When you are loading the stack segment register (SS) with a standard MOV instruction instead of the preferred LSS instruction, the 80386 ignores hardware interrupts, including NMI, until the *next* instruction is completed successfully. The next instruction is usually a MOV instruction that loads register ESP.

Exception 3—Breakpoint.
Class: Trap. Error Code: No

This exception is taken when the 80386 encounters a software breakpoint (opcode CC). This is not related to the hardware breakpoint exception discussed previously, except that both are used for debugging.

Exception 4—Overflow.
Class: Trap. Error Code: No

An exception 4 is generated when the 80386 encounters an INTO instruction while OF (overflow flag) in EFLAGS is set. This exception is typically used by compilers to trap arithmetic overflow in signed arithmetic. It is a somewhat more spectacular way of handling numeric overflow than a JO instruction.

Exception 5—Bound.
Class: Fault. Error Code: No

This exception handler is invoked if a BOUND instruction fails its test. The BOUND instruction takes three operands. If the first one is not numerically between the other two, an exception 5 is generated.

Exception 6—Invalid Opcode.
Class: Fault. Error Code: No

The 80386 raises this exception whenever it fetches from the code segment one or more bytes that do not correspond to valid 80386 instructions. Note that this is not limited to instructions in which the primary opcode byte is undefined; it also includes valid instructions with illegal secondary opcode bytes or an illegal addressing mode specifier.

Exception 7—Device Not Available.
Class: Fault. Error Code: No

This exception is generated whenever the 80386 fetches an 80287 or 80387 instruction and neither of these devices is present (EM=1). It also occurs when a coprocessor *is* present but a task switch has occurred since the last time it was used (MP=1 and TS=1). The former case allows you to either terminate the misinformed program or emulate the floating-point functions in software. The latter case allows you to save the previous task's coprocessor state before the current task modifies it.

Exception 8—Double Fault.
Class: Abort. Error Code: Yes

Exception 8 signals a grave system failure. A double fault is just this side of a shutdown. As the name implies, a double fault is when one fault occurs while the 80386 is trying to handle another

Table 7-4. Causes of a Double Fault

First Exception		Second Exception
0	Divide error	0, 9, 10, 11, 12, 13
9	Coprocessor overrun	0, 9, 10, 11, 12, 13
10	Invalid TSS	0, 9, 10, 11, 12, 13
11	Segment not present	0, 9, 10, 11, 12, 13
12	Stack fault	0, 9, 10, 11, 12, 13
13	General protection fault	0, 9, 10, 11, 12, 13
14	Page fault	0, 9, 10, 11, 12, 13, 14

one. This does not mean that any exception that occurs while an ISR is running will cause a double fault. Such faults happen only if a fault occurs while the 80386 is still performing its reflex operations at the very beginning of exception processing. Specifically, while the 80386 is vectoring to a gate in the IDT or locating the ISR code segment, it is vulnerable to certain exceptions that will cause a double fault. A summary of double-fault syndromes is shown in Table 7-4. The error code for a double fault is always 0.

Exception 9—Coprocessor Segment Overrun. Class: Abort. Error Code: No

This exception is roughly equivalent to a general protection fault for coprocessors. Because the operands for floating-point functions tend to be large, you have a better-than-usual chance of trying to load or store a floating-point number beyond the limit of a data segment. Certain Intel literature claims that this exception will never occur on the 80386. This is not true.

Exception 10—Invalid TSS.
Class: Fault. Error Code: Yes

An invalid TSS fault occurs if an attempt is made to switch to a task that has a bad TSS. Depending on what part(s) of the target TSS the 80386 takes exception to, this fault is reported either in the current task, aborting the switch, or in the new task, after the switch. Conditions that cause an invalid TSS fault are summarized in Table 7-5. It is strongly recommended that invalid TSS faults be handled through task gates.

Exception 11—Segment Not
Present.
Class: Fault. Error Code: Yes

This exception is raised if the 80386 makes reference to a descriptor that is marked not present. Typically, this occurs when a program tries to load a segment selector that points to a not-present segment. Because descriptors are used for more than just memory segments, however, this exception can also occur when an attempt is made to use a not-present gate, load a not-present LDT, or switch to a not-present TSS. Exception 11 is not related to the not-present page fault.

Aside from loading segment selectors under program control, the 80386 can also load segments when performing intersegment transfers (caused by a FAR CALL instruction or an exception) or as part of a task switch. For these reasons, it is recommended that you handle exception 11 with a task gate.

Table 7-5.   Causes of an Invalid TSS Fault

Check	Error Occurs In
New TSS Size $\geq$ 104 bytes	Old task
LDT selector is valid	New task
LDT is present	New task
CS selector is valid	New task
CS selector RPL = code descriptor DPL	New task
SS selector is valid	New task
SS selector RPL = stack descriptor DPL	New task
SS selector RPL = code descriptor DPL	New task
Data segment selectors are valid	New task
Data segment descriptors DPL $\geq$ CPL	New task
Data segments are readable	New task

Exception 12 — Stack Fault.
Class: Fault. Error Code: Yes

Exception 12 is a special form of exceptions 11 and 13. As a rule, whenever the 80386 detects a memory-related exception and the stack segment (SS) is involved, it reports it as a stack fault. These exceptions include segment overruns or underruns, which would normally be reported as exception 13, and segment not-present faults, which are exception 11, if they pertain to anything other than the stack segment. One nice side effect of reporting stack faults separately is that it is easier for operating system software to determine when an application program needs more stack space. This exception almost requires a task gate unless you can guarantee a privilege change when this exception occurs.

Exception 13—General Protection Fault.
Class: Fault. Error Code: Yes

The general protection fault is the "none of the above" category for the 80386. If an error occurs that does not have its own vector (0 through 16), it usually comes here. The following is a partial list of possible causes:

- Overrunning the end of a segment
- Underrunning the beginning of a segment
- Loading a segment descriptor of the wrong type
- Attempting to write to a read-only segment
- Attempting to read from an execute-only segment
- Loading a data segment register with an unreadable segment
- Using a null selector to reference memory
- Using a selector that is beyond the end of the appropriate descriptor table
- Using a selector that points to an LDT when no LDT is currently defined
- Attempting to switch to a busy task
- Fetching an instruction that is longer than 15 bytes
- Violating privilege rules

Since the 80386 will push an error code with a general protection fault, your ISR may be able to determine the cause of the fault and remedy it. If the error code is null, it usually indicates a problem you can't fix anyway.

Exception 14—Page Fault.
Class: Fault. Error Code: Yes

The 80386 raises this exception only if paging is enabled. During page translation, this fault occurs if either the PDE or PTE used in the translation is marked not present. A page fault also occurs if page-level privilege protection is violated, for example, a PL 3 program attempts to write to a protected page. The error code that the 80386 pushes for this fault contains only 3 significant bits. Fortunately, the 80386 also copies the linear address that was being translated into register CR2. This register is not used for any other purpose. Your page fault handler can use this information to decide whether to swap in secondary storage or terminate the offending program.

Exception 15—Reserved.
Class: Trap. Error Code: No

This exception is not currently defined by Intel. No internal error on the 80386 is assigned this vector. It is possible that it may be defined at a later time, perhaps on the 80486. Chances are, however, that it will remain undefined. Most currently available peripheral I/O chips can be programmed to supply any desired interrupt vector. If none is specified, it is customary for the device to send a vector of 0F (15 decimal). Thus, the exception handler for this vector might want to assume that it has been invoked because an as-yet-uninitialized peripheral device has generated a spurious interrupt request.

Exception 16—Coprocessor
Error.
Class: Fault. Error Code: No

In a sense, this is an external, hardware-initiated exception. When the 80287 or 80387 coprocessor detects an error condition of its own, it signals the 80386 through the ERROR pin that they share. Because of the heavily overlapped nature of numeric coprocessing on the 80386, this signal is not sampled regularly, as INTR and NMI are. Instead, the 80386 checks for coprocessor errors only when new coprocessor instructions are executed or when it is asked to do so with the WAIT instruction.

Exceptions 17 Through 31

Intel has reserved these 15 vectors for future expansion.

Exceptions 32 Through 255

You are free to use these exceptions. It is recommended that all of your hardware interrupts produce vectors of 32 (20 hexadecimal) or greater. The same goes for INT n instructions.

8

80286 EMULATION

The previous chapters have dealt with the newest, best, and most exciting features of the 80386. Ironically, one of the most useful features of the 80386 is its ability to use software written for earlier microprocessors in the iAPX 86 family. Older, 16-bit software written before the 80386 became available is abundant and is still very valuable. Obviously, this kind of previous-generation software was not written to take advantage of the 80386's newest features; it was designed for an entirely different microprocessor.

Because of the family resemblance between successive generations of the iAPX 86 microprocessors, a certain amount of compatibility is built in. As the distance between the earliest member (the 8086) and the latest (the 80386) increases, however, this compatibility becomes more and more difficult to maintain. Particularly since the 80286 introduced the Protected Virtual Address mode of operation, 8086-style memory segmentation has become very difficult to emulate (personal computers of the IBM AT class avoid this problem by not operating in Protected mode—they run in Real Address mode). With the 80386's expanded register file, addressing modes, and instruction set, executing unmodified 8086-era programs like an 8086 seems nearly impossible. The 80286 is a much closer match to the current state of the art. Therefore, the 80386 is able to execute Protected mode 80286 programs with very little trouble. This chapter describes exactly how you can accomplish this. To run 8086 code, the 80386 must operate in a special emulation mode, described in the next chapter.

On the 80386, 32-bit code is stored in code segments, data is stored in data segments, and stacks are stored in data or stack segments. These segments are defined by descriptors. The first time your program uses a new segment, the 80386 determines what type of segment it is by reading the segment descriptor's Access Rights byte. The descriptor also contains base address and limit information and two other bits that determine limit granularity and default operand size. These are bits 55 and 54, respectively. When the descriptor defines a code segment and the default operand-size bit (D bit) is set, the 80386 treats all information contained within that segment as 32-bit 80386 instructions. If a code segment descriptor has bit 54 clear, the segment is assumed to hold 16-bit 80286 code. Whenever control is passed to such a 16-bit segment, the 80386 will fetch, decode, and execute the opcodes within it as though it were actually an 80286 running in Protected mode.

Thus, merely by setting or clearing the D bit of a code descriptor, you can change the entire complexion of a segment of code. You can freely intermix 16-bit 80286 and 32-bit 80386 code segments in the same system, and you can pass control from one to the other and back. You can even define call gates between procedures of different sizes, so that you can build an operating system piecemeal and reuse older, 16-bit code. The D bit definition seems like a deceptively simple way to emulate an 80286. Actually, there is more to it than just that. Code interpretation is only one element. You must also consider stack usage, parameter passing, data sharing, and other problems that arise when one or more of your segments are defined to be 80286 compatible.

To execute 80286 code

- The 80286 code must occupy its own segment
- The segment descriptor must be defined as 16-bit code
- Descriptor bit 54 determines 16-bit versus 32-bit code
- The 80386 will fetch and execute all opcodes like an 80286

OPERAND SIZING

Let's continue the previous discussion by examining how 16-bit code segments work. To do that, you need to understand how "normal" 32-bit code is executed by the 80386. Because the 80386 has 32-bit registers (unlike any previous iAPX 86 processor), you have a much larger register size and operand size than ever before. This is something that the original 8086 instruction set was never designed for. On the 80386, you can use an 8-bit register (such as AL or AH), a 16-bit register (such as AX), or a 32-bit register (such as EAX) in most operations. All previous processors had only 8-bit and 16-bit registers. If you look closely at how 80386 instructions are encoded, you will see that all instructions that transfer data to or from a register or memory have a byte-size form and a full-size form. The byte form, of course, transfers 8 bits of data, as shown below:

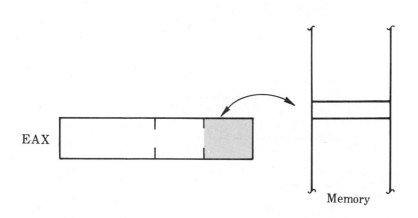

EAX

Memory

The processor's interpretation of the full-size form depends on the setting of the D bit of the code segment descriptor. If D = 1 (indicating 32-bit code), the 80386 will read or write 32 bits of data, as follows:

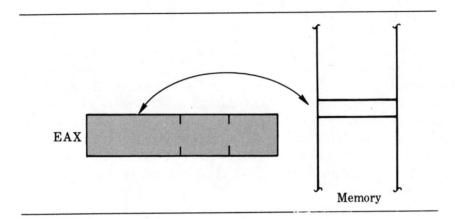

If D = 0 (indicating 16-bit, 80286 code), the 80386 interprets the full-size form to be 16 bits only and will transfer 16-bit operands, as follows:

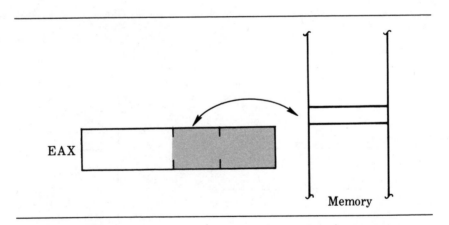

All 80386 instructions that transfer data have, at most, only these two forms. Many can use only one size of operand. (Instructions that load and store segment selectors always move 16 bits, for example.) There is no intermediate-size form of transfer instruction. How then does the 80386 handle 16-bit registers in a standard 32-bit code segment?

To allow the 80386 to use a nonstandard size of register or memory operand, you (or your assembler or compiler) must insert a special *operand-size override prefix* immediately before the instruction's opcode(s). The operand-size override prefix byte is 66 (102 decimal, 01100110 binary). When this prefix byte appears before an instruction that would normally use a full-size operand, the 80386 toggles its internal idea of full size for that instruction. For a 32-bit code segment, it allows you to use a 16-bit register or store a 16-bit value to memory, as shown here:

```
66 A1 12 34 56 78      MOV     AX, WORD PTR DS:[12345678h]
66 8B D9               MOV     BX, CX
66 4A                  DEC     DX
```

The operand-size prefix does not always force 16-bit operands to be used. Rather, it changes the interpretation of a full-size operand transfer. The same 66 prefix that causes an instruction in a 32-bit segment to transfer a 16-bit operand causes an instruction in a 16-bit segment to transfer a 32-bit operand. The operand-size prefix cannot be used to change the operand size of a byte-size instruction; it affects only full-size instructions.

Two or more operand-size prefixes before an instruction will not cause the 80386 to bounce back and forth between operand sizes trying to resolve your intended size; when the prefix is encountered during instruction prefetch, it enables operand-size override. Fetching two in a row neither reinforces the first one nor turns it back off. Operand-size prefixes also have a limited life span: one instruction. If you want multiple instructions to utilize irregular-size operands, you must insert a prefix before every one:

```
66 F7 E1               MUL     CX
66 8B C1               MOV     AX, CX
66 26 A3 12 34 56 78   MOV     WORD PTR ES:[12345678h], AX
```

The operand-size override prefix affects only the transfer of data. When a register is used as the source or destination of a data transfer instruction, the presence or absence of a prefix determines how much of the register will be used. If data is being transferred to or from memory, the prefix determines whether 2 bytes or 4 bytes of memory are accessed. If the instruction is transferring data between a register and memory, the prefix affects both.

Operand-size override prefix

- Is used as a 1-byte instruction prefix (66H)
- Reverses the native operand size for the subsequent instruction
- Allows 16-bit code to use 32-bit operands
- Allows 32-bit code to use 16-bit operands
- Affects register size, memory size, or both

ADDRESS SIZING

In addition to its new 32-bit data registers, the 80386 also has 32-bit address registers. In fact, with the 80386's extended instruction set, every register can be an address register. Because the 80286 had only 16-bit address registers (and fewer of them), it would appear that the 80286 emulation breaks down here. Not so.

The operand-size override prefix has a twin: the *address-size override prefix*. Like the operand-size override, the address-size override must be placed immediately before the affected instruction. It forces the 80386 to invert the sense of the D bit for the next instruction, but only for matters related to memory addressing. For instance, if you place an address-size override prefix before the following instruction:

```
MOV     EAX, DWORD PTR DS:[ESI]
```

it will be interpreted as

```
MOV    EAX, DWORD PTR DS:[SI]
```

Note that an address-size prefix does not affect the amount of data transferred to memory or its value. It only affects *how* the memory address is calculated. In the full 32-bit form, the linear memory address is given by the base of segment DS plus the 32-bit offset in register ESI. In the second, 16-bit example, the linear address is calculated in the same way, but only the lower 16 bits of ESI (register SI) contribute address offset information. If the upper half of ESI contains nonzero data, it is ignored. If it contains 05, for example, the 16-bit address override has no observable effect. In either case, all 32 bits of EAX are stored.

By adding an address-size override prefix to a memory load or store instruction, you limit the offset address to FFFF. Such an instruction is unable to reference more than the first 64KB in any one segment. It is important to note that this enforces a limit only on *logical* addresses. It does not affect linear or physical addressing. For example, if segment DS had a base address of 124000, you could still reference memory from 124000 to 133FFF (124000 + FFFF).

The opcode for the address-size override prefix byte is 67 (103 decimal, 01100111 binary). Both 66 and 67 were previously illegal opcodes on the 8086, 80186, and 80286 family processors.

Both an address-size override and an operand-size override can be used in the same instruction. The following example shows the four possible permutations:

```
    8B 06 MOV    EAX, DWORD PTR DS:[ESI]    ;default 32-bit form
  668B 06 MOV    AX, WORD PTR DS:[ESI]      ;operand size prefix
  678B 06 MOV    EAX, DWORD PTR DS:[SI]     ;address size prefix
66678B 06 MOV    AX, WORD PTR DS:[SI]       ;both prefixes
```

Note that the last form (both operand-size and address-size overrides) would be the default, normal case in a 16-bit code segment (D=0). This shows that, between the two override prefixes, you can temporarily turn 32-bit code into 16-bit code or vice versa, or you can do something in between.

Whenever 16-bit addressing is in effect, either because of a temporary address-size override or because that's the default addressing size for the segment, the abbreviated addressing mode extends to all memory addressing operations, some of which may not be obvious. The 16-bit instruction pointer, register IP, is used instead of EIP. Therefore, it is not possible to transfer control to any offset greater than FFFF. This is true for JMP and CALL instructions as well as for RET and IRET instructions and changes in flow caused by interrupts or exceptions. This aspect of 80286 compatibility will be dealt with in a later section. Non-standard addressing also affects instructions with implied memory addresses, such as LODS, STOS, CMPS, MOVS, SCAS, and XLAT.

Address-size prefix

- Is used as a 1-byte instruction prefix (67H)
- Reverses native address size for the subsequent instruction
- Allows 16-bit code to use 32-bit addressing
- Allows 32-bit code to use 16-bit addressing
- Affects most memory references and instruction fetch

STACK SIZING

An important change in stack operations takes place when non-standard addressing is used. You must keep especially close track of addressing modes when any kind of stack operation is performed, including CALL and RET instructions. The most important distinction to make regarding stack-related addressing is that the default addressing mode (16-bit or 32-bit) for stack operations is *not* set by the D bit of the code segment descriptor. Instead, it is set by the D bit of the *stack segment* descriptor. In other words, the D bit of the code segment descriptor sets the default operand size and the default addressing size for all memory references except stack operations. The default addressing mode for stack operations is set by the descriptor you use for a stack segment. This does not have to be an actual stack segment per se. As always, any writable data segment can be used for a stack. Using a stack-type segment does have some advantages, especially if stack growth will be supported (see Chapter 2).

Another distinction that must be made for stack operations is that the D bit of the stack segment descriptor affects only automatic or implicit stack references. Explicit references to the stack segment are not treated as stack references and use the form of memory addressing determined by the D bit of the code segment descriptor. *Automatic stack references* are those that the 80386 performs as part of its automatic response to interrupts or exceptions. *Implicit stack references* are those that always reference the top of the stack, at SS:[ESP] or SS:[SP], depending on the stack addressing mode. Instructions that make this type of reference include CALL, RET, IRET, INT *n*, ENTER, and LEAVE. *Explicit stack references* are programmed memory references that just happen to use the stack segment or the stack pointer to define an address.

Stack address size

- Stack references are not affected by address prefix
- Stack address size is determined by the stack segment

Stack descriptor

- Descriptor bit 54 determines 16-bit versus 32-bit stack
- Affects all automatic stack references
- Does not affect memory references within the stack segment

BRANCHING BETWEEN
16-BIT AND 32-BIT CODE

An intersegment (FAR) JMP instruction can be encoded in either of two ways. One form consists of the JMP opcode followed by a segment selector and an offset. The other consists of a 2-byte JMP opcode with a memory address. The contents of that memory are supposed to hold the target segment and offset. See Figure 8-1.

Consider the case of a 32-bit program that wants to transfer control to a 16-bit program. Either form of the FAR JMP instruction could be used with identical results. The selector portion would refer to a code descriptor that has its D bit cleared (a 16-bit code segment). The offset portion would specify the desired address within the new segment, from 0 to FFFF. Any offset larger than that would be ignored by the 80386. If no privilege rules are violated, the transfer would occur uneventfully.

Now consider the case of a 16-bit program branching to a 32-bit program. If the destination offset within the target code is within the first 64KB, your 16-bit code will have no problem specifying both a segment and offset. This represents the standard

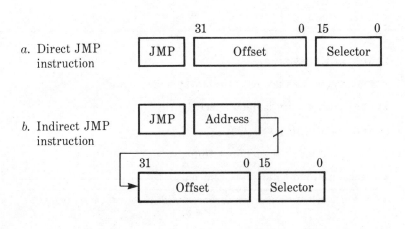

Figure 8-1.   Intersegment JMP instructions

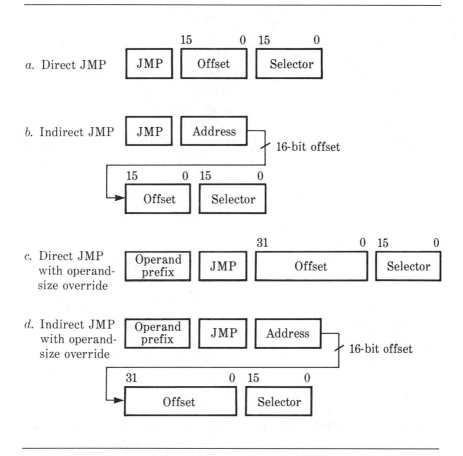

Figure 8-2.   Intersegment JMP from 16-bit code segments

case, shown in Figure 8-2a and b. But what if your 16-bit program needs to branch to offset 47E008 in the 32-bit segment? Your 16-bit code can give a 32-bit target offset by using an operand-size override prefix with the JMP instruction. In the first form of the instruction, an operand-size prefix will cause the 80386 to interpret the next 6 bytes after the JMP opcode as a 4-byte offset and a 2-byte selector, instead of the normal 2 and 2. See Figure 8-2c. Similarly, an operand-size prefix with the second form of JMP instruction, shown in Figure 8-2d, will cause the 80386 to fetch a 6-byte operand from memory and use it as a segment:offset pair.

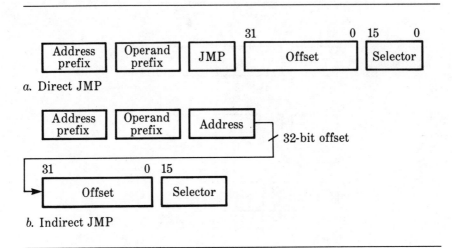

a. Direct JMP

b. Indirect JMP

Figure 8-3.   Intersegment JMP from 16-bit code with address-size override

Even though the pointer referenced by the indirect JMP instruction will be used as an address in the new code segment, you must use an operand-size override, not an address-size override. An address-size override will have no effect on the first type of JMP instruction illustrated, because no memory references are being made. An address-size override may affect the second form by causing the 80386 to look elsewhere for the selector and offset parameters. The effects are shown in Figure 8-3.

CALLING BETWEEN 16-BIT AND 32-BIT CODE

The problem with mismatched offset addresses also occurs when you use CALL and RET instructions to transfer control between 16-bit code segments and 32-bit code segments. The problem in this case is compounded, however, because call and return procedures involve implicit stack references. You must therefore pay careful attention to the default address size defined for your current stack segment.

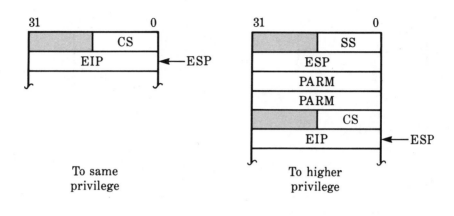

Figure 8-4.   32-bit call/return stack

32-Bit Code Calling 32-Bit Code

When a program in a 32-bit code segment executes an intersegment CALL instruction that targets another 32-bit code segment, using a 32-bit stack segment (the case assumed throughout this book), the 80386 pushes the current CS selector and EIP onto the stack. The stack pointer is then decremented by 8 (two 32-bit words = 8 bytes). If the destination code segment is of a higher privilege level than your calling code, the CALL instruction must reference a call gate, and the 80386 pushes your original SS selector and ESP, along with the specified number of 32-bit parameters. These cases are illustrated in Figure 8-4. When the destination code executes a RET instruction, this process is automatically reversed. The important points to remember are

- The CALL instruction specifies a 32-bit offset into the target code because the default operand size is 32 bits.
- All registers (EIP, ESP) are saved as 32-bit quantities because the default operand size is 32 bits.

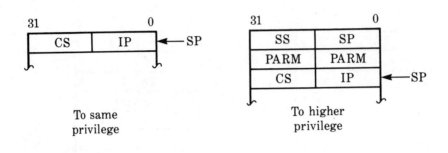

Figure 8-5.   16-bit call/return stack

- All data is pushed using a 32-bit stack pointer (ESP) because the stack address size is 32 bits.

- All parameters copied from the outgoing stack to the incoming stack are 32-bit quantities because the call gate is a 32-bit gate. (This is described later.)

- When the destination code returns, it removes 32-bit registers (EIP, ESP) from the stack because its default operand size is 32 bits.

- The destination code uses a 32-bit stack pointer (ESP) because the stack address size is 32 bits.

16-Bit Code Calling 16-Bit Code

If you invert the previous case and have all 16-bit code and all 16-bit data, everything will run smoothly. In fact, the 80386 will operate as though it were an 80286. The arrangement of the stack after such transfers is illustrated in Figure 8-5. As before, the determining characteristics are

- The CALL instruction specifies a 16-bit offset to which to transfer control.

- All registers (IP, SP) are saved as 16-bit quantities.

- The stack pointer is contained in SP.
- All parameters are 16 bits each.
- 16-bit return pointers are restored upon return.
- Return pointers are located through SP.

32-Bit Code Calling
16-Bit Code

The previous two cases represent "pure" 80386 code and "pure" 80286 code. Both are trivial and operate without any special consideration on the part of the programmer. When you want to call 16-bit (80286) code from 32-bit (80386) code, you must take some special steps to ensure that your stack is maintained properly.

When transferring control with a CALL or RET instruction between code segments with dissimilar sizes (16-bit versus 32-bit), you must consider five attributes:

- The operand size of the calling code, which determines the offset address to which control is to be transferred and also the size of the return pointers pushed on the stack
- The address size of the calling code, which may affect how parameters are addressed on the stack
- The operand size of the target code, which determines the size of the operands to be removed from the stack, including return pointers
- The address size of the target code, which might affect how parameters are addressed
- The address size of the stack segment, which determines which stack pointer is used, SP or ESP

Clearly, if the calling procedure pushes a 32-bit instruction pointer, the returning procedure must restore it correctly. Likewise, if a privilege change has taken place, a 32-bit ESP will need to be retrieved from the stack.

Either one side or the other must be made to conform. If the CALL is not going to change privilege levels or pass through a call gate, this consists mainly of inserting a well-placed operand-size override. It can be placed either before the CALL instruction (making it a 16-bit CALL) or before the RET instruction (making it a 32-bit RET). This forces operand alignment and agreement between the two procedures. If you are going to use a 16-bit CALL (operand prefix before the CALL, no prefix before the RET), be certain that your CALL instruction is executing within the first 64KB of the code segment. Because only the lower 16 bits of EIP will be saved, it is impossible to return to any address greater than FFFF.

Using Call Gates

If you are using a call gate, the solution is much different,

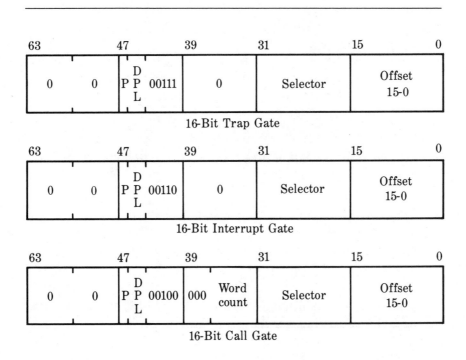

Figure 8-6.   16-bit gate descriptors

although no more difficult. Most gates are assigned sizes, just as code and stack segments are. Thus far, only one size of call gate, interrupt gate, and trap gate has been covered. In fact, there are two forms of each of these gates, 16-bit and 32-bit. The gates presented in Chapters 3, 4, and 5 were all 32-bit gates. Figure 8-6 shows the format of the three 16-bit versions.

When an intersegment CALL instruction references a call gate instead of a code segment selector, the operand size enforced is not determined by the default operand size of the calling segment, nor by any operand-size prefixes that may appear with the CALL. Instead, the 80386 uses the operand size determined by the call gate itself. The gate descriptor's size attribute (16-bit versus 32-bit) provides the 80386 with one overriding operand size. When a 16-bit call gate is used, all offsets are 16 bits, 16-bit registers are pushed and popped from the stack, and 16-bit parameters are copied from caller to callee. When the target 16-bit code returns, it naturally uses 16-bit operands because it is in a 16-bit segment.

When you move from 32-bit code to 16-bit code, be sure that you are executing within the lowest 64KB of the 32-bit segment. The 16-bit caller cannot return to an address greater than FFFF. Because only half of EIP is saved, any overflow is truncated, and the 80386 may return to an improper address. If the call gate will copy parameters, remember that a 16-bit gate will copy 16-bit parameters, regardless of any operand-size overrides you try to use. If the gate causes a change in privilege, a 16-bit gate will preserve only the lower half of the caller's ESP. Be sure that the caller's stack pointer is not above this limit.

Call gates

- Gates can be 16-bit size or 32-bit size

- Gate size overrides all other operand and address sizes

- Gate size should match destination code size

- 16-bit call gates copy 16-bit parameters

16-Bit Code Calling
32-Bit Code

All of the same problems arise when 16-bit (80286) code is calling 32-bit (80386) code. One problem is reversed, however. Whereas a 16-bit procedure cannot return control to a 32-bit address that is greater than 64KB, a 16-bit caller is not able to specify a target offset above the first 64KB in the 32-bit code segment.

Again, a call gate is useful here, even if no privilege change is anticipated. By using the gate, you can ensure that all parameters that are passed match, both coming and going. This is true as long as the operand size of the gate matches the default operand size of the destination code segment. There is an added advantage to using a 32-bit gate when you are calling from 16-bit code to 32-bit code: the gate descriptor has a 32-bit Offset field, and so you can transfer control to any desired target offset in the 32-bit code segment. An RET instruction in a 32-bit code segment can, of course, return control to any valid offset in a caller's 16-bit segment.

16-BIT INTERRUPT
HANDLERS

Just as you can create 16-bit and 32-bit versions of the call gate, you can create either 16-bit or 32-bit interrupt and trap gates. When you place 16-bit gates in the IDT, the 80386 performs a 16-bit transfer to 16-bit code whenever an exception or interrupt occurs that vectors to one of these gates. This feature allows you to use older, existing exception handlers that may have been written or debugged on an 80286. Because the error codes for exceptions 8 and 10 through 14 are all only 16 bits wide, they can easily be put on the stack of a 16-bit exception handler.

As nicely as this appears to work, there is one thing that a 16-bit exception handler cannot do, and that is return to a 32-bit program that was executing beyond the first 64KB of its code. Since most exceptions, and especially hardware interrupts, can occur at unpredictable moments, it is unwise to use 16-bit exception handlers and 16-bit IDT gates unless *all* of your code segments are smaller than 64KB.

16-BIT DESCRIPTORS

The deciding factor when you are creating a 16-bit code, data, or stack segment is clearing the Default operand-size bit (D bit) in the segment descriptor. If your goal is complete 80286 emulation, you need to zero a couple of other descriptor fields as well.

When the 80286 is operating in Protected mode, it enforces some addressing limitations that the 80386 doesn't have. Specifically,

- Segment base addresses are limited to 24 bits (16MB).
- Segment limits are limited to 16 bits (64KB).
- The operand/address-size bit is always 0 (16-bit).
- Segment limit granularity is always set to units of 1 byte.

If you review how code and data segment descriptor fields are arranged, you will see that all of these criteria are met at once if the upper 2 bytes of the descriptor are both 0. The experienced 80286 programmer will recall that all Protected mode 80286 segment descriptors required these 2 bytes to be 0 for future 80386 compatibility.

16-BIT TASKS

Just as there are 16-bit code and data segments and 16-bit trap, interrupt, and call gates, there are also 16-bit task state segments (TSSs). A 16-bit TSS represents the ultimate in 80286 compatibility. If your older, 16-bit 80286 code involves multitasking and you don't want to port it to a full 80386 environment, you can host your 80286 code on an 80386 using 16-bit TSSs. The format of an 80286 TSS and TSS descriptor is shown in Figure 8-7. Experienced 80286 programmers will recognize this format. Those who have never used an 80286 are advised that an 80286 TSS is not merely half of an 80386 TSS.

In an 80286 TSS, only the least significant half of the eight general-purpose registers is stored. Consequently, any extended, 32-bit operations that you might perform (using operand-size override prefixes) will be lost after a task switch. Of course, if you

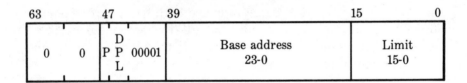

LDT Selector	DS	28
SS	CS	24
ES	DI	20
SI	BP	1C
SP	BX	18
DX	CX	14
AX	FLAGS	10
IP	SP2	0C
SS2	SP1	8
SS1	SP0	4
SS0	Back link	0

31   15   0

63   47   39   15   0

| 0 | 0 | D P P L | 00001 | Base address 23-0 | Limit 15-0 |

Figure 8-7.   80286 TSS and TSS descriptor

are running true 80286 code without modification, there will be no 32-bit operations to worry about. The 80286 TSS does not save registers FS or GS. Again, this will not be a problem unless you add segment override prefixes to your code.

Because the 80286 does not have a paging MMU, no provision is made for storing CR3 (the page directory base register) in a 16-bit TSS. Therefore, switching into or out of 80286 tasks will not change CR3 when paging is enabled. The 80286 task will inherit the page tables of the task that preceded it. You should either give all tasks the same page tables or carefully control use of the 80286 tasks.

An 80286 TSS is also missing the I/O bit map offset field and the Trap flag bit. Neither of these features was supported on the 80286. If an 80286 task does not have permission to perform I/O operations (CPL > IOPL), it will generate a general protection fault. Because there is no Trap bit, the 80386 will not notify your debug handler (exception 1) when an 80286 task is awakened.

There is no 16-bit form of task gate. When a task gate is placed in the GDT or IDT, the 80386 refers to the TSS descriptor to determine the type of task.

80286 COMPATIBILITY

Over time, Intel has made enormous improvements in the performance and capabilities of the iAPX 86 microprocessor family. At the same time, every attempt has been made to maintain compatibility at every level, particularly with respect to binary (object) code. Because the original 8086 instruction set was extremely lopsided and nonorthogonal, it is increasingly difficult to make improvements without giving up some measure of compatibility. Because the 80286 and 80386 microprocessors are so similar, there were very few trade-offs. Unless your original 80286 code was dependent on undocumented quirks of the 80286's microcode, you should not encounter any anomalous behavior when porting to an 80386 environment. The following is a brief list of some things you may need to watch out for.

16-Megabyte Address Wrap

The 80286 has 24 external address bus pins, giving it a 16MB physical address range. As is the case with all segmented memory processors, it is possible to produce a linear address on the 80286 that is greater than the physical limit. If an address goes beyond

FFFFFF, it is internally truncated, effectively wrapping around the upper end of the address space and reappearing at the low end. If you want to emulate this effect in the 80386, you can do so with paging. Simply create your page tables such that the first 16MB of the 80286 task's linear address space is identity-mapped. Then map the seventeenth MB into the same physical memory as the first MB. Although the linear address will no longer truncate and wrap, the physical address will.

Be forewarned that 80286 TSSs do not keep their own page tables, so if you are going to use this feature, it will unfortunately have to be in effect for all tasks.

Descriptor Differences

Obviously, the 80286 has no 32-bit segment or gate descriptors. These values in the Access Rights byte of a descriptor are invalid and cause a fault if used. On the 80386, of course, they define valid 32-bit descriptors. If your 80286 code uses any of these previously undefined values, depending on the processor to generate a fault, it will need to be changed. Intel has guaranteed that Access Rights byte values of 00 and 80 will always be invalid.

As was mentioned before, the most significant 2 bytes of every 8-byte descriptor are reserved on the 80286. It has been heartily recommended that the systems programmer store 0s in them. If, instead, your code stores miscellaneous information in the upper 2 bytes of working segment descriptors, you will almost certainly get bizarre errors when you attempt to run it on an 80386. The 80386 will read and interpret all 8 bytes of a descriptor, even if the Default operand- or address-size bit is set for 80286 compatibility.

Previously Undefined Opcodes

The 80386 has several new instructions. If your 80286 code uses illegal opcodes to generate faults, look closely at which values you used. The new 80386 instructions and their opcodes are as follows:

LSS/LFS/LGS	0F B2/0F B4/0F B5
Conditional JMP	0F 80 through 0F 87
BSF/BSR	0F BC/0F BD
BT/BTC/BTR/BTS	0F BA/0F A3/0F BB/0F B3/0F AB
MOV to/from control registers	0F 20/0F 22
MOV to/from debug registers	0F 21/0F 23
MOV to/from test registers	0F 24/0F 26
MOVSX	0F BE, 0F BF
MOVZX	0F B6, 0F B7
IMUL reg, reg/mem	0F AF
Conditional SET	0F 90 through 0F 97
SHLD/SHRD	0F A4, 0F A5/0F AC, 0F AD

Prefixes:	
FS	64
GS	65
Operand Size	66
Address Size	67

Restrictions on the
LOCK Prefix

You can use the LOCK prefix (F0) to ensure an indivisible read-modify-write bus cycle when updating memory in a multiprocessor system. Previously, the LOCK prefix could be used with any instruction, whether it performed a memory cycle or not. It could be scattered freely throughout the code and could cause no harm. The 80386 is considerably more finicky about where the LOCK prefix can be used. Only the following instructions can legitimately be locked:

BTS/BTR/BTS

XCHG

ADD, ADC, SUB, SBB, INC, DEC

OR, AND, XOR, NOT, NEG

The 80386 generates an invalid-opcode fault (exception 6) if a LOCK prefix precedes any other instruction.

This concludes the discussion of 16-bit Protected mode support (80286 emulation). In the next chapter you will see how to undertake the much more involved task of 8086 emulation.

9

8086 EMULATION

Since its commercial introduction in 1981, the 8086 microprocessor (and its twin, the 8088) has found immediate acceptance and widespread use throughout the world. The most visible and most highly publicized use of the 8086/88 was in second-generation personal computers, notably the IBM Personal Computer and Personal Computer XT. These small, popular machines fueled a wave of personal computer purchases by small businesses, students, homeowners, and hackers who could afford them.

At first, little or no software was available for these machines, which used an unusual microprocessor (unusual defined as anything other than a 6502) and the equally unusual MS-DOS operating system. A cottage industry soon developed to supply add-in Z80 microprocessors so that PC owners could run the then-dominant CP/M operating system and popular applications programs.

Whether for good or ill, MS-DOS caught on and is currently the de facto standard for small business machines. Consequently, an enormous amount of software has been developed to operate on 8086/88-based machines running MS-DOS or some variation.

When Intel released the 80286 in 1983, it represented a quantum leap in performance and capabilities over the 8086. The 80286 was instantly snapped up by personal computer makers and appeared in the IBM Personal Computer AT and its ilk. In particular, the 80286 introduced the Protected Virtual Address mode of operation, very similar to that used today in the 80386. Unfortunately, the prevailing software of the time was in no way capable of exploiting any of the new features of the 80286, least of all Protected mode addressing, and users were understandably loath to abandon their operating system and applications for something totally new. Consequently, the great majority of 80286-based machines in use today are running in Real Address mode as speedier 8086s.

The design of the 80386 undoubtedly posed something of a dilemma to the engineers at Intel. Many new enhancements to the iAPX 286 standard were planned, not the least of which was a full 32-bit architecture and the addition of a paging MMU. Clearly, however, they couldn't afford to turn their backs on 8086 and 80286 compatibility, or a large portion of the 80386's intended market would never materialize.

Because the 80286 introduced Protected mode, providing compatibility with the 80286 was not particularly difficult (as long as it too is running in Protected mode). This subject was covered in Chapter 8. Providing 8086 emulation proved considerably more difficult. For this reason, the 80386 has a separate, distinct 8086 compatibility mode, which will be referred to here as Virtual 8086 mode, or VM86. This chapter explores how 8086 compatibility is achieved, how you can run 8086, 80286, and 80386 code concurrently, and how you can create multiple virtual 8086s at the same time. It also points out flaws in the 80386's emulation.

Most readers will want to use the 80386's 8086 emulation mode to run older, unmodified programs that they do not wish to recompile or are not able to recompile without access to the source code. If so, multitasking can be used in conjunction with VM86 to create the impression of several 8086-based machines on one 80386. This might be more appealing than actually having multiple 8086 processors, both from a cost point of view and because it reduces space requirements and eliminates networking restrictions. With a properly designed 80386 system, you can have multiple 8086 "processes" instead of several 8086 "processors." You might also use the 80386 merely as a faster single-processor 8086 system. Depending on external hardware design factors (such as memory bandwidth), speed improvements of 2400% (25×) over popular 8088 systems are not unusual.

Because the advanced 80386 programmer can easily intermix 16-bit 8086 code, 16-bit 80286 code, and 32-bit 80386 code on the same processor and communicate among tasks, it is possible to create 8086 applications that run under an 80386 operating system. Likewise, you can have 80386 applications running under an 80286 operating system and making calls to an 8086 library. Some combinations are more difficult to implement than others, but almost anything is possible.

VIRTUAL 8086 TASKS

On the 80386, emulation of the 8086 processor is task oriented. That is, 8086 emulation is defined on a task-by-task basis. A task is either a VM86 task or it is not. The program or programs that are defined to be part of that task can freely transfer control into and out of various segments and make intersegment procedure calls, but it is all done 8086-style, between 8086-style code segments using 8086-style data and stack. This is not to say that VM86 tasks cannot interface or cooperate with other, non-8086 tasks, but they must do so using the task-to-task communication procedures outlined in Chapter 6. A VM86 task cannot execute a FAR CALL instruction to a 32-bit 80386 procedure and have the procedure return to it. When you create a task to run in Virtual 8086 mode, it's there to stay.

In the previous chapter, you saw how to define 80286-style code on a segment-by-segment basis. By defining a code segment's descriptor with the D (Default operand-size) bit cleared, you can control how the 80386 interprets and executes the contents of that segment. Similarly, data and stack segments can be defined with the 16-bit (D=0) attribute to create 80286-style data segments and stack space. Apart from these segment definitions, no other work is necessary to create a virtual 80286.

The mechanism for enabling 8086 emulation is much different. Rather than being merely an attribute of the currently executing segment, 8086 characteristics are in effect for an entire task, regardless of segment usage, as was mentioned previously. Specifically, Virtual 8086 mode is enabled when the VM flag (bit 17) in the EFLAGS register is set. When VM is reset, the 80386 reverts to Protected mode, and the 16-bit/32-bit definition of the current code segment's D bit holds sway.

Because the VM bit is held in the EFLAGS register, any instruction that can manipulate EFLAGS can potentially enable or disable Virtual 8086 mode. Typically, this is done only as a result of a task switch, although an IRET instruction works just as well. A POPF instruction will not affect the current setting of the VM bit; it is specifically microcoded not to do so. A later section covers transitions between Protected mode and Virtual 8086 mode in more detail.

Ordinarily, a program can push a copy of EFLAGS onto the stack and then examine it to determine the status of various flags, including VM. Because the VM flag is in the upper word of EFLAGS, however, 16-bit 8086 programs are not able to examine that bit to determine its status. Presumably, carried-over 8086 programs would not be written to do so anyway. Any program that *can* push all 32 bits of EFLAGS must not be running in a VM86 task, and so again the point is moot.

MEMORY SEGMENTATION

Before delving too deeply into the hows and whys of enabling Virtual 8086 mode, let's examine what 8086 emulation gets you. First, you will take a look at the memory model used in a VM86 task and see how segmentation works.

As you might expect, the segmentation system that the 80386 uses in Virtual 8086 mode is exactly like the system an 8086/88/186/188 would use. That is, there are no descriptor tables, no descriptors, no segment selectors, and no RPL fields. Segment registers become plain old paragraph base registers. You can load any value you want, from 0000 to FFFF, into any of the segment registers, and it will be treated as the paragraph-aligned base address of a segment, as it would be by the 8086. All segments are exactly 64KB long—no more, no less.

All of the protection- and privilege-related information associated with Protected mode segment descriptors completely vanishes once the 80386 enters Virtual 8086 mode. Your descriptor tables will not be destroyed, of course—just temporarily rendered superfluous. Memory space that might have been undefined by segment descriptors is now perfectly accessible. Segments that had been defined with privileged DPLs are completely unprotected, and read-only segments can be written into. Remember, you're dealing with an 8086 now; it just happens to be housed in a 132-pin package. When (or if) your software returns to Protected mode, order will be restored.

As they are with a standard 8086 family processor, all segments are 64KB long and can begin at any paragraph (16-byte) boundary. Because the segment (base) registers are themselves 16 bits wide, this gives you an address space of exactly 1MB (20 bits). For example, if you were to load segment register DS with the value 0000, you could directly address memory from 00000 to 0FFFF through that segment. Similarly, if DS holds F000, you can produce addresses from F0000 through FFFFF. If a segment register holds a paragraph base greater than F000, it is possible to produce addresses greater than the 1MB limit. How this is handled on the 80386 is discussed in a later section.

Obviously, the major goal of the Virtual 8086 mode of operation is to duplicate the functions of a five-year-old 16-bit processor as accurately as possible on a 32-bit processor with a radically different addressing mechanism. At the same time, the 80386 operating in Virtual 8086 mode offers some features that the original 8086 never had. A complete list of the differences will be presented later on, but one bonus worth noting here is that a VM86 program has access to the 80386's two newest segment registers, FS and GS.

If you want, you can write your 8086-compatible software to take advantage of these two new segments. Obviously, older 8086/88 software would never use these segments, since they were nonexistent before the introduction of the 80386. If they prove useful, help yourself. Just as they are in Protected mode, the FS and GS segments are never used by default on any operation. They must be requested explicitly with the FS or GS segment overrides (64 and 65, respectively). Keep in mind that any new

software you write, and any older software you modify to take
advantage of this 80386 bonus (or any of the other 80386-only features discussed in this chapter), will no longer be backward compatible. If you try to run such a program on a genuine 8086, it will
bomb with an illegal opcode exception. Being able to modify old
code to use the two new segment registers can be a real lifesaver
if you are segment bound, but it's a one-way trip.

Virtual 8086 mode addressing

- All memory segments are created equal.

- All segments are exactly 64KB long.

- Memory is not protected (no types or privilege levels).

- Descriptors and descriptor tables are ignored.

- Segment registers do not hold selectors.

PRIVILEGE AND PROTECTION

The 8086 family of processors had no means of implementing
memory protection, and so it is with the 80386 running a Virtual
8086 program or task. No distinction is made between code space,
data space, and stack space. There are no upper or lower bounds
on segments, other than what you can address with your segment
and index registers. There is no such thing as a not-present segment or a privileged segment. All of the careful planning you did
to restrict access to private code and data is for naught when the
VM bit in EFLAGS is set. To a VM86 program, an address is an
address is an address. One consolation is that VM86 programs are
limited to the first 1MB of the linear address space, since an 8086
cannot generate addresses greater than that. As you will see, a
VM86 program's access to the physical space is a very different
matter.

No privilege levels are enforced on the code or data used by a Virtual 8086 program. Instead, the 80386 enforces a kind of group privilege level on all VM86 tasks. Whenever VM is set (the processor is operating in Virtual 8086 mode), your effective CPL is always 3. This is important to keep in mind when your VM86 tasks need to interact with Protected mode tasks or programs. It also effectively limits your ability to execute certain instructions. Recall from the discussion of privilege protection in Chapter 3 that certain 80386 instructions are privileged; they can be executed only if CPL equals 0. This precludes VM86 programs from executing any of the following instructions:

HLT
CLTS
LGDT
LIDT
LLDT, SLDT
LTR, STR
LMSW
LAR, LSL
ARPL
VERR, VERW
MOV to/from control registers
MOV to/from debug registers
MOV to/from test registers

Note that the majority of these are instructions that did not exist on the 8086 anyway, and so they are not likely to cause compatibility problems.

The 80386 also implements several IOPL-sensitive instructions. Recall that IOPL is a 2-bit field in EFLAGS that specifies the minimum privilege level required to execute certain I/O-related instructions. Even though IOPL resides in EFLAGS, it is not easily changed by applications software. This aids in the building of a secure, protected system.

Because a VM86 program has a fixed privilege level of 3, it is never able to alter the IOPL bits and so might be granted or denied I/O permission when its TSS is first created. In Protected mode, a task that has been denied I/O permission (CPL > IOPL) might still be able to access certain I/O locations if an I/O Permission bit map has been defined in its TSS.

In Virtual 8086 mode, both the IOPL field and the I/O Permission bit map are used, but both have very different functions than they do in Protected mode. In Virtual 8086 mode, IOPL controls the right to execute the following instructions only:

CLI, STI
PUSHF, POPF
LOCK
INT n
IRET

Note that the actual I/O instructions, namely IN, OUT, INS, and OUTS, are not controlled by IOPL. Instead, these four instructions are controlled solely by the VM86 task's I/O Permission bit map (if one is defined). If the bits corresponding to the I/O locations being accessed are clear, I/O access is permitted. Otherwise, the I/O instruction causes a general protection fault.

Why the change in the function of IOPL? This was done to accomplish two things: to protect EFLAGS and to control interrupts. Note that all of the newly IOPL-sensitive instructions just listed affect either the processor flags or the return stack, or both. The rationale for this is that 8086 programs are used to running alone, and they enjoy complete control of the processor and system. On an 80386-based system, this may no longer be true, and you might not want a transplanted 8086 application running under a shiny new 80386 multitasking operating system to disable interrupts whenever it feels like it. By the same token, the 80386 does not handle interrupts and exceptions in the same way an 8086 would, even in Virtual 8086 mode, and so software-generated exceptions must be handled with care. This subject will be expanded on later.

Privilege protection in Virtual 8086 mode

- The IOPL field controls execution of sensitive instructions.

- I/O instructions are not affected by IOPL.

- The I/O Permission bit map field in TSS controls I/O access.

80386 ENHANCEMENTS

When the 80386 operates in Virtual 8086 mode, it implements a superset of 8086 functions and capabilities. A VM86 program can do everything a native 8086 program can do and a little bit more. The ability to use the two 80386 segment registers, FS and GS, is one example. This does not compromise 8086 compatibility in any way, since no capabilities are being removed, only added. A transplanted 8086 program will be blissfully unaware of the fact that it is running on an 80386 with some additional features. If you want to develop new software that runs in Virtual 8086 mode, you may be able to avail yourself of some of the bonus features.

In addition to the two extra segments, a VM86 program has access to the 80386's 32-bit register set. For example, it is possible to perform 32-bit multiplication, division, and logic instructions, as shown here:

```
MUL     ESI                 ;EDX:EAX = EAX x ESI
NOP
DIV     EBP                 ;EAX = EDX:EAX / EBP; EDX = remainder
NOP
AND     EBX, ECX            ;EBX = EBX (AND) ECX
```

A VM86 program can also perform 32-bit memory accesses. In short, all operations that can be either byte or word sized can also be dword-sized. You use the nonstandard operand size in the same way as an 80286-compatible program does: with an operand-size override prefix byte (66). Whenever the 80386 encounters an operand-size override immediately before a 16-bit operation, it temporarily converts the word-wide reference to a dword-wide reference. Just as it is in Protected mode, an operand-size override is in effect for one instruction only, and it does not affect byte-wide operations.

Virtual 8086 mode does not grant you access to any of the new 80386 memory management or debugging registers. The control registers CR0 through CR3, test registers TR6 and TR7, and debug registers DR0 through DR7 are not accessible from a VM86 program. Oddly, GDTR, IDTR, and MSW (CR0 bits 0 through 15) can be read from a VM86 program. Their contents cannot be altered, however. The reason the new registers are not generally accessible is that they are protected. Only PL 0 programs can alter the debugging and MMU registers. Because a VM86 program is perpetually running with an effective privilege level of 3, these registers are off-limits.

In addition to the increased operand size, a VM86 program can use the extended instruction set of the 80386. The three lists that follow give the incremental enhancements made to the original 8086 instruction set that can be utilized by a VM86 program.

The following instructions first appeared on the 80186:

BOUND
ENTER, LEAVE
INS, OUTS
PUSHA, POPA

The next instructions first appeared on the 80286:

PUSH immediate data
IMUL immediate data
SAL, SAR, SHL, SHR, RCL, RCR, ROL, ROR immediate
    count

These instructions first appeared on the 80386:

MOVZX, MOVSX
SET*cc*
J*cc* with 32-bit displacement
BT, BTC, BTS, BTR
BSF, BSR
SHLD, SHRD
IMUL with any destination register
LFS, LGS, LSS

Of course, when you are operating in Virtual 8086 mode, you lose the ability to reference memory using 80386-style addressing modes. Not all registers can be used as indirect address pointers, and scaled addressing is not supported. For those readers who have been spoiled by the 80386's addressing options, the following table summarizes the addressing modes available on an 8086 (virtual or otherwise). Choose one from the first column, one from the second column, and one from the third column.

Base Register	Index Register	Immediate Displacement
None	None	None
BX	SI	0-FF
BP	DI	0-FFFF

Memory addressing options in Virtual 8086 mode

- Segment registers FS and GS are available.

- 32-bit offset addresses can be used.

- 32-bit quantities in memory can be used directly.

- New 80186, 80286, and 80386 instructions are available.

- Only 8086 addressing modes can be used.

ENTERING VIRTUAL 8086 MODE

The 80386 begins operating in Virtual 8086 mode whenever bit 17 (the VM flag) in the EFLAGS register is set. This is not as easy as it may sound. A normal PUSHF instruction followed by some stack manipulation and a POPF instruction won't do it. POPF is specifically constructed so that it will not alter the current status of VM. The only other ways to alter EFLAGS are through a task switch or an interrupt return.

Task switching is the preferred method for initiating Virtual 8086 mode operation. Typically, your 8086 programs will need to be kept separate from Protected mode code and data. By segregating all 8086 programs into one or more tasks, you make things much easier on yourself. When VM86 interrupts and exceptions are discussed in a later section, the benefits will become more evident.

When you create a TSS that will be used by a virtual 8086 task, simply set the VM bit in the EFLAGS image (byte offset 36, bit offset 17). When the 80386 switches into this task, it finds VM set and loads all segments and interprets all addresses and instructions 8086-style. Ironically, all VM86 tasks must be defined by an 80386 TSS descriptor. 80286 TSSs store only the lower 16 bits of the CPU registers, including EFLAGS. Because the VM flag is in the upper half of EFLAGS, an 80286 TSS cannot be used to store an 8086 task's state!

When the 80386 performs a task switch into an 80386 TSS (even one marked for Virtual 8086 mode), it loads the full 32-bit registers EAX through EDX and ESI through ESP. If your VM86 task uses the extended registers, their contents will be saved and restored on every task switch, unlike an 80286 task, which loses the upper half of its registers on every swap-out.

Remember to create the TSS with the desired values in each segment register and in EIP. You need not initialize the FS and GS register images if you don't want to. Likewise, the privilege level 1 and 2 stacks do not need to hold anything meaningful. Zeros are recommended. The privilege level 0 stack (SS0 through ESP0) is critical, however, and must point to a valid Protected mode PL 0 stack segment. This requirement is explained in the section on interrupts and exceptions.

The LDT register image should be initialized properly. Even though VM86 tasks do not use descriptor tables, interrupts that occur in the task might. Register CR3 is also loaded when the 80386 invokes a VM86 task. If paging is enabled, CR3 must hold the physical address of the base of your page directory, just as it must in Protected mode. As was pointed out earlier, the IOPL field and I/O Permission bit map serve somewhat different functions in Virtual 8086 mode, so consider how you want to treat them when initializing your TSS.

The other way to begin operating as an 8086 is to push data onto the stack and issue an IRET instruction. Because IRET pops EFLAGS off of the stack right after the return address, it can be made to force a transition into Virtual 8086 mode. This is somewhat trickier than a normal interrupt return because the return stack for a VM86 program or task is different than that for a normal Protected mode program or task; all of the extra information will have to be duplicated before you execute the IRET.

Although it is not as clean as simply task-switching into your 8086 code, an IRET is useful if you are not using multitasking or if a Protected mode program wants to convert itself to Virtual 8086 mode.

INTERRUPTS AND EXCEPTIONS

Hardware interrupts, software exceptions, and processor aborts, traps, and faults are handled differently in Virtual 8086 mode than they are in Protected mode. Technically, exceptions aren't handled in Virtual 8086 mode at all. The 80386 automatically switches from Virtual 8086 mode to Protected mode as the first step in handling any exceptional condition. The exception is then handled by a Protected mode interrupt service routine (ISR). The 80386 will return to Virtual 8086 mode when the ISR executes its final IRET instruction. All of this is more or less transparent to the VM86 program that was interrupted or that generated the exception, unless the VM86 code is itself an interrupt service routine. If you really need to maintain 8086-style ISRs, there is a way to use them, which will be covered shortly. For now, let's take a closer look at the normal case, with a VM86 program using Protected mode ISRs.

Changing from Virtual 8086 Mode to Protected Mode

Every VM86 program must be part of a task; that is, it must have a TSS associated with it. Several virtual 8086 programs can share a task, or each one can be assigned its own task, just like Protected mode programs. How you partition your programs and tasks is up to you.

When a Virtual 8086 program (or a real 8086) needs to push or pop information from the stack, it uses the SS (stack segment) register to locate the base of the stack segment and the SP (stack pointer) register to select a particular offset into that segment. Subroutine calls and returns are typical examples of automatic uses of the stack. You can also use the stack to store variable information temporarily. On a genuine 8086, the stack is also used automatically to store CS, IP, and FLAGS whenever an interrupt or exception occurs. This is one instance in which a VM86 program on the 80386 differs from an actual 8086 implementation. Instead of using the VM86 program's stack (SS:SP), the 80386 pushes all exception information onto the *Protected mode stack for privilege level 0*. The VM86 program's stack is ignored and will not be altered in any way during exception processing. The stack segment selector and 32-bit stack pointer for the PL 0 stack are taken from the VM86 program's TSS. Figure 9-1 highlights the location of the PL 0 stack pointer image in a TSS.

At the time the 80386 recognizes the exception (acknowledges an external interrupt request or discovers a software error), it first switches from Virtual 8086 mode to Protected mode. Then, it locates the current task's TSS (pointed to by TR) and reads the privilege level 0 stack selector and stack pointer. Onto this stack it pushes the current (8086-style) CS, EIP, and EFLAGS. Note that all 32 bits of EIP and EFLAGS are saved. This is necessary, or

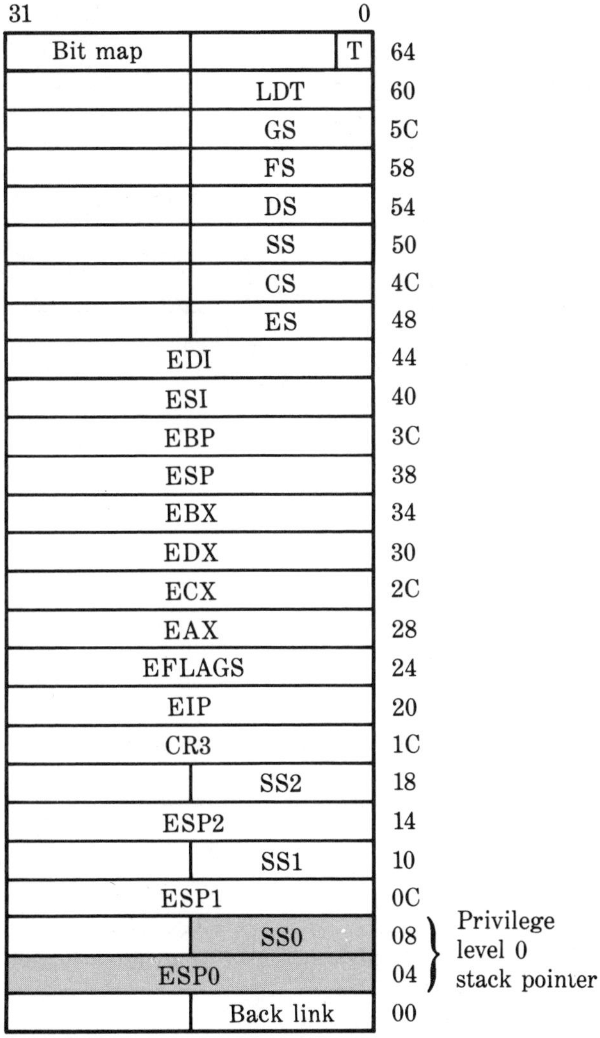

31			0	
Bit map		T		64
	LDT			60
	GS			5C
	FS			58
	DS			54
	SS			50
	CS			4C
	ES			48
EDI				44
ESI				40
EBP				3C
ESP				38
EBX				34
EDX				30
ECX				2C
EAX				28
EFLAGS				24
EIP				20
CR3				1C
	SS2			18
ESP2				14
	SS1			10
ESP1				0C
	SS0			08
ESP0				04
	Back link			00

} Privilege level 0 stack pointer

Figure 9-1.   Location of PL 0 stack pointer in TSS

else the 32-bit Protected mode handler might alter the upper half of either register. Because a privilege transition is about to take place (from level 3 to level 0), SS and ESP are also pushed. If the

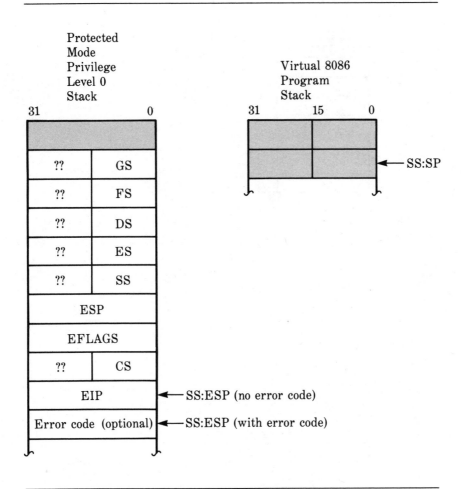

Figure 9-2.   Stack switch from VM86 to Protected mode

exception generated an error code, it is pushed onto the PL 0 stack as well.

One additional step is taken whenever a VM86 program is interrupted. All four data segment registers (DS, ES, FS, and GS) are pushed onto the PL 0 stack, and then these four registers are loaded with 0s. Figure 9-2 shows the finished product after an exception has been taken but before the ISR has begun execution.

> ### Virtual 8086 mode exception processing
>
> - The 80386 automatically changes from Virtual 8086 to Protected mode.
>
> - The Protected mode PL 0 stack is used at all times.
>
> - The Virtual 8086 stack remains unused.
>
> - The 32-bit register contents are saved.
>
> - The four data segment registers are saved.

Why are the four data segments saved and modified? Consider the differences between VM86 memory segmentation and Protected mode segmentation. In Virtual 8086 mode, all segment registers hold simple 16-bit paragraph addresses. Any value from 0000 to FFFF is valid. By contrast, Protected mode segment registers hold selectors. Thirteen bits of the selector select a segment descriptor, one bit selects a descriptor table, and two more bits determine or affect privilege level protection. Not all possible values are valid or even meaningful. If a Protected mode ISR were to begin execution with Virtual 8086 mode values still in its segment registers, it would almost certainly generate memory faults. Therefore, the 80386 must flush all six segment registers during the transition from Virtual 8086 mode to Protected mode. Registers CS and SS are taken care of by the interrupt or trap gate and the VM86 task's TSS, respectively.

Interrupt and trap gates do not hold enough information to specify new values for DS, ES, FS, and GS, and so the 80386 must make a compromise. Obviously, the 8086-style segment registers can't be left as they are, but there is no way for the processor to know what valid Protected mode selectors you want loaded. The only segment selectors that are guaranteed to be valid, regardless of the arrangement of your descriptor tables, are the null selectors. That is why these segments are zeroed during the mode transition. The net result is that your Protected mode ISR begins execution with a valid CS:EIP and SS:ESP, but all other segment registers are 0 if a VM86 program was interrupted. Of course, if the 80386 was running in Protected mode when the exception occurred, the four data segment registers will be unharmed.

For this reason, you must take a few extra steps in your interrupt service routines if there is any possibility of the ISR being invoked from within a VM86 program. Ideally, you should push all segment registers at the beginning of the ISR and then load them with the desired values. Then, at the end of the ISR, you can pop the original segment values before returning, as shown in the following code fragment:

```
        PUBLIC  handler

handler PROC    FAR

        PUSH    DS                      ;save all four data segment
        PUSH    ES                      ;registers/selectors
        PUSH    FS                      ;just in case we are called
        PUSH    GS                      ;from a VM86 task or program

        PUSH    AX                      ;save work register
        MOV     AX, data_segment_selector_1
        MOV     DS, AX                  ;load new selector value
        MOV     ES, AX                  ; "    "    "    "
        MOV     AX, data_segment_selector_2
        MOV     FS, AX                  ;load new selector value
        MOV     GS, AX                  ; "    "    "    "

; Begin servicing exception here ...

        POP     AX                      ;restore work register
        POP     GS                      ;
        POP     FS                      ;restore four data segment
        POP     ES                      ;registers/selectors
        POP     DS                      ;

        IRET                            ;return from exception

handler         ENDP
```

If this ISR is invoked from a Protected mode program or task, it will merely save and then restore the interrupted code's selectors, which is a good idea anyway. If the ISR is invoked by a VM86 program or task, it will push four null selectors and then load valid new selectors. Before returning, the ISR will pop the four null selectors, which is harmless and will not cause any segmentation or privilege violations. By adding this simple preamble and postamble to all 256 ISRs, you can guarantee that they will run regardless of the operating mode at the time of the exception.

If it is important that your ISR code know whether or not it was invoked by a VM86 program, there are two simple tests you can use. First, if all four data segment registers are 0, it's a pretty good bet that they were cleared by an automatic mode transition. Statistically, this is a fairly accurate scheme, but it is not fool-proof. A much better and more reliable test is to examine the VM bit of the EFLAGS image near the top of your stack. If it is set, the 80386 was running as a virtual 8086 when the interrupt, fault, or exception occurred. If it is not, the 80386 was operating in Protected mode (either native 80386 or 80286 compatibility).

The 80386 itself checks this bit when it encounters an IRET instruction. If it finds VM set as it pops EFLAGS off of the stack, it knows that it must restore the four 8086-style segment registers before returning to a VM86 program.

Because of the extra amount of processing involved, interrupt latency is increased somewhat over purely Protected mode operation. The amount of extra time required depends mostly on the memory speed in your computer.

One final note regarding Protected mode ISRs for VM86 programs: if trap or interrupt gates (as opposed to task gates) will be used to handle exceptions, they must meet the following criteria:

- The gate must be an 80386 gate.
- The gate's DPL must equal 3.
- The target code segment's DPL must equal 0.

Control must pass through an 80386 trap gate or 80386 interrupt gate (no 80286 gates) with a gate privilege level of 3, or a general protection fault will result. Additionally, the ISR *must* be in a PL 0 code segment. This ensures that the inevitable IRET instruction will execute at privilege level 0. Only a PL 0 IRET can alter the VM bit in EFLAGS. This is why the PL 0 stack is always used for VM86 exception handling. Since VM86 exceptions must be handled by PL 0 code, and since the same IDT is used by all tasks, whether virtual or protected, this last requirement essentially forces you to place some or all of your interrupt service routines in PL 0 code segments. Specifically, if a particular ISR could ever be invoked while a VM86 program was running, it must be placed in a PL 0 code segment. This list usually includes all external hardware interrupts, NMI, and general protection faults.

Terminating Virtual 8086 mode exception processing

- The interrupt service routine executes an IRET instruction.
- The 80386 removes information from protected PL 0 stack.
- The VM bit in EFLAGS identifies the Virtual 8086 mode caller.
- The 80386 restores four data segment registers.

If you want, you can have one or more exceptions handled by separate tasks by putting a task gate descriptor into the IDT slot corresponding to that exception. When an exception is handled through a task gate, the 80386 automatically initiates a task-switch operation before exception processing begins. After the task switch, execution commences at the instruction to which the new task's EIP points. The interrupted task and the interrupt service task are essentially unrelated. The ISR task can be a native 80386 Protected mode task, an 80286-compatible task, or even another virtual 8086 task.

No stack operations take place when an exception is handled through a task gate; there is no need, since all of the outgoing task's state is saved in its TSS. However, if the offending exception produced an error code, the 80386 is thoughtful enough to push it onto the top of the handling task's stack. If the handling task is also a virtual 8086 task, the stack top is located through SS:SP.

Exceptions vectored through task gates do not have the same restrictions that trap and interrupt gates impose. The privilege level of the handling task does not need to be 0. If the handling task is another VM86 task, its privilege level will be 3. You can freely use 80286 TSS and 80286-compatible tasks to handle virtual 8086 exceptions, if you want. The DPL of the task gate must, however, be set to 3, or the failing VM86 program will not be privileged enough to use the gate.

Using 8086 Exception Handlers

If you want, you can run some of your interrupt and exception handlers in Virtual 8086 mode. The previous section, for instance, described how an exception might vector to a task gate that switches to another Virtual 8086 task. Whenever an exception causes a task switch like this, the 80386 automatically sets the NT (Nested Task) bit in the new task's EFLAGS register, signifying that this task is nested inside another. The new task's TSS will also get a new Back Link field identifying the parent task. This way, the 80386 can determine whether a subsequent IRET instruction should return to another task or to code within the same task.

Unfortunately, the NT bit is checked only when IRET is executed in Protected mode. NT is ignored in Virtual 8086 mode. The net result is that IRET can be used only to set VM, not clear it, and so a Virtual 8086 task cannot return to its parent task with an IRET instruction. This casts some serious gloom over the prospect of maintaining old 8086 exception handlers. Since the only way to invoke an 8086 exception handler directly is through a task gate, and because nested 8086 tasks cannot return to their callers properly, you must use either a Protected mode task (an 80386 task gate or 80286 task gate) or a Protected mode procedure (an 80386 trap gate or 80386 interrupt gate) to handle all Virtual 8086 mode exceptions.

All is not lost, however. Even though the ISR must run in Protected mode, there is no reason why it can't invoke a VM86 program or task as part of its work. This VM86 code can be the original 8086 exception handler. When the 8086 code returns to the Protected mode ISR, the ISR can then execute an IRET instruction to return to the interrupted program. The Protected mode ISR simply acts as a "wrapper" around your original 8086 code.

While this concept is relatively straightforward, the actual execution can be pretty tricky. The steps go something like this:

1. The VM86 program is interrupted or generates an exception. Control is turned over to a PL 0 Protected mode ISR. The VM86 program's state is pushed onto the top of the ISR's stack.

2. Copy IP, CS, and FLAGS (only 16 bits apiece) from the ISR's stack onto the VM86 program's stack, and modify the VM86 program's stack pointer. This simulates the automatic stack operations of an 8086. Note that this step requires a Protected mode program (the ISR) to correctly interpret an 8086-style segment reference (the interrupted program's SS).

3. Store all of the information on the ISR's stack somewhere safe. It is all going to be destroyed soon.

4. Push a 32-bit copy of EFLAGS with bit 17 (VM) set and bits 12 and 13 (IOPL) cleared. Push an 8086-style CS segment and EIP. These should point to the beginning of the desired 8086 code.

5. Execute an IRET instruction. This terminates the Protected mode ISR. When the 80386 pops the return address and EFLAGS, it will appear that you are returning to a Virtual 8086 program within the same task, which is true. However, it will "return" you to the 8086 exception handler, not to the interrupted program.

6. The 8086 ISR should now operate normally. The trick is getting it to return to the Protected mode ISR. Because the current IOPL equals 0, the final IRET instruction will generate a general protection fault. Assuming that your general protection fault handler uses the same PL 0 stack as the first Protected mode ISR, you have just lost the VM86 program information pushed in step 1.

7. Your general protection fault handler (itself a Protected mode program or task) must now turn control over to the first ISR.

8. Remove the three registers pushed in step 2 from the VM86

program's stack, and adjust SP accordingly. This simulates an 8086's execution of an IRET.

9. Restore the information saved in step 3 onto the ISR's stack. Execute another IRET instruction. This terminates your Protected mode ISR, this time popping the return address and EFLAGS register of the originally interrupted program.

10. Execution of the interrupted program resumes.

Variation 1: steps 2 and 8 can be omitted if you know that the 8086-style ISR will not examine the stack. Note that you will never need to copy parameters from stack to stack, as Protected mode call gates do. This is because the interrupted program and the 8086-style ISR share the same stack. If the interrupted program pushed any parameters prior to the exception, they will still be there for the ISR to use.

Variation 2: you can eliminate steps 7, 8, and 9 if you don't mind your 8086 code running unprotected. In step 4, you can push a copy of EFLAGS with bits 12 and 13 (IOPL) both set. This sets IOPL to 3. Execute an IRET instruction. Now the 80386 will "return" to your VM86 ISR, but it will not generate a general protection fault when it executes its final IRET. Instead, the 80386 will return directly to the interrupted program. This is considerably simpler to implement but has the disadvantage that the VM86 ISR must operate with IOPL equal to 3, allowing it to manipulate the Interrupt flag directly, among other things. You may wish to refer back to the list of IOPL-sensitive instructions in Virtual 8086 mode.

Although it should be obvious, it is worth pointing out that a virtual 8086 program does not use an 8086-style interrupt vector table. All interrupts and exceptions are handled through the IDT. If your 8086 programs make a habit of modifying their idea of an interrupt vector table, your Protected mode ISRs that act as wrappers for the Virtual 8086 mode ISRs should keep up-to-date on any changes that are made.

Using 8086 interrupt service routines

- The 80386 cannot directly utilize 8086 ISR code.

- The exception handler must run in Protected mode.

- The exception handler can "reflect" the interrupt to an 8086 ISR.

- The 8086 ISR must return to the Protected mode exception handler.

- The exception handler returns to the interrupted code.

USING IOPL FOR EMULATION

As you know, several instructions in Virtual 8086 mode are IOPL-sensitive. Because CPL equals 3 in Virtual 8086 mode, if IOPL is not equal to 3 and any of the listed instructions are executed, a general protection fault results. Note that none of these instructions perform I/O. Instead, they were chosen to prevent transplanted 8086 programs, which usually have the luxury of owning the entire machine on which they are running, from bombing an otherwise secure 80386 system. Generally, the IOPL-sensitive instructions are related to interrupts and the Interrupt flag. The rationale here is that a multitasking system usually uses hardware interrupts to determine when it is time to schedule a new task (a process known as time-slicing). If a VM86 program disables interrupts for an inordinately long period of time, all manner of bad things might happen.

The CLI, STI, PUSHF, and POPF instructions might be used to examine or modify the Interrupt flag, as was mentioned earlier. By trapping these instructions, you can effectively fool the VM86 program by keeping a side copy of EFLAGS just for its use. This "virtual FLAGS" register can be substituted for the real thing on the stack when a PUSHF is executed, and so forth.

The INT *n* instructions are also trapped because they are often used as calls to an operating system that in all probability doesn't exist anymore. By trapping these, you can choose to either duplicate their functions with new 80386 code or reflect them back onto their original 8086 ISRs, as was outlined in the previous section. Note that the INTO (interrupt on overflow) and INT 3 (breakpoint) instructions are not trapped. Both of them perform identical functions on the 8086 and 80386, so there is no need to do so.

The actual I/O instructions IN, OUT, INS, and OUTS are not IOPL-sensitive, but they are protected. The instructions themselves are not privileged, but the I/O locations they may access are controlled by the current task's I/O Permission bit map, so the effect is the same. By controlling the I/O Permission bit map, you can selectively choose whether to allow physical access to I/O or to trap it. If you trap it, you can provide a number of responses. The I/O address can be remapped, or you can provide "virtual data" or return an error status.

USING PAGING IN VIRTUAL 8086 MODE

Although Protected mode memory segmentation is not used while the 80386 is operating in Virtual 8086 mode, the paging portion of the MMU does work. Recall from the discussion of paging in Chapter 4 that it can be used for address translation, page-level protection, and demand paging. This is still true for virtual 8086 tasks. This section dwells mainly on the usefulness of address translation.

A Virtual 8086 task can generate linear addresses only up to 1MB (plus a little bit, as you will see). Because of this, you may have problems if you are running more than one VM86 task at a time. They're going to contend for the same memory. If you put each VM86 program in a separate TSS and assign each of these TSSs a different set of page tables, you can effectively map each VM86 task anywhere in the 4GB physical space of the 80386. See Figure 9-3. One VM86 task's address 1000 does not have to be another task's 1000. If you desire, you can have the VM86 tasks share some portion of their address spaces, such as ROM or reentrant code.

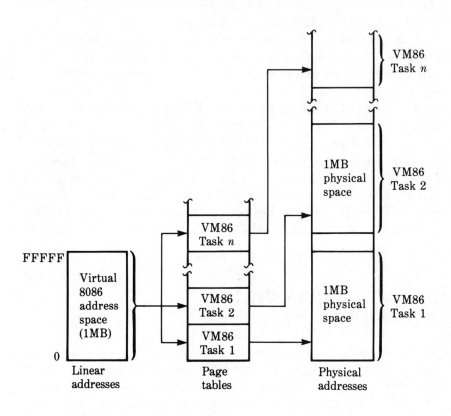

Figure 9-3.   Page translation of multiple VM86 tasks

Each segment register in a VM86 program can hold the paragraph-aligned base address of a different segment of memory. When the segment register is used, its contents are shifted left by 4 bits (multiplied by 16) and added to a 16-bit offset address. This form of addressing is illustrated in Figure 9-4.

If a segment register holds a value greater than F000, it is possible to generate linear addresses greater than 1MB. In fact, if a segment register holds a value of FFFF, it's difficult not to do this. See Figure 9-5. The greatest linear address possible is

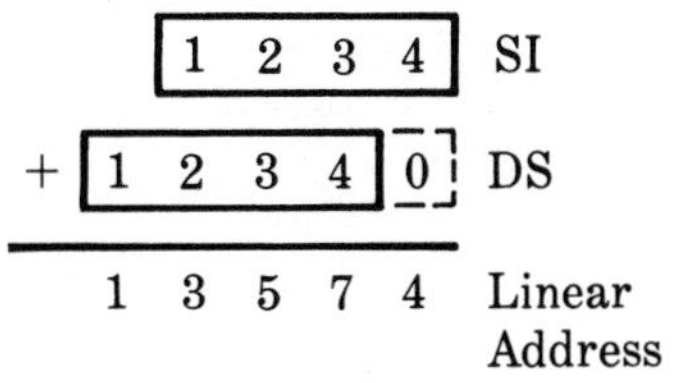

```
            ┌─────────────┐
            │ 1  2  3  4  │  SI
            └─────────────┘
         ┌──────────────┬──┐
      +  │ 1  2  3  4   │0 │  DS
         └──────────────┴──┘
         ────────────────────
            1  3  5  7  4     Linear
                              Address
```

Figure 9-4.   Linear address calculation in Virtual 8086 mode

10FFEF. Because the 8086 had 20-bit-wide address logic, the most significant bit would be dropped, making addresses greater than FFFFF appear to "wrap around" the end of the address space and reappear at the low end. Thus, an address of 10FFEF would actually become FFEF. More than one 8086 programmer has been known to exploit this quirk. Because the 80386 has 32-bit-wide address logic, no such wrap will occur. The address space in Virtual 8086 mode is therefore nearly 64KB larger than on a real 8086. More to the point, programs that rely on a narrow address bus will not work. You can overcome this shortcoming through the judicious use of paging tables. If you map the extra 64KB of linear space to the same physical memory as the first 64KB, the net result is the same. Figure 9-6 shows a sample memory map.

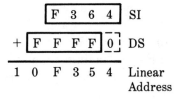

Figure 9-5.   Linear address overflow in Virtual 8086 mode

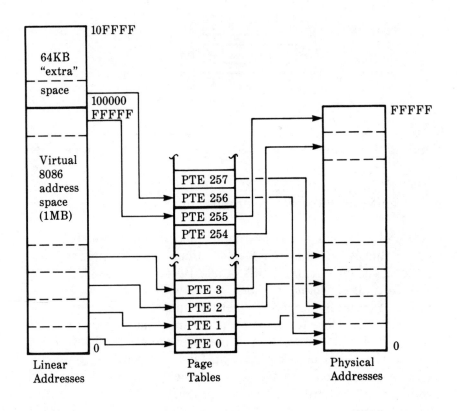

Figure 9-6.   Simulating 1MB address wrap

Because there is no segment-level memory protection in Virtual 8086 mode, the only means available to restrict memory accesses from VM86 programs is through page-level protection. If you mark various PTEs as having supervisor privilege, those pages will not be accessible to VM86 programs, which always run at PL 3. In addition, you can mark PTEs with user privilege but make them read-only. Only if the PTE and its corresponding PDE are both marked user and read/write will full access be allowed.

Paging in Virtual 8086 mode

- Paging MMU functions normally in Virtual 8086 mode.

- Page translation can be used for multiple 8086 tasks.

- Page translation can emulate 1MB "wrap" of an 8086.

- Page-level protection can be used to protect memory.

DIFFERENCES FROM A REAL 8086

Inevitably, there are some features of the 8086 microprocessor that the 80386 does not emulate properly. Often, this is because the 8086 had a bug or other undesirable feature that has since been cleaned up. Other times, the nature of the 80386's 32-bit architecture prohibits precise emulation. At any rate, none of the differences listed here should create severe compatibility problems. Some may even be cause for minor celebration. In no particular order, the differences are as follows:

Divide Error Pointer Is Correct   Divide errors (exception 0) on the 80386 push the address of the offending DIV or IDIV instruction onto the handler's stack. The 8086 would save the address of the instruction *after* the divide. This should aid your divide error handler considerably.

IDIV Range Extended   The 8086 would generate an exception 0 if the IDIV instruction produced a quotient of 80 (-128) for byte division or 8000 (-32768) for word division. This no longer occurs on the 80386.

Address Wrap at 1MB   The 8086's 20-bit address bus could not produce physical addresses greater than FFFFF. Linear addresses above this range would appear to "wrap around" to lower addresses. This no longer occurs on the 80386, but you can duplicate its effect with page translation.

Offset Wrap at 64KB   An 8086 program could not generate logical offset addresses greater than FFFF by virtue of its 16-bit registers. On the 80386, however, a VM86 program can use a size prefix byte to specify 32-bit registers. This enables a VM86 program to produce offsets as great as 4GB. Because all memory segments are exactly 64KB long when the processor is operating in Virtual 8086 mode, the 80386 generates a general protection fault if an offset greater than 64KB is attempted for DS, ES, FS, or GS. A stack fault is generated for offsets greater than 64KB in SS.

Push SP Changed   Pushing SP (the stack pointer register) onto the stack presents something of a chicken-and-egg problem. Do you push the value of SP before or after the push? The 8086 pushed the value of SP after the push operation; the 80386 pushes the value before the push. A simple workaround is shown here:

```
;Simulate an 8086-style "PUSH SP" instruction...

PUSH    BP                          ;save work register and push
MOV     BP, SP                      ;BP gets new stack top pointer
XCHG    BP, WORD PTR SS:[BP]        ;restore BP and copy SP
```

LOCK Instruction   The LOCK instruction prefix can no longer be used haphazardly. The 80386 generates an undefined opcode fault (exception 6) unless LOCK is followed by one of the instructions shown here:

    BT, BTS, BTR, BTC
    XCHG
    ADD, ADC, SUB, SBB
    AND, OR, XOR, NOT, NEG
    INC, DEC

FLAGS Register   The 8086's FLAGS register did not define bits 12, 13, 14, or 15. They would generally be stored as 1s after a PUSHF instruction. On the 80386, bits 12 and 13 are the IOPL field, and bit 14 is the NT flag. These will be stored as their correct values. Bit 15 is still undefined but will be stored as 0.

Coprocessor Error Pointer   A coprocessor (8087) instruction that failed would generate an interrupt, which would cause the address of the coprocessor instruction to be pushed onto the stack. The 80386 operating in Virtual 8086 mode pushes the address of the coprocessor instruction minus any prefix bytes that may have been present. This makes it much easier to restart the failed instruction.

Coprocessor Error Vector = 16   Because the 80386 and 80387 are tightly coupled, the 80387 ERROR signal does not need to be routed through an interrupt controller (typically an 8259). Instead, an 80387 error directly generates an exception 16. Previously, the interrupt controller could assign any vector desired.

Shift and Rotate Instructions   The 8086 bit-shift and rotate instructions could shift or rotate an operand by up to 255 bits. Obviously, anything over 15 was wasted. However, since the processor checks for external hardware interrupts only between instructions, this could unnecessarily lengthen interrupt response time. The 80386 treats all shift and rotate counts modulo 32.

NMI Interrupting NMI   When the 80386 recognizes and services a nonmaskable interrupt, it does not act on any further NMI inputs until the first NMI handler executes an IRET instruction. It "remembers" exactly one incoming NMI during that time, should one occur. In that case, the second NMI will be serviced directly after the first one returns.

Repeated String Instructions   If a repeated string instruction sequence is interrupted, the return address saved on the stack takes into account any instruction prefixes that were present. The 8086 excluded prefixes.

Instruction Length Limit No single instruction encoding can be longer than 15 bytes or the 80386 will generate a general protection fault. This can occur only if you place redundant prefixes in the object code.

Single-Stepping ISRs If an interrupt occurs while single-stepping is enabled, the 80386 suspends single-stepping until the interrupt handler is done executing.

Previously Undefined Opcodes The 80386 has many more instructions than the 8086. Therefore, many previously undefined opcodes now execute valid 80386 instructions. Some of these are legal in Virtual 8086 mode and some are not, but none is likely to do what an 8086 program intended.

Speed Perhaps the most apparent difference between a given program running on an 8086 and under Virtual 8086 mode on an 80386 is speed. 80386 microprocessors start at 16MHz operating frequency and can go higher than 30MHz. By contrast, most common 8086/88-based machines run at between 4 and 6 MHz. Add to this the fact that an 80386 can often execute the same instructions as an 8086 in fewer clock cycles, and the difference is even more marked. By and large, this is not considered a problem. You must be careful about programs that have software timing or wait loops. Communications programs and games are notorious for these. As a rule of thumb, you can expect unmodified 8086 object code to run 5 to 25 times faster on an 80386.

In this chapter you have seen how the 80386 can be made to emulate the operation of an 8086 microprocessor. The Virtual 8086 mode of operation, creation of VM86 tasks, transitions into and out of 8086 mode, VM86 interrupt handling, and special 80386-only features were covered. Now, of course, you can create or port

8086, 80286, and 80386 software and watch it run flawlessly the first time. If, perchance, your code develops some "undocumented features" in the process, the next chapter will provide you with some useful tools for exorcising them.

10

DEBUGGING

Any first-time computer user soon learns what every programmer already knows: computers do what they're told, not necessarily what you want them to do. Computers are wonderful machines capable of performing tasks that would be impossible for a person to do alone, but they are not endowed with common sense. If just one bit is wrong in an otherwise flawless and inspired application program, it's usually not long before the entire computer system takes a one-way trip to never-never land. Locating that inverted bit can be a tedious and time-consuming endeavor. (They all look the same.)

As any software engineer can tell you, the great majority of computer errors are caused by hardware failures. Nevertheless, it is often the task of the programmer to track down and cure the problem. Oftentimes the computer has taken innocent programs or data down with it, making diagnosis that much more difficult.

Traditional debugging methods have involved single-stepping (tracing) through object code, one assembly-level instruction at a time, looking for something out of place. Another tactic is to scatter diagnostic messages throughout the program ("I'm at line 309" or "I'm going to load a file now") in hopes of narrowing down the points of interest. You can also insert breakpoints at strategic locations, in an attempt to catch the computer doing something untoward.

All of these time-honored debugging methods are well supported by the 80386 microprocessor. What makes the 80386 truly
unique in its field is its built-in hardware support for more
advanced debugging features. Not only will the 80386 single-step
through object code, it will break execution on particular task
switches, allow breakpoints in ROM or other unwritable space,
and even monitor variables in memory and notify you when they
are modified. The 80386 provides a unique set of tools that has
never before been available on any machine, except for the occasional VAX. In this chapter you will see how you can take full
advantage of the 80386's self-debugging features.

The types of debugging tools available directly from the processor can be divided into these types:

Memory segment limits

Memory segment type checking

Four-level privilege protection

Single-step (trace)

Software breakpoint instructions

Break on task switch

Hardware instruction breakpoints

Hardware data reference breakpoints

Debug register access protection

By taking each of these features and building some software
around it to report and control it, you can accumulate a respectable set of functions to aid in software debugging. Some of the
features listed are common among contemporary microprocessors
and should be familiar to those who have ever seen their programs behave in unexpected ways. Others are simply useful side
effects of the iAPX 86 memory model. Some features, however,
are unique to the 80386 and will be the most interesting ones
covered in this chapter.

MEMORY SEGMENTATION

Although the segmented memory architecture of the 80386 is not generally considered a debugging tool at all, it should be your first line of defense against unruly code. Because of the many restrictions Protected mode imposes on how and when your programs can use memory, segmentation acts like a screen, weeding out all sorts of memory-related errors. Since segment-level protection is an integral part of the 80386, you don't have to enable it or do anything special to get it to work for you. Indeed, avoiding general protection faults in even the smallest programs sometimes seems like more trouble than it's worth.

The segment-related protection is best at catching addressing errors. If an array subscript goes astray, you are likely to overstep the limits of the data segment in which the array is stored. Because all addresses are unsigned 32-bit numbers, a subscript that goes negative looks like a very large offset address to the 80386 segmentation hardware. The more strictly you enforce tight-fitting segment limit definitions in your segment descriptors, the more effective this kind of diagnostic tool is going to be. Instead of arbitrarily making all data segments, say, 1MB long, make each one exactly long enough to hold your data structures and no more. An extreme case would be to define separate data segments for each different data structure in your program. That way, you are guaranteed that the 80386 will automatically abort any reference to the data that is not within bounds. The smaller your segments, the better.

Another advantage to using segmentation faults for debugging is that they occur *before* the actual memory reference takes place. Instead of not finding out until later that bad data has been read because an address, pointer, or subscript was corrupted, you can set it up so that a segment violation is generated immediately when the bogus data starts to cause problems. This allows you to stop and examine the guilty code at precisely the moment it goes awry.

Segment-related errors consist mainly of general protection faults. Most errors that would cause a general protection fault for segments CS, DS, ES, FS, or GS will cause a stack fault instead for segment SS. Segment-not-present faults may also pop up if you use the Present bit in segment descriptors. Page faults will occur if you are using paging, although these are generally not considered errors. They might be symptomatic of programming errors in your environment if you so choose. For instance, you might decide to use the page-level privilege protection in lieu of segment-level protection. Invalid TSS faults are a good indication that something is amiss in your task-scheduling software. They often indicate that an intertask JMP or CALL instruction tried to reference something other than a TSS descriptor or task gate. These faults can also occur if some unauthorized modification of the NT bit in EFLAGS has occurred. If NT is set when it shouldn't be, the next IRET instruction will usually cause a fault as the 80386 tries to return to a task specified by an invalid Back Link field.

Two important things to note about all of the above-mentioned errors are that

- They are all classified as faults.
- They all push error codes.

Because they are all faults, the 80386 pushes a code segment selector and offset address that·point directly to the instruction that caused the fault, complete with code prefixes, if it had any. This makes identifying the source of the fault (if not necessarily the source of the error) absolutely trivial.

Faults are also restartable. The return address on the handler's stack already points to the faulting instruction, and the copy of EFLAGS right behind it is made at the time the fault occurred. All you have to do is execute an IRET instruction, and the 80386 will pick up where it left off, with no ill effects. This assumes, of course, that you've fixed the problem. If a program generates a memory fault, you may just want to terminate it.

The best part about memory faults is that they push error codes. The error code is, more often than not, a segment selector.

This is invaluable. Illegal control-transfer instructions cause the new value for CS to be pushed. Illegal data references (caused by reading when you should be writing, and so on) push the data segment selector. Bad task switches report the intended TSS or gate selector that was used. In short, memory faults not only catch many programming errors, they turn in the evidence as well.

Memory faults as debugging tools

- Happen automatically in Protected mode

- Are always enabled and active

- Trap addressing errors before they happen

- The faulting instruction can be restarted

- The 80386 pushes a 16-bit error code with all memory faults

---

Stack Errors

Bad subscripts or address references are just one kind of memory-related error that the 80386 will trap. Stack misman-agement can be a particularly nasty and pervasive kind of bug to track down, especially in high-level languages in which stack usage is heavy but not always obvious. Stacks may be used to hold temporary data values that are passed between functions or when you (or the compiler) simply run out of registers. Obviously, stacks are also used for storing and retrieving return addresses. When a selector is popped into a segment register, the 80386 performs all of the same tests it does when selectors are loaded with a MOV instruction. The segment type is checked (code versus stack versus data), privilege levels are compared, and descriptor tables are read. A segment descriptor is recached and reevaluated when a segment register is popped, even if it is being reloaded with the same value. All of this serves to trap bad segment selectors *before* they are used.

If items on the stack are not popped in the reverse order in which they were pushed, or if too many or too few parameters are removed from the stack before a return, chances are good that segment registers will be loaded with items that were never meant to be selectors. The most common result is a general protection fault. As is the case with all other memory faults, the suspect selector will be turned over to the fault-handling software.

Stack faults as debugging tools

- Checked automatically in Protected mode
- May be caused by incorrect parameter handling
- Segment registers are checked as they are popped
- Return addresses are checked as they are popped
- The 80386 pushes a 16-bit error code with all stack faults

Privilege Violations

Some addressing errors show up as privilege violations rather than as out-of-bounds addresses. These are usually caused by bad selectors being loaded into a segment register. Since moves into and out of the segment registers are not privileged instructions, any program (or programmer) is allowed to experiment with them without limit.

The general protection fault is something of a garbage can; every exception that doesn't have its own vector becomes a general protection fault. A good rule of thumb is that a memory-related general protection fault pushes a valid selector for an error code, and miscellaneous privilege-related errors and exceptions push null error codes. If a general protection fault occurs and the error code is 0, don't assume that your program tried to jump to segment 0. You may need to examine the failing instruction (its address is on the stack) to figure out what went wrong.

Privilege violations as debugging tools

- Privileges are checked automatically in Protected mode
- Privilege violations cause general protection faults
- Violations are usually caused by selector handling errors
- Privilege violation instructions can be restarted
- The 80386 pushes a null error code for privilege violations

---

SINGLE-STEPPING

Perhaps the most familiar form of microprocessor debugging (and the most dreaded) is single-stepping. When you single-step, or trace, a program, you execute it one machine instruction at a time. After each instruction you are usually free to examine memory, register contents, I/O status, or whatever, looking for something that isn't as it should be. Although this is an extremely slow process, it is also very thorough. Single-stepping represents the proverbial fine-toothed comb. It has also been compared to looking for a needle in a haystack. As programs get larger and larger, single-stepping through them becomes more and more tedious. If the program interacts with hardware or depends on interrupts, single-stepping may not even work. Because the program under scrutiny is not running in real time, single-stepping could very well cause it not to behave properly in relationship to the outside world. In short, single-stepping sometimes violates the first rule of debugging tools: to solve more bugs than you create.

Single-stepping has been around for a long time and is supported by almost every device even loosely defined as a microprocessor. Even 8048s, which are found inside the keyboards of most PCs, can single-step. On the 80386, single-stepping is implemented through a combination of hardware and software. The

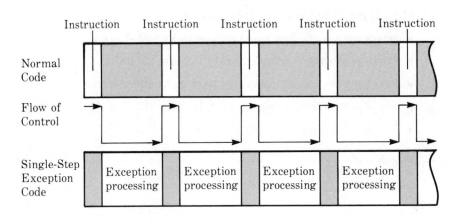

Figure 10-1.   Single-step traps

processor will tell you when a single machine instruction has been executed; the rest is up to you.

To enable single-stepping, set the TF (Trace Flag) bit (bit 8) in EFLAGS. As long as single-stepping is enabled, the 80386 will automatically generate a debug trap (exception 1) after every instruction it executes. The resulting jerky execution sequence is shown in Figure 10-1. Because they are generated after an instruction executes, single-step exceptions are considered traps. The code segment selector and offset address pushed on the exception handler's stack will point to the instruction following the one just executed. If the traced instruction changed the flow of control, the return address will point to the next instruction to have been executed, not necessarily the next instruction in lexical sequence.

When the debug exception is taken, the return address is pushed onto the stack, as was mentioned earlier, and EFLAGS is saved, with TF set. At that time, the 80386 clears TF itself. Otherwise, your single-step handler would be single-stepped and you would get nothing done. TF must then be set again to reenable single-stepping. This is done in the normal course of an IRET, since the EFLAGS image saved on the handler's stack will already have that bit set. If you want to disable single-stepping, have your exception handler clear the TF bit in the saved EFLAGS image before returning, as shown:

```
  . . .
AND      BYTE PTR SS:[ESP] +9, 0FEh      ;clear TF
IRET                                     ;interrupt return
```

When single-stepping is in effect, the 80386 generates a single-step trap after every instruction it executes *except* the one that sets TF. This could be either a POPF or an IRET instruction. Both instructions can also be used to clear TF and disable single-stepping.

If you perform a task switch to a task that has TF set in its TSS, that task will generate a single-step fault after the 80386 executes the first instruction of the new task.

The 80386 automatically clears TF in the process of handling any interrupt or exception that does not switch tasks (that is, one for which there is no task gate in the IDT). Single-step exceptions are included in this category, as was mentioned previously. This is a change from the way in which the 8086 handled single-step traps. By automatically resetting the TF bit after EFLAGS is saved, the 80386 circumvents the problem of single-stepping hardware interrupts that happen to occur when TF is set. Now all exception handlers execute at full speed. If you want to debug an exception handler, you will need to jump to it, call it like a subroutine, or place a breakpoint (discussed later) at the beginning of it to arrest execution so that single-stepping can be enabled.

Single-stepping

- Setting the TF bit in EFLAGS starts single-stepping
- The 80386 generates exception 1 after every instruction
- Exception processing automatically clears TF
- The exception handler's IRET instruction sets TF again

SOFTWARE
BREAKPOINTS

After single-stepping, breakpoints are probably the most common debugging feature generally available. In a way, breakpoints work like single-stepping except that the microprocessor stops execution only after specified instructions (breakpoints) instead of after every one. By specifying breakpoints at strategic locations throughout the suspect code, you can take "snapshots" of program execution at various points.

Breakpoints have the advantage that they do not slow down execution of the entire program. They also do not subject the program's author to the endless repetition of single-stepping. A common tactic is to scatter breakpoints throughout a program (this is known as the "shotgun" approach) and then single-step the portion that behaves erratically.

Breakpoints are actually just 80386 instructions. To place a breakpoint, you simply exchange a byte of code with a breakpoint instruction. The breakpoint opcode is CC (11001100 binary). Because the breakpoint opcode is only 1 byte, you can use it to replace any instruction. If you want to use a breakpoint in place of a multiple-byte instruction, you should place it on the first byte of the instruction, including any prefixes it may have.

When the 80386 encounters the breakpoint opcode in the instruction stream, it fetches it and executes it like any normal instruction. When this instruction is executed, its sole purpose is to generate a breakpoint trap (exception 3). It does not affect any registers or flags. Normal exception processing proceeds, with EFLAGS, CS, and EIP pushed on the exception 3 handler's stack. Breakpoints do not push an error code.

After the trap is taken, your breakpoint handler can then allow you to look around and examine memory, registers, I/O, or whatever. What you do at this point is up to you. Since the breakpoint is a trap, the instruction pointer saved on the stack will point to the byte immediately following the breakpoint's CC opcode. This is not necessarily the beginning of the next instruction. If the breakpoint was placed at the beginning of a multibyte instruction, EIP is likely to point into the middle of a meaningless byte sequence. In no event will your original instruction have been executed.

For these reasons, restarting a breakpoint trap is a little more difficult than restarting a single-step fault. If you want to execute your original instruction after the breakpoint has been taken, you will need to swap the breakpoint opcode with the first byte of your original instruction stream. Then you must back up the saved EIP image by one, to point to the beginning of your instruction again, and issue an IRET. The breakpoint will be removed and your original code will be restarted.

A nice feature of breakpoints is that you can put as many or as few in your code as you wish. For lack of a better strategy, you may want to insert a breakpoint at the beginning of every function or subroutine or at every conditional branch.

Breakpoint instructions

- Single-byte opcode (CC hexadecimal)

- A breakpoint's only function is to generate exception 3

- A breakpoint can be exchanged with a byte of object code

- Any number of breakpoints can be used

The major drawback of using breakpoints is that they require you to modify your object code. At the very least, this means that you must alias the target code segment with a writable data segment, or your own debugger will generate general protection faults.

Breakpoints cannot be used at all to debug code that is not writable. For instance, any program in ROM cannot be breakpointed. When you are placing a breakpoint, make a habit of reading back from the modified address to be sure it took. Writable data segment aliases will not work; you will still be trying to write into ROM.

Code that is swapped out in a demand-paging system may also

be immune to breakpoints. As was discussed in Chapter 4, it is
sometimes expedient to swap out code space without writing it out
to secondary storage first, since code is usually unmodifiable. If
code with a breakpoint is swapped out in this way, your breakpoint may mysteriously disappear after awhile. This is a case in
which proper alias management becomes important.

The following sample program illustrates how to set a breakpoint, given a selector and offset to the desired instruction.

```
data    SEGMENT RW PUBLIC USE32
EXTRN   brkpt:BYTE                                      ;storage for instruction
data    ENDS


code    SEGMENT ER PUBLIC USE32

        ASSUME  CS:code
        ASSUME  DS:data
        ASSUME  FS:NOTHING
        ASSUME  GS:gdt_alias

gdt_base        EQU     00                              ;base address of your GDT

breakpoint_set  PROC    FAR

        AND     BL,11111100b                            ;drop RPL bits and...
        MOVZX   EBX,BX                                  ;zero-extend selector
        LSL     ECX,EBX                                 ;ECX gets segment limit
        CMP     ECX,EAX                                 ;compare limit to offset
        JL      error                                   ;Sorry, offset too large!

        MOV     DL,92h                                  ;AR byte for data segment
        MOV     DH,0CCh                                 ;breakpoint opcode

; Convert target code segment descriptor to a data segment
; descriptor temporarily...

        PUSHFD                                          ;save current EFLAGS
        CLI                                             ;disable interrupts
        XCHG    BYTE PTR GS:gdt_base[EBX]+5,DL
        MOV     FS,BX                                   ;cache new descriptor

; Swap instruction byte with a breakpoint opcode byte...

        XCHG    DH,BYTE PTR FS:[EAX]

; Convert segment back to code...

        XCHG    BYTE PTR GS:gdt_base[EBX]+5,DL

        POPFD                                           ;restore EFLAGS
        MOV     brkpt,DH                                ;store displaced opcode
        RET


breakpoint_set  ENDP

code    ENDS
```

BREAK ON TASK SWITCH

A variation of the breakpoint mechanism allows you to trap task switches into predetermined tasks. This can be useful for debugging on a larger scale in a multitasking system. You may want to trap certain task switches in order to examine their state just before they begin executing. You could also use the task-switch trap to perform other chores, such as updating shared resource lists, saving the 80387 state, or taking statistical measurements.

You enable the task-switch trap by setting the T bit (task-switch trap) in the target TSS. This bit is near the I/O Permission bit map field, in bit 0 at byte offset 64 (100 decimal). Whenever the 80386 discovers this bit set in an incoming TSS, it performs the task switch normally but generates a debug trap (exception 1) before the first instruction of the new task is executed. This implies that the task-switch trap handler will run in the context of the new task, assuming that the debug exception is not handled with a task gate. If you do decide to handle debugging tasks with a distinct task (a topic covered later), do not set the T bit in the debug task's TSS; you won't like the outcome.

The T bit is never reset by the 80386; it does not correspond to any processor register. To disable trapping of this task, you must deliberately reset the T bit in the TSS.

Even though a task-switch trap is classified as a trap, it occurs *before* the first instruction of the new task is executed. From the processor's point of view, it is trapping the instruction that caused the task switch. The values of EFLAGS, CS, and EIP saved on the debug handler's stack point to the first unexecuted instruction of the new task and should therefore be equal to the EFLAGS, CS, and EIP values stored in the TSS itself.

Setting the T bit in a task's TSS has no effect on any of the task's other debug conditions. Trapping a task switch does not enable single-stepping (tracing) or other debug activity in that task. You can use the T bit as a kind of preemptive single-step, however. Since normal single-stepping (TF=1) causes debug traps *after* each instruction, you can use the T bit to forestall the first instruction of a new task.

Task-switch trap

- Each task can be trapped individually
- Each task has a task switch trap bit in its TSS
- The 80386 generates exception 1 when the task switch trap bit is set
- The exception occurs before the first instruction of the new task
- The task switch trap bit is not cleared automatically

DEBUG REGISTERS

Both single-stepping and task-switch trapping cause an exception 1. How is a lowly debug handler to tell them apart? On the 8086, 80186, and 80286, exception 1 was used for single-stepping only, and so there was no problem. The 80386 supports many more debug features, however, all of which share the exception 1 vector. The single-step and task-switch traps are just two examples. More will be discussed later. To differentiate between the various causes of a debug exception, the 80386 provides a debug status register located in debug register 6 (DR6). Figure 10-2 shows the various bits defined in DR6.

Whenever a debug exception (exception 1) is generated, the 80386 sets one or more of the bits in DR6 to indicate the cause of the debug exception. Your debugger can use this register to distinguish single-step traps from task-switch traps.

Bits 0, 1, 2, and 3 of DR6 are related to the four hardware breakpoints, which are covered later. Bit 13 is used for debug register protection, also covered later. It is the flags in bits 14 and 15 that are of interest now. Note also that there is no bit in DR6 that corresponds to the breakpoint trap. Breakpoints have their own

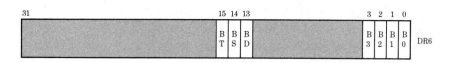

Figure 10-2. Debug register 6

vector (3), however, which is not shared, and so there shouldn't be any confusion.

The BS flag (bit 14) is set in DR6 when the 80386 begins exception processing for a single-step trap. The BT flag (bit 15) is set when a trap on a task switch occurs. Your exception handler/ debugger can test these bits with a logical AND instruction or a 32-bit bit test instruction, as illustrated here:

```
  • • •
MOV      EAX,DR6              ;read status from DR6
AND      EAX,0000C000h        ;drop all except BT & BS
CMP      EAX,8000h            ;BT = 1 & BS = 0 ?
JE       task_switch
CMP      EAX,4000h            ;BT = 0 & BS = 1 ?
JE       single_step

  • • •
MOV      EAX,DR6              ;read status from DR6
BT       EAX,15               ;BT = 1 ?
JC       task_switch
BT       EAX,14               ;BS = 1 ?
JC       single_step

  • • •
```

The only 80386 instruction that operates directly on the debug registers is MOV. Therefore, reading or writing any of the 80386's special purpose registers, including DR6, is at least a two-step process.

The processor never clears the status bits in DR6 automatically, so you must do so yourself. Otherwise, debug status bits will accumulate in DR6, and you won't be able to determine the actual cause of the debug exception. The best procedure is to clear all of the status bits immediately after you read DR6, so that any subsequent debug exceptions will have a clean slate to work with. Who knows, your debug handler may need to be debugged someday!

To clear status bits in DR6, simply write 0s on top of the bits you want to clear. Writing a 1 bit into any position of DR6 has no effect. For now, the easiest thing to do is simply to MOV a 32-bit zero into the register after reading it, like this:

```
   . . .
   XOR     EAX,EAX                    ;zero out EAX
   MOV     DR6,EAX                    ;move into DR6
   . . .
```

Because most of the bits in DR6 are officially undefined, it might be a good idea to write only 0s into bits 0 through 3 and 13 through 15. That way, you can avoid any grief when the 80486 comes along.

Debug status register (DR6)

- The DR6 identifies the cause of exception 1 faults or traps

- Register has 7 status bits

- The 80386 sets one or more bits when exception 1 occurs

- Status bits must be cleared by software

Conflicting Debug Status Indicators

It is possible to have more than one debug status flag set in DR6 when a debug exception occurs. This is especially prevalent when hardware breakpoints are enabled, as described in the next section. It's also possible to have your exception 1 handler invoked with none of the debug status flags set. If that happens, your debugger must assume that either of the following conditions has occurred:

- A hardware interrupt device passed a vector of 1.

- An INT 1 instruction was executed.

Hardware interrupts can legally pass any vector from 00 to FF during an interrupt acknowledge cycle (discussed in Chapters 7 and 14), although the numbers 00 through 1F (31 decimal) are not recommended to avoid confusion with software exceptions. The same is true for INT *n* instructions. Telling hardware interrupts and INT *n* instructions apart may require a little creativity.

HARDWARE INSTRUCTION BREAKPOINTS

A few pages back you learned about breakpoint instructions and how they can be inserted into an ailing program to take samples while it runs. This technique works very well, but it has some drawbacks, which center around the fact that the object code must be modified. To modify code, you must create a data segment alias. If the code is being shared, the newly inserted breakpoint will affect every program or task that uses that code. While the breakpoint is being inserted or removed, you must ensure that no other programs are using the target code and that no interruptions take place. Finally, you can never place breakpoint instructions in unwritable storage such as ROM.

A unique, 80386-only feature takes care of all of these problems in one fell swoop. You can have the processor itself monitor its instruction stream and generate a debug exception when a predetermined instruction is fetched. In fact, the 80386 can watch four different instructions simultaneously. Furthermore, you can enable and disable these four breakpoints independently on a per-task basis and use them to debug programs in ROM or other immutable substances. All you have to do is specify the linear address of the instructions you want monitored.

Figure 10-3 illustrates the arrangement of five more debug registers: DR0 through DR3 and DR7. Debug registers DR4 and DR5 are undefined and are never used. Registers DR0 through DR3 hold the 32-bit linear address of your four breakpoints. Register DR7 is used to selectively enable and disable the four hardware breakpoints, as well as to set some other options. The 80386 interprets the bits in DR7 as follows:

L0 (bit 0), Local Enable 0	When you set this bit, hardware breakpoint 0 is enabled, but only in the current task. If the 80386 fetches an instruction from the address contained in register DR0, it generates a debug exception. When a task switch occurs, the 80386 clears this bit (as well as L1, L2, and L3), and the breakpoint is no longer active.
G0 (bit 1), Global Enable 0	This works exactly like the L0 bit, except that it is not affected by task switches. That is, it is global across all tasks. It is perfectly all right to have L0 and G0 set at the same time. To disable breakpoint 0, you must clear the G0 bit manually.
L1, G1 (bits 2 and 3), Local and Global Enable 1	Same as L0 and G0, except that the breakpoint address is contained in register DR1.

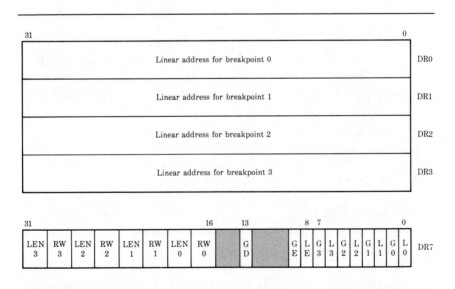

Figure 10-3. Debug registers DR0-DR3, DR7

L2, G2 (bits 4 and 5), Local and Global Enable 2	Same as L0 and G0, except that the breakpoint address is contained in register DR2.
L3, G3 (bits 6 and 7), Local and Global Enable 3	Same as L0 and G0, except that the breakpoint address is contained in register DR3.
LE, GE (bits 8 and 9), Local and Global Exact	These bits affect data reference breakpoints, discussed in the next section.
GD (bit 13), General Detect	This bit affects the debug register protection feature, discussed in a later section.
RW0 (bits 16 and 17), Read/Write 0	This 2-bit field determines the type of breakpoint to enforce for hardware breakpoint 0. This will be covered in more detail in the next section. For instruction breakpoints, this field should be set to 00.
LEN0 (bits 18 and 19), Length 0	Like the RW0 bit-field, this field is used mainly by the data reference breakpoint features. For instruction breakpoints, this field should be set to 00.
RW1, LEN1 (bits 20 through 23), Read/Write 1 and Length 1	Same as RW0 and LEN0, except that the breakpoint address is contained in register DR1.
RW2, LEN2 (bits 24 through 27), Read/Write 2 and Length 2	Same as RW0 and LEN0, except that the breakpoint address is contained in register DR2.
RW3, LEN3 (bits 28 through 31), Read/Write 3 and Length 3	Same as RW0 and LEN0, except that the breakpoint address is contained in register DR3.

To use one of the new hardware breakpoints, you need to store the instruction's linear address in one of the breakpoint address registers (DR0 through DR3), clear the appropriate RW and LEN fields, and set either the local or global enable bit for that breakpoint. After the enable bit has been set, the 80386 begins to monitor its own instruction prefetch address logic. If it finds a match between the address of an instruction and one of the enabled breakpoint address registers, it generates a debug exception. As part of the exception processing, the 80386 sets the status flag in DR6 that corresponds to the breakpoint that was hit. Bit 0 in DR6 is set if the last instruction was fetched from the address in DR0, for example.

Unlike "normal" breakpoint opcodes, the four hardware breakpoints do not modify any code. The program under test is not modified in any way. This makes placing the breakpoint much easier and also circumvents the problem mentioned earlier of code being paged out. Since nothing is modified, no changes need to be stored.

The address you store in the breakpoint address register must be a full 32-bit linear address, not a segment offset or a physical location. This may require that your debugger calculate the linear address of an instruction from its offset plus the linear base address of its segment. Specifying a linear address is actually the ideal situation: it is unique and unambiguous, yet it is independent of paging. In fact, if a portion of code was swapped out to secondary storage, it could be swapped back in and remapped to an entirely different physical page of memory, and the hardware breakpoint would still work.

If you want to place a hardware breakpoint on a multibyte instruction (which is not unreasonable), the linear address must specify the very first byte of the instruction, including any prefixes. This is an artifact of the way in which the 80386 instruction pipeline works. If you do not abide by this rule, the hardware breakpoint will not be recognized.

Hardware-supported instruction breakpoints

- Four different breakpoints can be used simultaneously
- The linear addresses of instructions are stored in DR0 through DR3
- Breakpoints are enabled through DR7
- Instruction breakpoints are treated as faults
- Object code is never modified

Handling Hardware Instruction Breakpoints

Hardware instruction breakpoints are classified as faults, not traps. Because the hardware breakpoints are based on addresses, and because the 80386 fetches instructions before they are used, it is able to determine when a breakpoint has been reached before the specified instruction is actually executed. Therefore, the values of CS and EIP pushed onto your debug exception handler's stack will point to the as-yet-unexecuted "breakpoint" instruction. Your instruction, of course, will not be modified. The following program listing shows how you can implement a simple routine to set and remove hardware instruction breakpoints:

```
code    SEGMENT ER PUBLIC USE32

        ASSUME  CS:code

; Clear a hardware instruction breakpoint.
; Called with an ASCII number from 1 to 4, indicating the
; breakpoint to be cleared.

breakpoint_clear        PROC    FAR

        CMP     AL,'1'
        JB      error                   ;Sorry, out of range!
        CMP     AL,'4'
        JA      error                   ;Sorry, out of range!
```

```
        SUB     AL,'O'                  ;remove ASCII bias
        SHL     AL,1                    ;AL = AL * 2
        SUB     AL,01h                  ;AL = 1/3/5/7
        MOV     EBX,DR7                 ;read debug control bits
        BTR     EBX,EAX                 ;reset Global Enable n
        MOV     DR7,EBX                 ;update DR7
        RET

breakpoint_clear        ENDP

; -----------------------

; Set a hardware instruction breakpoint.
; Called with the instruction offset in EAX,
; code segment selector in BX.
; Uses function in Chapter 2 which returns the base address
; of a segment in EAX.

breakpoint_set          PROC    FAR

        PUSH    EAX                     ;save offset
        PUSH    EBX                     ;save selector

        MOV     EAX,DR7                 ;read debug control bits
        MOV     ECX,4                   ;check four breakpoints
next:   TEST    AL,00000011b            ;either Ln or Gn set ?
        JZ      open                    ;unused breakpoint found
        ROR     AL,2                    ;try next breakpoint
        LOOP    next                    ;repeat as necessary
        JMP     not_open                ;Sorry, all breakpoints in use

; Convert selector and offset into a linear address...

open:   POP     EBX                     ;restore selector
        POP     EAX                     ;restore offset
        XCHG    EAX,EBX                 ;swap selector, offset
        CALL    getbase                 ;call Chapter 2 function
        ADD     EAX,EBX                 ;EAX gets linear address


; Now set the breakpoint in register DR7 and DR0-DR3.
; ECX holds 3,2,1 or 0, for DR0, 1, 2 or DR3, respectively.
; EAX holds the 32-bit linear address.

brkpt0: CMP     ECX,3
        JNE     brkpt1
        MOV     DR0,EAX                 ;store linear address
        MOV     EAX,DR7                 ;read control register
        AND     EAX,0FFF0FFFFh  ;clear LEN0, RW0 fields
        OR      EAX,000000002h  ;set Global Enable 0 bit
        MOV     DR7,EAX                 ;update DR7
        JMP     exit

brkpt1: CMP     ECX,2
        JNE     brkpt2
        MOV     DR1,EAX                 ;store linear address
        MOV     EAX,DR7                 ;read control register
        AND     EAX,0FF0FFFFFh  ;clear LEN1, RW1 fields
        OR      EAX,000000008h  ;set Global Enable 1 bit
        MOV     DR7,EAX                 ;update DR7
        JMP     exit

brkpt2: CMP     ECX,1
        JNE     brkpt3
        MOV     DR2,EAX                 ;store linear address
        MOV     EAX,DR7                 ;read control register
        AND     EAX,0F0FFFFFFh  ;clear LEN2, RW2 fields
        OR      EAX,000000020h  ;set Global Enable 2 bit
        MOV     DR7,EAX                 ;update DR7
        JMP     exit

brkpt3: CMP     ECX,0
        JNE     error                   ;should never get here
        MOV     DR3,EAX                 ;store linear address
        MOV     EAX,DR7                 ;read control register
        AND     EAX,00FFFFFFFh  ;clear LEN3, RW3 fields
```

```
        OR      EAX,000000080h  ;set Global Enable 3 bit
        MOV     DR7,EAX                 ;update DR7
        JMP     exit

exit:   RET

breakpoint_set          ENDP

code    ENDS
```

One of the advantages of hardware breakpoints is that they can be enabled for only a certain task or group of tasks, if you wish. If you enable one of the breakpoints by setting its local enable bit (bit 0, 2, 4, or 6 for registers DR0, DR1, DR2, or DR3, respectively), that address will be monitored only until the next task switch. The 80386 clears all four of the local breakpoint-enable bits during every task-switch operation at the same time that it sets TS in the EFLAGS register. However, since DR7 is not saved as part of a task's TSS, there is no record of its former status, and the local enable bits will not be restored when the task being debugged resumes. Once the 80386 clears the local break-point-enable bits, you must restore them manually.

One good technique for accomplishing this is to set the T bit in the TSS of the task (or tasks) in which you have enabled breakpoints. When the 80386 switches into such a task, it raises a debug exception with the BT flag in DR6 set. At that time, you can restore the local enable bits in DR7 to their desired states and resume task execution. If you store a copy of DR7 in an extension to the TSS, you can easily copy it into the real DR7. In fact, if you store DR0 through DR3 in the TSS as well, you can have four completely different breakpoints in every task. The task-switch trap can be used to change the breakpoint addresses and enables for each one.

One last point to remember is that the code that sets the local enable bits must run in the same task as the code you're debugging. Otherwise, the breakpoints will be disabled almost as soon as you enable them!

If you are not using multitasking, you can set the global breakpoint-enable bits (bit 1, 3, 5, or 7 for register DR0, DR1, DR2, or DR3, respectively) instead of using the local enable bits. The global enable bits are unaffected by task switches. If you are using multitasking but the tasks' linear address spaces do not overlap, you can still use global enables and not have one task's breakpoints interfere with another task. On the other hand, you may want to know when a certain instruction sequence is executed regardless of which task is currently running.

Task-specific breakpoints

- Hardware breakpoints can be global or single-task

- Global breakpoints affect all tasks

- Single-task breakpoints are disabled at every task switch

The RF Flag

Because the hardware instruction breakpoints are faults, the 80386 pushes the address of the instruction causing the fault (the "breakpointed" instruction), which has not yet been executed. When your debug exception handler performs an IRET instruction, the processor resumes execution by fetching the instruction pointed to on the stack—which has a breakpoint on it. Because hardware instruction breakpoints are taken before the instruction that has the breakpoint on it, it would appear that the 80386 has shot itself in the foot. How do you ever get past an instruction whose address is defined as a breakpoint? This is where a little-used bit in EFLAGS comes in.

The Resume flag (or RF, bit 16) is set automatically during the handling of any fault, including hardware instruction break-points. RF is not set by hardware-related interrupts, nor by exceptions classified as traps or aborts. Recall that faults are those exceptions that push the address of the faulting instruction and are restartable. When RF is set, the 80386 ignores further hardware instruction breakpoints. Therefore, since RF is set automatically when the breakpoint occurs, it will be stored in the EFLAGS image on the debug exception handler's stack and restored when execution restarts. Finding RF set as it begins executing the breakpointed instruction, the 80386 suppresses a second debug fault, and execution proceeds normally.

The RF bit has an extremely limited life span. Every instruction that executes without error clears RF. That is, RF will remain set for only one full instruction before being cleared automatically by the processor. The only exceptions to this are instructions that cause EFLAGS to be loaded, such as POPF, IRET, and task-switch instructions. These load RF with whatever the EFLAGS image on the stack or in the incoming task indicates.

RF does not mask other exceptions, only hardware instruction breakpoints. It is certainly possible that an instruction that has been designated as a breakpoint will also cause, say, a stack fault or a general protection fault. Because of the Resume flag, the breakpoint will be reported only once, no matter how many exceptions that instruction causes or the number of times it is restarted. RF is cleared only after the successful execution of an instruction.

Resume flag

- Maintained in EFLAGS register

- 80386 sets RF when it handles a fault

- 80386 clears RF after every successful instruction

- RF masks hardware instruction breakpoints

Selective Breakpoints

The only thing better than hardware-supported breakpoints are breakpoints that stop program execution only when you want them to. Suppose, for instance, that you're debugging a program loop that makes 1138 iterations through a data array. Something is going wrong somewhere within the loop, but you don't know where, and so you enable a breakpoint on one of the instructions in the loop. If the problem doesn't occur until after 1000 or so iterations, you're going to have a lot of breakpoints to examine. This is almost as tedious as single-stepping. It might be nice to have the breakpoint take effect only every 100th pass over the breakpointed instruction. Then, when the range of the problem has been narrowed down, you could let the breakpoint operate normally and examine every iteration through the loop.

A "macro breakpoint" like this is certainly possible with the hardware breakpoint features of the 80386, but it requires a little software on your part. Normally, when your debug exception handler is called and determines that an instruction breakpoint has occurred, you will want to have the handler report it. You may have it print a big message and provide a register dump. You can then prompt the user to either continue execution or abort the program. If you continue, you need only execute an IRET, and the 80386 will restart the program from its point of interruption (the breakpoint).

There is nothing to prevent you from implementing a macro breakpoint like the kind mentioned above merely by keeping breakpoints a secret. When your debug exception handler is called because of a hardware instruction breakpoint, it can simply decrement a counter. If the counter has not reached 0, you can silently return to the interrupted program with no fanfare. Only when the skip count is exhausted will the breakpoint be announced.

An example of this is shown in the following program. It assumes that the main part of the debug exception handler has already determined the cause of the exception by examining DR6.

```
data      SEGMENT RW PUBLIC USE32
EXTRN     counter:DWORD                        ;break skip counter
data      ENDS

code      SEGMENT ER PUBLIC USE32

          ASSUME  CS:code
          ASSUME  DS:data

          . . .

          DEC     counter                      ;count off a hit
          JZ      announce                     ;count exhausted ?
          IRETD                                ;no -- do nothing
```

```
announce:
        NOP                             ;print messages etc.

        . . .

code    ENDS
```

You can be more elaborate if you want and create selective breakpoints that occur only when an instruction is executed and certain other conditions are true. For example, you could choose to stop the program loop mentioned previously after exactly 1043 iterations. To do this, your breakpoint handler would test the current value of your loop counter (usually register ECX) and return to the program if it isn't equal to 1043.

You can also test the value of other registers and variables when debug exceptions occur. Depending on how complex you want your debugger to be, it is possible to implement breakpoints with several levels of trigger equations. The only limit is your imagination and tolerance for complexity.

HARDWARE DATA REFERENCE BREAKPOINTS

Generally speaking, programming errors fall into two categories: program code going where it shouldn't and data being clobbered. Breakpoints and single-stepping are the ideal way to ferret out the first kind of bug, because you can follow the program's flow of control, at whatever level of scrutiny you like, and see just when things begin to go amiss.

These tracing and trapping tools are not quite so ideally suited for finding out when variables have been written into incorrectly or when data has been read from the wrong address. Bugs like these can crop up in unlikely places, and so it is often necessary to single-step an entire program or pepper it with breakpoints until the culprit can be found. Ideally, there would be a tool that monitored data and could trap an unwanted update.

The 80386 implements just such a data-monitoring facility

with the debug registers. You can have the processor monitor up to four different locations in memory and generate a debug trap when any one of them is read from or written to. Using this feature, you can often dispense with breakpoints entirely and go directly to the instruction that is erroneously modifying your data.

The four data reference breakpoints are implemented in much the same way as the four hardware-supported instruction breakpoints are. In fact, they are one and the same. You can have at most a total of four data reference breakpoints and instruction breakpoints. The two functions share debug registers DR0 through DR3, DR6, and DR7. You can split them in any way desired (4 and none, 2 and 2, and so on).

To use a data reference breakpoint, load one of the breakpoint address registers (DR0 through DR3) with the 32-bit linear address you want monitored. The four sets of local and global enable bits operate just as they do for instruction breakpoints. Set the local enable bit corresponding to the address register used if you want to monitor data references in the current task, or set the global enable bit to monitor data references made by all tasks.

To distinguish between instruction breakpoints and data reference breakpoints, the 80386 uses the RWn bit-fields. For instruction breakpoints, RWn must be set to 00, as was mentioned previously. If RWn is set to 01, the 80386 traps all writes to the linear address in register DRn. If RWn is set to 11, traps occur for both reads and writes. A value of 10 will not trap reads; it is undefined and should not be used. Table 10-1 summarizes the interpretation of the RW bit-field.

You are allowed another option when using data reference breakpoints. Besides specifying the address to monitor, you can

Table 10-1. RW Bit-Field in Debug Register DR7

00	Instruction breakpoint
01	Data write operations
10	Undefined; do not use
11	Data read and write operations

Table 10-2.   LEN Bit-Field in Debug Register DR7

00	1-byte field (and all instructions)
01	2-byte field
10	Undefined; do not use
11	4-byte field

specify how big an area to monitor. That is, the data reference breakpoints are sized. The four LENn bit-fields determine the intrinsic size of the data item you want to monitor. If LENn is set to 00, the 80386 monitors 1 byte. The byte address is given in breakpoint address register DRn. A LENn value of 01 specifies a word field, and 11 is used to monitor a dword field. The value 10 is undefined. The LEN field is summarized in Table 10-2.

Data Operand Alignment

When the 80386 is monitoring a word field (LEN=01) or a dword field (LEN=11), the address of the data field must be aligned according to its size. Word fields must be 16-bit-aligned, and dword fields must be 32-bit-aligned. The 80386 ignores the least significant bit of breakpoint address register DRn when LENn equals 01, and it ignores the two least significant bits when LENn equals 11. Therefore, the processor enforces this alignment even if you try to specify an unaligned address.

If you must monitor an unaligned word or dword field, you must set two separate breakpoints. One should monitor the lower-addressed part, and the other should cover the higher-addressed portion.

A nice feature of the data reference breakpoints is that the 80386 will report a trap even if a memory access only partly hits the monitored addresses. For example, if you have enabled a data reference breakpoint to monitor a dword from 1000 to 1003, the 80386 will generate a debug exception if a word write to 1003 and 1004 is performed. If any portion of the monitored address space is involved, a trap is reported.

One last option available is the exact bit. Bits 8 and 9 in DR6 are the Local and Global Exact reporting bits, respectively. The exact bits affect all data reference breakpoints simultaneously. They do not affect instruction breakpoints, and both LE and GE should be cleared if no data reference breakpoints are defined. As you might expect, LE is cleared at every task switch, whereas GE must be reset manually.

The exact bits slow down memory references slightly so that a data reference breakpoint can be reported exactly as it occurs. The high-performance design of the 80386 is such that two or more instructions are usually in progress at any given time. This is especially true of instructions that are not computational in nature but simply move data to or from memory. These are banished to a separate section of the processor to run while the next instruction begins to execute. Because of this overlap, or pipelining, a data reference breakpoint is often not recognized until a few instructions after it actually occurred. In extreme cases, the breakpoint is not reported at all. The trade-off is that your program executes more slowly as long as either LE or GE is set.

It is usually wise to set an exact bit whenever you are using a data reference breakpoint. A debugging tool is no good if you can't trust it. Just be sure to reset it before taking any benchmarks.

Handling Data Reference Breakpoints

Data reference breakpoints are classified as traps. Unlike the hardware-supported instruction breakpoints, which use the same registers but are treated as faults, a data reference breakpoint causes the 80386 to push copies of EFLAGS, CS, and EIP as they existed *after* the memory reference was made. If neither of the exact bits (LE or GE) was set, this may be quite a while afterward. If the memory access was a write to memory, the old contents will already be lost when the debug exception handler is invoked. If the previous contents of that location are important to you, save them before setting the breakpoint; you're guaranteed to be notified the first time it changes.

The following program listing shows a simple routine to enable and disable a data reference breakpoint, given a segment and offset to the operand, along with its size.

```
code    SEGMENT ER PUBLIC USE32

        ASSUME  CS:code

; Clear a data reference breakpoint.
; Called with an ASCII number from 1 to 4, indicating the
; breakpoint to be cleared.

data_breakpoint_clear   PROC    FAR

        CMP     AL,'1'
        JB      error                   ;Sorry, out of range!
        CMP     AL,'4'
        JA      error                   ;Sorry, out of range!
        SUB     AL,'0'                  ;remove ASCII bias
        SHL     AL,1                    ;AL = AL * 2
        SUB     AL,01h                  ;AL = 1/3/5/7
        MOV     EBX,DR7                 ;read debug control bits
        BTR     EBX,EAX                 ;reset Global Enable n

        CMP     BL,0                    ;last breakpoint ?
        JNZ     exit                    ;no -- done
        AND     EBX,0FFFFFCFFh          ;clear GE, LE flags

exit:   MOV     DR7,EBX
        RET

data_breakpoint_clear   ENDP

; ------------------------

; Set a data reference breakpoint.
; Called with the instruction offset in EAX.
; Code segment selector in BX.
; DL holds ASCII "R" for read/write, "W" for write only.
; DH holds ASCII "B" for byte, "W" for word, "D" for dword.
; Uses function from in Chapter 2 which returns the base address
; of a segment in EAX.

data_breakpoint_set             PROC    FAR

        PUSH    EAX                     ;save offset
        PUSH    EBX                     ;save selector

        MOV     EAX,DR7                 ;read debug control bits
        MOV     ECX,4                   ;check four breakpoints
next:   TEST    AL,00000011b            ;either Ln or Gn set ?
        JZ      open                    ;unused breakpoint found
        ROR     AL,2                    ;try next breakpoint
        LOOP    next                    ;repeat as necessary
        JMP     not_open                ;Sorry, all breakpoints in use

; Convert selector and offset into a linear address...

open:   POP     EBX                     ;restore selector
        POP     EAX                     ;restore offset
        XCHG    EAX,EBX                 ;swap selector, offset
        CALL    getbase                 ;call Chapter 2 function
        ADD     EAX,EBX                 ;EAX gets linear address

        XOR     EBX,EBX                 ;zero work register

type11: CMP     DL,'R'                  ;read/Write breakpoint ?
        JNE     type01
        OR      BL,0011B                ;set temp RWn field to 11
        JMP     size00
type01: CMP     DL,'W'                  ;write only breakpoint ?
        JNE     error                   ;Sorry, parameter error!
```

```
        OR        BL,0001B              ;set temp RWn field to 01
size00: CMP       DH,'B'                ;byte size breakpoint ?
        JNE       size01
        OR        BL,0000B              set temp LENn field to 00
        JMP       brkpt0
size01: CMP       DH,'W'                ;word size breakpoint ?
        JNE       size11
        OR        BL,0100B              set temp LENn field to 01
        JMP       brkpt0
size11: CMP       DH,'D'                ;dword size breakpoint ?
        JNE       error                 ;Sorry, parameter error!
        OR        BL,1100B              set temp LENn field to 11

; Now set the breakpoint in register DR7 and DR0-DR3.
; ECX holds 3,2,1 or 0, for DR0, 1, 2 or DR3, respectively.
; EAX holds the 32-bit linear address.
; BL holds LENn and RWn bits fields.

brkpt0: MOV       EAX,DR7               ;read debug control bits
        CMP       ECX,3
        JNE       brkpt1
        MOV       DR0,EAX               ;store linear address
        AND       EAX,0FFF0FFFFh        ;zero LEN and RW for now
        SHL       EBX,16
        OR        EAX,EBX               ;store correct LEN and RW
        OR        EAX,02h               ;set Global Enable 0

brkpt1: CMP       ECX,2
        JNE       brkpt2
        MOV       DR1,EAX               ;store linear address
        AND       EAX,0FF0FFFFFh        ;zero LEN and RW for now
        SHL       EBX,20
        OR        EAX,EBX               ;store correct LEN and RW
        OR        EAX,08h               ;set Global Enable 1

brkpt2: CMP       ECX,1
        JNE       brkpt3
        MOV       DR2,EAX               ;store linear address
        AND       EAX,0F0FFFFFFh        ;zero LEN and RW for now
        SHL       EBX,24
        OR        EAX,EBX               ;store correct LEN and RW
        OR        EAX,20h               ;set Global Enable 2

brkpt3: CMP       ECX,0
        JNE       error                 ;should never get here
        MOV       DR3,EAX               ;store linear address
        AND       EAX,0FFFFFFFFh        ;zero LEN and RW for now
        SHL       EBX,28
        OR        EAX,EBX               ;store correct LEN and RW
        OR        EAX,80h               ;set Global Enable 3

a204:   BTS       EAX,9                 ;set GE bit
        MOV       DR7,EAX               ;update DR7
        RET

data_breakpoint_set     ENDP

code    ENDS
```

Data reference breakpoint exceptions don't necessarily mean that the data being monitored has actually been changed, only that the address held in the debug register was written to. The value written may be the same as what was there before. You can, if you want, build up some software to implement intelligent breakpoints, which report a debug exception to the user only when the new data is different or if it falls outside a certain range. This would be an extremely useful and powerful debugging tool.

Hardware Breakpoint Limitations

Advanced system designers and programmers who are contemplating multiprocessor systems with shared memory should understand how the debug registers work. Both the data reference breakpoints and the instruction breakpoints work by comparing the 80386's own internal address bus to the four debug address registers simultaneously. An exception is generated if there is a match, qualified by the conditions in DR7 and EFLAGS. The point is that the processor does not actually monitor the target memory itself, only its own attempts to reference it. Therefore, the 80386 cannot act as a watchdog in a multiprocessing, shared-memory system. It has no "bus snoop" capability and is not omniscient.

MULTIPLE BREAKPOINT HITS

If an instruction that modifies a monitored location (a data reference breakpoint) is itself the target of an instruction breakpoint, the 80386 will correctly generate two debug exceptions. The first one reported will be the instruction breakpoint, since it is a fault. Assuming that it is restarted and executes without generating any spurious exceptions, the 80386 will then report the data reference breakpoint as a trap.

From the point of view of the exception handler, DR6 is used to indicate the cause of the exception. In this case, both breakpoints will be indicated for both exceptions. This is an artifact of the way in which the 80386 detects hardware breakpoints. How you handle multiple breakpoints that appear simultaneously is up to you.

It is also possible to get breakpoint hit indications in DR6 for breakpoints that are not even enabled. The 80386 is rather sloppy about filtering breakpoint conditions when more than one could occur at a time. If a hardware breakpoint hit occurs (either an instruction fetch or a data reference), the 80386 sets the flag bit in DR6 that corresponds to that breakpoint as well as the flag bits for any breakpoints that are not enabled but might also happen to be true at that instant.

To filter out these extraneous breakpoint hit indications, your debug exception handler must compare the breakpoint enable bits with the alleged breakpoint hits. If neither a local nor a global enable bit is set for a given breakpoint, its hit bit should be ignored. The following program fragment illustrates an easy way to do this:

```
          . . .

          MOV     EAX,DR6           ;read debug status bits
          MOV     EBX,DR7           ;read debug control bits

          MOV     ECX,4
next:     TEST    BL,00000011b      ;either Ln or Gn set ?
          JNZ     repeat            ;yes -- no alternation
          AND     AL,11111110B      ;drop this hit bit
repeat:   ROR     BL,2              ;rotate control bits
          ROR     AL,1              ;rotate status bits
          LOOP    next
          ROL     AL,4              ;realign status bits

          . . .
```

Multiple breakpoint exception status bits

- DR6 may indicate multiple hardware breakpoint hits

- A breakpoint may be indicated if true but not enabled

- Software must consider the enable bits when analyzing hits

DEBUG REGISTER
ACCESS PROTECTION

The final feature of the debug registers to be covered is the Global Debug, or GD, flag in bit 13 of DR7. When this bit is set, the 80386 refuses all further access to any of the debug registers, including attempts to clear GD. Why do this? No good reason.

The GD bit is used primarily by Intel's in-circuit emulator, ICE-386. Designed for those developers who actually enjoy using

Table 10-3.   Debug Exceptions

Debug Exception	Class	Identification
Single-step	Trap	BS = 1
Software breakpoint instruction	Trap	Vector = 3
Break on task switch	Trap	BT = 1
Hardware instruction breakpoint	Fault	Bn = 1
Data reference breakpoint	Fault	Bn = 1
Debug register access	Fault	BD = 1

n = 0, 1, 2, or 3, depending on which breakpoint occurred

emulators, this flag is intended to keep your software from interfering with the ICE's work.

Attempts to read or write any of the 80386 debug registers when GD is set result in a debug exception. The processor sets the BD flag (bit 13) in DR6 to indicate the cause of the exception. It also clears the GD bit so that the exception handler can read DR6. This is the only way to clear GD once it has been set. Debug register access exceptions are classified as faults and, as such, can be restarted.

Summary of Debug Exceptions

Table 10-3 summarizes all of the debugging exceptions discussed in this chapter. It shows whether the exception is classified as a fault or a trap and tells how to recognize one when it happens.

DEBUGGING WITH A SEPARATE TASK

So far this chapter has assumed that the debug exception handler (exception 1) and the software breakpoint handler (exception 3) have run as interrupt procedures in the currently running task.

You may want to consider handling your debug exceptions with task gates. By performing all debug exception handling in another task, you can gain several benefits.

One of the biggest advantages of using task gates is that the program under test will automatically be saved in its entirety for later scrutiny. A prime goal of any debugger should be to be as noninvasive as possible. If the presence of a debugger affects the performance of a program under test, the results may not be reliable when the debugger is removed. Unless the program under test can run in a real-world situation, the debugger may be next to useless. By performing all debug operations in a different task, you can keep the amount of contamination to a minimum. On the 80386, total separation of tasks is the rule rather than the exception, and this suits the design of a good debugger well.

Because all debugging-related exceptions cause a task switch, it becomes easy to examine the registers and flags of the debugged task. If necessary, you can modify those registers by writing into the TSS before restarting the task. This is helpful if you choose to implement the selective breakpoints described earlier.

A major consideration when you are implementing debug tools is robustness. Presumably, you will be debugging programs that don't work right. If the unruly program has problems with its segment registers or its stack, it may very well take the debugging handlers down with it. This is particularly frustrating because you can't tell why your code isn't working if the debugger isn't either. Keeping debug code in a separate task adds considerably to the robustness of the entire system. Almost no amount of fouling up can crash a well-written debugger that has its own task and address space. The only event that the debugger cannot guard against is a processor shutdown.

One pitfall of using a separate debug task is that it makes it tricky to reenable local debug enable bits in DR7. Somehow, you need to set them on the other side of the task switch, into the program under test.

The 80386 provides programmers with a unique set of tools for self-hosted debugging. The data reference breakpoints should prove particularly useful. Only a small amount of exception processing code is necessary for you to realize the benefits of the debug registers. If you choose to write more elaborate debugging software, as has been outlined in this chapter, the 80386's debugging features will really shine. Considering the complexity of the microprocessor itself and its elaborate memory- and task-management hardware, it seems that the internal, hardware-supported debug features have arrived just in time.

After you feel you've mastered the 80386, move on to the next chapter, where you will see how to run two processors at once.

11

THE 80387 NUMERIC PROCESSOR EXTENSION

The 80387 is a companion processor for the 80386 and is dedicated to mathematical functions. Although the 80386 is a versatile and capable microprocessor, as you have seen, its instruction set is not particularly strong in the mathematical realm. For instance, how would you program it to calculate the hyperbolic arctangent of 130 degrees, or the square root of pi? Most laypeople consider the ability to solve mathematical problems such as these to be a computer's strong point, yet performing these kinds of calculations with the 80386's instruction set would be a complex and tortuous task for the average programmer. Only a select few mathematically minded software engineers can produce accurate and reliable answers to such problems using the basic four functions of the 80386.

This is not to say that the 80386 has somehow been cheated out of real computational muscle. Its instruction set is quite typical of contemporary microprocessors. The general-purpose nature of most commercial microprocessors, including the 80386, prohibits the inclusion of a high-end instruction set and registers as standard equipment. Instead, number-crunching capability is usually available in an additional integrated circuit closely mated to the main processor. Ninety-nine percent of all microcomputers today perform their floating-point operations using a numeric coprocessor; the 80386 is no exception.

The 80387 numeric processor extension (NPX) greatly broadens the horizons of the programmer. It means that you literally have two microprocessors running in parallel, one that executes normal logic and flow-of-control instructions and one devoted entirely to floating-point numeric processing. Tasks that were previously impossible can be performed easily, quickly, and accurately with an 80387. Mathematical or scientific tasks that would take hours to compute on an 80386 can be done in a matter of minutes—and almost certainly with greater accuracy and repeatability than if you had done the work completely in software.

The 80387 NPX equips your system for such complex chores as navigation, graphics, solids modeling, simulation, data transformation, encryption and decryption, and more. Because the 80387 hardware performs many complex mathematical functions as a matter of routine, you (and your software) don't need to be concerned with the mechanical aspects of the task at hand. You can devote your time and energy to developing program flow, logic, and user interface.

80387 advantages

- Ease of use
- Repeatability of results
- Speed of execution
- International standard number notation
- Simple add-in component

WHY FLOATING POINT?

Just as important as the mathematically inclined instruction set of the 80387 is its unique register set. The data registers allow the 80387 to directly manipulate numbers that are several orders of magnitude larger, and smaller, than those the 80386 can handle. Because of the way in which the 80387 interprets its data, it is able to deal with fractional values, exponentiation, scientific notation, and several "imaginary" numbers familiar only to mathematicians.

Recall how the 80386 interprets and represents numbers stored in memory or in its internal registers. An 8-bit quantity can represent decimal values from -128 to 127. A 16-bit number can range from $-32,768$ to $32,767$, and 32-bit numbers reach maximum extents of $-2,147,483,648$ and $2,147,483,647$. Although these numbers are certainly large enough for everyday life, they are all integers. The standard two's-complement system of binary numbers is incapable of representing fractional values. A task as simple as balancing a checkbook requires some number juggling on the 80386 just to deal with the decimal point. (Normally you would multiply everything by 100 and treat all quantities as pennies instead of dollars.) Even a simple pocket calculator can handle decimal points and fractions. This highlights a fundamental inability of the basic 80386 to deal with real-world scientific and mathematics problems.

The 80387, on the other hand, does not use the two's-complement format to represent numbers. Instead, it uses an 80-bit (10-byte) format defined by the Institute of Electrical and Electronics Engineers (IEEE). IEEE standard 754 specifies (among other things) a globally accepted way to represent extremely large and extremely small numbers in binary notation. By using this format, the 80387 not only circumvents the problems associated with a two's-complement system, it guarantees data compatibility with other machines worldwide that also conform to the IEEE standard.

As an example of the flexibility of the 80387's numeric range, consider that it is able to represent numbers as large as 1.21×10^{4932}. (That's 121 followed by 4930 zeros!) For comparison, the number of electrons in the universe is estimated at about 10^{87}. Likewise, the 80387 is able to handle numbers as small as 3.3×10^{-4932} (33 preceded by a decimal point and 4930 zeros). The 80387 does not maintain a fixed number of decimal places. As values get smaller, more decimal places are used; as values get larger, decimal places are dropped. Thus, the decimal point "floats," hence the term "floating point."

THE 80387 REGISTER SET

Because it is a microprocessor, the 80387 practically requires some internal registers with which to work. Like the 80386, the 80387 has data registers for storing intermediate results, constants, and so on. There are eight of these registers. The 80387 also has three control and status registers that can be read from or written to in order to control various aspects of operation or check up on its state. The usable register set is shown in Figure 11-1; the 80387 also contains many programmer-invisible

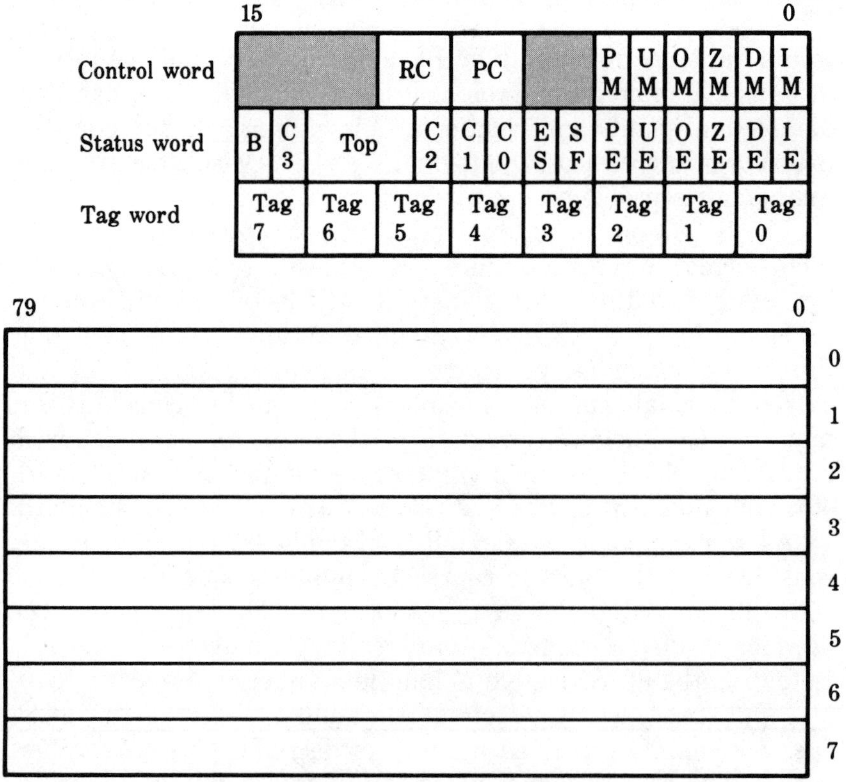

Figure 11-1. 80387 registers

registers which will not be discussed here. Following is a description of the various registers and the fields within them.

Control Word

The 80387 control word, shown at the top of Figure 11-1, can be used to set various numeric processing options. The control word is logically divided into an upper and lower byte. The 2 fields in the upper byte control accuracy, and the 6 bits defined in the lower byte control exception processing. These 6 bits correspond to the six possible exceptions that the 80387 can encounter. Each exception is individually maskable. If a particular exception is generated and its respective mask bit is clear, the 80387 actively signals that exception. If the mask bit is set, however, the 80387 deals with that exception as it sees fit, and no exception is reported. This register is readable and writable at all times. The control word is divided as follows:

RC (Rounding Control, bits 10 and 11)

This field determines the way in which imprecise results are rounded, for those instructions that do rounding. The four combinations are shown here. When the 80387 is reset or initialized, RC is set to 00.

00 Round to nearest, or nearest even number

01 Round down (toward negative infinity)

10 Round up (toward positive infinity)

11 Truncate

PC (Precision Control, bits 8 and 9)

This field can be used to decrease the standard number of significant bits (and therefore the precision) of internally stored numbers. This may produce a slight speed advantage, but its primary use is for deliberately emulating the reduced precision of other numeric processors. The 80387's interpretation of this field follows. When the 80387 is reset or initialized, PC is set to 11.

00   24 bits (single precision)

01   Reserved; do not use

10   53 bits (double precision)

11   64 bits (extended precision)

PM (Precision Mask, bit 5)

Setting this bit masks precision exceptions. Whenever the 80387 is not able to represent the infinitely exact value of a calculation in the destination register, it raises a precision exception. As accurate as the 80387 is, its precision is not infinite, so this exception can occur relatively often, depending on the kind of work you're doing. If this exception is masked, the 80387 rounds the result according to the RC field instead of reporting it. There is no speed advantage in doing this. It is mainly a convenience feature.

UM (Underflow Mask, bit 4)

Setting this bit masks underflow exceptions. Underflow exceptions occur when a number becomes so small that it can no longer be stored accurately. If this exception is masked, the 80387 stores either 0 or a denormalized representation of the number (described later).

OM (Overflow Mask, bit 3)

This bit is used to mask overflow exceptions. Overflow is the corollary to underflow; it occurs when the result of a floating-point operation is too large to be represented in the destination register or memory operand. The 80387's reaction to a masked overflow exception depends on the current setting of the RC (Rounding Control) field. The following table shows how the overflowing number is converted. Note that the 80387 has special ways of storing positive and negative infinity, described later.

Rounding Mode	If Result Is Positive	If Result Is Negative
00 Nearest	+ infinity	− infinity
01 Down	Largest possible	− infinity
10 Up	+ infinity	Smallest possible
11 Chop	Largest possible	Smallest possible

ZM (Divide-by-Zero Mask, bit 2)   When this bit is set, the 80387 does not report divide-by-zero exceptions. Instead, it returns an answer of infinity, with the sign (positive or negative infinity) determined by the sign of the operands involved and by the type of the operation.

DM (Denormalized Mask, bit 1)   This bit masks denormal exceptions. When denormal exceptions are enabled, the 80387 signals an exception when any arithmetic operation is attempted with one or more denormal operands. If this bit is set, the 80387 proceeds with the operation and does not report denormal exceptions. Denormal numbers are discussed in a later section on special numbers.

IM (Invalid Operation Mask, bit 0)   This bit is used to mask invalid floating-point operations, as defined by IEEE 754. This exception is not related to the reporting of invalid 80387 opcodes, which the 80386 reports as exception 6. Rather, this exception flags those numerical calculations that are generally considered meaningless. As such, the occurrence of an invalid-operation exception is a good indication of a program error. When this exception is masked, the 80387 returns a standard response. This normally consists of a special "indefinite" number.

Status Word

The 80387 status word provides a quick look at the current status of the coprocessor. When exceptions occur, it also allows your 80386 code to determine the cause, since all six coprocessor exceptions raise an exception 16 on the 80386. The status word is divided up as follows:

B (Busy, bit 15)   This bit is provided only for compatibility with the 8087. It does not reflect the actual status of the 80387's BUSY output pin. Instead, it is an echo of the ES bit (bit 7).

C3 (Condition Code 3, bit 14)   This is one of the four 80387 condition code flags. The condition codes are similar to the EFLAGS bits on the 80386. They change constantly as the 80387 executes floating-point code. You can use conditional instructions to examine them to determine the outcome of the last 80387 instruction.

TOP (Top of Floating-Point Stack, bits 13, 12, and 11)   This 3-bit field identifies which floating-point data register is currently at the top of the stack. The floating-point stack system is discussed in a later section.

C2 (Condition Code 2, bit 10)	Like C3, this is one of the 80387's condition code flags.
C1 (Condition Code 1, bit 9)	Like C3.
C0 (Condition Code 0, bit 8)	Like C3.
ES (Exception Summary, bit 7)	This bit is a software-readable indication of the 80387's external ERROR pin. It is a logical OR of the 6 low-order status bits.
SF (Stack Fault, bit 6)	This bit distinguishes invalid operations that occurred because of stack conditions from other invalid conditions. When this bit is set, condition code C1 further distinguishes between stack overflow (C1=1) and underflow (C1=0).
PE, UE, OE, ZE, DE, IE (Exception Flags, bits 5, 4, 3, 2, 1, and 0)	Each of these bits is controlled by the corresponding exception mask bit in the control word. When the 80387 detects an exception that is not masked, it sets the appropriate exception flag and drives the ERROR pin to inform the 80386 of the exception. ES will also be set.

Tag Word

Each of the eight floating-point data registers has a 2-bit tag associated with it. The tag makes it much easier for user software (and for the 80387 itself) to determine what kind of value is stored in a particular register. All eight tag values are available as a tag word. The four possible tag values are listed in the following table. The tag fields in the tag word are the *only* place in which the 80387 refers to actual, physical registers instead of the standard floating-point stack notation. For example, the 2 least significant bits of the tag word always apply to data register 0, regardless of which register is currently at the top of the floating-point stack.

00	Valid
01	Zero
10	Infinity, NaN, denormal, or unsupported format
11	Empty

Floating-Point Data Registers

The 80387 contains eight separate data registers ideally suited for storing extended-precision, 80-bit floating-point numbers. The registers are called register 0 through register 7. However, except in the case of the tag word, the 80387's eight data registers are treated exactly like an on-chip stack and are named according to their positions relative to the current top of the stack. The TOP field in the status word indicates which register is currently at the top of the stack. For example, if TOP equals 010, register 2 is at the top of the stack and would be referred to as register ST(0), or ST. Register 3 would be directly "below" it on the stack and would be termed ST(1). Register 1 would be at the very bottom of the stack at ST(7). See Figure 11-2.

   All 80387 instructions deal with the register set in this way. At no time are you allowed to operate on an actual physical register, even in assembly language. All operations either push or pop floating-point operands by copying values to or from the register designated as the top of the stack and then incrementing or decrementing the TOP field in the status word. Furthermore, the majority of 80387 instructions either do not allow register addressing or have no-operand forms. Instead, they take as many operands as they need, starting from ST(0). An FMUL instruction, for instance, multiplies ST(0) by ST(1) and leaves the result in ST(0) by default. This kind of operand allocation takes a little getting used

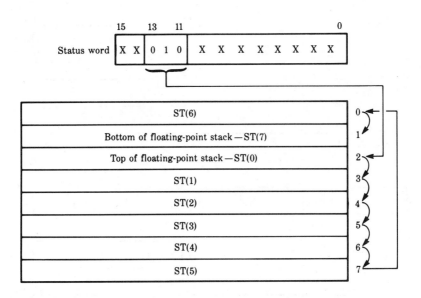

Figure 11-2.   Floating-point stack

to, but it turns out to be ideal for implementing reverse Polish notation.

One final note: the eight data registers really are implemented as a stack, not a circular queue. If you attempt to push more than eight operands, the 80387 generates an invalid-operand exception (which may or may not be masked). The SF flag will indicate a stack fault, and C1 will indicate an overflow. You will also get an error if you try to pop too many operands from the register stack.

THE 80387 NUMBER SYSTEM

Perhaps the trickiest part of understanding the 80387 is getting the hang of the way in which it represents numbers. If you are going to use the 80387, you need to know how to format floating-

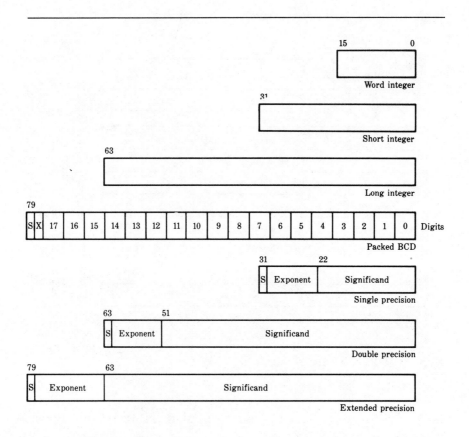

Figure 11-3.   80387 storage formats

point values in memory so that you can load numbers into the coprocessor. Learning the IEEE format will also help you understand the results.

The 80387 can actually load and store numbers in any of seven different formats, illustrated in Figure 11-3. Three of these are true floating-point formats, three are for integers only, and one is in binary-coded decimal, or BCD (which is also limited to integers) to make numbers more readable to humans.

The word integer and short integer formats are stored in the familiar two's-complement notation. These are absolutely identical to the 80386's word and dword formats. If your 80387 calculations deal with integers in this range only, then your task is easy—the 80386 and 80387 can freely exchange data in either of these formats. The other five formats, however, are completely undecipherable to an 80386.

Long integers are merely an extension of short integers. These integers are still in two's-complement notation, but they occupy 64 bits in memory. This allows the 80387 to store signed integers that are 4 billion times larger than those the 80386 can store.

The packed BCD format allows the 80387 to read and write a limited range of integers in a format close to ASCII. The BCD load and store instructions take a relatively long time to execute because the BCD format is so drastically different from the 80387's native form, but they are very handy for printing floating-point numbers.

Single precision, double precision, and extended precision are the three actual floating-point notations. One of these formats must be used to store any nonintegral value. All three are similar, the only difference being the range of values accommodated. Each one trades off precision and magnitude for memory space.

Now is a good time to point out two facts about the 80387's number system. First, all values stored in the 80387's eight internal data registers are always stored in extended (80-bit) precision. All calculations involving registers use all 80 significant bits, and any time a number is loaded into an 80387 register, it is automatically converted to extended precision. It is only when data is read or stored to outside memory that the other six formats are used. The format is determined by your selection of floating-point MOV instructions.

The second point to keep in mind is the difference between a number with a large magnitude and one with a large value. A large magnitude implies many digits before the decimal point. A large value implies that the number is positively signed. A large-magnitude number may have an extremely negative value. A small-magnitude number is one that is extremely small and has many digits after the decimal point. These may, of course, also be positive or negative.

The three floating-point formats are each divided into three fields. The most significant bit is the sign bit. If the sign bit is 0, the number is positive; otherwise, the number is negative. Next comes the exponent field. This is similar to the superscript numbers used in scientific notation. The size of the exponent field varies with the format used and determines how many bits to the left or right the binary point is to be moved. The last field is the *significand*. This is analogous to a mantissa in scientific notation. The size of this field also varies with the format used, and it determines the number of significant bits that can be held. Note that the significand field in extended-precision notation is 64 bits long.

The significand field holds all of the significant bits in a number, both before the decimal point (if any) and after (if any). In extended precision, there are 64 significand bits total. Because the decimal point floats, large numbers are not necessarily limited to a few decimal places. Rather, the only restriction is that all of the significant digits must be consecutive. Because there is only one significand field, you cannot store the integral portion and fractional portion of a number separately. There can be only one string of digits. Consequently, when numbers have several significant digits before the decimal point, an inverse number of digits is available after the decimal point, and vice versa. The larger the format, the greater the possible spread between the first and last significant digits.

To save precious storage space, none of the three floating-point formats stores leading zeros in the significand. For values before the decimal point, this is only natural. Only banks write leading zeros before numbers. For values after the decimal point, this allows the 80387 to represent extremely small quantities without having to waste memory on leading zeros between the decimal point and the first "real" (nonzero) digit. Instead, the significand field always starts with the first nonzero digit of the floating-point number, and the exponent field is used to place the decimal point relative to the beginning of the significand. It is common to place the decimal point completely outside the scope of the significand, resulting in implied leading or trailing zeros. Figure 11-4 illustrates this concept.

To save more space, the significand field does not hold the very first 1 bit in the number's significand. Since all numbers except

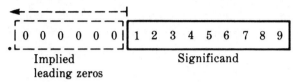

Floating-Point Number with Negative Exponent

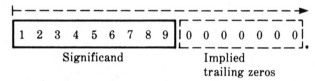

Floating-Point Number with Positive Exponent

Figure 11-4.   Decimal point placement

exactly 0.00 must have at least one 1-bit in them, there will always be a "first" 1 bit. Omitting this first bit, like omitting leading zeros, saves space in the significand field. In a binary system, gaining a bit allows a twofold increase in magnitude, and so the miserly attitude toward memory is warranted.

The extended-precision format does not drop the first 1 bit as single precision and double precision do. Apparently, the IEEE decided that enough was enough.

As already mentioned, the exponent field places the decimal point within (or without) the significand. Actually, since a binary number system is involved, it places a binary point. The binary point is assumed to begin immediately before the first bit in the significand, after the "phantom" 1 bit. In extended precision, it begins after the "real" first 1 bit. If the exponent is positive, the binary point is moved down the bit stream (or to the right, if you prefer), resulting in a larger number. If the exponent is negative, the binary point is moved "upstream" (to the left), making the number smaller.

Just to keep things from being easy, the exponent field is not stored as a normal signed number. Instead, each exponent is *biased*. The amount of the bias depends on the format. In the single-precision format, the 8-bit exponent is added to 7F (127) before being stored. You must subtract this bias to determine the true exponent. For example, an exponent of 0 would be stored as 7F, an exponent of 1 would be written as 80, and so on. In double precision, the bias is 3FF (1023), and in extended precision it is 3FFF (16,383).

Although this may seem like a useless annoyance, it does have a nice side effect. You can write a trivial 80386 program to do signed comparisons between floating-point numbers without knowing anything about the floating-point storage format. If you begin scanning the bits of two floating-point numbers, beginning with the sign bit and working down, the first bit position that differs provides an accurate indication of which number is numerically greater.

The last step in interpreting floating-point number formats is learning how to read those bits that may remain to the right of the binary point. Significand bits to the left of the binary point are interpreted as a normal binary integer. Those on the right represent the real number's fractional component and are interpreted differently.

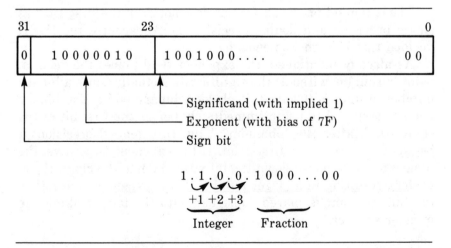

Figure 11-5. Single-precision example

Figure 11-5 provides an example of how fractions are interpreted. The decimal number 12.5 is shown represented in single-precision floating-point format. It shows the biased exponent field followed by the significand field, with the phantom 1 bit and binary point. After the bias of 7F is subtracted, you can see that the exponent is actually +3. If the binary point is moved three places to the right and the missing bit is inserted, the integral portion becomes 1100 and the fractional portion becomes 1000...0. The quantity 1100 in binary is 12, so there is your integer.

Now comes the fun part. Each bit position in the fractional portion of a real number represents 1 over successive powers of 2. The first "fraction bit" is equal to 1/2, the next to 1/4, and then to 1/8, 1/16, and so on. In the example, only a single bit is set after the binary point, and its value is 1/2. Therefore, the final value is 12 1/2. The program listing that follows shows how you can convert extended real floating-point numbers to a straight ASCII representation suitable for printing:

```
; Define some miscellaneous variable storage...
data      SEGMENT RW PUBLIC USE32 'data'
          EXTRN    string_ptr:BYTE            ;ASCII string (32 characters)
          EXTRN    power_ptr:WORD             ;power of ten (decimal placement)
          EXTRN    status:WORD                ;temp storage for 80387 status word
          EXTRN    power_two:WORD
          EXTRN    power_ten:WORD
          EXTRN    fraction:TBYTE
          EXTRN    bcd_value:TBYTE            ;final storage for BCD value
data      ENDS

FIELD_SIZE        EQU    18                   ;maximum number of ASCII decimal digits

INFINITY          EQU    6                    ;these constants will be used
NAN               EQU    4                    ;to keep track of our progress
INDEFINITE        EQU    3                    ;as we try to determine what kind
EXACT             EQU    2                    ;of number we are dealing with.
MINUS             EQU    1                    ;
NORMAL            EQU    0                    ;
EMPTY             EQU    -2                   ;
ZERO              EQU    -4                   ;
DENORMAL          EQU    -6                   ;
UNNORMAL          EQU    -8                   ;


code      SEGMENT ER PUBLIC USE32

          ASSUME  CS:code
          ASSUME  DS:data, ES:data, SS:data

; --------------------------------------------
power_table       DQ     1.0,    1.0E1,  1.0E2,  1.0E3,  1.0E4
                  DQ     1.0E5,  1.0E6,  1.0E7,  1.0E8,  1.0E9
                  DQ     1.0E10, 1.0E11, 1.0E12, 1.0E13, 1.0E14
                  DQ     1.0E15, 1.0E16, 1.0E17, 1.0E18
; --------------------------------------------
```

```
status_table      DB        UNNORMAL, NAN,      UNNORMAL +MINUS, NAN +MINUS
                  DB        NORMAL,  INFINITY, NORMAL +MINUS,   INFINITY +MINUS
                  DB        ZERO,    EMPTY,    ZERO +MINUS,     EMPTY
                  DB        DENORMAL, EMPTY,   DENORMAL +MINUS, EMPTY
; ------------------------------------
const10           DW        10

        PUBLIC  float

; Procedure will convert the value on the top of the 80387
; floating-point stack to an ASCII string of 0 - 19 characters.
; All 80387 registers will be destroyed.
; All 80386 registers are preserved, except:
; EAX = return code, EBX = char count, ECX = power of 10 (decimal placement).

float   PROC    NEAR

        PUSH    EDX                         ;save work registers
        PUSH    ESI                         ;
        PUSH    EDI                         ;

; Initialize some variables...
        MOV     ECX,32
@001:   MOV     string_ptr[ECX]-1,0
        LOOP    @001                        ;zero out ASCII string buffer
        MOV     power_ptr,0

        CALL    tos_status                  ;compress C3, C2, C1, C0 into EAX
        MOV     DL,status_table[EAX]        ;DL gets status code
        CMP     DL,EMPTY                    ;register empty ?
        JE      found_empty
        CMP     DL,INFINITY                 ;number = infinity ?
        JGE     found_infinity
        CMP     DL,NAN                      ;number = NaN ?
        JGE     NAN_or_indefinite

        MOV     ECX,FIELD_SIZE -1
        MOV     EAX,0

        FABS                                ;take absolute value of ST(0)

        CMP     DL,UNNORMAL + MINUS         ;number = unnormal ?
        JLE     found_unnormal
        CMP     DL,DENORMAL + MINUS         ;number = denormal ?
        JLE     found_denormal
        CMP     DL,ZERO + MINUS             ;number = zero ?
        JLE     real_zero

        FXTRACT                             ;else normal number
        JMP     normal_value

found_empty:
        MOV     DL,1                        ;return code
        JMP     exit

found_infinity:
        JMP     exit                        ;return code

NAN_or_indefinite:
        TEST    DL,MINUS
        JZ      exit                        ;positive sign, must be NaN
        FSTP    fraction
        FWAIT                               ;wait for fractional part to be stored
        MOV     EBX,0C0000000h
        SUB     EBX,DWORD PTR fraction +4   ;compare to upper half of fraction
        OR      EBX,DWORD PTR fraction +0   ;compare to lower half of fraction
        JNZ     exit                        ;zero fractional part, must be NaN
        MOV     DL,INDEFINITE               ;else indefinite
        JMP     exit

found_unnormal:
        MOV     DL,8                        ;return code
        JMP     exit

real_zero:
        SUB     DL,ZERO
        JMP     convert_integer
```

```
found_denormal:
        FLD1
        FXCH
        FPREM
        FXTRACT                                 ;separate significand and exponent

        FXAM                                    ;examine ST(0)
        FSTSW   AX                              ;AX gets 387 status word
        FXCH                                    ;swap ST(0), ST(1)
        FXCH    ST(2)                           ;swap ST(0), ST(2)
        SUB     DL,DENORMAL
        TEST    AX,4400h                        ;C3 = 0 and C2 = 0 ?
        JZ      found_unnormal                  ;fraction is an unnormal
        FSTP    ST(0)                           ;remove 1.0 from ST(0)

normal_value:
        FSTP    fraction                        ;store significand
        FIST    power_two                       ;store binary exponent
        FLDLG2
        FMUL
        FISTP   power_ten                       ;store decimal exponent
        FWAIT                                   ;pause...
        MOV     AX,power_ten
        SUB     AX,CX
        JA      adjust_result
        FILD    power_two
        MOV     DH,DL                           ;save return code in case of failure
        SUB     DL,NORMAL - EXACT
        FLD     fraction
        FSCALE
        FST     ST(1)                           ;duplicate ST(0)
        FRNDINT                                 ;take integer
        FCOMP                                   ;compare number to integer self
        FSTSW   status
        TEST    status,4000h                    ;integer ?
        JNZ     convert_integer                 ;yes
        FSTP    ST(0)                           ;no...
        MOV     DL,DH                           ;restore old return code

adjust_result:
        MOV     power_ptr,AX                    ;store power of ten
        NEG     AX
        CALL    get_power_10
        FLD     fraction
        FMUL
        FILD    power_two
        FADDP   ST(2),ST
        FSCALE
        FSTP    ST(1)                           ;remove exponent, lift stack


; Test magnitude of final result to see if it will fit in a BCD field...
test_power:
        FCOM    power_table[ECX*8] + TYPE power_table
        FSTSW   AX
        TEST    AX,4100hfrom                    ;C3 = 0 and C0 = 0 ?
        JNZ     test_for_small

        FIDIV   const10                         ;too big, divide by 10
        AND     DL,NOT EXACT                    ;mark inexact status
        INC     power_ptr                       ;increment power of 10
        JMP     in_range

test_for_small:
        FCOM    power_table[ECX*8]
        FSTSW   AX
        TEST    AX,0100h                        ;C0 = 0 ?
        JZ      in_range

        FIMUL   const10                         ;too small, multiply by 10
        DEC     power_ptr                       ;decrement power of 10

in_range:
        FRNDINT                                 ;drop all fractional bits

convert_integer:
        FBSTP   bcd_value                       ;store integer portion
```

```
        MOV     ESI,OFFSET bcd_value +8  ;BCD numbers begin 8 bytes into TBYTE
        MOV     EDI,OFFSET string_ptr
        MOV     BL,1                     ;character count = 1 (plus/minus sign)
        CLD
        MOV     AL,'+'
        TEST    DL,MINUS
        JZ      positive_result
        MOV     AL,'-'

positive_result:
        STOSB                            ;store sign character
        AND     DL,NOT MINUS
        FWAIT

skip_leading_zeroes:
        MOV     AH,BYTE PTR DS:[ESI]     ;read a BCD byte (2 digits)
        MOV     AL,AH
        SHR     AL,4
        AND     AL,0Fh                   ;read high nibble
        JNZ     enter_odd
        MOV     AL,AH
        AND     AL,0Fh                   ;read low nibble
        JNZ     enter_even
        DEC     ESI                      ;read backwards
        CMP     ESI,OFFSET bcd_value
        JAE     skip_leading_zeroes      ;repeat while still numbers left

        MOV     AL,'0'
        STOSB                            ;all zeroes, write out one zero
        INC     BL                       ;count a character
        MOV     AL,DL                    ;AL gets return code
        JMP     exit

digit_loop:
        MOV     AH,BYTE PTR DS:[ESI]     ;read a BCD byte (2 digits)
        MOV     AL,AH
        SHR     AL,4

enter_odd:
        ADD     AL,'0'
        STOSB
        MOV     AL,AH
        AND     AL,0Fh
        INC     BL                       ;count a character

enter_even:
        ADD     AL,'0'
        STOSB
        INC     BL                       ;count a character
        DEC     ESI                      ;read backwards
        CMP     ESI,OFFSET bcd_value
        JAE     digit_loop               ;repeat while more BCD bytes
        MOV     AL,DL                    ;AL gets return code

exit:   MOVSX   ECX,power_ptr            ;ECX = power of 10 (decimal placement)
        MOVZX   EBX,BL                   ;EBX = character count
        MOVZX   EAX,DL                   ;EAX = return code
        POP     EDI
        POP     ESI
        POP     EDX
        RET

float   ENDP

;---------------------------------
get_power_10    PROC    NEAR

        CMP     AX,18
        JA      out_of_range
        PUSH    EBX
        MOVZX   EBX,AX
        SHL     EBX,3                    ;table entries = 8 bytes each
        FLD     power_table[EBX]
        FXTRACT
        POP     EBX
        RET
```

```
out_of_range:
        FLDL2T
        ENTER   4,0
        MOV     [EBP -2],AX              ;save power of 10
        FIMUL   WORD PTR [EBP -2]        ;ST(0) = log2(10) * P
        FSTCW   WORD PTR [EBP -4]        ;store control word
        MOV     AX,WORD PTR [EBP -4]     ;read it back
        AND     AX,0F3FFh
        OR      AX,0400h                 ;force round-down mode
        XCHG    AX,WORD PTR [EBP -4]     ;swap old,new control words
        FLD1
        FCHS                             ;ST(0) = -1.0
        FLD     ST(1)
        FLDCW   WORD PTR [EBP -4]        ;load new control word
        FRNDINT
        MOV     WORD PTR [EBP -4],AX
        FLDCW   WORD PTR [EBP -4]        ;restore original control word
        FXCH    ST(2)
        FSUB    ST, ST(2)
        MOV     AX,[EBP -2]
        FSCALE
        F2XM1
        LEAVE
        FSUBR
        FMUL    ST,ST(0)
        RET

get_power_10    ENDP

;--------------------------------
tos_status      PROC    NEAR

        FXAM
        FSTSW   AX
        MOV     AL,AH
        AND     EAX,4007h
        SHR     AH,3
        OR      AL,AH
        MOV     AH,0
        RET                             ;compress C3, C2, C1, C0

tos_status      ENDP
; --------------------------------
code    ENDS
        END
```

Special Numbers

In the realm of true mathematics, some classes of numbers are not representative of anything you might encounter in the real world. These are represented in the 80387 by special formats. The 80387 also has special formats for representing infinity and zero. You should familiarize yourself with these formats, if only so that you will be prepared should one crop up unexpectedly in your calculations.

Zero   The value of zero can be either positive or negative, although the sign has no conceivable significance to any calculations the 80387 might perform. Typically, the 80387 will produce a positive zero during processing. If a zero is located in one of the eight data registers, that register is tagged as zero. Zero is represented by an exponent field of all 0s, and a significand of all 0s.

Infinity   The value of infinity can also be either positive or negative, and positive infinity is greater than negative infinity, if you check such things. This is known as *affine closure*. The 80287 supports a system whereby both infinities are considered exactly equal (*projective closure*). Infinity is represented by a significand of 100...00 and an exponent of all 1s.

Denormal Numbers   These are not as strange as they might sound. As was mentioned previously, the 80387 does not store the leading zeros of a very small fractional number. Instead, it stores the significand beginning with the first nonzero number, and an exponent calculated to place the binary point a sufficient distance to the left of the first bit in the significand. As immense as the range of the 80387's number system is, it is always possible to create a number that is smaller than can be represented with the most negative exponent possible. In these cases, the 80387 uses the most negative exponent possible for the chosen format and inserts leading zeros in the significand. This increases the range of extremely small numbers that are representable without losing accuracy, as long as all significant bits still fit in the significand field. This conversion will cause a denormal exception unless it is masked. Figure 11-6 illustrates the format of a denormal number.

Not a Number   Because of the carefully formatted way in which IEEE numbers are represented, it is possible to create bit strings that are impossible to interpret as valid numbers. These are flagged as NaN (Not a Number). Out of this has grown a special format reserved for defining undefinable numbers. There are even two kinds of NaNs: *quiet* and *signaling*. A signaling NaN can have any significand between 100...01 and 101...11. A quiet NaN can have any significand from 110...01 to 111...11. Both kinds of NaN have an exponent of all 1s.

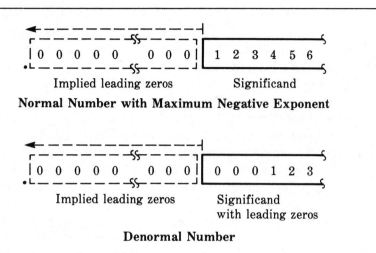

Figure 11-6.   Denormalizing a number

Indefinite   The indefinite number is the default response to several otherwise insoluble problems. In every 80387 storage format, including the integer formats, one encoding is reserved for the indefinite number. It is normally the most negative number that that format can represent. In the three floating-point real formats, indefinite is represented with a significand of 110...00 and an exponent of all 1s.

THE PROCESSOR-TO-COPROCESSOR INTERFACE

Even though the 80387 is a full-fledged processor unto itself, designed to run concurrently with the 80386, it appears to the programmer that the 80386 instruction set has merely been enhanced. The programmer can ignore the fact that the 80387 is an autonomous processor residing on a different chip. (The 80387 will probably be the last separate NPX in the family—the

80486/487 combination is expected to be fabricated on one chip.) In fact, the way in which the 80386/387 combination works is quite elaborate and may be important for you to understand if you are designing for maximum performance.

The 80386 communicates with the 80387 through two I/O ports. One is a command/status port, and the other is a data port. When it encounters an instruction intended for the 80387, the 80386 copies that instruction to the 80387's command port, which is at I/O address 800000F8. The 80386 can recognize all coprocessor instructions because the first 5 bits of the primary opcode are always 11011. The 80386 then fetches its next instruction and continues executing normally. If the 80387 requires more information before it can proceed (if it needs an operand from memory, for example), it asserts the PEREQ (Processor Extension Request) pin, which the two components share. At the next break between instructions, the 80386 reads the 80387's command/status port to determine the coprocessor's need. If the request involves the transfer of operands, the 80386 reads or writes data between memory and the 80387's data port at I/O address 800000FC. If the 80387 requires still more service, it continues to drive PEREQ; otherwise, the 80386 can go about its business. As you can see, the 80387 does not fetch opcodes or operands from memory itself. Instead, it requests that the 80386 do the work for it. Indeed, the 80387 has no external address bus pins or other necessary hardware to perform bus cycles. It is entirely a slave to the host processor.

80387 coprocessor interface

- Completely automatic and transparent to the user
- The 80387 occupies two dedicated I/O addresses
- The 80386 services 80387 requests for data transfers
- The 80387 notifies the 80386 of service requests and errors

While the 80387 is executing an instruction, it drives its external BUSY pin to inform the 80386 that it cannot yet accept a new instruction. Should the 80386 fetch a new 80387 instruction while the 80387 is busy with the previous one, the 80386 will wait patiently until the BUSY signal is gone. Although both processors can execute in parallel, each can execute only one instruction at a time. For maximum performance, you should avoid bunching floating-point instructions together. Otherwise, your 80386 will be nothing more than a very expensive servant for the 80387. Ideally, a new 80387 instruction would be fetched just as the previous one was finishing. This kind of perfect parallelism is virtually impossible, and effective numeric processing consists in large part of trying to achieve this goal.

If the 80387 should detect an unmasked exception, it drives its ERROR pin. The 80386 will not recognize this condition until it fetches another 80387 instruction, at which time it will report the coprocessor error as an exception 16. Your coprocessor exception handler may then examine the 80387 status word to determine its cause.

The 80387 instruction set consists entirely of arithmetic, trigonometric, and transcendental functions. There are no conditional or flow-of-control instructions, only floating-point forms of test and compare instructions. These affect the 80387 status word flags C0 through C3. Your 80386 code must examine the outcome of numeric comparisons by reading these bits. The 80387 instruction FSTSW AX (store status word in AX) is ideal for this. Better still, follow this with an SAHF (store AH into FLAGS) 80386 instruction, and you're all set up for a conditional JMP or SET instruction. By no coincidence, the 80387 condition codes mate with three of the 80386 flags, as shown here:

Bit Position	80386 Flag	80387 Flag
6	ZF	C3
2	PF	C2
0	CF	C0

The 80386 is able to communicate with an 80287 instead of an 80387, if you so desire. The two parts are largely compatible (naturally), the major difference being the 80287's 16-bit data bus. Partly because of this and partly because of technology changes, an 80287 operates at about 20% of the speed of an 80387. If the ET (Extension Type) bit in CR0 is set, the 80386 uses 32-bit 80387 communication protocol. If ET is reset, the 80386 uses the older, 16-bit 80287 protocol. By an interesting trick of hardware, the 80386 is able to tell the difference between an 80287 and an 80387 when the parts are first reset. If an 80387 is installed in your 80386 system, the processor will set ET for you automatically as it comes out of reset. If ET is not set, it means there is either an 80287 installed or no coprocessor at all.

Two other bits in CR0 also determine the 80386's actions when it encounters a coprocessor instruction. The EM (Emulate) bit should be set if you want to emulate 80387 functions in software. If the 80386 fetches a coprocessor instruction while EM equals 1, it generates an exception 7, coprocessor not available. The MP (Math Present) bit is a sort of corollary to EM. It is meant to indicate whether or not a coprocessor (80287 or 80387) is actually attached. EM and MP should never be set at the same time. Whereas the 80386 can set ET by itself, you must set or clear EM and MP in software.

DIFFERENCES AMONG THE 80387, 80287, AND 8087

First, the differences between the 80387 and 80287 will be detailed. After that is a list of additional changes you should watch for if you are familiar only with the 8087. In no particular order, the differences are as follows:

Error Status   When the 80387 is reset, it comes up with an "artificial" invalid-operation exception. Bits IE and ES in the 80387 status word are set, and the ERROR pin is driven active. You must execute an FNINIT instruction before the 80387 is usable.

Unsupported Formats   The 80387 does not recognize or support four data formats supported by the 80287. These are pseudo-zero, pseudo-infinity, pseudo-NaN, and unnormal. The 80387 generates an invalid-operation exception if it encounters one of these.

Unsupported Tags   The 80287 tags pseudo-zero and unnormal as valid (tag = 00). Pseudo-infinity and pseudo-NaN are tagged invalid (tag = 10). The 80387 tags all four as invalid.

Inconsistent Tags   It is possible to load the tag word with a tag value that does not correctly reflect the value in the data register it is tagging. An 80287 will believe the tag while the 80387 will examine the register. One exception is an empty tag (tag = 11). In such cases, the 80387 believes the register to be empty.

Stack Fault   The Stack Fault bit in the status word is new to the 80387.

Infinity Control   The 80287 supports both affine closure (negative infinity < positive infinity) and projective closure (negative infinity = positive infinity). The 80387 supports only affine closure. Bit 13 of the control word is now undefined.

Condition Codes   Flags C0 through C3 are cleared by a reset, an FINIT instruction, or an incomplete FPREM instruction. The 80287 does not modify these bits.

Quiet NaN   The 80387 supports the concept of a quiet NaN, which does not generate exceptions.

Operations on Denormals   An FSQRT, FDIV, or FPREM instruction, or a conversion to integer (including BCD) on a denormal number causes an invalid-operation exception on the 80287. The 80387 simply normalizes the value.

Denormal Exceptions   The FXTRACT instruction and all transcendental instructions never raise a denormal exception on the 80287. The 80387 can raise denormal exceptions in these cases.

New Instructions The following mnemonics are new to the 80387:

FPREM1	Partial remainder
FUCOM, FUCOMP, FUCOMPP	Unordered comparisons
FSIN, FCOS, FSINCOS	Sine and cosine

FSETPM The 80387 treats the FSETPM instruction as an FNOP. The 80386/80387 interface is such that it always knows when the main processor is operating in Protected mode.

Differences from the 8087

All of the following changes should be considered in addition to those listed above when you are transporting 8087 code to the 80387.

FENI and FDISI The 80387 treats the FENI and FDISI instructions as FNOPS.

Exception 16 The 80387 uses a dedicated ERROR pin to signal exceptions to the 80386. This has a fixed vector of 16. The 8087 generated standard hardware interrupts and was handled accordingly.

Exception 7 The 8086/87 combination did not support the coprocessor not available fault (exception 7). You may have to write a new handler for this fault.

Operand Wrap The 80386 does not wrap addresses around the 64KB "barrier," as an 8086 does, so be sure that 8086/87 code does not make use of this feature.

Instruction Prefixes   When an 8087 generated an interrupt because of an unmasked exception, the 8086 would push the segment and offset of the coprocessor instruction, sans prefix bytes, if any. The 80387 state includes all instruction prefixes.

Loosened WAIT Requirements   For both the 8086/87 and 80286/287 combinations, the programmer was required to insert a WAIT instruction whenever there was the possibility of the main processor and coprocessor reading from or writing to the same location in memory. This is no longer the case. The only requirement is that you insert a WAIT opcode or any other coprocessor instruction between the 80387 instruction that writes an operand to memory and the 80386 instruction that tries to read it. This ensures that the floating-point result has, in fact, been completely stored.

In this chapter, you have seen that the addition of an 80387 floating-point coprocessor can make a great amount of difference in the overall performance of your system. Indeed, the integration of an 80387 is not usually considered an option: you either need it or you don't. If you do need one, there's no getting along without it. When the 80386 and 80387 are working well together, you truly have two processors operating at once.

   In the next chapter, you will see how you might be able to make some more prosaic improvements in the performance of your software.

12

PROGRAMMING
FOR PERFORMANCE

The 80386 is unquestionably one of the highest-performance microprocessors available today. Its 32-bit address and data buses allow it to manipulate nearly limitless amounts of memory directly and to gobble up data 4 bytes at a time. The 80386's instruction set is ideally suited for memory-to-memory transfers or comparisons, substring searches, or area fills. With the help of an 80387 numeric coprocessor, your 80386 system can rival the number-crunching capability of many mainframes less than ten years old.

Everybody has their own ideas about what makes a computer or a microprocessor fast, and every application is different. An architecture that yields ideal results for one application may perform terribly with another. Some computer tasks may be processor-bound (tying up the CPU), while others are I/O-bound (waiting for disks, tapes, terminals, and so on). Benchmark claims and comparisons are made regularly by silicon manufacturers, systems integrators, and software vendors, but unless the benchmark conditions reflect your intended application fairly accurately, their numbers are nearly meaningless. What really counts is how *your* software performs in the real world.

The number of factors that can affect the performance of a running computer is equal to the number of electronic compo-

Table 12-1.   Benchmarking Factors

Hardware Considerations

Memory speed	Affects code, data, and stack references
Memory bus width	A 32-bit bus is twice as fast as a 16-bit bus
Disk performance	May affect program and overlay load time
RAM size	Insufficient RAM may force swapping
CPU frequency	Directly affects execution time
Interrupt frequency	Servicing interrupts adds overhead

Software Considerations

Size of program	May not fit into available RAM
Compiler and/or assembler	Can greatly affect efficiency of code
Integer/floating mix	Floating point is slow without an 80387
Multitasking	Task-switch overhead takes time

nents it contains. Almost anything can have an adverse (or beneficial) effect on how quickly and smoothly the finished system runs. Even the fastest machine is not going to perform well, however, if the software is no good. Poorly written software can drag down an otherwise phenomenal machine. Likewise, well-written software can rescue mediocre hardware. Examples of both of these cases abound in the commercial market. Table 12-1 summarizes some items to watch for.

The techniques for writing good software are far beyond the scope of this book. Instead, this chapter shows how you might be able to squeeze extra performance out of your programs. The suggestions and examples in this chapter are not so much generic practices for good programming as they are 80386-specific tricks or tweaks.

Assuming that your code already does what it is supposed to, the goal now is to optimize it. Usually you optimize for speed. Sometimes, however, you want to decrease the size of object code.

This might be the case if you're trying to shoehorn too much code into a limited space, such as an EPROM. Here you will learn various ways to speed up 80386 code, as well as a few ways of decreasing code size.

OPTIMAL ADDRESSING

To be able to trim execution time, you must understand how the 80386 fetches and executes code. It also helps to understand how operands are transferred to and from memory. Sometimes simply rearranging instructions in your code can save a little time without changing the work done.

The 80386 is always fetching instructions. It continually fills an instruction pipeline with object code. Newly fetched instructions go in one end of the instruction pipeline, and the microprocessor executes instructions that it pulls out of the other end. The instruction pipeline is 16 bytes long, so it will typically hold four to eight complete instructions. See Figure 12-1.

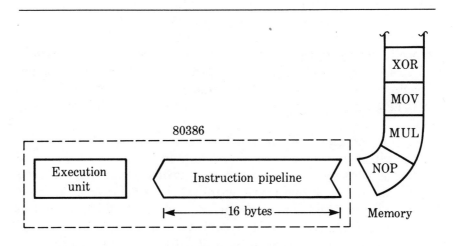

Figure 12-1. Instruction pipeline

To keep the pipeline constantly filled (or nearly so), a portion of the 80386 does nothing but 32-bit reads from memory. These reads are always 32-bit-aligned. That is, the prefetch unit (as it is called) reads 4 bytes, increments its address counter by 4, reads 4 more bytes, and so on. It pays no attention to what it is fetching or what other activity might be going on. It makes no attempt to fetch multibyte instructions in one piece; it simply reads the next 4 bytes. Therefore, if the majority of your instructions begin on 4-byte-aligned addresses, more complete instructions will fit into the pipeline. If most instructions are misaligned, the instruction pipeline will hold fewer complete instructions and more frag- mented ones. Because 80386 instructions come in all sizes, from 1 byte to more than a dozen bytes in length, it is just about impossi- ble to write a usable program that is completely aligned in this way, but it is something to keep in mind. An occasional NOP instruction to align major subroutines or often-used loops can pay off. Figure 12-2 shows how proper code alignment can save an entire code fetch cycle.

Whenever you read or write data items to or from memory, the 80386 suspends automatic code prefetching to carry out the data transfer. During this time the instruction pipeline is being drained but not refilled. If your memory or I/O device is particu- larly slow to respond, the pipeline may run dry. At that point, the 80386 must execute at reduced capacity. This problem is related more to hardware than to software, but you should be aware of it. If you must do several memory transfers, you might consider spacing them out, with non-memory-transfer instructions in between. This will give the prefetch mechanism a chance to catch up.

As is the case with instructions, you will see better perfor- mance if your memory operands are aligned. The 80386's 32-bit data bus allows you to transfer 4 bytes to or from memory at once, but only if all 4 bytes are within the same dword address. Transferring 4 bytes to or from an unaligned address, such as 1D063, requires twice as much time as an aligned transfer. A 16- bit transfer need only be 16-bit-aligned to run at top speed, and 8-bit transfers need not be aligned at all. Unlike instruction alignment, operand alignment is usually under the control of the

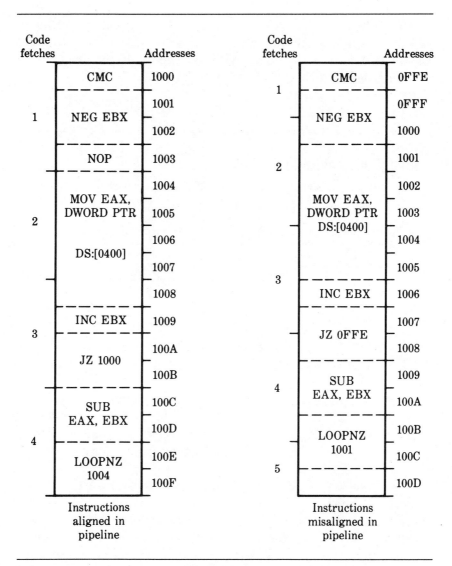

Figure 12-2. Code alignment

assembly language programmer, and so you may want to consider this option.

Everything that is true for data operand alignment is doubly true for stacks. A misaligned stack will have immediate and obvious effects on your execution time. Stack operations occur all of the time, and once a stack is misaligned it tends to stay that way. A 32-bit stack should be dword-aligned; a 16-bit stack can be word-aligned, but dword alignment won't hurt.

80386 instruction prefetch

- Prefetching instructions increases CPU performance
- The 80386 attempts to keep 16 bytes of code in the pipeline
- Instruction alignment affects prefetch performance
- Operand alignment affects memory performance
- Stack alignment affects subroutine and exception-handling performance

---

USING REGISTERS

One way to avoid data alignment problems is, of course, not to use memory. Unfortunately, all but the smallest utilities need some place to store data, intermediate results, output strings, and so forth. Whenever possible, you should try to store as much data as you can in registers.

The 80386 has eight general-purpose registers, each 32 bits wide. With the exception of ESP, you can use any one of them for random storage with no ill effects. Every 80386 operation that can work with either registers or memory operates faster if a register is used. How much faster depends on your memory speed, but a factor of two is a minimum for most instructions.

All eight 32-bit registers can be broken into an upper and a lower half, with the lower half instantly addressable as its own register. For example, the lower 16 bits of register ESI are usable as SI. Very few operations on the lower half of a register will disturb the upper half.

Although the upper halves of the registers have not been assigned names, they are usable nonetheless. All it takes is a 16-bit rotate instruction to swap the upper and lower halves of any 32-bit register; you then have access to a second half-register.

Four of the eight general-purpose registers can also be treated as byte quantities. For example, the least significant byte of register EDX is DL. Better still, the second-least-significant byte is also addressable directly, in this case as DH. All told, you have eight single-byte registers useful for holding ASCII characters, small constants, table indexes, and so on.

Register usage

- Register storage is two to ten times faster than memory

- The 80386 has seven general purpose 32-bit registers *or*

- Seven general-purpose 16-bit registers *or*

- Eight general-purpose 8-bit registers

- Unused halves of registers can be used with rotate instructions

---

INSTRUCTION EXECUTION TIME

Not all 80386 instructions take the same amount of time to execute, just as not all instructions require the same number of bytes. Some functions are more complex than others and consequently take longer for the processor to resolve. The amount of time it takes to execute every possible permutation of every possible instruction can be found in the *80386 Programmer's Reference Manual* (Intel order number 230985).

The amount of time a given instruction takes to execute is usually expressed as a number of clock cycles. The amount of real time a clock cycle represents depends on the operating frequency of your 80386 microprocessor. You can find the elapsed time for a single clock cycle by taking the inverse of the frequency. For a 16-MHz 80386, the operating frequency is 16 MHz, or 16,000,000 cycles per second. The inverse of this number is 0.0000000625, or 62.5 nanoseconds. Therefore, one clock cycle equals 62.5 nanoseconds for a 16-MHz processor. A clock cycle takes 50 nanoseconds for a 20-MHz processor and 40 nanoseconds at 25 MHz.

The quickest instructions take at least two clock cycles to execute, and so the maximum rate at which a 16-MHz 80386 can do anything is 8 million instructions per second. Mind you, this is not doing very much actual work. Most instructions in an average program take longer than two clock cycles to execute, so a figure of about 3 million instructions per second is more realistic. This is where the acronym "MIPS" comes from: million instructions per second. It has also been described as "meaningless indicator of performance."

Execution speed

- Speed is often rated in MIPS (million instructions/second)
- Processor operating frequency affects speed rating
- Memory speed affects execution speed
- Alignment of code, operands, and stack all affect execution speed
- 80386 processors average about 3 to 5 MIPS

Selecting the Right Instructions

Given that various instructions take varying amounts of time to execute, the trick is to get your work done using the instructions that execute in the least amount of time. In this section, you will see some nonstandard ways of doing things that can buy you greater speed, more-compact object code, or both.

Conditional JMPs   The conditional JMP instructions (JNE, JO, JNC, and so on) are the basis of almost every program ever written. Conditional execution on the evaluation of a Boolean expression is a fundamental characteristic of any digital computer. If you are programming for speed, you may want to take a close look at your use of conditional JMP instructions.

If the conditional JMP is *not* taken (that is, if flow of control "falls through"), the 80386 requires three clock cycles to process the instruction. If the JMP *is* taken, the number of clock cycles required varies but is always at least eight. The exact time depends on the size (in bytes) of the instruction that is the destination of the JMP. The longer it is, the longer the JMP takes.

A conditional JMP takes longer to execute when the Boolean expression is true because the new destination instruction is not already in the instruction pipeline. The 80386 blindly fetches ahead sequentially, and when it executes code out of sequence, it must flush the pipeline and fetch a new set of instructions. This also explains why the size of the target instruction affects execution time. See Figure 12-3.

XOR versus MOV   If you want to move the quantity 0 into a register, use the XOR instruction to exclusive-OR the register with itself instead. Regardless of the contents of the register, an XOR with itself will always produce a 0. This technique will not save you any time at all (both forms take two clock cycles), but it does save space. It also tends to confound people who are reading your code, so always include a comment.

AND versus BTR   The 80386 has added four bit-test instructions to the instruction set. These test and sometimes modify a single bit either in memory or a register and return its status in the Carry flag. The same functions can sometimes be performed with generic logic routines, which execute two to three times fast-

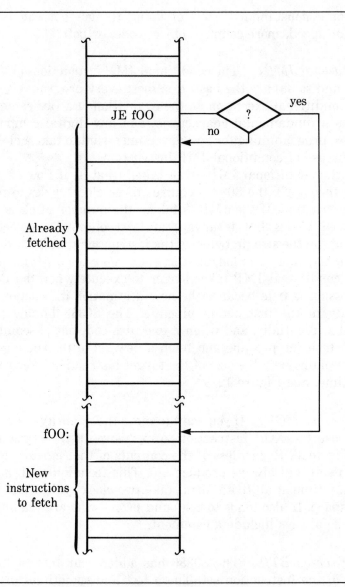

Figure 12-3.   Effects of conditional JMP instructions

er. For example, you might replace the BTR instruction with an AND instruction that has a 0 bit in the operand field, representing the bit to be reset.

```
; Using BTR instruction...
        BTR     EAX, 7                         ;test bit 7, and clear it
        JC      true                           ;jump if bit was set

        BTR     WORD PTR DS:[1234], 4          ;test bit 4, and clear it
        JC      true                           ;jump if bit was set
; Using AND instruction...
        AND     EAX, 01111111B                 ;clear bit 7
        JZ      true                           ;jump if result is zero

        AND     WORD PTR DS:[1234], 11101111B  ;clear bit 4
        JZ      true                           ;jump if result is zero
```

OR versus BTS   Similarly, you can sometimes replace the BTS instruction with an OR instruction that has a 1 bit representing the bit you want to set:

```
; Using BTS instruction...
        BTS     EAX, 7                         ;test bit 7 and set it
        JC      true                           ;jump if bit was set

        BTS     WORD PTR DS:[1234], 4          ;test bit 4 and set it
        JC      true
; Using OR instruction...
        OR      EAX, 10000000B                 ;set bit 7
        JPO     true                           ;jump if only 1 bit

        OR      WORD PTR DS:[1234], 00010000B  ;set bit 4
        JPO     true                           ;jump if only 1 bit
```

XOR versus BTC   The XOR instruction inverts those bits in the destination register or memory that are paired up with a 1 bit in the source operand. The following illustrates this:

```
; Using BTC instruction...
        BTC     EAX, 7                         ;test bit 7, then swap it
        JC      true                           ;jump if bit was set

        BTC     WORD PTR DS:[1234], 4          ;test bit 4, then swap it
        JC      true                           ;jump if bit was set
; Using XOR instruction...
        XOR     EAX, 10000000B                 ;toggle bit 7
        JZ      true                           ;jump if result is zero

        XOR     WORD PTR DS:[1234], 00010000B  ;toggle bit 4
        JZ      true                           ;jump if result is zero
```

The MOV instructions   Very few forms of the MOV instruction alter the EFLAGS register in any way. Because of this, you can insert as many MOV instructions as you want between a comparison or testing instruction and the conditional JMP or conditional SET that acts on it. Although doing this may not save any execution time, it might save code space if the MOV instructions were going to be done in both halves of the conditional branch anyway.

LEA versus MUL   This is probably one of the most obscure speed tricks and one of the most useful. The LEA instruction loads an effective address into a register. That is, it causes the 80386 to evaluate the memory addressing mode for the source operand, simplify it, and load the simplified effective address (offset) into the destination register. Nothing is ever transferred to or from that memory address; the 80386 simply calculates where it is. You can use any addressing mode to specify the source operand.

Because the 80386 has doubly indirect addressing modes, which use two registers, and scaled addressing, you can put together addresses like this:

    DWORD PTR DS:[EAX][EAX * 4]

If you were to use this kind of addressing mode in an LEA instruction, the destination register would be loaded with a value representing the contents of EAX times 5. Best of all, LEA always executes in two clock cycles, making it one of the quickest operations the 80386 can perform. A normal multiply by 5 would take up to 41 clock cycles! The following code fragment shows some samples of multiplication done with LEA:

```
LEA     EAX, DS:[EAX][EAX * 4]      ;EAX gets EAX times five
LEA     EBX, DS:[ECX * 8]           ;EBX gets ECX times eight

LEA     EDX, DS:[ESI][ESI * 2]      ;EDX gets ESI times three

LEA     EAX, DS:[EBX][ECX * 8]      ;EAX = EBX + (ECX X 8)

LEA     ECX, DS:[ECX][ECX * 4]      ;ECX gets ECX times five ...
LEA     ECX, DS:[ECX][ECX * 4]      ;times five again (25 X) ...
LEA     ECX, DS:[ECX * 4]           ;times four (100 X)
```

CBW and CWDE versus MOVSX   The CBW instruction sign-extends AL into AX, and CWDE sign-extends AX into EAX. The new 80386 instruction MOVSX performs the same function but offers two advantages: MOVSX will work with any register, not just the accumulator, and the source operand can be in memory. Also, MOVSX can directly sign-extend an 8-bit quantity to 32 bits. This would otherwise require a CBW followed by a CWDE.

Shift versus multiply and divide   As any practiced assembly language programmer knows, you can multiply a number by shifting it to the left, and you can divide a number by shifting it to the right, as long as you are multiplying or dividing by a power of 2. If you know that multiplication and division operations in your program will be thus constrained, you can save yourself a lot of time. Figure 12-4 and the following program listing illustrate this concept.

```
MOV     EBX, DWORD PTR DS:[1234]        ;read from memory
SHL     EBX, 4                          ;multiply by 16

MOV     EBX, DWORD PTR DS:[1234]        ;read from memory
SAR     EBX, 3                          ;divide by 8
```

LOOP versus DEC and JNZ   The LOOP instruction decrements ECX and performs a conditional branch depending on whether or not it equals 0. Other forms of LOOP check EFLAGS also. The LOOP instruction is very handy but not particularly efficient. You can do better by using a simple DEC instruction followed by a JNZ (or any other conditional branch, as you see fit). The advantages are reduced clock cycle count, and the fact that you can use any register or memory operand you want for a loop counter.

There are doubtless other techniques for trimming execution time or code size. Every programmer has a few favorites that get sprinkled into programs now and again. Programming is as much an art as a science, and every practitioner has a unique style.

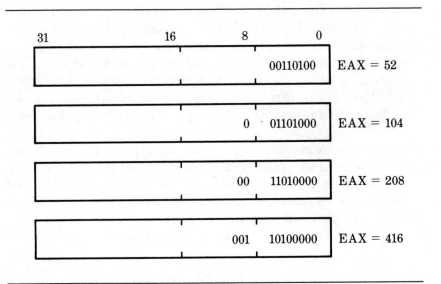

Figure 12-4.   Multiplication using the SHL instruction

In the next chapter, you will see how the 80386 looks as it comes to life after a power-up reset. As you will see, it behaves very differently than it does in Protected mode, and no small amount of software is required to get it fully up and running.

13

RESET AND REAL MODE

So far, this book has dealt almost exclusively with the 80386's Protected Virtual Address mode of operation. Chapter 9 detailed another mode of operation, Virtual 8086 mode. This chapter covers the third and final operating mode of the 80386: Real Address mode.

Real Address mode, or simply Real mode, is the simplest and most basic operating mode that the 80386 supports. Real mode is much like an 8086's normal (and only) style of operation or like Virtual 8086 mode on the 80386. When the 80386 is first turned on, or reset, it always begins operating in Real mode. For this reason, the systems programmer must become familiar with Real mode operation, if only to prepare the processor to operate in Protected mode. This chapter covers the state of the 80386 as it comes out of reset, Real mode operation, and the transition from Real mode to Protected mode (and back, if desired).

RESETTING THE 80386

Any time the 80386 receives an active level on its RESET input pin, it immediately terminates all processing, memory activity, exception handling, and so forth, and resets itself. Similarly, when an 80386-based machine first receives power, the 80386 initiates internal reset procedures. A power-up reset is indistinguishable from a hardware reset.

Self-Test

Reset processing consists of several stages. First, all current program execution ceases. Next, the processor may or may not begin a self-test of its internal functions. This test is initiated by external hardware. If the 80386's BUSY input pin is held in the active (low-voltage) state by external hardware at the proper moment, the 80386 will perform the self-test. Otherwise, the self-test is skipped. The precise hardware requirements for generating a self-test are detailed in the next chapter.

The internal self-test takes from 20 to 35 milliseconds to complete and can detect roughly 90% of common "random logic" failures, according to Intel. If the self-test is requested and the 80386 passes the test, register EAX will contain all 0 bits when your software begins to execute. A nonzero value in EAX indicates some form of self-test failure, although there is no way to determine the cause.

80386 self-test

- The 80386 can perform a self-test when it is reset
- A self-test is requested by driving BUSY active
- Approximately 90% of processor logic failures are found

Designing your hardware to initiate a processor self-test (if you have that luxury) is heartily recommended. When your power-up or reset code starts to execute, one of the first things you should do is to check EAX against 0. If it is equal to 0, all is well. If it is not, you may have a faulty processor. If so, the next step is up to you. Because the capabilities of a faulty processor are never certain, don't write anything elaborate to signal a self-test failure. One reasonable action is simply to turn an LED on and halt. Especially, avoid a lot of memory references, since the external address and data bus control may be suspect.

One final point to remember is not to check EAX unless your hardware requested a self-test. Without the self-test, the value of EAX is indeterminate, but experience has shown that it is rarely 0.

Processor and Revision ID

In addition to updating the contents of register EAX after the optional self-test, the 80386 alters register DX whenever it is powered up or reset. When your software begins executing, DH will always contain the binary value 3 (00000011). This is intended to identify the processor as an 80386. The 80286 does not put a 2 in DH on reset, nor does the 80186 store a 1. Presumably, this is a new feature intended to aid in super-compatibility with future iAPX 86 family processors (the 80486 and so on). By examining the contents of DH shortly after reset, your software can determine exactly what kind of processor it is running on. For now, this action has limited use. You could, if you wanted, write reset code to distinguish an 80386 from an earlier-generation processor, but that's about all.

After reset, register DL contains a value that identifies the revision of the 80386 silicon you are using. Every time a change is made to an integrated circuit (such as the 80386 microprocessor), one or more new "masks" must be created for the silicon wafer-fabrication process. New masks are typically generated only to fix bugs in the device or to enhance performance, since the process is incredibly expensive.

Part of the 80386's mask determines the value left in DL after reset. Generally, when changes are made to the 80386, the value in DL is incremented. This gives your software a "fast and loose" way to determine the revision level of your processor. Intel makes no guarantees that all mask changes will store a unique value in

DL or that the values that are stored will proceed in any logical sequence. All you can determine with certainty is that two processors that produce different values in DL are not of the same revision.

This feature might be useful for anticipating known bugs in certain revisions of the silicon (there are several), or you can just ignore it completely. Keep in mind that the part number in DH and the mask revision in DL are independent of the self-test request. Register DX is updated automatically after every reset.

Automatic 80387 Detection

One particularly nice feature of the 80386 is its ability to sniff out an 80387 numeric processor extension (NPX) on reset, if one is present. Recall that the Extension Type bit (ET, bit 4) in CR0 determines whether the 80386 uses the 80287 or 80387 protocol to communicate with a coprocessor. If you set ET, the 32-bit 80387 protocol is used. If ET is not set, the 80386 uses 16-bit 80287-style communication.

When the 80386 is being reset, it samples its ERROR input pin. If this pin is in the active (low-voltage) state, the 80386 deduces that an 80387 is connected to it (since all 80387s place an error indication in the status word when they are reset). This being the case, the processor automatically sets ET for you, selecting 80387 communication. If ERROR is not active, ET is cleared.

In the latter case, there is no way, without a little software testing, to determine whether an 80287 is connected, an 80387 is connected in a nonstandard way, or no coprocessor is present at all.

The following program listing shows a simple way to distinguish between an 80287 and no coprocessor at all. First, the coprocessor (if any) is reset, and then the status word is copied into AX. After initialization, a coprocessor's exception flags should all be clear. If no coprocessor is connected, the 80386 will typically read a "floating bus" and return all 1s. By performing a simple check on the returned data, you can determine with a high degree of confidence whether or not a coprocessor is connected.

```
FNINIT                        ;initialize NPX
FSTSW        AX               ;AX gets status word
CMP          AL, 0            ;AL = 0 ?
JE           okay             ;yes -- NPX present
```

Initial Register Contents

In addition to the values stored in the three registers mentioned previously (EAX, DX, and CR0), the 80386 stores constant values in most general-purpose registers. Figure 13-1 shows the state of the 80386 register set after power-up or reset.

An EFLAGS value of 2 indicates that all flags are clear, including IF. (Bit 1 is always set and performs no function.) All segment registers are 0, effectively limiting access to the lowest 64KB of memory after reset. The 16-bit instruction pointer, IP, is set to FFF0, and so the 80386 will fetch its very first instruction 16 bytes from the end of the initial code segment (more on this later). Even though an interrupt descriptor table is not used in Real mode (the 80386's operating mode after reset), the IDTR is initialized for a base address of 0 and a limit of 03FF (1023 decimal). Registers marked with X's are undefined after reset. All debug and test registers are undefined as well.

Fetching the First Instructions

After the 80386 is reset and has completed the steps described in the previous section, it is operating in Real Address mode and begins fetching and executing instructions. After reset, the 80386 always fetches its first instruction from a fixed address. After that, it is under control of your software. The physical address at which the first instruction must be placed is FFFFFFF0. This is exactly 16 bytes before the absolute high end of the 80386's 4GB address space.

You can put any instruction you like at this location, but if it is not a JMP, one of the next few instructions following it must be. Sixteen bytes is not a lot of room, and the 80386 is near the end of

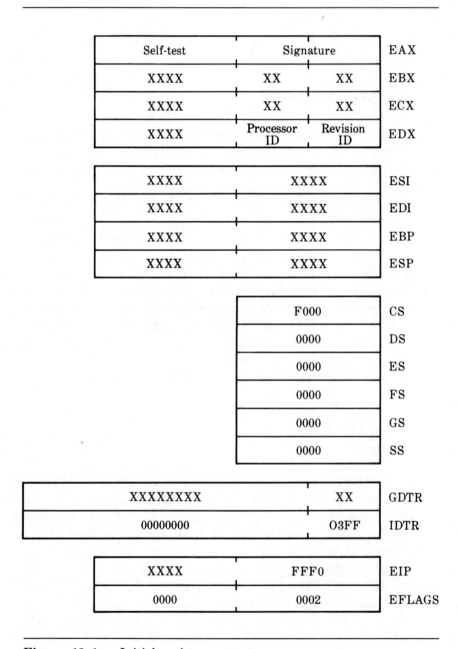

Figure 13-1.   Initial register contents

its address space as it is. Do not attempt to wrap around the end of this address space on power-up or reset—the 80386 will shut down. That's much too elaborate a trick for a processor that has just begun to run.

The first instruction is fetched from FFFFFFF0, even though the reset value of CS is F000 and IP is FFF0. This value would normally select an address of 000FFFF0, which is 16 bytes from the end of a 1MB address space. In fact, the 8086/88 and 80186/88 do select this address. However, when the 80386 is reset, the address pins for A20 through A31 are automatically driven high for instruction fetches and other references to the code segment (CS). This creates a physical address that is much higher than the linear address that CS and IP would indicate. By automatically boosting CS-relative addresses in this way, the 80386 makes it easy to place a bootstrap ROM at the extreme upper end of the 80386's 4GB address space, instead of in the middle, around the 1MB boundary.

Recall that the stack segment and four data segment registers all contain 0. Therefore, after reset, they all point to a 64KB segment at the extreme low end of the memory space. Of course, you can alter these registers to allow access to any address in the low 1MB of memory. Memory references that use any of these five segment registers are not boosted, as code-segment-relative references are. The resulting memory map is shown in Figure 13-2.

The automatic boosting of CS-relative memory references (including instruction fetch) has another advantage. Besides being able to place startup code in a ROM at the high end of the address space, you can also place constant data in the ROM and copy it to low memory by using MOV instructions with CS override prefixes. This is extremely useful for copying things like descriptor tables and TSSs from the boot ROM before you enable Protected mode.

This peculiar memory map, in which CS-relative memory references use the extreme high end of memory, lasts only until the first time CS is changed. After that, address boosting is turned off permanently, and a more normal and familiar 1MB address map is used. You will no longer be able to access your bootstrap ROM or anything else addressed above 1MB.

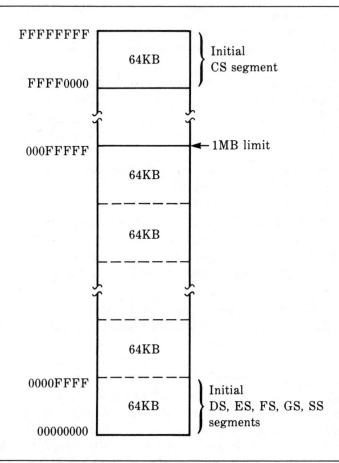

Figure 13-2.   Initial memory map

As always, the only way to alter CS in Real mode is to perform a FAR (intersegment) control transfer. This could be a FAR JMP, a FAR CALL, or a FAR RET instruction. NEAR (intrasegment) control transfers do not affect code segment address boosting, but the very first intersegment control transfer turns it off permanently. Typically, you will want to write your power-up and reset code (the bootstrap code) to perform a FAR JMP shortly after any necessary memory and I/O initialization is completed.

Address map after reset

- The 80386 boosts all CS-relative addresses after reset
- Boosting causes the first instruction to be fetched from FFFFFFF0
- Segments DS, ES, FS, GS, and SS are not affected by boosting
- The first intersegment transfer instruction cancels boosting

REAL MODE OPERATION

Real Address mode is the third mode of 80386 operation, the other two being Protected mode and Virtual 8086 mode. In capabilities, Real mode is like Virtual 8086 mode, which is to say it is much like an 8086. Real mode is somewhat more rudimentary, however, for it does not allow the programmer to use many of the 80386 features available in Virtual 8086 mode. Multitasking and paging, for example, cannot be used in Real Address mode.

Whenever the 80386 is reset or powered up, it begins operating in Real mode. You can continue to operate the processor in Real mode, if you want, or your startup code can initialize the 80386 for Protected mode or Virtual 8086 mode (which requires Protected mode operation first). The transition from Real mode to Protected mode is covered in detail in the next section. The remainder of this section looks at the capabilities of the 80386 in Real mode.

Of the 80386's three major operating modes, Real mode most closely approximates an actual 8086/88. This is the mode in which most 80386 microcomputers run today. The MS-DOS operating system was never designed to deal with flexible segmentation, privilege protection, multitasking, paging, or any of the other features available in Protected mode or even in Virtual 8086 mode, and so Real mode is the easiest solution. Commercial software products are available that place a Real mode MS-DOS machine into Protected mode in order to run special applications, but these are currently the exception rather than the rule.

Real Mode Registers and Instructions

Like Virtual 8086 mode, Real mode represents an 8086 processor with a plus. In addition to all of the standard 8086 registers, a Real mode program has access to the 80386's 32-bit register set, including the control, debug, and test registers. You access the 32-bit registers by using an operand-size override prefix byte (66) immediately before a normal 16-bit operation. The special-purpose registers are available through the normal MOV instructions used in Protected mode to access the control, debug, and test registers. The only two registers not available in Real mode are those specific to Protected mode, namely TR (task register) and LDTR (local descriptor table register). Data segment registers FS and GS are also available in Real mode and can be used through the two corresponding segment override prefix bytes, 64 and 65.

Almost the entire 80386 instruction set is available to you in Real mode. As is the case with the registers, only those instructions that are specific to Protected mode operation cannot be used, namely,

    VERR, VERW
    LAR, LSL
    LTR, STR
    LLDT, SLDT
    ARPL

These instructions generate an exception 6 (invalid opcode fault). All of the other 80386 enhancements to the instruction set can be used, such as bit-manipulation instructions, conditional JMP instructions with 32-bit displacements, and so on.

Even though privilege levels are not used in Real mode, the effective CPL, for all intents and purposes, is 0. This is why the special-purpose registers are available from Real mode and not from Virtual 8086 mode. Because CPL is essentially 0 during Real mode execution, the IOPL (I/O Privilege Level) field in EFLAGS has no effect. Like those in an 8086, I/O operations in

Real mode are always legal. Because Real mode does not support multitasking and therefore does not support TSSs, there are no I/O Permission bit maps, either.

Real mode protection

- The CPL in Real mode is always 0 (most privileged)

- The control, debug, and test registers are accessible

- All privileged instructions are allowed

- All I/O instructions are allowed

- Protected mode-only instructions are restricted

- No access is allowed to local descriptor tables or task registers

---

Real Mode Addressing

Memory segment descriptors are not used in Real mode. Instead, the 80386 forms addresses as an 8086 would, using the contents of a segment register as a paragraph base address and adding a 16-bit offset. This is also the mechanism used in Virtual 8086 mode. With this system, a logical offset address cannot exceed 16 bits (FFFF), and the final physical address will never be greater than 10FFEF. Unlike an 8086, the 80386 will not wrap physical addresses greater than 1MB, because it has a 32-bit-wide address bus. This gives the programmer working in Real mode on the 80386 an address space almost 64KB larger than the 8086's 1MB. You may need to be mindful of this difference if you are porting 8086/88 or 80186/88 applications that depend on 1MB wrap-around.

You are allowed to use address-size override prefix bytes (opcode 67) to generate 32-bit addresses in Real mode. However, the usefulness of this is questionable, considering how Real mode addresses are formed. Regardless of whether 16-bit or 32-bit addressing is used, you can never generate a logical offset greater than FFFF. If an offset greater than 64KB is used, the 80386 generates a general protection fault (exception 13) or a stack fault (exception 12). These exceptions, like all exceptions in Real mode, do not push an error code, as they do in Protected mode. They merely cause the 80386 to push CS, IP, and FLAGS onto the stack (16 bits apiece).

In addition to performing 8086-style address calculation, the 80386 in Real mode executes instructions with 8086 addressing modes. Only SI and DI can be used as index registers, and only BX and BP can be used as base registers for memory addressing. The other general-purpose registers cannot be used as address registers, nor is scaled addressing supported.

Paging is not enabled in Real Address mode, nor are any multitasking features. Like an 8086, an 80386 in Real mode executes only one program, and that one program has complete control over the processor and the resources of the computer.

No address translation is possible in Real mode, so all linear addresses in Real mode are also physical addresses. A Real mode program is restricted to the first megabyte of physical memory plus the last 64KB, which is available during bootstrap procedures only. The vast majority of the 80386's potential 4GB address space is unusable.

Page-level privilege protection is also unavailable in Real mode. No page descriptors or tables need to be defined, and the effective CPL is always 0. Again, as is true on an 8086 or 80186, the currently running program has complete control of the processor and system. Obviously, since paging is not supported, demand-paged virtual memory techniques do not work in Real mode either.

Address generation in Real mode

- No descriptors or selectors are used

- Linear addresses are limited to 1MB plus about 64KB

- Page translation is not allowed

- Only limited 8086-style index and base register usage is allowed

- No memory protection is available

Exception Processing

When the 80386 is operating in Real mode, it handles interrupts and other exceptions just as an 8086 would; in fact, in this respect, Real mode is closer to a true 8086 than Virtual 8086 mode is. When the processor recognizes an exception in Virtual 8086 mode, the 80386 immediately switches to Protected mode. All exception processing is performed by Protected mode ISRs, and then the 80386 switches back to Virtual 8086 mode to resume the interrupted program. This is not the case at all in Real mode. Instead, the 80386 performs all exception processing without any changes in operating mode. Locating the exception vector, executing the ISR, and handling the stack are all done just as an 8086 or 80186 would.

The biggest difference in the way the 80386 handles exceptions in Real mode, as opposed to Protected mode, is the way in which it locates the ISR. In Protected mode, the interrupt descriptor table (IDT) contains 256 eight-byte gate descriptors. Each interrupt

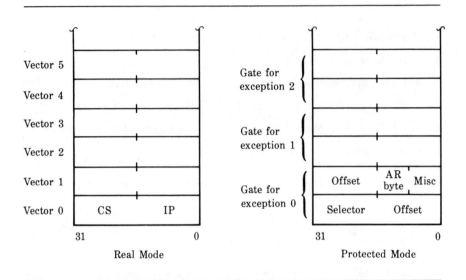

Figure 13-3. Real mode vector table versus Protected mode descriptor table

descriptor points indirectly to an interrupt service routine. (In the case of a task gate, it points *very* indirectly.) By contrast, the 80386 uses a simple interrupt vector table while it is in Real mode, just as the 8086 does. The vector table is simply 256 segment:offset pairs, each of which identifies the first instruction of an ISR. Essentially, the interrupt vector table is a series of intersegment JMP instructions, with the JMP supplied by the processor. Figure 13-3 illustrates the differences between a Protected mode IDT and a Real mode vector table.

Programmers familiar with interrupt service routines for the 8086 or 80186 will recognize the format of the 80386's Real mode vector table. Don't be lulled into complacency, however; there is one critical difference between the 80386 implementation of a vector table and everyone else's implementation. The 80386 still uses IDTR (interrupt descriptor table register) to locate the base of the vector table and determine its length. On 8086s and so forth, the vector table was always placed at physical address 0 and could not be moved. A given exception vector was always stored at a fixed address. This fact made it easy to locate the beginning of an ISR by reading its pointer from the vector table, or to change ISRs by writing a new segment and offset address into low memory.

The default value that the 80386 loads into IDTR defines a base address of 0 and a limit of 03FF (1023 decimal). This mimics perfectly the standard arrangement of previous iAPX 86 generations. If you want, you can change either or both of these values to suit your needs.

Increasing the limit beyond 03FF is pointless, since 1024 bytes is exactly enough to house 256 interrupt vectors, and no more than 256 vectors can be generated. Decreasing the limit serves to truncate the vector table. If an interrupt or exception generates a vector whose entry would be beyond the limit of the vector table, the 80386 takes exception 8. This exception signifies a double fault in Protected mode but is used solely for vector table overrun in Real mode. If the vector table is so short that vector 8 would be beyond the vector table limit too, the 80386 shuts down.

You can change the 32-bit Base Address field of IDTR to relocate the entire vector table to more convenient quarters, if you want. Obviously, you shouldn't move it higher than 000FFC00, or the 80386 will not be able to address the entire table. Whenever an interrupt is received or an exception occurs, the 80386 locates the appropriate vector table entry relative to this address. Although this technique might be handy for your application, bear in mind that any transplanted 8086 code isn't going to look at IDTR before it tries to read or write the vector table. Any code that uses absolute memory addresses to massage vector entries will have to be rewritten if you change IDTR in this respect. Use this feature with caution.

Interrupt handling in Real mode

- Interrupt, trap, and task gates are not used

- The 80386 uses an interrupt vector table with 256 entries

- Vectors specify the segment and offset of the interrupt handler

- The interrupt descriptor table register defines the base and length of the vector table

- IDTR is initialized with a base of 0 and a limit of 03FF

PREPARING FOR
PROTECTED MODE

So far, this book has assumed that you will be operating the 80386 in Protected mode and writing code to take advantage of the many unique features available on the 80386. It should by now be apparent that the 80386 requires you, the systems programmer, to set up many complex data tables for Protected mode operation to work. Descriptor tables are required for memory segmentation and protection, task state segments are needed for task coordination, and page tables are necessary for virtual memory management, to name a few. All of these tables are too complex for the 80386 to set up automatically or for it to operate temporarily on some default values, yet Protected mode operation is not possible without them. This is largely the reason why the 80386 begins operating in Real Address mode after power-up or a reset.

If you plan always to operate in Protected mode, you need remain in Real mode only long enough to build your Protected mode data structures and make the mode transition. Technically, the 80386 begins operating in Protected mode when the PE bit (Protection Enable, bit 0) in CR0 (or the machine status word, if you prefer) is set by software. However, in practical terms there is much more to it than that. If you randomly set PE without making the proper preparations, you are likely to shut down your processor. Although there are very few hard and fast rules about preparing for Protected mode operation, this section details some procedures you may wish to follow.

First, of course, the 80386 fetches its first instruction from physical address FFFFFFF0. It is customary to place an unconditional NEAR (intrasegment) JMP instruction here, although you can squeeze in a few others first, if you like. Remember, all four data segments (DS, ES, FS, and GS) and the stack segment (SS) will be pointing to a 64KB address range from 00000000 to 0000FFFF. The code segment will be artificially boosted to cover an address range from FFFF0000 to FFFFFFFF. This arrangement remains in effect until your code performs a FAR (intersegment) JMP, CALL, or RET. You can modify the five non-code-segment registers at run time in any way you want to expand your addressable range to the lower 1MB of memory, plus about 64KB because the 80386 does not perform 1MB wraparound.

While you are executing code in this special 64KB code segment, you may wish to perform simple diagnostic or confidence testing on your system. This might include checking the 80386's self-test signature in EAX or testing low memory before building descriptor tables. Next, you will usually want to copy one or more Protected mode descriptor tables from ROM into low RAM. Note that because it is not possible to address memory above 1MB, your descriptor tables will have to be kept in this range. If this is inconvenient, you will have to move them or build new ones after you've made the transition into Protected mode.

Copying descriptor tables from the bootstrap ROM into low RAM is the easiest and most efficient way to create them. You can build the tables on your software development system and burn them into the ROM as constant data, along with your reset code. Then all you have to do is copy them en masse to the desired location in low RAM at reset, and you're all done. An alternative is to have your reset code manufacture descriptors one by one and store them individually. Choose the method that works for you. Figures 13-4 and 13-5 illustrate the steps involved in enabling Protected mode. Figure 13-4 shows the automatic activity of the 80386, over which you have little control. Figure 13-5 shows a recommended flowchart for enabling Protected mode.

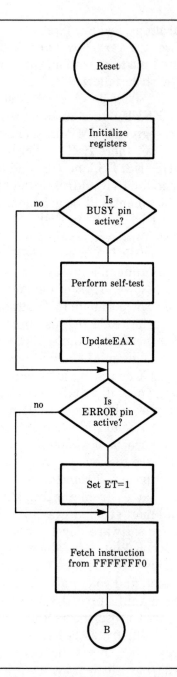

Figure 13-4.   Hardware activity after reset

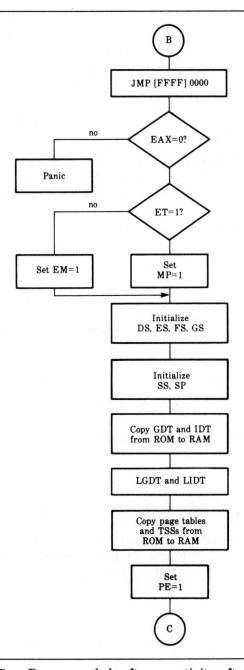

Figure 13-5.   Recommended software activity after reset

GDT and IDT

At the very least, you need to create a GDT and an IDT before entering Protected mode. LDTs and TSSs are necessary only if you are going to use them right away. It might be simpler to create them later, after you are running in Protected mode. GDTR must be loaded with the linear base address and limit of your GDT, and IDTR will need to be loaded as well.

Loading IDTR may pose something of a problem, depending on your system. Recall that in Real mode the 80386 uses IDTR to locate the base of an interrupt vector table, but in Protected mode it defines an interrupt descriptor table, which looks very different. Between the time you load IDTR and when you enable Protected mode, you are going to be using an interrupt table that is inconsistent with the current operating mode. Unfortunately, since you can't change IDTR and CR0 at the same time, this window of vulnerability is unavoidable. If a hardware interrupt (including NMI) or software exception occurs during this window, the 80386 will not behave in a predictable fashion. About all you can do is cross your fingers and hope for the best.

To minimize the risk, you should load IDTR as late as possible before entering Protected mode. You might also consider loading IDTR with a Limit field of 0. That way, you are guaranteed that any exception will cause a shutdown. This might not seem like an ideal solution, but at least its results are predictable.

Paging

Paging can be enabled either simultaneously with Protected mode or after Protected mode is already enabled. The latter is recommended. To enable paging and Protected mode at the same time, simply set PG (paging enable, bit 31) along with PE when you load CR0. As always when enabling paging, some precautions are in order.

First, register CR3 must already have been loaded with the physical base address of the page directory. A page directory and as many page tables as are necessary must also be created beforehand for CR3 to point to.

Second, the page translation should be arranged so that the code that enables paging occupies the same linear space after page translation as it did before. In other words, the currently executing page must be identity mapped.

Third, immediately after the MOV instruction to CR0, which enables paging (LMSW will not work here), you should execute a NEAR JMP instruction to force a flush of the 80386's instruction prefetch queue. This guarantees that all instructions executed after paging is enabled will use the new, page-translated memory addresses.

Enabling Protected Mode

After you have taken care of all of the preparations described in the previous sections, you can set PE with a MOV instruction to CR0. You can also use LMSW if you prefer, but LMSW alters only the lower 16 bits of CR0 and so cannot be used to enable or disable paging. Immediately after completing the instruction that sets PE, the 80386 begins operating in Protected mode.

The next instruction should be a NEAR JMP instruction to flush the prefetch queue. This should be done whether or not paging was enabled. It assures that all subsequent instructions are interpreted as Protected mode code and not Real mode code.

All six segment registers continue to hold the values they did in Real mode, even though these values are likely to make poor Protected mode segment selectors. Likewise, all six segments continue to point to the same 64KB address spaces they did in Real mode. Memory is still addressable as it was before the transition. Each of the six segment registers remains "in Real mode" until its contents are altered.

Once you disturb a segment register in Protected mode, the 80386 loads a selector from the GDT (or LDT, as appropriate) and caches the descriptor internally. That segment will then address memory as determined by its respective descriptor. It is wise to load all of the segment registers with Protected mode descriptors as soon as possible. This not only cuts down on confusion, it also alleviates the problem of exception processing with Real mode segment registers. If a segment register that is lingering in Real

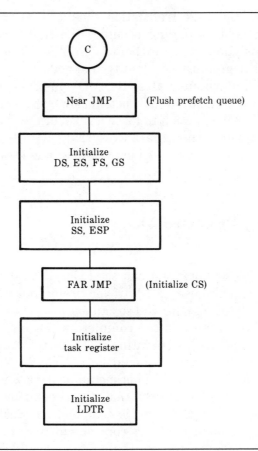

Figure 13-6. Recommended software activity in Protected mode

mode is pushed onto the stack, you will almost certainly get a general protection fault when it is popped again, because the 80386 will attempt to treat it as a selector.

Reloading CS is a bit tougher than loading the other segments, but it is no less important. A FAR JMP to the next instruction is a common technique for doing this.

Finally, you may want to reload your stack pointer (ESP) after segment SS is changed. Otherwise, the 80386 will use your Real mode stack pointer (SP) to reference a Protected mode stack segment. The LSS instruction is perfect for this because it alters both parts of the stack pointer at once. Figure 13-6 shows some recommended steps for ensuring a smooth transition into Protected mode.

Multitasking

If you are going to use multitasking, you will need to define your TSSs and TSS descriptors. You can do this in Real mode at the same time you create the GDT and IDT, or you can postpone it until you are already in Protected mode. Either way, the final step cannot be performed until the processor is operating in Protected mode. Before the first task switch takes place, you must load TR (task register) with an initial value. This must be a selector to a TSS descriptor in the GDT. The 80386 requires an initial TSS so that it can save the current state of the processor when it switches to a new task. If the current state of the processor is not worth saving, define a throwaway TSS for the 80386 to use. The task register must be initialized in Protected mode because LTR raises exception 6 in Real mode.

Now you're under way! The 80386 is operating in full Protected Virtual Address mode. All functions are operational, and you can use as many of them as you like. The next section deals with the transition from Protected mode back to Real mode.

RETURNING TO REAL MODE

If you want to return the processor to Real mode without turning off the power or resetting the system, you can simply clear PE in CR0. As is the case with enabling Protected mode, however, disabling it successfully involves more than a single MOV instruction.

If paging is enabled, it should be disabled first. Do this by clearing PG in CR0. Just as to enable paging, you must disable paging from a page that is identity mapped. It is also wise to zero out CR3 so that the paging cache will be cleared.

Table 13-1.   Real-Mode-like Segment Descriptions

Attribute	Value	
Limit	FFFF	(exactly 64KB)
Granularity	0	(byte granular)
Expansion direction	0	(expand up)
Writable	1	(writable)
Present	1	(segment present)

The next major step is to use segment descriptors that look as much like Real mode segments as possible. To do this, you must load selectors to descriptors with the attributes shown in Table 13-1 into all four data segment registers (DS, ES, FS, and GS) and the stack segment register (SS).

You should also load CS with a selector to a code descriptor having these attributes, except for the writable attribute, before disabling Protected mode. This is best accomplished with a FAR JMP instruction.

After clearing PE, you should immediately execute a FAR JMP instruction to flush the 80386's instruction prefetch queue.

You are now operating in Real Address mode. As before, there will be a certain amount of time where the interrupt table is inconsistent with the current operating mode; you can minimize this by building your Real mode vector table ahead of time and by disabling interrupts during the mode transition. Figure 13-7 shows a flowchart that outlines the procedure for disabling Protected mode.

TESTING THE TLB

This final section deals with the 80386's mechanism for testing the paging MMU's translation lookaside buffer (TLB). Although this doesn't have anything to do with Real mode in particular, you may want to perform TLB testing as part of system initialization or power-up diagnostics. Before proceeding too much further, it

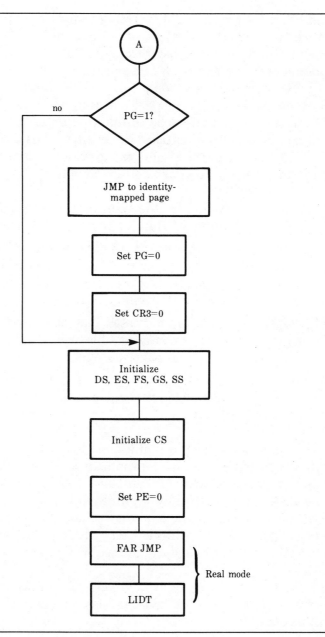

Figure 13-7.   Recommended procedure to disable Protected mode

should be pointed out that TLB testing requires a fair amount of software and a similar measure of understanding of cache management. Moreover, Intel has disclaimed any responsibility for the method used to test the TLB, and it may not be the same on future processors. You may want to weigh the investment against the advantages before sinking a lot of time into MMU testing.

The page translation cache is maintained as a four-way set associative cache with 32 entries. Each entry holds a 20-bit linear address, the 20-bit physical address to which it is mapped, and four tag bits. The tag bits are defined as follows:

V (Valid)   When set, the V bit indicates that this entry is valid. If this bit is clear, this cache entry is unused and all remaining bits are undefined.

D (Dirty)   When set, this bit indicates that the physical page (4KB) of memory identified by this cache entry has been written to.

U (User)   This bit indicates that the physical page of memory is accessible from PL3 code. Otherwise, the page has supervisor protection.

W (Writable)   This tag bit indicates that write permission is available for the page identified by this cache entry.

In normal use the TLB is maintained by the 80386 and is completely transparent, even to the sophisticated user. However, for testing purposes, registers TR6 and TR7 provide a "window" into the 80386 TLB. By carefully reading and writing to these two registers, you can manually load the cache or have the 80386 perform lookup operations on it. Registers TR6 and TR7 are shown in Figure 13-8. The bit-fields are defined as follows:

Linear (Linear Address, bits 12 through 31)   This 20-bit field holds the linear address used in TLB write and lookup operations.

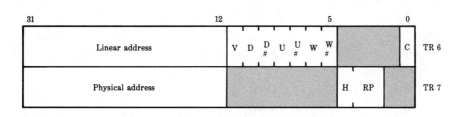

Figure 13-8.   Test registers

V (Valid, bit 11)	For TLB writes, this bit sets the V bit of the selected cache tag entry. For lookups, it determines whether or not to restrict the search to valid tags.
D (Dirty, bit 10)	For TLB writes, this bit sets the D bit of the selected cache tag entry. For lookups, it determines whether or not to restrict the search to dirty tags.
D# (Not Dirty, bit 9)	For writes, this bit must always be set to the opposite state of the D bit. For TLB lookups, it determines whether or not to restrict the search to nondirty tags.
U (User, bit 8)	Similar to D.
U# (Not User, bit 7)	Similar to D#.
W (Writable, bit 6)	Similar to D.
W# (Not Writable, bit 5)	Similar to D#.

C (Command, bit 0)	This bit distinguishes a TLB write (C=0) from a TLB lookup (C=1).
Physical (Physical Address, bits 12 through 31)	This 20-bit field holds the physical address used in TLB write and lookup operations.
H (Hit, bit 4)	For lookup operations, this bit indicates whether or not a cache hit occurred. For TLB writes, it determines how cache sets are selected.
RP (Replacement Pointer, bits 2 and 3)	For lookups, this field indicates which cache set was hit. For writes, it determines which cache set to use.

You can either perform TLB writes into the cache or have the 80386 perform a TLB lookup from the cache. The operation is determined by bit 0 of TR6. Before any testing begins, be sure that paging is disabled or you will wreak havoc on your page tables.

To write a TLB entry, follow these steps:

1. Write into TR7. You should write the new physical address to which you want the selected cache entry to map. Clear the H flag (bit 4) if you want the 80386 to select the cache set (1 of 4) to use, or set the H flag if you want to write into the set selected by the RP field.

2. Write into TR6. The values you give for V, D, U, and W are stored in the new tag field. D#, U#, and W# must be set to complement their respective positive-logic counterparts. The C flag (bit 0) should be clear to indicate a TLB write.

3. A new cache entry will be written. The linear address in TR6 will now be mapped (at least in the cache) to the physical address in TR7. You can repeat this process as often as you like.

After one or more TLB entries have been written, you can perform TLB lookups by following these steps:

1. Write into TR6. The linear address field should contain the upper 20 bits of the hypothetical linear address you are looking up, and the tag fields are used to qualify the lookup. The V flag should always be set so that invalid cache lines are not searched. The other three attributes can be set as desired. For example, if D equals 1 and D# equals 0, the 80386 searches only tags that are marked dirty. The opposite arrangement matches only tags that are marked not dirty. If both D and D# are zero, the Dirty field always matches; it becomes a "don't care." If both D and D# are set, the Dirty field always misses, and therefore the entire TLB lookup will always miss. This four-way logical arrangement works for U/U# and W/W# as well. When you are writing to TR6, be sure to set bit 0 for a TLB lookup request.

2. Read TR7. If the H flag (bit 4) is set, a cache hit occurred. The Physical Address field will be set to show the physical address that was mapped to the linear address given in TR6, and the RP field will show the cache set in which the entry was found. If H is not set, a cache miss occurred and the rest of TR7 is undefined.

By carefully mixing TLB writes with lookups, you may be able to determine whether or not the page table cache logic is functioning correctly. The precise methodology and thoroughness of this procedure is left to you.

This chapter has covered the behavior of the 80386 as it begins operation in Real mode. You can continue to operate in Real mode if you want, using the 80386 as a kind of "turbo" 8086. You have also seen how to prepare the 80386 for Protected mode operation, with some recommended steps for getting there. In Protected mode, you can exercise the true power of the 80386.

This is the last chapter in this book that deals exclusively with software-related issues. The next chapter uncovers some of the hardware mysteries of the 80386, including memory and I/O addressing, the causes of wait states, the effects of code and operand alignment, and more.

14

HARDWARE

Much to the dismay of most programmers, software is not possible without hardware. You can't boot up and run your latest whiz-bang software masterpiece if there's no disk, no memory, or no processor. Just as an excellent race car driver can make the difference between winning and losing but can't increase the basic performance of the car, software can run only as fast as the hardware that hosts it. Many software engineers are indebted to the ingenuity of their computer's hardware designer for making their programs look good. Undoubtedly, the reverse is also true.

The basic design of a computer system, at the hardware level, fundamentally determines what that machine is or is not capable of. The speed of the processor, the amount and type of memory, and the available peripheral or I/O devices dictate what the machine will be used for and its cost, and they also define the options open to the programmer. After all, what's the difference between a Cray X/MP and an Apple II besides a little hardware? You can program them both in C.

This chapter covers some basic hardware topics relevant to 80386-based computers. Although it will probably not make a hardware engineer out of you, it may help take the mystery out of such things as memory addressing, wait states, I/O space, and so forth.

THE MICROPROCESSOR

The 80386 is fabricated on a semiconductor wafer (a silicon chip) and is roughly 1/4-inch square and extremely thin. In this small space more than 275,000 transistors are packed. After being tested, the 80386 is mounted into the center of a 1 1/2-inch-square ceramic holder, vaguely purplish in color, and a protective, air

+5v	GND	A8	A11	A14	A15	A16	A17	A20	A21	A23	A26	A27	A30
GND	A5	A7	A10	A13	GND	+5v	A18	GND	A22	A24	A29	A31	+5v
A3	A4	A6	A9	A12	GND	+5v	A19	GND	A25	A28	+5v	GND	D30
		A2									GND	+5v	D29
+5v	GND	+5v									D31	D27	D26
GND											D28	D25	GND
+5v	INTR										+5v	+5v	D24
ERROR	NMI	PEREQ									GND	D23	+5v
GND	BUSY	RESET									D20	D21	D22
+5v	W/R	LOCK									GND	D17	D19
D/C	GND	GND									D15	D16	D18
M/IO		+5v	+5v	BE0	CLK2	+5v	D0	GND	D7	+5v	D10	D12	D14
BE3	BE2	BE1	NA			READY	D1	GND	D5	D8	+5v	D11	D13
+5v	GND	BS16	HOLD	ADS	GND	+5v	D2	D3	D4	D6	HLDA	D9	GND

Figure 14-1. 80386 pinout

Table 14-1.   Data Bus Voltage Levels

Data Pin	Logic Level	Voltage
D31 through D08	0	0 V
D07	0	0 V
D06	1	+5 V
D05	0	0 V
D04	0	0 V
D03	1	+5 V
D02	0	0 V
D01	0	0 V
D00	1	+5 V

tight lid is sealed over it. On the bottom of the ceramic holder, or chip carrier, are 132 pins, arranged in a grid pattern. Before the lid is sealed, very thin wires are attached between the pins of the chip carrier and strategic locations on the 80386 chip itself. This packaging allows the 80386 to be handled and mounted easily on a normal printed circuit board with standard soldering equipment. Figure 14-1 shows all 132 pins of the 80386 as you would see them if you flipped the package over. The address pins are toward the top, with the data pins on the right. Those pins without names perform no function.

The Data Bus

Thirty-two of the 132 pins are the processor's data lines. One data pin is assigned to each bit of data, from bit 0 to bit 31. Whenever the 80386 reads or writes data to or from memory or an I/O device, the information is transferred through these pins. Logical 1 bits are represented by a +5-volt level on the appropriate data pin, and logical 0 bits are represented by a 0-volt, or ground, level. For example, if you wrote a line of code that stored the byte value 49 (01001001 binary) to some memory address, the voltage on the 80386's data pins would be as shown in Table 14-1. The entire microprocessor (and, indeed, most computers today) operates on no more than 5 volts, less than the output of a typical transistor radio battery.

Data bus

- 32 data pins carry data to and from the 80386
- Each pin represents 1 bit of data
- 1 bits carry +5 volts on the pin
- 0 bits carry 0 volts on the pin

The Address Bus

Thirty-four more pins are wired to the 80386's address bus. There is one pin for each address bit from A31 down to A02. There are no pins for address bits A0 or A1. Instead, there are four *byte-enable pins*, BE0, BE1, BE2, and BE3. That explains why there are 34 address pins and not 32. But why does the 80386 use byte enables instead of the two least significant address bits? This has to do with the technical problems involved in addressing more than one byte of memory at a time.

In software, if you want to write to a word (two consecutive bytes) in memory, you simply write an instruction such as

MOV WORD PTR DS:[1000h],1234h

This writes the 16-bit value 1234 to address 1000. Actually, you would be writing the byte value 34 to address 1000 and the value 12 to address 1001, but this is not readily apparent. You would write a dword (four consecutive bytes) to memory in a similar manner:

MOV DWORD PTR DS:[1000h],12345678h

This writes four bytes to four different byte addresses. Granted, this is a trivial matter in software. But how does the 80386's address bus show that it wants to write to address 1000 *and* address 1001? Or that it wants to read a dword from addresses 1000, 1001, 1002, and 1003? Which address should it show on its address pins, and how should it indicate that it wants to read or write more than the one byte at that address?

All of these problems are solved when you dispense with the two address pins A0 and A1 and replace them with four byte-enable pins. Without the two least significant address pins, the 80386 can produce only addresses that are even multiples of 4. The address 1003 looks exactly like 1000 (or 1001 or 1002) if A0

Table 14-2.   Aligned Transfers

Desired Address	A31 through A02	BE0	BE1	BE2	BE3
	Single-Byte Transfers				
00001000	00001000	On	Off	Off	Off
00001001	00001000	Off	On	Off	Off
00001002	00001000	Off	Off	On	Off
00001003	00001000	Off	Off	Off	On
00001004	00001004	On	Off	Off	Off
00001005	00001004	Off	On	Off	Off
	Double-Byte (Word) Transfers				
00001000	00001000	On	On	Off	Off
00001001	00001000	Off	On	On	Off
00001002	00001000	Off	Off	On	On
00001003	(See Table 14-3)				
00001004	00001004	On	On	Off	Off
00001005	00001004	Off	On	On	Off
	Quad-Byte (Dword) Transfers				
00001000	00001000	On	On	On	On
00001001	(See Table 14-3)				
00001002	(See Table 14-3)				
00001003	(See Table 14-3)				
00001004	00001004	On	On	On	On
00001005	(See Table 14-3)				

and A1 are missing. To distinguish between these four addresses, the 80386 also drives (produces voltage on) one or more of its byte-enable pins. If the desired byte of data is at 1000, it drives byte-enable 0 (BE0). This essentially means, "I want the data at address 1000 plus 0." If the 80386 is referencing a byte from 1001, it drives BE1 instead. A read or write from 1002 drives BE2, and 1003 produces a response from BE3. If you want to reference address 1004, the "normal" address pins drive the binary address for 1004, and BE0 is enabled again, and so on. Table 14-2 summarizes the use of the four byte-enable pins with the address pins. Six consecutive addresses each are shown for byte, word, and dword transfers.

So far, this is pretty tame stuff. Where the system really shines is when you, the programmer, want to read or write more than one byte at a time. Say you wanted to write a word to 1000, as in the previous example. To do that, the 80386 drives the address for 1000 on its address pins and also drives BE0 *and* BE1. This is interpreted as "I want the data at address 1000, plus 0 and plus 1." If you wrote a word to 1001, the 80386 would respond by driving BE1 and BE2. Writing to 1002 would cause BE2 and BE3 to be driven. Of course, the same is true when you're reading from memory as well. Writing a word to 1003 is a bit trickier; that case will be discussed later.

Transferring dwords to and fro is simply an extension of the previous example. To read or write 32 bits of data, the 80386 drives all four byte-enable pins to their active state at the same time.

Address bus

- The 80386 uses 30 address pins to carry address information
- Each pin represents 1 bit of the address
- Address bits 0 and 1 are not represented
- Four byte-enable pins are used to solve multibyte addressing problems

Unaligned Transfers

All of the examples so far have assumed that you are transferring to or from memory an operand that is on an aligned address. That is, they assume that the word or dword you are referencing (bytes don't have this problem) did not cross an address that is a multiple of 4. For instance, word transfers from 1000, 1001, and 1002 are aligned. A word from 1003 is not aligned because it also implicitly references address 1004, which is a new multiple of 4. A dword read or write from 1000 is aligned, but ones from 1001, 1002, and 1003 are not, because they each cross a 4-byte boundary.

When this type of transfer occurs, the 80386 services your request by splitting it into two different transfers. First, it transfers the higher-addressed portion of your data, and then it transfers the lower-addressed portion. To return to the previous example, if you are writing a word to 1003, the 80386 performs a single-byte write to 1004 (address = 1004, BE0 = on) followed by a single-byte write to 1003 (address = 1000, BE3 = on). Table 14-3

Table 14-3.   Unaligned Transfers

Desired Address	A31 Through A02	BE0	BE1	BE2	BE3
	Double-Byte (Word) Transfers				
00001003	00001004	On	Off	Off	Off
	00001000	Off	Off	Off	On
	Quad-Byte (Dword) Transfers				
00001001	00001004	On	Off	Off	Off
	00001000	Off	On	On	On
00001002	00001004	On	On	Off	Off
	00001000	Off	Off	On	On
00001003	00001004	On	On	On	Off
	00001000	Off	Off	Off	On
00001005	00001008	On	Off	Off	Off
	00001004	Off	On	On	On

illustrates those transfers not shown in Table 14-2 because they cannot be completed in one bus cycle.

Because two separate bus cycles are required, it takes twice as much time to read an operand from or write an operand to a badly aligned address as it does to work with an aligned one. Fortunately, all of this is completely transparent to your software. The only effect you will ever notice is in your program's execution time. Since this alignment rule is in effect for every reference you make to memory or I/O, including code fetches and stack operations, you may indeed notice some real changes if you juggle often-used operands.

Miscellaneous Pins

Twenty pins on the 80386 package are used solely for supplying power to the microprocessor. Twenty-one more are for ground connections. Three pins are used to communicate with an 80287 or 80387 floating-point coprocessor. They are PEREQ, BUSY, and ERROR, and they are normally connected to the coprocessor's pins of the same names. The 80386 has two interrupt input pins, INTR and NMI, a RESET pin, 11 data bus control pins, and eight pins that perform no useful function whatsoever.

ADDRESS DECODING

Your computer is useless without memory. There usually isn't enough storage space in the processor's registers to hold all of the data you need, and besides, where would the program code be stored?

It is taken for granted that any 80386 machine you will program will have some quantity of memory, maybe 64KB, maybe 2MB or more. Normally, once you know how much memory is at your disposal and where it is addressed, you can use it as you see fit. Reading and writing memory locations are two of the most basic functions of assembly language. But how does the 80386

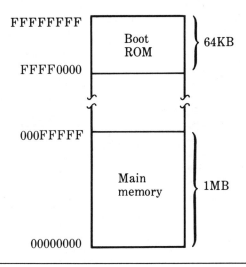

Figure 14-2.   Sample memory map

actually find this memory? Given an address, how is the data stored or retrieved? What happens to the empty spaces in the memory map?

It is the responsibility of the hardware designer to build a circuit that can determine what address or addresses in memory the 80386 is referencing and to route the data appropriately. This is called *address decoding logic*.

The decoding logic works by monitoring the address pins of the processor every time it (the processor) reads or writes from memory. By comparing the high and low voltage levels on these pins to fixed patterns built into the circuit, the decoding logic can quickly tell whether the address the 80386 is producing selects the system's main memory, an I/O device, a cache, or nothing at all.

A sample memory map is given in Figure 14-2. It shows a simple system with 1MB of memory starting at address 0 and a 64KB ROM at the very high end of the address space, used for bootstrap loading at power-up or reset. The majority of the

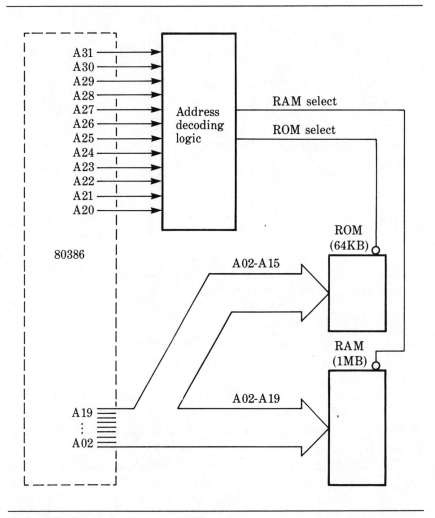

Figure 14-3. Address decoding logic

80386's 4GB address range is unused in the system (which is not remarkable, since all 80386 systems combined probably don't have 4GB of memory in them). In the next figure (Figure 14-3), you see the 80386 on the left, with its 30 address pins, and the memory on the right, with the address decoding logic in between. Notice that only the 12 most significant address pins are connected to the decoding circuit. The remaining 18 go directly to the RAM chips. Of these, the low 14 go to the ROM as well.

The way this memory map is arranged, the addresses of the RAM start at 00000000 and go through 000FFFFF. The next address after that, 00100000, selects nothing at all. This void continues until you reach FFFF0000, the beginning of the ROM. The ROM covers 64KB, ending exactly at the end of the 80386's address range. Given this arrangement, it is easy to determine whether or not the 80386 is referencing low RAM by monitoring the 12 most significant address pins. If these address bits are all 0s (the pins are at low-voltage level), the address must be within the low 1MB. If any are not 0, the address must be either a ROM address or an illegal address. This logic can be implemented with a simple 12-input NOR circuit. As long as none of the input terms (address bits) is true (has a high-voltage level), the output term (RAM select) is true. The remaining low-order address bits and the four byte-enable lines are routed directly to the RAM memory chips, where they will determine which byte (or bytes) in RAM to read or write.

You can decode the address space of the ROM in one of two ways: the good way or the quick-and-dirty way. Using the quick-and-dirty method, you could simply invert the RAM select signal and use that to select the ROM. Then the ROM decoding logic becomes "if not RAM, then ROM." This works just fine if you have only two memory resources from which to choose. It has the interesting side effect that the ROM can be referenced at *any* address that is not a RAM address.

A somewhat more elegant solution is to build into the decoding logic another circuit that looks specifically for ROM addresses. Because the ROM occupies the extreme upper 64KB of the address space, it is correct to say that if the upper 16 address bits are all 1s, this reference must be to the ROM. This can be implemented with a 16-input AND circuit. As long as all 16 inputs (address bits) are true (have a high-voltage level), the output (ROM select) is true.

Alas, reality strikes. Suppose, for example, that you can't connect all 16 high-order address pins to your decoding logic device.

It is a 16-pin IC, and only 12 pins are available for inputs. Of the remainder, two are needed for outputs, and two more serve as power and ground connections. What do you do?

A compromise arrangement would be to monitor only the existing 12 address pins, instead of the desired 16, and design a 12-input AND circuit to select the ROM. Then, any address in which the upper 12 bits are high (FFF00000 to FFFFFFFF) will be treated as a reference to the ROM. As you could with the quick-and-dirty arrangement, you could then address the ROM in multiple locations (16 to be exact), but unless you really need to use that space for something else, it shouldn't cause any problems.

This technique is known as shadowing, and it is used regularly as an expedient means of implementing address decoding in a limited amount of space. The low-order address pins should be connected directly to the ROM device (or devices), as they were to the RAM. The ROM should not require all of the remaining address lines, because it occupies only a 64KB space. The remaining address lines can remain disconnected. They become "don't care" as far as the ROM is concerned, which is why it will appear 16 times in the address space.

DIFFERENT KINDS
OF MEMORY

Usually the greatest determinant of your computer's performance, apart from CPU frequency, is the amount and type of memory you have. It is a programming axiom that code will always expand to fill up the available memory, so more is usually better. Most retail computer advertisements emphasize the amount of RAM installed in a system as the primary feature, although a great percentage of their readers probably have no idea what that means. Although the amount of usable RAM available in a system is certainly important in terms of the kind of work that can be done, the type of memory used is much more important in determining performance.

The generic term "memory" covers a lot of things, from RAM to floppy disks to magnetic tapes. This section deals with main, workspace RAM, the kind you can address with a MOV instruction, and how it affects system performance and cost.

The memory in a typical 80386-based machine is made up of several identical RAM chips. Each one adds a little to the capacity of the machine. Commercial RAM chips come in two basic types: static and dynamic. Static RAM chips (SRAMs) are much faster and therefore provide better performance, but dynamic RAM chips (DRAMs) are much less expensive and so are more common. Roughly 85% of all 80386-based personal computers use DRAM exclusively. The ratio of SRAM to DRAM is somewhat higher in performance-sensitive applications such as workstations.

Dynamic RAM chips are slower, consume more power, produce more heat, and are more difficult to interface than SRAMs. In short, they have absolutely no redeeming virtues except that they are about one-fourth the cost of SRAMs. For the same amount of money and in about the same amount of space, you can get about four times as much memory in your system by using DRAMs. This is why they are so popular for most applications.

One of the most annoying features of DRAM chips is that they must be refreshed periodically. If they are not refreshed, dynamic memories "forget" what they were supposed to remember (hence the term "dynamic"). Refreshing takes time, and the memory in a DRAM is not usable by the 80386 while a refresh is taking place. This is one of the factors that gives DRAMs their generally lower performance compared with SRAMs, which do not need to be refreshed.

Another factor that degrades the performance of DRAMs is that they need to recover after being read from or written to. This means that after the 80386 accesses memory it may have to wait for the memory to recover before accessing it again. This would normally occur only with multiple transfers or during stack operations, but it is also possible during code prefetch, since the 80386 likes to keep the instruction pipeline as full as possible. Even so, DRAM is overwhelmingly the memory of choice.

Dynamic RAM versus static RAM

- DRAM consumes more electricity
- DRAM must be refreshed periodically
- DRAM produces more excess heat
- SRAM is faster
- SRAM is more expensive

Caches

To combat these problems, high-performance 80386 systems are often designed with a small amount of fast, trouble-free SRAM in addition to the main DRAM array. This small SRAM area is called a *cache*. A cache adds to the performance of the computer, one hopes by an amount that justifies the added cost of the SRAM.

Like the descriptor cache or page-translation cache within the 80386 itself, a memory cache is used to keep a copy of something that is in main memory. The cache is not located at a different address than the main memory. In fact, it has no address at all. It merely holds a copy of the data that was most recently read from or written to main memory. If that data is needed again soon, chances are good that it can be found in the cache so that the 80386 will not have to wait for the slower DRAMs (which may need to recover from a previous access or may be getting refreshed).

A typical cache is between 16KB and 64KB in size. The effect it has on the performance of your system depends in large part on the software you are running. Most cache management is based on a theory known as *locality of reference*. It involves the fact that if your program has used a constant, variable, or other memory item recently, it will more than likely use it again soon. Furthermore, the memory items in use at any given point in a program tend to be clustered together in nearby addresses. This is also true of program instructions themselves. After the 80386 has fetched one instruction, chances are good that it will want another instruction from a nearby address (usually the subsequent one). Based on this theory, even a small cache, over time, can hold a great amount of useful data.

Wait States

Although fast memory helps to increase overall system performance, a main memory system that is twice as fast as another will not double the overall speed of your system. This is true simply because the 80386 does not spend all of its time reading and writing memory operands.

The ideal memory design would keep up with every request for data transfers. When this is not the case (and it usually isn't), the 80386 must wait and do nothing while the memory responds with data or stores information. This idle time is completely wasted and is known as a *wait state*. The more wait states a particular memory design requires, the more time your processor is spending "twiddling its thumbs."

A 16-MHz 80386 is capable of requesting a memory read or write every other clock cycle, that is, 8 million times per second. Ideally, during one clock cycle, the 80386 would drive its address pins with the logic levels indicating the address your program wishes to reference, and the memory would respond in the next clock cycle. The 80386 could then initiate a new memory cycle immediately afterward. At 16 MHz, that gives your memory about 60 to 75 nanoseconds to either store or provide data. If the memory can't comply that fast, external memory-control hardware must inform the 80386 that more time is required. The 80386 would then wait for one clock cycle (62.5 nanoseconds at 16 MHz) and try again. If, after that cycle, the memory-control logic signaled that the memory cycle had completed, the 80386 could then start a new memory cycle if it needed to. This is an example of a memory cycle with one wait state.

Memory wait states

- Occur when the 80386 is faster than its memory

- Slow down memory read and write operations

- Cause the processor to wait unnecessarily

- Have a variable impact on overall system performance

If, on the other hand, the memory-control logic did not indicate success after one wait state, the 80386 would wait for another clock cycle, check again, and so on. The 80386 will wait literally forever until the memory it is addressing can comply with its read or write request. As was mentioned previously, a perfect memory cycle requires two 80386 clock cycles, or 125 nanoseconds, to complete. This represents the best case, without any wait states. If one wait state is required, the total time stretches to three clock cycles. Two wait states require four clock cycles, and so on. Therefore, an 80386 computer with a memory design that requires one wait state is running at 66% efficiency, at least as far as memory references are concerned.

A memory design that runs at only two-thirds the speed of the CPU does not mean that the machine as a whole will run a third slower than an "ideal" model, because the 80386 does other things besides store and fetch from memory. The actual ratio of memory speed to final, useful speed depends on many factors. Not the least of these is the presence and size of a cache. Memory speed can help or hinder your total execution speed, depending on the programs or tasks the 80386 is running. Figure 14-4 shows a graph of the relationship between relative CPU performance and the number of memory wait states. These numbers assume that no cache is present.

The graph in the figure can be used to find the effect of fractional wait states as well. Fractional wait states are possible, as an average, because not all memory designs incur the same number of wait states all the time. A system based on dynamic RAM, for

Relative
performance

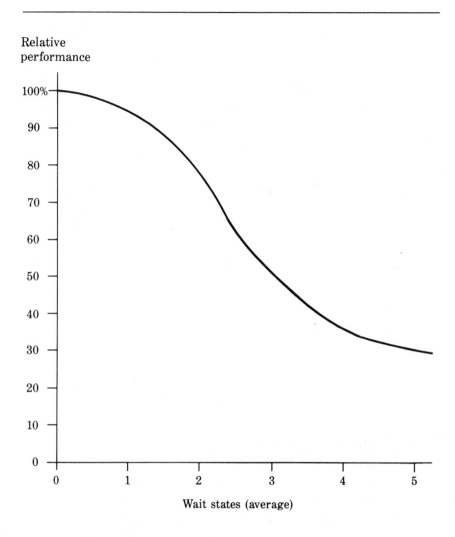

Figure 14-4.   Performance impact of wait states

example, might need one wait state normally but require two or three when a refresh is in progress. The average might work out to 1.15 or so.

The graph has such a peculiar curve because of the workings of the instruction prefetch pipeline. Because instructions are fetched ahead of time as much as possible, a few wait states do not affect the 80386 very much. It always has plenty of code handy to execute, and only data read and write operations are slowed. As the number of wait states increases, however, the situation is reversed. Now the code prefetch function is waiting so long for memory that both it and the data transfer operations are forcing the 80386 to wait. It must empty and refill the instruction pipeline regularly and consequently spends a lot of its time with nothing to do.

Performance impact of wait states

- The relationship of wait states to performance is not linear
- Wait states affect memory read and write operations first
- Several wait states will adversely affect code fetching as well
- DRAM usually requires more wait states than SRAM
- Cache misses usually force wait states

BUS LOCKING AND READ-MODIFY-WRITE CYCLES

Several instructions on the 80386 can be used to modify the contents of a memory location. The MOV and STOS instructions are two of the simplest. They simply store a new value in a memory operand, replacing the old value stored there before. Other instructions perform an operation on the existing memory contents and then store the updated result. Examples of this kind of instruction are ADD, SUB, XOR, NOT, and XCHG. Although it is not obvious from a software point of view, this second class of instruction is treated very differently by the 80386.

Whereas MOV instructions simply perform a write cycle to memory (like the write cycles described earlier), an instruction like XCHG or BTS must read the original operand from memory, alter it inside the processor in some way, and then write the result back out. Two separate memory transfers are thus required for one instruction. These transfers make up what is called a *read-modify-write cycle*. From the programmer's point of view, such a cycle is only one simple instruction. As far as the 80386, the system's memory, and the memory control circuits are concerned, however, the cycle is two separate and distinct memory transactions that simply happen to reference the same address.

Read-modify-write instructions are frequently used in systems that have more than one microprocessor. The microprocessors usually share some amount of memory so that they can communicate with one another. Sometimes this communication is as simple as a yes/no message sent to indicate status. For example, one processor might set a shared status bit to 1 to indicate that it is using the system's floppy disk drive. The other processor(s) would then have to wait until that bit was cleared again before attempting to use the drive. This bit is called a *semaphore*.

The BTS instruction is ideal for checking this kind of semaphore bit. The 80386 reads the current status of the bit, stores the result in the Carry flag, and then unconditionally sets the bit and writes the new value back out. A subsequent instruction that tests the Carry flag will tell you whether or not the semaphore was set originally. If it was not, the shared resource (such as a disk drive) is yours, and the semaphore has already been set to indicate to the other processors that it is in use. If the semaphore was already set, you will have to wait, and resetting it with the BTS instruction didn't hurt.

The problem with shared memory and semaphores lies in the way in which the 80386 performs the read-modify-write cycle mentioned earlier. It is possible, although unlikely, that another processor could sneak in and alter the semaphore bit between the time the 80386 reads the bit and when it writes it back. (The reverse is also true, of course, but that's the other programmer's problem, not yours.)

To avoid this, you can use the LOCK instruction prefix byte with certain instructions to prevent memory from being altered. When the LOCK prefix (opcode F0) appears with an instruction that performs a read-modify-write cycle, the 80386 turns on a special LOCK pin on the outside of the device until the instruction is complete. As long as LOCK is asserted, no other processor should be allowed access to memory. Of course, your memory-control circuits have to be designed to honor the LOCK signal, or no locking is possible.

INTERRUPT ACKNOWLEDGE CYCLES

As part of all exception processing, the 80386 assigns a vector number to each exception so that it can select one of the 256 gate descriptors in the IDT. If the exception is caused by a software error (privilege violation, stack fault, and so on), a fixed vector number is assigned, depending on the cause of the error. General protection faults, for instance, are always assigned vector 13. If the 80386 receives an external nonmaskable interrupt (NMI), it assigns it vector 2 and begins executing the service routine indicated by gate number 2 in the IDT. External maskable interrupt sources are not given fixed vectors.

When the 80386 receives an interrupt on its INTR pin, and interrupts are not masked (IF=1), it begins an automatic interrupt acknowledge cycle. This cycle is intended to allow the source of the interrupt to choose its own vector.

The processor begins the cycle by performing a 1-byte read from address 00000004. Certain other pins on the 80386 are driven as well, to distinguish this from an actual read cycle. This is the beginning of the interrupt acknowledge cycle and is not intended to transfer any data. After the first bogus read cycle terminates, the 80386 initiates another 1-byte read, this time from address 00000000. At this time, the interrupting hardware device is expected to produce 1 byte of data. The 80386 reads this byte as the interrupt vector and terminates the cycle.

The interrupt vector is used as an index into the IDT to select a gate descriptor. Alternatively, you could say that the vector is multiplied by 8 and used as a byte offset from the beginning of the IDT. Only the chip designers know for sure. Note that all interrupt vector values from 00 to FF are possible, so you could conceivably have your floppy-disk interrupt pass the vector for a stack fault, but this is not recommended. Start your hardware interrupt vectors from 20 (32 hexadecimal), and work up from there.

SELF-TEST REQUEST AND COPROCESSOR SENSE

A nice feature of the 80386 hardware design is its ability to perform an internal self-test every time it is reset, as described in Chapter 13. The self-test is optional and takes several milliseconds to run. To request that a self-test be performed, your external hardware must hold the 80386's BUSY input pin at a 0-volt (ground) potential just before the RESET pin is allowed to go low, signaling the end of a reset request. The BUSY pin is normally an output from the 80387 or 80287 numeric coprocessor, but it serves double duty in this case. The pin does not have to be held low for very long, only about half a microsecond.

Another nice feature of the 80386 is that it is able to detect the presence of an 80387 by monitoring its ERROR pin. The 80387 always drives ERROR active when it is reset, whereas the 80287 never does. Near the very end of its internal resetting procedures, if the 80386 detects an active ERROR pin, it automatically sets the ET (Extension Type) bit in CR0 for you, indicating the presence of an 80387.

Although both of these features are semiautomatic and helpful, one may interfere with the other. For some unknown reason, the 80386's BUSY pin must be held high for it to detect correctly the state of its ERROR pin. Therefore, if you plan to make use of the self-test request feature, be sure to hold the BUSY pin low only for as long as is necessary, or you'll get an erroneous indication of your coprocessor type. Experience has shown that it tends to err on the side of an 80287 in this case. Currently, this interesting timing requirement is not mentioned in any of Intel's technical literature, but it does appear briefly in a timing diagram in an introductory booklet.

In this chapter, you have seen some ways in which the hardware design of an 80386-based system might affect the performance of your software. With these points in mind, it may be possible for you to avoid problem areas and code more wisely to get the maximum possible performance out of your hardware. Hopefully, the information in the rest of this book has shown you how to get the most flexibility, the greatest power, and the best performance out of the 80386.

A

GLOSSARY

Accumulator   Another name for the most-often-used register in the 80386, EAX. On the 8086, 80186, and 80286, this was AX. Before that, it was simply register A, for Accumulator.

Address Bus   The hardware pins on the outside of the 80386 that carry the addresses generated by your programs to external circuitry.

Alias   A memory segment that spans the same physical address range as another segment. Because segment descriptors in Protected mode have usage restrictions, it is sometimes useful to define two or more segment descriptors for the same address range so that the memory can be used in multiple ways.

Breakpoint   A location within a program where the processor is to stop executing. Breakpoints help the programmer find bugs in programs by stopping the processor at various points so that the programmer can examine the state of the machine.

Byte   Eight binary bits of data. One byte is capable of representing 256 different binary patterns. How these patterns are interpreted is up to the program code.

Cache   A small store of memory. Caches are used to hold often-used pieces of information in a readily accessible place for quick reference. The 80386 has one cache internally in which it holds active segment descriptors and another in which it holds selected page-translation table entries.

CISC   Complex Instruction Set Computer. "Complex" is a relative term, but it usually implies a processor that has 100 or more assembly-level instructions. The 80386 is an example of a CISC machine.

Coprocessor   A second processor that runs concurrently with a main processor. The 80387 Numeric Processor Extension chip is an example of a coprocessor.

CPL   Current Privilege Level. While the 80386 is running in Protected mode, the CPL is usually determined by the DPL field of the code segment descriptor that defines the segment of memory from which the 80386 is currently fetching its instructions. If that descriptor has the "conforming" attribute set, it does not determine CPL. Instead, CPL is determined by the DPL of the last nonconforming code segment that was used. CPL determines what instructions the 80386 can or cannot execute.

Data Bus   The 32 external hardware pins on the outside of the 80386 that carry data into and out of the microprocessor. They are usually connected to the computer's memory and I/O devices.

Descriptor   An 8-byte object in memory that describes the beginning and end of a segment and what it can be used for. In Protected mode, each segment must have a descriptor associated with it. It is possible to create two or more descriptors that describe that same range of addresses; this is called aliasing.

DPL   Descriptor Privilege Level. This is a 2-bit field within a descriptor. The DPL field of a code segment descriptor determines CPL. The DPL field of a data or stack segment descriptor determines the privilege level of the data stored within that segment.

DRAM   Dynamic Random Access Memory. This is a type of IC used to store code and data within a computer. Dynamic RAM chips are the most prevalent kind because of their low cost per megabyte.

Dword   Double word. Thirty-two bits of data.

EPROM   Erasable Programmable Read-Only Memory. This is a type of IC used to store permanent data, such as bootstrap code or constant data. EPROMs can be erased and reprogrammed, but this requires special equipment.

Exception   The generic term used to describe interrupts and software errors. Anything that causes the 80386 to stop what it is doing and refer to the interrupt descriptor table is an exception.

Gate   A type of segment descriptor that defines a special, protected entry point for software, instead of a range of memory.

GB   Gigabyte. Roughly 1 billion bytes; technically 1,073,741,824 bytes. This number is the closest power of 2 (2^{30}) to 1 billion.

GDT   Global Descriptor Table. All memory segment descriptors must reside in either the GDT or an LDT. Descriptors in the GDT are available to all tasks, whereas those in an LDT are available only to some tasks. There can be only one GDT, and its starting address and length must be loaded into GDTR.

GDTR   Global Descriptor Table Register. This is a 48-bit register in the 80386 that allows the processor to find the GDT. It can be read or written only with the SGDT and LGDT instructions, respectively.

IC   Integrated Circuit. A small, black, rectangular device that contains electronic circuits etched into the surface of a semiconductor, such as silicon.

IDT   Interrupt Descriptor Table. This is a table of descriptors, much like the GDT or an LDT. The IDT holds only gate descriptors, which in turn allow the 80386 to locate exception-handling software. There are usually 256 gate descriptors in the IDT, one for each possible exception.

IDTR   Interrupt Descriptor Table Register. This is a 48-bit register in the 80386 that allows the processor to find the IDT. It can be read or written only with the SIDT and LIDT instructions, respectively.

Interrupt   An exception caused by hardware. When a device in a complete computer system needs to get the attention of the 80386, it can generate an interrupt by signaling on either the INTR pin or the NMI pin of the 80386.

Intersegment   Involving two segments of memory. An intersegment control transfer means a FAR JMP, CALL, or RET instruction, which causes the 80386 to begin fetching instructions from a different code segment.

Intrasegment   Occurring within one segment of memory. An intrasegment control transfer means either a NEAR or a SHORT JMP, CALL, or RET instruction, which causes the 80386 to begin fetching instructions from a different offset within the current code segment.

IOPL   Input/Output Privilege Level. This is a 2-bit field within the 80386 register EFLAGS. The relationship between IOPL and CPL determines whether or not the 80386 can perform I/O-related instructions, such as IN, OUTS, and so on.

KB   Kilobyte. Roughly 1000 bytes; technically 1024 bytes. This is the power of 2 (2^{10}) nearest to 1000.

LDT   Local Descriptor Table. This is a table of segment descriptors, much like the GDT. Descriptors placed in an LDT are available only to the task or tasks using that LDT. A task can use an

LDT if the selector to the descriptor that defines the LDT itself is in that task's TSS. Any descriptors in the LDT can be used in addition to those already in the GDT.

LDTR Local Descriptor Table Register. This is a 16-bit register within the 80386 that holds the selector to the current LDT. This register is loaded from the incoming task's TSS whenever a task switch is performed. LDTR can also be manipulated through the LLDT and SLDT instructions.

Linear Address A linear address is halfway between a logical address and a physical address. Program code generates logical, or offset, addresses. The 80386 segmentation mechanism adds the base address of the appropriate segment to produce a linear address. If page translation is in effect, the linear address can be altered to produce a physical address. If paging is not enabled, the physical address is the same as the linear address.

Logical Address Logical addresses are the segment-relative offset addresses produced by program code. Applications programmers need only be concerned with logical addresses; the segmentation and paging considerations are transparent to all but systems programmers.

MB Megabyte. Roughly 1 million bytes; technically _,048,576 bytes. This is the power of 2 (2^{20}) nearest to 1 million.

Microcode The 80386 is permanently programmed at a level even lower than assembly language code. This level is known as microcode. The microcode is what allows the individual logic gates of the 80386 to interpret the assembly-level instructions it fetches.

MMU Memory Management Unit. This is the section of the 80386 that performs logical-to-linear and linear-to-physical address translation. The 80386 is somewhat unusual in that the MMU is built into the microprocessor.

Mnemonic   The short English abbreviations used for assembly language instructions, such as MOV, ADD, or LSL. Since a microprocessor cannot understand mnemonics directly, it is the job of an assembler to translate programmer-written mnemonics into machine-readable opcodes.

MSW   Machine Status Word. Another name for register CR0.

NMI   Nonmaskable Interrupt. This is one of two hardware interrupt pins on the outside of the 80386.

NPX   Numeric Processor Extension. The common abbreviation for a numeric coprocessor like the 80387.

Opcode   The binary, machine-readable form of an assembly language instruction.

Page   A 4KB range of memory addresses. When the paging function of the 80386 MMU is enabled, several page-related protection features are available. All paging functions operate on memory as units of one page, or 4KB.

PDBR   Page Directory Base Register. This 32-bit register within the 80386 is used to locate the beginning of the page translation tables. PDBR is another name for register CR3.

PDE   Page Directory Entry. The first tier of page-translation and protection information is in the PDEs. PDEs, in turn, refer to tables of PTEs.

Physical Address   The final stage of address translation. If paging is enabled, linear addresses are translated into physical addresses through PDEs and PTEs. If paging is not enabled, linear addresses become physical addresses directly.

PTE   Page Table Entry. This is the second tier of page-translation and protection information. A PTE points directly to a page of memory.

RAM   Random Access Memory. The main memory, or workspace, of a computer. The 80386 is able to address up to 4GB of RAM directly.

RISC   Reduced Instruction Set Computer. A computer that has very few assembly-level instructions but executes them very rapidly is a RISC machine.

ROM   Read-Only Memory. This is a type of IC used to hold permanent information, such as bootstrap code or constant data. ROMs cannot be erased or reprogrammed.

RPL   Requestor's Privilege Level. This is a 2-bit field in every segment selector. The RPL field of a selector is used by the 80386's memory protection mechanism.

Selector   A 16-bit item used to specify a segment descriptor and therefore a segment of memory. In Protected mode, anything loaded into the six segment registers is considered a selector.

Segment   The 80386's basic unit of memory. Using segment descriptors, the systems programmer is able to define a memory segment to be anything desired. Segment size, base address, and usage attributes are all defined by the programmer when a segment descriptor is created.

SRAM   Static Random Access Memory. This is a type of IC used for storing programs and/or data. Static RAM chips are normally faster than dynamic RAMs and don't need to be refreshed, but they cost more.

Task   A program or related group of programs. On the 80386, a task is defined by a TSS. Every TSS implies a task. Programs that are parts of different tasks cannot normally communicate or interfere with one another.

TLB   Translation Lookaside Buffer. A cache within the 80386 used to store recently used page-translation information. The operation of the TLB is generally transparent to the programmer, but it can be tested with registers TR6 and TR7.

TSS   Task State Segment. A special segment of memory used to define the current state of a dormant task. Exactly one TSS must be defined for every task. TSSs are sometimes not required if multitasking is not desired.

Word   Sixteen bits. Halfway between a byte and a dword.

B

NEW INSTRUCTIONS

The 80386 has more than 200 instruction mnemonics in its instruction set. Because of the 80386's architectural compatibility with previous generations of Intel processors, most of these instructions can be found in the instruction sets of the 8086/88, 80186/88, or 80286. This appendix lists only those instructions that are totally new or that have been enhanced enough to warrant being treated as new instructions. They are listed alphabetically by their common mnemonics. For a complete reference to all 80386 instructions, see *80386 Microprocessor Handbook* by Pappas and Murray (Berkeley: Osborne/McGraw-Hill, 1988) or *80386 Programmer's Reference Manual* (Intel publication number 230985-001).

Each instruction is presented in the same easy-to-read format. First, the common mnemonic is listed, followed by a description. Next, the opcode byte or bytes for the instruction is given in hexadecimal. Often, a new 80386 instruction is 2 or more bytes long. In cases where opcode bytes might be embedded in a subsequent addressing byte, the addressing byte is given in binary notation, with the pertinent opcode bits shown and the addressing bits appearing as x's. The next line lists the addressing forms that are allowed. The addressing forms are abbreviated as follows:

R   Register
M   Memory operand
I   Immediate operand
D   Relative displacement

Numbers that follow the initial letter indicate the size of operand allowed. For example, R16 indicates a 16-bit register, such as AX or BP.

Mnemonic

BSF

Operation

Bit Scan Forward

Opcode(s)

0F BC

Addressing

| R16, R16 | R16, M16 |
| R32, R32 | R32, M32 |

Description The BSF instruction finds the first 1 bit in the source operand, starting from the least significant bit (bit 0) and working up. If the entire source operand has no 1 bits, that is, if it equals 0, ZF is set, and the destination operand is undefined. Otherwise, ZF is cleared, and the destination operand gets the bit index of the first 1 bit.

Example

```
MOV    EAX, 03004000h    ;load constant into EAX
BSF    EBX, EAX          ;EBX gets 14
JZ     zero              ;EAX = 0 ?
```

Mnemonic

BSR

Operation

Bit Scan Reverse

Opcode(s)

0F BD

Addressing

R16, R16	R16, M16
R32, R32	R32, M32

Description The BSR instruction operates exactly like the BSF instruction, except that it begins scanning from the most significant bit of the source operand and works toward bit 0. The most significant bit may be either bit 15 or bit 31, depending on the operand size in effect at the time.

Example

```
MOV    EAX, 00000F00h    ;load constant into EAX
BSR    EBX, EAX          ;EBX gets 11
JZ     zero              ;EAX = 0 ?
```

Mnemonic

BT

Operation

Bit Test

Opcode(s)

0F A3
0F BA xx100xxx

Addressing

R16, R16	M16, R16
R32, R32	M32, R32
R16, I8	M16, I8
R32, I8	M32, I8

Description   The BT instruction reports the status of a bit in the operand by setting or clearing CF to match it. The operand under test may be either a register or a memory location. The operand is not harmed. The second operand specifies which bit in the first operand to test. Because 32-bit registers can be used here, it is possible, and perfectly permissible, to test the 4,294,967,296th bit of a memory operand.

Example

```
BT    EAX, 5        ;test bit 5 of EAX
JC    foo           ;jump if bit 5 was set
```

Mnemonic

BTC

Operation

Bit Test and Complement

Opcode(s)

0F BB
0F BA xx111xxx

Addressing

R16, R16	M16, R16
R32, R32	M32, R32
R16, I8	M16, I8
R32, I8	M32, I8

Description   The BTC instruction operates exactly like the BT instruction, except that the bit being tested is inverted after the test is performed, and its condition is saved in CF. If the bit under test resides in memory, the 80386 performs a read-modify-write operation.

Example

```
BTC  DWORD PTR DS:[4E4Ch], 9  ;test and invert bit 9
JC   foo                      ;jump if bit used to be 1
```

Mnemonic

BTR

Operation

Bit Test and Reset

Opcode(s)

0F B3
0F BA xx110xxx

Addressing

R16, R16	M16, R16
R32, R32	M32, R32
R16, I8	M16, I8
R32, I8	M32, I8

Description   The BTR instruction operates exactly like the BTC instruction, except that it always clears the bit being tested.

Example

```
BTR EAX, 0                    ;test and clear bit 0
JC   foo                      ;jump if it was set
```

Mnemonic

BTS

Operation

Bit Test and Set

Opcode(s)

0F AB
0F BA xx101xxx

Addressing

R16, R16	M16, R16
R32, R32	M32, R32
R16, I8	M16, I8
R32, I8	M32, I8

Description   The BTS instruction operates exactly like the BTC instruction, except that it always sets the bit being tested.

Example

```
BTS     DWORD  PTR  DS:[840621],  3     ;test and set bit 3
JC      foo                             ;jump if it was set
```

Mnemonic

CDQ

Operation

Convert Double to Quad

Opcode(s)

99

Addressing

(None)

Description   The CDQ instruction sign-extends register EAX into EDX. This has the effect of filling EDX with all 1s or all 0s, depending on the sign bit of EAX (bit 31).

Example

```
MOV     EAX, 4A696D57h    ;EAX = positive number
CDQ                       ;EDX = 0
```

Mnemonic

CWDE

Operation

Convert Word to Double, Extended

Opcode(s)

98

Addressing

(None)

Description The CWDE instruction sign-extends AX into EAX. This is different from the original CWD instruction, which extends AX into DX.

Example

```
MOV     AX, 1234h         ;AX gets positive number
CWDE                      ;EAX gets positive number
```

Mnemonic

IMUL

Operation

Integer Multiply

Opcode(s)

0F AF

Addressing

R16, R16	R16, M16
R32, R32	R32, M32

Description Although the IML instruction is certainly not new to the 80386, it has been made considerably more general-purpose. It is now possible to multiply any register by any other register or by a memory operand.

Example8

```
MOV    EBX,     12345678h
MOV    ESI,     87654321h
IMUL   EBX,     ESI          ;EBX = EBX * ESI
```

Mnemonic

Jcc

Operation

Jump on condition code

Opcode(s)

0F 80 through 0F 8F

Addressing

D32

Description The 80386 has extended the normal conditional JMP instructions by allowing 32-bit address displacements. This makes it possible to perform a conditional JMP instruction that transfers control to any address in a program, even with 4GB-long code segments.

Example

```
CMP    AX, 4357h    ;compare AX to constant
JNE    far_away     ;jump if not equal
```

Mnemonic

JECXZ

Operation

Jump if ECX equals Zero

Opcode(s)

E3

Addressing

D8

Description   The JECXZ instruction is a 32-bit extension of the JCXZ instruction. Even though it tests all of register ECX, you must still specify only an 8-bit relative displacement. Because JECXZ is normally used at the tops of iterative loops, this isn't often a big restriction.

Example

```
    MOV     ECX, loop_counter    ;load ECX from memory
    JECXZ   foo                  ;skip loop if ECX = 0
```

Mnemonic

LFS

Operation

Load FS segment register

Opcode(s)

0F B4

Addressing

R16, M32
R32, M48

Description   The LFS instruction operates exactly like the LDS and LES instructions, except that segment register FS is loaded along with a register of your choice.

Example

    LFS   EDX, mem_pointer   ;load FS and EDX

Mnemonic

LGDT, LIDT, LLDT

Operation

Load Global Descriptor Table register
Load Interrupt Descriptor Table register
Load Local Descriptor Table register

Opcode(s)

0F 01 xx010xxx
0F 01 xx011xxx
0F 00 xx010xxx

Addressing

M48		(LGDT, LIDT)
R16	M16	(LLDT)

Description   The LGDT, LIDT, and LLDT instructions are not entirely new to the 80386; they first appeared on the 80286. However, for the 80386, LGDT and LIDT require 48-bit operands. The first 16 bits specify the limit of the descriptor table, while the upper 32 bits hold a linear base address. LLDT requires a valid LDT selector as an operand, which may come from a register or from memory.

Example

    LGDT   mem_pointer_1
    LIDT   mem_pointer_2
    LLDT   BX

Mnemonic

LGS

Operation

Load GS segment register

Opcode(s)

0F B5

Addressing

R16, M32
R32, M48

Description   The LGS instruction operates exactly like the LFS instruction, except that it operates on GS.

Example

    LGS   EBP, mem—pointer   ;load GS and EBP

Mnemonic

LSS

Operation

Load SS segment register

Opcode(s)

0F B2

Addressing

R16, M32
R32, M48

Description   The LSS instruction operates exactly like the LFS instruction, except that it operates on SS. This is the perfect instruction for changing your stack pointer and segment selector at the same time, avoiding inconsistent stack references.

Example

```
LSS     ESP, mem_pointer     ;load SS and ESP
```

Mnemonic

MOV

Operation

Move to/from control, debug, test registers

Opcode(s)

0F 20
0F 21
0F 22
0F 23
0F 24
0F 26

Addressing

R32, CR*n*	CR*n*, R32
R32, DR*n*	DR*n*, R32
R32, TR*n*	TR*n*, R32

Description   The MOV instruction has been expanded to cover the new 80386 control, debug, and test registers. Only 32-bit general-purpose registers can be used as source or destination operands for these MOV instructions.

Example

```
MOV     EAX, CR0     ;read CR0
OR      AL, 1        ;set bit 0
MOV     CR0, EAX     ;store new value
```

Mnemonic

MOVSX

Operation

Move with Sign Extend

Opcode(s)

0F BE

0F BF

Addressing

R16, R8	R16, M8
R32, R16	R32, M16
R32, R8	R32, M8

Description   The MOVSX instruction performs a MOV operation between two operands of dissimilar size. The source operand is sign-extended as it is copied into the larger, destination operand.

Example

```
MOV      BL, 55h      ;BL gets positive number
MOVSX    ECX, BL      ;ECX = 00000055h
```

Mnemonic

MOVZX

Operation

Move with Zero Extend

Opcode(s)

0F B6

0F B7

Addressing

R16, R8	R16, M8
R32, R16	R32, M16
R32, R8	R32, M8

Description The MOVZX instruction operates just like the MOVSX instruction, except that the source operand is zero-extended into the destination operand. If the source operand is positive (the sign bit equals 0), this has the same effect as a MOVSX.

Example

```
MOV     DH, 89h        ;DH gets negative number
MOVZX   EAX, DH        ;EAX = 00000089h
```

Mnemonic

POPAD

Operation

Pop All, Double

Opcode(s)

61

Addressing

(None)

Description The POPAD instruction pops all eight 32-bit general-purpose registers from the top of the stack. This is distinct from the POPA instruction, which pops 16-bit values. POPAD works in conjunction with PUSHAD.

Example

```
POPAD       ;pop 32 bytes off stack
```

Mnemonic

POPFD

Operation

Pop EFLAGS, Double

Opcode(s)

9D

Addressing

(None)

Description   The POPFD instruction is equivalent to the POPF instruction, except that it pops all 32 bits of the EFLAGS register. This works in conjunction with the PUSHFD instruction.

Example

    POPFD   ;pop 4 bytes from stack

Mnemonic

PUSHAD

Operation

Push All, Double

Opcode(s)

60

Addressing

(None)

Description   The PUSHAD instruction is the functional opposite of the POPAD instruction; it causes all 32 bits of the eight general-purpose registers to be pushed onto the stack. This works in conjunction with POPAD.

Example

   PUSHAD   ;push 32 bytes on stack

Mnemonic

PUSHFD

Operation

Push EFLAGS, Double

Opcode(s)

9C

Addressing

(None)

Description   The PUSHFD instruction pushes all 32 bits of the EFLAGS register onto the stack. This works in conjunction with POPFD.

Example

   PUSHFD   ;push 4 bytes on stack

Mnemonic

SET*cc*

Operation

Set byte on condition code

Opcode(s)

0F 90 through 0F 9F

Addressing

R8 M8

Description   The SET*cc* instructions store a byte of 1 bits (FF hexadecimal) into the destination operand if the condition is true. Otherwise, they store a byte of 0 bits (00 hexadecimal). All conditions that can be used for conditional JMP instructions can be used for conditional SET.

Example

```
CMP     DH, AL                      ;compare two values
SETNE   BYTE PTR DS:[100]           ;store FF if not equal
```

Mnemonic

SHLD

Operation

Shift Left, Double

Opcode(s)

0F A4
0F A5

Addressing

R16, R16, I8	M16, R16, I8
R32, R32, I8	M32, R32, I8
R16, R16	M16, R16
R32, R32	M32, R32

Description   The SHLD instruction shifts the first operand to the left. The second operand provides bits to shift in from the right. The third operand specifies the shift count as an 8-bit immediate number. If the two-operand form is used, register CL is used for the shift count. A normal SHL instruction always shifts 0 bits into the destination operand, whereas SHLD allows the programmer to specify a source bit stream to shift in. The source/operand is never modified.

Example

    SHLD   EAX, EBX, 13   ;shift 13 bits EAX ≤ EBX

Mnemonic

SHRD

Operation

Shift Right, Double

Opcode(s)

0F AC

0F AD

Addressing

R16, R16, I8	M16, R16, I8
R32, R32, I8	M32, R32, I8
R16, R16	M16, R16
R32, R32	M32, R32

Description The SHRD instruction operates exactly like the SHLD instruction, except that the destination operand is shifted to the right, and the source operand specifies bits to shift in from the left.

Example

    SHRD   EBX, EAX, 9   ;shift 9 bits EBX ≥ EAX

C

MEMORY STRUCTURES
AND 80386 REGISTERS

This appendix reviews some of the most-often-used memory structures and 80386 registers. You may wish to keep these pages handy when building descriptor tables or writing memory management code. Shown first are the various forms of segment descriptor, starting with a "generic" descriptor format. All segment descriptors are 8 bytes (64 bits) long, even those for describing 80286-compatible segments and tasks. Samples of 80386 and 80286 Task State Segments follow the segment descriptors. After the TSSs are the two forms of page descriptors, and a sample of a not-present page descriptor.

The second section of this appendix reviews the newest 80386 registers. The EFLAGS register is shown first, followed by the Control registers, the Debug registers, and the Test registers.

SEGMENT DESCRIPTORS

63 56	55 52	51 48	47 44	40	39 16	15 0
Base bits 31-24	G X D U	Limit bits 19-16	D P P S L	T Y P E A	Base address bits 23-0	Limit bits 15-0

Segment Types
000   Data, read only
001   Data, read/write
010   Stack, read only
011   Stack, read/write
100   Code, execute only
101   Code, execute/read
110   Code, execute only, conforming
111   Code, execute/read, conforming

Segment descriptor format (Figure 2-2)

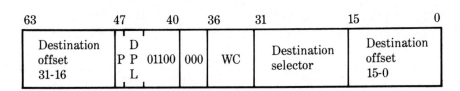

63	47	40	36	31	15	0
Destination offset 31-16	D P P L	01100	000	WC	Destination selector	Destination offset 15-0

Selector   Destination code segment
Offset   Offset within destination code segment
WC   Word count, 0-31
DPL   Descriptor privilege level
P   Descriptor Present flag

Call gate descriptor (Figure 3-1)

63	47	39	31	15	0
Offset 31-16	D P P 01111 L	Reserved	Selector	Offset 15-0	

Trap Gate

63	47	39	31	15	0
Offset 31-16	D P P 01110 L	Reserved	Selector	Offset 15-0	

Interrupt Gate

Trap gate and interrupt descriptors (Figure 7-4)

63	47	39	31	15	0
Available	D P P 00101 L	Available	Selector	Available	

Task gate descriptor (Figure 5-3)

63	55	51	47	39	15	0
Base 31-24	G X D U	Limit 19-16	D P P 01001 L	Base address 23-0	Limit 15-0	

Task state segment descriptor (Figure 5-1)

63	55	51	47	39	15	0
Base address 31-24	0000	Limit 19-16	P 0000010	Base address 23-0	Limit 15-0	

LDT descriptor (Figure 2-10)

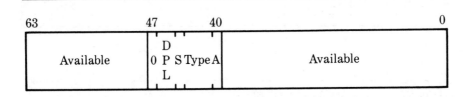

63	47	40	0
Available	0 DPL P S Type A	Available	

Not-present segment descriptor (Figure 2-4)

TASK STATE SEGMENTS

63	55	51	47	39	15	0
Base 31-24	G X D U	Limit 19-16	P DPL 01001	Base address 23-0	Limit 15-0	

80386 task state segment (Figures 5-1 and 5-2)

31			0	
I/O permission bit map →		X	T	64
X		LDT		60
X		GS		5C
X		FS		58
X		DS		54
X		SS		50
X		CS		4C
X		ES		48
EDI				44
ESI				40
EBP				3C
ESP				38
EBX				34
EDX				30
ECX				2C
EAX				28
EFLAGS				24
EIP				20
CR3				1C
X		SS2		18
ESP2				14
X		SS1		10
ESP1				0C
X		SS0		8
ESP0				4
X		Back link		0

80386 task state segment (Figures 5-1 and 5-2), *continued*

31	15	0	
LDT Selector	DS		28
SS	CS		24
ES	DI		20
SI	BP		1C
SP	BX		18
DX	CX		14
AX	FLAGS		10
IP	SP2		0C
SS2	SP1		8
SS1	SP0		4
SS0	Back link		0

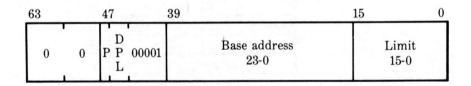

63	47	39	15	0
0	0	D P P L 00001	Base address 23-0	Limit 15-0

80286 task state segment (Figure 8-7)

PAGE DESCRIPTORS

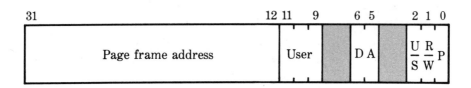

Page directory entry (Figure 4-3a)

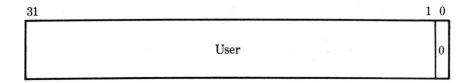

Page table entry (Figure 4-3b)

31   1 0

| User | 0 |

Not-present page descriptor (Figure 4-3c)

SELECTED 80386 REGISTERS

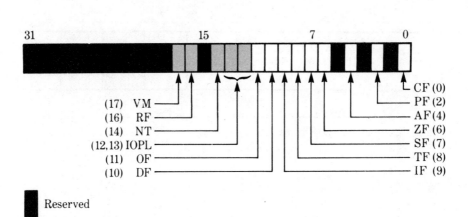

EFLAGS register (Figure 1-6)

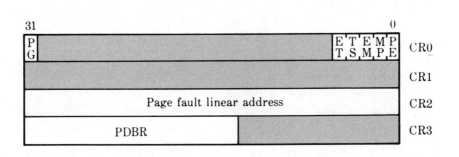

Control registers (Figure 1-9)

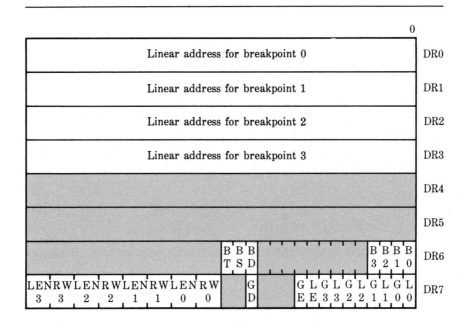

Debug registers (Figure 1-10)

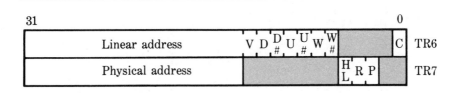

Test registers (Figure 1-11)

D

EVOLUTION OF
THE 80386

Over the years that the 80386 has been in development, several changes have been made to the microprocessor. When the 80386 was first released for sampling in late 1985, it was somewhat different from the part you are probably using today. Some of the changes were intentional, and some were not. In other words, any component as complex as the 80386 is bound to have a few "undocumented" features. As time went on, the bugs became fewer, farther between, and more obscure.

Currently, some bugs still remain in the 80386. This appendix lists some evolutionary changes that have been made to the processor. The bugs and alterations are listed chronologically, by "stepping" ID. A stepping is Intel's term for a silicon mask change, the kind reported in register DL after reset. You can normally identify the stepping revision of your 80386 by examining the outer case. A two-character ID should be printed there.

A1 STEPPING

This is the first revision after the initial (A0) introduction of the

80386. The A1 stepping became available around the first of the year in 1986.

Hardware Peculiarity Unless pin F13 of the 80386 is connected to the +5-volt power supply, the 80386 never terminates a memory cycle, hanging the processor.

Loading LDTR with a Null Selector If you load the local descriptor table register with a null selector (0000 through 0003) without performing a memory read immediately afterward, the 80386 behaves erratically. LDTR can be loaded either as the result of an LLDT instruction or as part of a task-switch operation if the incoming TSS has a null selector in its LDT field.

Loading Bad Stack Selectors The 80386 does not check the privilege level of the desired stack segment selector during an LSS instruction. Normally, the RPL of the selector and the DPL of the segment must exactly equal the DPL of the currently executing code segment.

Misaligned Selectors If a 16-bit memory operand is loaded into a segment register, the 80386 hangs if the selector is not word-aligned. This can happen with a MOV instruction and with the LDS, LES, LFS, LGS, and LSS instructions.

Testing Null Selectors The 80386 hangs if an LAR, LSL, VERR, or VERW instruction is used to test a null selector.

Popping Selectors When popping a segment selector from the stack, the 80386 performs all of the privilege-related checks backward. That is, you are allowed to pop a selector to a segment with more privilege, but not to one with less privilege.

Indirect FAR JMP to Same Privilege Level An indirect JMP instruction is one in which the new segment selector and offset are stored in memory. If the new code segment is at the same privilege level as the current code segment, the 80386 does not read the selector portion of the JMP operand. The result is a NEAR JMP to a new offset within the current code segment.

Spurious Breakpoint Exceptions   A MOV instruction into or out of the debug registers while hardware breakpoints are enabled may cause a breakpoint fault to be reported. You should temporarily disable the hardware breakpoints while reading or writing the debug registers and then execute a JMP instruction to flush the prefetch queue before reenabling them.

Successive Floating-Point Instructions   If two floating-point instructions are executed close together, the 80386 may force the coprocessor to start the second one too soon if the first one did not require any memory operands.

Bad Floating-Point Instructions   The execution of certain undefined floating-point instructions causes the 80386 to hang rather than reporting an invalid instruction fault.

Misaligned Floating-Point Instructions   If 80287 and/or 80387 instructions are not word-aligned, the 80386 passes the wrong instruction to the coprocessor, causing unpredictable behavior.

Misaligned Descriptor Tables   All segment descriptors should be dword-aligned, or the 80386 may not read them correctly.

Incorrect Interrupt Vector   If a maskable interrupt occurs immediately after the 80386 has executed an instruction with an 8-bit operand, the interrupt is always assigned a vector number of 0.

Handling Exceptions with 80286 Tasks   If an exception that pushes an error code is handled through a task gate to an 80286 task, the 80386 generates a double fault (exception 8) as soon as the 80286 task switch is completed.

Page Fault During Task Switch   If the new task uses different page tables than the old task and a page fault occurs during the task-switch operation, the 80386 hangs instead of reporting the page fault.

Returning from a Nested Task   If you execute an IRET instruction when the NT (Nested Task) flag in EFLAGS is set, the 80386 returns to your "parent" task. However, it will neglect to clear NT in the outgoing task's TSS.

Task-Switch Trap Bit   When a task switch occurs and the incoming TSS has its task-switch trap bit set, the 80386 generates a debug fault (exception 1). However, it will neglect to set the BT flag in register DR6 before invoking the exception 1 handler.

Invalid TSS Faults   When an invalid TSS fault (exception 10) occurs as the result of a task-switch operation, the 80386 pushes wrong values for EIP and ESP onto the error handler's stack.

Wrong Paging Information During Task Switch   When a task switch occurs and the new task uses a different set of page tables than the old task (that is, CR3 in the TSS is different), the 80386 reads the new TSS descriptor and updates the old TSS using the page tables of the new task.

Masking NMI   If an NMI is serviced through a task gate, the 80386 neglects to reenable NMI inputs after the NMI-handling task terminates. The 80386 normally does not recognize NMI inputs while it is servicing an NMI.

Incorrect Error Code   If an exception that pushes an error code is handled through a task gate, the 80386 may push an error code of 0 instead of the correct error code.

Not-Present LDT   If a task switch occurs and the new task's TSS selector selects an LDT descriptor that is marked not present, the 80386 reports a not-present fault (exception 11), instead of an invalid TSS fault (exception 10).

Self-test   The self-test feature does not work on the A1 stepping of the 80386.

Interlevel Transfers   If you perform a control transfer to a higher privilege level and the procedure at that level uses an expand-down stack segment for its stack, as opposed to an expand-up data segment, the 80386 generates a spurious stack fault (exception 12).

Debug Access Fault   If an attempt is made to read or write the debug registers while GD is set in DR7, the 80386 generates a debug fault (exception 1). However, the wrong value for EIP will be pushed onto the exception handler's stack.

Multiply and Divide Errors   If the 80386 executes a MUL, IMUL, DIV, or IDIV instruction with a memory operand and a general protection fault (exception 13) occurs, the processor hangs rather than reporting the fault.

Intersegment Transfers   If the last 2 bytes of a direct FAR JMP or FAR CALL instruction are beyond the end of the code segment, the 80386 hangs rather than reporting a general protection fault.

Intersegment Transfers II   If the last 2 bytes of a direct FAR JMP or FAR CALL instruction lie on the other side of a page boundary, the 80386 hangs, regardless of whether the other page is present or not. Remember, a page boundary occurs every 4KB.

Bit-Test Instructions The bit-test instructions that perform read-modify-write cycles to memory (BTC, BTR, and BTS) do not work properly unless your memory runs without wait states.

Bit Scan Forward Instruction If a BSF instruction is executed with a memory operand, and a general protection fault (exception 13) or a page fault (exception 14) occurs, the 80386 hangs rather than reporting the fault.

Accessing CR3, TR6, and TR7 Reading or writing registers CR3, TR6, or TR7 produces incorrect results if your memory requires wait states. This is particularly obscure, since these instructions do not reference memory.

B0 STEPPING

The B0 stepping became available around the middle of 1986. As is the case with earlier steppings, the "B0" marking can sometimes be found on the outside of the device. If not, the code "S40336" or "S40337" may appear. Starting with the B0 stepping, the 80386 would leave the component identifier, 3, in DH and the revision identifier, also 3, in DL.

Interrupts and Privilege Violations If a hardware interrupt occurs immediately before an IOPL-sensitive instruction when CPL is greater than IOPL, the 80386 behaves erratically. Generally, it will produce spurious stack faults (exception 12). Note that this occurs only if the IOPL-sensitive instruction was going to fail.

Infinite Page Faults If a page fault (exception 14) occurs while the 80386 is attempting to invoke a page fault handler, it generates another page fault rather than reporting a double fault (exception 8).

Invalid TSS Fault   If an invalid TSS fault (exception 10) is caused by an attempt to switch to a TSS that is too small, and the exception is handled through a task gate, the 80386 shuts down.

Invalid TSS Fault II   If you execute an IRET instruction while the NT (Nested Task) flag is set in EFLAGS, and the "parent" TSS is too small, the 80386 generates a double fault (exception 8).

Invalid TSS Fault III   If the previous error occurs and the double fault is handled through a trap gate, the 80386 shuts down.

Invalid TSS Fault IV   If the gate descriptor for an invalid TSS fault (exception 10) is bad and an invalid TSS fault occurs for any reason, the 80386 shuts down.

Tracing a REP MOVS Instruction   The 80386 does not correctly single-step (trace) repeated string move instructions. Instead, it generates a debug trap after every *other* iteration of the repeated MOVS instruction.

Breakpointing a REP MOVS Instruction   If a data breakpoint is enabled and it is hit during a repeated string move instruction, the 80386 reports it only after an even number of iterations. This gives you a fifty-fifty chance of learning about your breakpoint one instruction late.

16-Bit and 32-Bit Control Transfers   Whenever control is transferred from 16-bit code to 32-bit code through a task gate or through a gate that causes a change in privilege level, the 80386 discards the upper half of the offset address in EIP. If the destination address was greater than 64KB, this will cause a program error.

16-Bit and 32-Bit Control Transfers II   When an IRET instruction that transfers control to a Virtual 8086 mode task is executed, the 80386 neglects to truncate the offset address on the stack to 16 bits.

16-Bit and 32-Bit Control Transfers III   If a 32-bit call, trap, or interrupt gate is used to transfer control from a 16-bit code segment to a 32-bit code segment without changing privilege levels, the 80386 treats the gate as a 16-bit gate.

Mixing Address Sizes   If a LOOP, MOVS, LODS, STOS, CMPS, INS, or OUTS instruction is followed by an instruction that uses a different address size, the 80386 may use the incorrect address size when updating either the loop counter or the string index.

B1 STEPPING

The B1 stepping became available in late 1986. It corrected many of the bugs in earlier versions, but new ones were either introduced or discovered. The best known of these was the widely publicized multiply failure discovered in mid-1987. The B1 stepping is identifiable either by the "B1" mark or by the code "S40343," "S40344," or "S40362." As is the case with the B0 stepping, the B1 revision leaves a binary three in DL after reset.

IBTS and XBTS Instructions Removed   The Insert Bit String (IBTS) and Extract Bit String (XBTS) instructions were removed from the 80386's instruction set. It was determined that they took up too much space on the microprocessor and that their functionality could be duplicated with the SHLD and SHRD instructions. The opcodes 0F A6 and 0F A7 now produce invalid opcode faults.

Multiplication Errors   Certain 80386 microprocessors produce erroneous results when performing multiplication. Not all B1 stepping 80386s suffer from this bug. It is aggravated by increases in the processor's operating frequency, elevations in the ambient temperature, or decreases in the power supply voltage. This failure is extremely pattern sensitive; certain operands will produce errors readily, while others never will.

The following sample program has been calculated to produce the error. An 80386 that fails one or more of these multiply instructions is obviously faulty. However, passing does not guarantee a perfect part. To their credit, Intel agreed to test all 80386s for a limited time and report on their success or failure. Since then, all 80386s have been tested before shipping. Those that fail have been marked "For Sixteen-Bit Software Only." Those that passed have been marked with a double sigma sign, shown below. All 80386s produced after the B1 stepping should be free of this defect.

```
; Perform various 16-bit and 32-bit multiply operations...

K1       DD      41h                          ;memory-based constant 1
K2       DD      81h                          ;memory-based constant 2

         MOV     EAX, 0042E8h                 ;load EAX with operand
         MUL     K1                           ;EAX = EAX * 41H
         CMP     EAX,10FCE8h                  ;check answer
         JNE     fail                         ;failure if not equal

         MOV     EAX, 085D00h
         MUL     K1
         CMP     EAX,021F9D00h
         JNE     fail

         MOV     EAX, 042E80000h
         MUL     K1
         CMP     EAX, 0FCE80000h
         JNE     fail
         CMP     EDX, 010h
         JNE     fail
```

```
        MOV     EAX, 0417A000h
        MUL     K2
        CMP     EAX, 0FE7A000h
        JNE     fail
        CMP     EDX, 0002h
        JNE     fail

        MOV     DX, 0AB66h              ;16-bit tests
        MOV     AX, 09AE8h
        MUL     DX
        CMP     AX, 0B070h
        JNE     fail

        MOV     DX, 0FDF3h
        MOV     AX, 09AE8h
        MUL     DX
        CMP     AX, 05238h
        JNE     fail

        MOV     DX, 0B554h
        MOV     AX, 0E8EAh
        MUL     DX
        CMP     DX, 0A4F9h
        JNE     fail

        MOV     DX, 0B4C6h
        MOV     AX, 0E8EAh
        MUL     DX
        CMP     AX, 0ACFCh
        JNE     fail
        CMP     DX, 0A478h
        JNE     fail

        MOV     DX, 0B318h
        MOV     AX, 0E8EAh
        MUL     DX
        CMP     DX, 0A2F1h
        JNE     fail

        MOV     DX, 0B438h
        MOV     AX, 0E8EAh
        MUL     DX
        CMP     DX, 0A3FAh
        JNE     fail
```

Double Page Faults   The bug that appeared in the B0 stepping regarding page faults that occurred during page faults has been made a permanent feature of the 80386, with one minor change. If a third page fault occurs while the processor is servicing the first two, the 80386 shuts down.

Disabling Page Translation   The 80386 does not stop translating linear addresses to physical addresses when paging is disabled. Any page-translation entries that are still in the cache will be used, regardless of the setting of PG in CR0. To completely disable paging, flush the TLB by clearing CR3.

Page Translation Affects I/O Addresses When paging is enabled, the MMU sometimes erroneously translates I/O addresses above 0FFF as well as memory addresses. Coprocessor references (which appear in the I/O space) are also affected. The I/O addresses are translated as though they were linear memory addresses, using the memory translation tables cached in the TLB. If the "linear" I/O address is not in the cache, no translation will take place; only cached entries produce this effect.

Page Fault Error Codes Under certain circumstances, the 80386 pushes an incorrect error code onto the page fault handler's stack.

Four-Gigabyte Code Segments If you define a 4GB code segment (limit = FFFFF, G = 1), the base address of that segment must be dword-aligned, or the 80386 generates a general protection fault (exception 13) when it fetches an instruction from the beginning of the segment. This feature is expected to become permanent.

Wrong Loop Counter After a REP INS instruction finishes its last iteration, register ECX holds the value FFFFFFFF instead of 0, if the next instruction after the REP INS references memory.

LSL Instruction and Stack Pointer If the LSL instruction is followed by an instruction that references the stack, register ESP may become corrupted.

Not-Present LDT If a task switch occurs to a Virtual 8086 mode task and the incoming task's TSS holds a selector to an LDT descriptor that is marked not present, the 80386 generates a not-present fault (exception 11) rather than reporting an invalid TSS fault (exception 10).

Reading from CR3, TR6, or TR7   If hardware breakpoints are enabled, reading from register CR3, TR6, or TR7 may cause spurious debug faults to be reported. It is recommended that you disable breakpoints and then execute the MOV instruction followed by a JMP instruction before reenabling breakpoints.

Privilege Checking a Null Selector   If you perform an LAR, LSL, VERR, or VERW instruction using a null selector (0000 through 0003), the 80386 actually checks the descriptor in slot 0 of the GDT instead of always failing.

Privilege Checking Bad Selectors   An LAR, LSL, VERR, or VERW instruction that checks an unreachable selector causes the 80386 to hang unless there is a JMP, CALL, or memory-related instruction already in the prefetch queue. An unreachable selector is one that either is beyond the limit of its descriptor table or references a nonexistent LDT. The processor will remain hung until it receives an interrupt.

Faulting Floating-Point Instructions   If the second byte of a floating-point instruction is located in the first byte of a page that will cause a page fault (either because it is not present or because of an impending privilege violation), the 80386 hangs. The processor will remain hung until it receives an interrupt.

TRADEMARKS

Advanced Micro Devices™	Advanced Micro Devices Corporation
Apple®	Apple Computer, Inc.
AT™	International Business Machines Corporation
Clipper®	Intergraph Corporation
COMPAQ®	COMPAQ Computer Corporation
COMPAQ DESKPRO®	COMPAQ Computer Corporation
CP/M®	Digital Research, Inc.
CRAY X-MP™	Cray Research, Inc.
Fairchild®	National Semiconductor Corporation
IBM®	International Business Machines Corporation
Intel®	Intel Corporation
Microsoft®	Microsoft Corporation
MS-DOS®	Microsoft Corporation
National Semiconductor®	National Semiconductor Corporation
OS/2™	International Business Machines Corporation
PS/2™	International Business Machines Corporation
SPARC™	Sun Microsystems, Inc.
Sun Microsystems®	Sun Microsystems, Inc.

UNIX®	AT&T Information Systems
VAX®	Digital Equipment Corporation
XENIX®	Microsoft Corporation
XT™	International Business Machines Corporation
Z80000™	Zilog, Inc.

INDEX

Order Today!
Call Toll-Free 800-227-0900
Use Your American Express, Visa, or MasterCard

Here's More Help From the Experts

Now that you've developed even better computer skills with *Advanced 80386 Programming Techniques*, let us suggest the following related titles that will help you use your computer to greater advantage.

Inside the Model 80
by Chris H. Pappas and William H. Murray, III

Serious programmers and software designers can take a look inside the IBM® PS/2™ Model 80 while exploring with Pappas and Murray, two 80386 masters. After a brief introduction to the Model 80 environment, Pappas and Murray discuss operating systems, DOS versus OS/2™, and consider the advantages and limitations of each. Next, the book deals with hardware features at the board and chip level, and with interfaces to disk drives, the monitor, mice, keyboards, and serial and parallel ports. As the authors of *80386/80286 Assembly Language Programming* and *80386 Microprocessor Handbook*, Pappas and Murray are uniquely qualified to write the chapters on assembly language techniques and applications. Specialized applications and workstation concepts, including desktop publishing, and CAD/CAM, are among the additional topics that are described in detail.

$22.95 p
0-07-881311-5, 500 pp., 7⅜ x 9¼

80386/80286 Assembly Language Programming
by William H. Murray and Chris Pappas

This comprehensive guide enables serious programmers to take full advantage of the unique design of the 80386 and 80286 microprocessors found in the IBM® PC AT, COMPAQ® Desk Pro 286, TANDY 6000,® and other major computer systems. Instructions for programming the 8087/80287/80387 coprocessor are also included. The authors carefully detail the use of assembler pseudo-ops; macros, procedures, and libraries; and testing and debugging techniques. You'll also find instructions for interacting with high-level languages such as BASIC, Pascal, and FORTRAN. Many practical programming examples show beginners how to implement assembly language, while experienced programmers have an invaluable reference to the 80386 and 80286 instruction set.

$21.95 p
0-07-881217-8, 400 pp., 6⅜ x 9¼

Order Today!
Call Toll-Free 800-227-0900
Use Your American Express, Visa, or MasterCard

80386 Microprocessor Handbook
by Chris H. Pappas and William H. Murray, III

Serious programmers can take an inside look at Intel's "next generation" 80386 chip with this comprehensive microprocessor handbook. Murray and Pappas, authors of *80386/80286 Assembly Language Programming*, zero in on 80386 technology and deliver complete details on the 80386 instruction set, as well as the 80387/80287 coprocessor and the 82385 cache controller chip. All operating modes are discussed — real, protective, and virtual — as are signals and timing, electrical specification, and packaging. If you're designing software for the IBM® PC AT, COMPAQ® Desk Pro 386, or other 386 systems, the *80386 Microprocessor Handbook* leads you through a complete investigation of 80386 architecture.

$19.95 p
0-07-881242-9, 550 pp., 7⅜ x 9¼

OS/2™ Made Easy
by Herbert Schildt

This "Made Easy" guide contains simple, clear instructions for using OS/2™, the new operating system from IBM and Microsoft that runs on the 386, and PS/2™ computer families. Schildt, the of numerous bestsellers, including *DOS Made Easy*, teaches the fundamentals to first-time O users, as well as experienced DOS users. Start OS/2 basics, such as formatting diskettes and up files. Schildt then pursues more advanced techniques. Learn to manipulate directories and use OS/2 commands, run DOS applications und OS/2, operate multiple tasks, and manage your disk. Like all the "Made Easy" books, each cha presents a step-by-step lesson that includes pl of examples and hands-on exercises.

$19.95 p
0-07-881360-3, 350 pp., 7⅜ x 9¼

Available at fine bookstores and computer stores everywhere.

For a complimentary catalog of all our current publications contact: Osborne/McGraw-Hill, 2600 Tenth Street, Berkeley, CA 94710

Phone inquiries may be made using our toll-free number.
Call 800-227-0900. TWX 910-366-7277.

Prices subject to change without notice.

The manuscript for this book was prepared and submitted to Osborne/McGraw-Hill in electronic form. The acquisitions editor for this project was Nancy Carlston, the technical reviewer was Kris Jamsa, and the project editor was Fran Haselsteiner.

Text body and display set in Century Expanded.

Cover art by Bay Graphics Design Associates. Color separation by Colour Image. Cover supplier, Phoenix Color Corp. Book printed and bound by R.R. Donnelley & Sons Company, Crawfordsville, Indiana.